THE
FUGITIVE
GAME

Jonathan Littman

THE

ONLINE WITH

FUGITIVE

KEVIN MITNICK

GAME

LITTLE, BROWN AND COMPANY
Boston   New York   Toronto   London

FIRST PAPERBACK EDITION

ISBN 0-316-52858-7 (hc) 0-316-52869-2 (pb)
Library of Congress Catalog Card Number 95-81109

10 9 8 7 6 5 4 3 2 1

MV-NY

Published simultaneously in Canada by Little, Brown & Company (Canada) Limited

Printed in the United States of America

For Sherry Lue
and Elizabeth Claire

Contents

Author's Note

This story grew out of a book that I was writing about another Kevin. His name was Kevin Poulsen and he, like Kevin Mitnick, was a computer hacker. The stories intertwined. In the spring of 1994, I began receiving phone calls from Kevin Mitnick. He was a fugitive, the FBI's most wanted computer hacker. Sometimes he called me at pay phones. Eventually he called me at home. Mitnick phoned me dozens of times over the next nine months. I suspected he was in the United States but I never knew where he was.

Within a month of his arrest in February of 1995, I began writing this book. I had already interviewed many of the key participants: the FBI informant sent to develop a case against Mitnick in 1992, the Assistant U.S. Attorney in charge, fellow hackers, a phone security officer, John Markoff of the *New York Times*, and numerous minor characters, including a pimp and an exotic dancer.

In the next few months I interviewed cellular phone investigators who had tracked Mitnick in Seattle, Washington, and Raleigh, North Carolina; an FBI agent; a U.S. Marshal; a second Assistant U.S. Attorney; the owner and managers of the Internet provider the Well; Tsutomu Shimomura; and many other individuals in the story. Several scenes in this book include dialogue. The dialogue is based on my interviews. The sources are listed in the back of the book.

·   ·   ·

My wife's faith made this book possible. She reminded me why I've spent a good portion of my life chasing and telling the stories of real people. You never know where a story may lead.

In the days after Mitnick's arrest, I was on the phone with my editor, Roger Donald, Little, Brown's editorial director. Roger had a tough choice. He'd already commissioned my book on Kevin Poulsen. He made a strategic decision. He put my Poulsen book on hold, and signed me up to write the Mitnick story as fast as possible. Without his support and that of Dan Farley, Little, Brown's publisher, the book would not have been written. My agent, Kris Dahl of ICM, helped me focus and ignore the hype.

I was ably assisted in interviews by Deborah Kerr, a journalist and writer. My friend Rusty Weston offered sage advice. I was lucky to be surrounded by skilled editors, chiefly Roger Donald, but I also benefited greatly from suggestions by Geoffrey Kloske, my wife, Rusty Weston, Rik Farrow, Deborah Kerr, David Coen, and Amanda Murray. My father provided sound counsel and perspective.

It is a journalist's job to make contact with the characters who bring a landscape and culture to life, and although this story presented unusual obstacles, I've found the journey exciting. I would like to thank Kevin Mitnick and the hackers, phone company investigators, federal prosecutors, and other individuals who gave generously of their time. They opened the doors to their worlds.

Mill Valley, October 18, 1995
JONATHAN LITTMAN,
jlittman@well.com

THE
FUGITIVE
GAME

Prologue

His straight black hair sweeps behind his ears past his shoulders. His face reveals a perfect Eastern mask: the broad nose, the full lips, the black eyes impenetrable even without the Oakley sunglasses balanced on his head. He wears khakis, a T-shirt with the name of a cross-country ski race, and Birkenstock sandals. It's around forty degrees, windy, the time shortly after 7 P.M. on Sunday, February 12, 1995. He walks through the airport concourse, carrying his Hewlett Packard palmtop computer with the custom interface that plugs into his modified Oki 900 cellular phone. He doesn't need to stop at baggage claim.

One of the Sprint technicians waits curbside at Raleigh-Durham Airport in the company Ram Charger. The other tech finds the man where he said he'd be, standing next to the bank of telephones.

His name is Tsutomu Shimomura. His press clippings speak for themselves. The *New York Times* has dubbed him one of the nation's "most skilled computer security experts." Attacked on Christmas Day by a mysterious hacker, Shimomura took it upon himself to solve the crime as a "matter of honor." He's been tracking the hacker virtually nonstop for the last five days.

The *New York Times* article that thrust Shimomura into the national spotlight less than two weeks ago is vague about his identity.

Shimomura has lived most of his life in the United States, but he is a Japanese citizen, a foreigner with extraordinary U.S. military and intelligence contacts. "Until last week, Mr. Shimomura, a 30-year-old computational physicist at the federally financed San Diego Supercomputer Center, was primarily known only to an elite circle of the country's computer security specialists." The *Times* reported that Shimomura writes software security tools that have "made him a valuable consultant to the FBI, the Air Force and the National Security Agency." What exactly Shimomura does, and for whom, is unknown.

In twelve days Shimomura has rocketed from relative anonymity to media darling, his press all the more remarkable because he was a victim, the latest target to be compromised by a brilliant, "darkside" hacker employing a novel attack that the *Times* warned puts the entire Internet at risk. The story is a trendy twist on Sherlock Holmes and Dr. Moriarty. It's followed by a quarter-page, neon-lit close-up of Shimomura in *Newsweek*. In the image superimposed above his own face, he sits cross-legged, Buddha-style, his eyes boring into the laptop on his knees: "Shimomura doesn't resemble your typical cybercop," wrote *Newsweek*. "With his shoulder-length hair, wraparound sunglasses and rollerblades, he's as creative in building and maintaining security as dark-side hackers are in breaking it."

Neither the *New York Times* nor *Newsweek* hints at the identity of Shimomura's opponent, but to those in the know there's a likely suspect. Someone talented and obsessed. Someone capable of cracking Shimomura's vaunted security. Someone like Kevin Mitnick, a grossly overweight demon hacker, who stared out from the front page of the *Times* the previous Fourth of July, a scruffy mass of dark hair, horn-rimmed glasses, heavy, remorseless face, and blank eyes.

CYBERSPACE'S MOST WANTED: HACKER ELUDES F.B.I. PURSUIT

Combining technical wizardry with the ages-old guile of a grifter, Kevin Mitnick is a computer programmer run amok. And law-enforcement cannot seem to catch up with him. . . .

The front-page placement was proof of the enduring power of Kevin Mitnick's legend. The hacker had not yet been captured or even sighted. Indeed, it was unclear that he had committed any new crime to justify the front-page story. But reading further in the article it was clear that Mitnick was a serial hacker, in and out of trouble since 1981. And now, Mitnick had crossed the ultimate line: "Last year, while a fugitive, he managed to gain control of a phone system in California that allowed him to wiretap the FBI agents who were searching for him."

But it was more than just the mockery Mitnick made of the FBI. In the same article, the *Times* declared Mitnick a one-man threat to the worldwide cellular phone revolution, and set the stage for a digital joust of immense proportions.

> Mr. Mitnick is now a suspect in the theft of software that companies plan to use for everything from handling billing information to determining the location of a caller to scrambling wireless phone calls to keep them private. Such a breach could compromise the security of future cellular telephone networks even as their marketers assert that they will offer new levels of protection.

Tsutomu Shimomura has barely slept the last hundred hours or so, moving rapidly from one Internet site to another, conferencing with the Assistant U.S. Attorney and FBI agents, logging intrusions to the Net, comparing the results of phone company traffic patterns, traps, and traces.

The Sprint techs whisk Shimomura from the airport, past the billboards hawking computers and cellular phones, to meet the local FBI agents at the Sprint cellular switch, where local airborne Sprint calls are switched to land phone lines. But the agents don't stay long.

About 11:30 P.M., Shimomura and one of the techs arrive at the Sprint cell site, a tiny one-room prefab building crammed with relay racks and radio gear. The cell site is a small hub, a local Sprint cellular link serving customers within a few square miles, logistically the best place to base their tracking operations. Phone records show Mitnick's calls originated in this sector of cellular airspace. He's probably just a few miles away.

The hunt begins with the Sprint tech's Cellscope, a high-quality scanner controlled by a laptop that only law enforcement, cellular providers, or licensed detectives can legally operate. By pressing a couple of keys on the laptop the tech can command the scanner to jump through the local cellular channels. He can also enter the unique identifier every cellular phone has: a mobile identification number, or MIN, and an electronic serial number, or ESN. The Cellscope picks up the portion of the call broadcast by the caller and received by the nearest cell site.

Once the scanner locks onto a call, the laptop displays the signal strength and the number dialed. That's where the directional antenna attached to the scanner comes into play. The tech sweeps the antenna in a circle, searching for the strongest reading displayed on the laptop. The signal strength increases as the Cellscope is moved closer and closer to the individual making the call.

Shimomura's brought along his own hacker's scanning rig. It's pretty basic, just an Oki 900 cellular phone and a hardware interface to his tiny HP Palmtop. One of Shimomura's friends — who happens to be under federal indictment for illegal hacking — cooked up the interface and helped write the software.

Shimomura likes his computer-controlled cellular phone, but its use for tracking is limited. Its main purpose is to lock on a call and eavesdrop. It is illegal to use it to eavesdrop on calls. That's why Shimomura needed immunity from prosecution when he demonstrated his Oki scanner before Congress a couple of years ago.

Around 1 A.M., Mitnick dials out on CellularOne's radio band. Within seconds, the tech at the Sprint switch gets a call from CellularOne and relays the three-digit channel to Shimomura and the tech.

They jump in the red Blazer. The tech punches in the frequency, and modem static crackles, the sound of Mitnick's digital signals coursing through the air as analog audio tones. The tech reaches into the back to adjust the Cellscope's volume control. Shimomura taps the number into his palmtop, but he's got his hands full. It's his job to sweep the small aluminum directional antenna in a circle. The laptop sits between them, the signal strength weak, only about -105 dBm (decibels per milliwatt). That's barely measurable, considering

-35 dBm is the maximum strength and -115 dBm is the minimum. Within minutes, the call goes silent.

Fifteen minutes later, they pick it up again on Highway 70. The signal's stronger now, -95 dBm to -90 dBm, but just after they turn left at Duraleigh Road, it goes dead again. They park in front of a little library in a small shopping center off of Duraleigh Road and they wait.

Minutes later, Mitnick's familiar MIN pops up on the laptop window. This time the call doesn't die. The signal's strong, around -90 dBm. Mitnick's online again, and he's not far away.

They turn off Duraleigh onto Tournament Drive. To the right, a sign reads "Player's Club," an upscale apartment complex. They turn in and follow the loop around the buildings, the meter jumping from -60 dBm to -40 dBm. Thirty minutes of active tracking, that's all it takes the Japanese master. He's narrowed down the hacker's location to an area not more than one hundred meters square.

Two days later, an FBI technical team from Quantico, Virginia, picks up where Shimomura left off and zeroes in on the cellular transmissions. A few minutes after 8:30 P.M. on Valentine's Day, Special Agent LeVord Burns and Assistant U.S. Attorney John Bowler stand in Federal Magistrate Judge Wallace W. Dixon's living room and ask him to sign search warrants.

Early the next morning, FBI agents and U.S. Marshals knock on apartment number 202. Ten minutes pass. Finally the most wanted hacker in cyberspace cracks the door.

I.

Agent Steal

Eric Heinz strolls down the windy, illuminated Sunset Strip, past the fantasy of pastel deco hotels, palm trees, and giant billboard maidens spotlit in their Calvin Kleins.

RAINBOW.

He walks under the vertical neon sign and by the red awning, opposite a dusty, sky blue wall plastered with rock posters. The crowd is restless, waiting to get into the popular bar and restaurant. He presses a little flesh and cuts to where he belongs, the front of the line.

Everybody knows Eric.

Those bedroom eyes, the sculpted nose, the tall, slender frame. He looks like a rock star. He's got the Farrah Fawcett chest-length shag with highlights. The smudged Maybelline shadow and liner with a hint of blush. The long, manicured nails. The whole package poured into skintight jeans and cowboy boots.

But to thousands of pimply, bug-eyed boys on the Internet, Eric's a bad-ass computer hacker. Agent Steal's his handle, the information superhighway his gravy train. He wiretaps for a slick Hollywood detective at two grand a pop. He wins thousands of dollars in radio contests by seizing stations' phone lines. He scams Porsches by setting up phony credit under false identities. He lives on stolen ATM and credit cards. And best of all, Eric knows that he never really hurts the little guy. He's a friendly rogue, just working corporations and nameless institutions, playing the System.

Eric cruises the red Naugahyde booths, pecking the cheeks of the Rainbow's silicone-enhanced, lingerie ladies, actresses, models, off-duty call girls, and strippers. He takes his spot up front by the stone fireplace that burns year round, cigarette smoke wafting, rock tunes blaring. White Christmas lights drape the oak paneling. Guitars and drums from Guns N' Roses, Bon Jovi, and Poison hang from the wall, their autographed, poster-size images peering down like Mexican roadside shrines.

Eric is in his element. The Rainbow Bar and Grill is a Hollywood legend. Decades ago Errol Flynn frequented the joint, and Marilyn Monroe kept Joe DiMaggio waiting here two hours for their blind date. John Belushi had his last supper at the Rainbow with De Niro and Robin Williams. Who will join Eric tonight at his table? A rocker? A star?

Eric's here for the sex. He plucks his kittens not only from the Rainbow, but from Hollywood strip clubs like the Seventh Veil, Crazy Girls, and the mud-wrestling venue, the Tropicana. Strippers can't resist his cool indifference.

But it's a numbers game. Quantity is Eric's ultimate goal. Sometimes the night's first catch is too drunk to last or a bit low on silicone, not worthy of a feature performance back home. A marginal opportunity like this calls for the Rainbow employees' bathroom. Not the upstairs bathroom next to the dance floor, but the one through the kitchen. The one where someone's puked. The cubicle with a single toilet and a peephole in the wall perfect for passing drugs or taking a peek. No time for foreplay. Someone's pounding on the door.

Up with the jeans, flash that winning grin, out to the parking lot post-party for a little mingling, and then on down a few blocks to Rock N' Roll Denny's. When the Rainbow exhales at two A.M., the all-night diner becomes an after-hours club, swelling with rockers and lounge lizards. Eric's got his choice of strippers, models, and off-night hookers who've washed in from the Rainbow. Or maybe he'll order up something fresh from the Hollywood menu, one of the new runaways looking for a free meal, a bed, and a little fun.

What will it be tonight?

Her name won't be important, or the color of her hair or her skin. She could be white, black, Asian, blond, brunette, or a redhead. She could be in her teens or over thirty. But she won't be forgotten. Every girl gets a number, a three-digit entry in Eric's black book. Soon, he'll break a thousand.

Once Eric believed in love. Her name was Frecia Diane and she had rich brown hair, a pretty face, a great figure, and a regular office job. All in all, a nice girl from New Mexico. When Eric hacked his first five-thousand-dollar radio contest, he cared for Frecia so deeply that he put his winnings up for her breast implants. Sure, she was great in bed, but it was more than that. She was Eric's friend and partner. That's why Eric had to wiretap her, because he loved her.

One day, it was bound to happen. She found the bondage photos Eric left carelessly in a desk drawer. But Frecia soon found that leaving Eric wasn't so easy. Eric would pop in on Frecia's phone line at work to freak her out, or just listen in the background. Eric knew everything about Frecia Diane: when she started stripping at Nudes, Nudes, Nudes on Century near the airport. When she took a woman as a lover. And when she began to star in lesbian bondage porn flicks.

·   ·   ·

Tonight's catch will be impressed by Oakwood Apartments at 3636 South Sepulveda. She'll walk by the tennis courts and the clubhouse, the palm tree–lined swimming pool and the spacious Jacuzzi. The thirteen-hundred-dollar-a-month apartment is furnished: a white-washed oak dining table with chairs in rose and gray floral, nearly everything in conservative teal and rose. She won't see much in the way of hacker gear, maybe a telephone lineman's butt set, a computer and modem, and perhaps a few three-ringed binders crammed with notes.

She may see the city lights from Eric's balcony, but this is a room with another view. It will start innocently. A little kissing, a little caressing, and then before she'll understand, her hands will be tied. Eric will slap duct tape over her lips, and she'll watch him drag a large black duffel bag from his closet across the carpet. She won't see the video camera, and she won't see his skin-toned prosthetic leg.

He'll start with one leg at the toes, wrapping the cellophane round and round her naked skin to her crotch. Then the other leg. Next her stomach, her breasts, pinching her with his alligator clips. He'll wrap her neck and face, leaving only a slit for her to breathe through her nose. Tight but not too tight, so she won't suffocate like the painted girl in *Goldfinger*.

The Call

Bathed in the smoky red lights, one palm wrapped around her metal pole, Erica dances above the crowd, the sweat streaming past her bikini. She's got the look: spiked blond hair, freshly siliconed breasts, high, laced boots from Trashy Lingerie. She smiles at Eric as he works the crowd, brushing cheeks Hollywood style, giving high fives. They're friends now. Erica got over the things he did to her that night.

This is the Red Light District, Henry Spiegel's hot new Sunset club. Live bands jam in one room, while strippers bump and grind in another. Then there's the VIP room, where the celebrities lounge in sixties beanbags and get high without being hassled for autographs.

Eric wants a favor. How can she refuse? She's forgiven him for the manacles, the handcuffs, the gag, and the alligator clips. And she remembers the night Eric warned her about the phone tap on Spiegel's telemarketing boiler room operation. Erica and Henry's ex-con bank robber buddies worked his phone lines selling suckers on fictitious gold mines and phony office products. If not for Eric, she and Spiegel would surely have been busted for the three dozen phone lines running into Spiegel's house and the $150,000 in unpaid long distance bills. Sure, the Secret Service agents roughed them up a bit, even threatened to beat Spiegel if she wouldn't spill the beans, but Erica knew they didn't have any evidence.

Eric wants an introduction to a legendary hacker.

.   .   .

"Hi, this is Kevin Mitnick," cracks the voice on Spiegel's answering machine in December of 1991.

Spiegel never answers the phone. Why pick up before he knows who's calling? Spiegel's a veteran Hollywood pimp who shot and dealt junk for a decade. He's an institution to LAPD vice. Spiegel knows all the angles.

"My brother, Adam, said some gal Erica said I should phone you," begins Mitnick. "Said somebody called Eric wants to talk —"

"Hi —"

It's Spiegel, picking up.

He's sitting at his paper-strewn desk in his bungalow on Martel off Sunset Boulevard. The rat Erica gave him is scurrying about a few feet away in its cage. The floor is unfinished plywood, the couch in the corner, stained and sagging. Computer magazines are piled around the PC. A girl with a silver nose ring and a parrot perched on her shoulder taps the names of clubgoers into Spiegel's computer.

"So who's this Eric dude?" Mitnick asks.

"He's a hacker," Spiegel says in his tired voice, lounging in his sandals, black sweatpants, muscle-man T-shirt, and gold necklace. Spiegel's been pumping iron with his personal trainer. He's fifty, still muscular, his salt-and-peppery mane tied back in a ponytail.

Spiegel can only imagine what Mitnick looks like, though he feels like he knows him. Susie Thunder, a hacker and one of Spiegel's former girls, told him all about Mitnick. The two had a falling out in the early 1980s when Mitnick exposed Thunder's double life as a hooker. Thunder sliced the phone cables to Mitnick's apartment building. Phone service was suddenly disconnected or forwarded. Threatening calls were made to friends and family on both sides. It raged into a full-scale hacker war.

Spiegel's got a stack of Mitnick's press clippings, arrests dating back to the early 1980s, nearly all of them bearing the same menacing photograph. Mitnick was seventeen when he first cracked Pacific

Bell's computers, according to a December 1988 *Los Angeles Times* article, altering telephone bills, penetrating other computers, and stealing $200,000 worth of data from a San Francisco corporation. He was released on probation after serving six months at a youth facility. "Suddenly, his probation officer found that her phone had been disconnected and the phone company had no record of it." Mitnick was omnipresent: "A judge's credit record at TRW, Inc. [the nationwide credit reporting agency], was inexplicably altered," reported the *Times*. "Police computer files on the case were accessed from outside." Finally, in December 1988, Mitnick was arrested on charges of "causing $4 million damage to a Digital Equipment Corp. [DEC] computer" and "stealing a highly secret computer system." U.S. Magistrate Venetta Tassopulos "took the unusual step of ordering the young Panorama City computer whiz held without bail, ruling that when armed with a keyboard he posed a danger to the community."

In the days after Mitnick's latest arrest, the accusations snowballed. Assistant U.S. Attorney Leon Weidman told the *Times* that "investigators believe that Mitnick, twenty-five, may have been the instigator of a false report released by a news service in April that Security Pacific National Bank lost $400 million in the first quarter of 1988."

On December 27, 1988, the *Los Angeles Daily News* reported that "in an effort to safeguard the nation's computer systems, a new federal agency plans to look closely" at Mitnick's case. "A guy like Mitnick can commit crimes all over the world in a 10-minute span." The article ended with the ultimate charge. "[LAPD Sergeant Jim] Black added that because Mitnick does not seem to be motivated by money he is more dangerous. . . . It is possible for a person with Mitnick's capabilities to commit nearly any crime by computer. 'You could even kill a person by using a computer. . . .' "

When U.S. District Judge Mariana R. Pfaelzer ruled Mitnick "a very, very great danger to the community" and renewed his imprisonment without bail, Mitnick's attorney complained to the Associated Press that Mitnick is "being held incommunicado" and is being treated more harshly than men charged with violent crimes. "My client is being portrayed as some sort of Machiavellian figure either out of government paranoia ... or some other government agenda I'm not aware of."

But it was the January 8, 1989, *Los Angeles Times* piece by John Johnson that cemented Mitnick's legend. Titled "Computer an 'Umbilical Cord to His Soul': 'Dark Side' Hacker Seen as 'Electronic Terrorist,' " the article was one of the first to explore the hacker's psyche:

> Mitnick's motive for a decade of hacking?
>
> Not money, apparently. An unemployed computer programmer, he drove a used car and was living with his wife in his mother's modest Panorama City apartment ... but within the subculture of computer hackers, Mitnick was a colorful figure, using the name "Condor," for a Robert Redford movie character who outwits the government. The final digits of his unlisted home phone were "007," reportedly billed to the name "James Bond."
>
> Mitnick had such a special feeling for the computer that when an investigator for the Los Angeles County district attorney's office accused him of harming a computer he entered, he got tears in his eyes. "The computer to him was more of an animate thing," said the investigator, Robert Ewen. "There was an umbilical cord from it to his soul. That's why when he got behind a computer he became a giant."
>
> ... Steven Rhoades, a fellow hacker and friend ... said he and Mitnick broke into a North American Air Defense Command computer in Colorado Springs, Colo., in 1979. The 1983 movie "Wargames" is based upon a similar incident, in which a young hacker nearly starts World War III.

Over time, newspapers codified the legend. Soon, the unchecked allegations of Mitnick's incredible feats were treated as fact. Kevin Mitnick was the "Condor," the dark-side hacker, enemy of the government and the public, a hacker too dangerous to be allowed near a computer or phone. He was fat, ugly, uneducated, a slave to junk food. Greed the government could understand. But a hacker who wielded power for its own sake, someone who played electronic pranks on probation officers, FBI agents, and judges?

Mitnick's intrusions spawned new laws to curb computer crime. He had an insider's understanding of the international phone system and the burgeoning Internet. He had the prerequisite obsessive streak. He had a quirky sense of humor, a love of sophomoric pranks. And he understood better than anyone who came before him that people make the computers, the phones, the networks. And nobody, nobody fooled people like Kevin Mitnick. He became one of those rare figures whose reputation grew so ominous that the government and the media seemed to act as one, ignoring any facts that might diminish his demonic image.

Defense attorneys argued that Mitnick was a computer addict, a novel legal theory accepted by the prosecution and the judge. By April of 1989, the prosecution had drastically changed its harsh view of Kevin Mitnick and accepted a plea bargain. U.S. Attorney James Sanders admitted to Judge Pfaelzer that Mitnick's damage to DEC was not the $4 million that had made headlines but $160,000. Even that amount was not damage done by Mitnick, but the rough cost of tracing the security weaknesses that his incursions had brought to DEC's attention. The government acknowledged it had no evidence of the wild claims that had helped hold Mitnick without bail and in solitary confinement. No proof Mitnick had ever compromised the security of the NSA. No proof that Mitnick had ever issued a false press release for Security Pacific Bank. No proof that Mitnick had ever changed the TRW credit report of a judge. "A lot of the stories we originally heard just didn't pan out," James R. Asperger, the Assistant U.S. Attorney, told the *Daily News*.

But the judge, perhaps influenced by the terrifying media coverage, rejected the plea bargain and sentenced Mitnick to a longer term than even the government wanted. "Mr. Mitnick, you have been engaging in this conduct for too long, and no one has actually punished you," U.S. District Judge Mariana Pfaelzer was quoted in the *Los Angeles Times*. "This is the last time you are going to do this."

The prosecution's admission that Mitnick's case had been hyped barely registered a blip on the Mitnick legend. Newspaper articles continued to quote the $4 million figure and recite the other myths as fact. And what angered Mitnick the most was that he suspected at least some of the reporters knowingly hid the truth.

.   .   .

He did his eight months in solitary at the Metropolitan Detention Center in Los Angeles and four months at Lompoc, up the coast, where he met Ivan Boesky. Then, after six months in a Jewish halfway house, Kevin Mitnick tried to reenter the workforce. He landed a programming job in Vegas, but his employer was so terrified of his reputation that he wasn't allowed to work unchaperoned in the computer room. By law, Mitnick had to tell them he was a convicted felon.

Finally, after he lost his Vegas programming job in June of 1991, Mitnick realized his efforts were in vain. Mitnick applied at all the heavily computerized Vegas casinos: Caesar's, the Mirage, the Sands. Mitnick believed they were all interested, until his probation officer would phone or write.

The federal government had decided Kevin Mitnick was a danger to society, and like a convicted rapist or child molester, Mitnick was being monitored. His probation officer would persistently contact Mitnick's prospective employers: "Does he have access to cash? . . . I want you to understand the danger. . . ."

The federal government didn't know what to do with Kevin Mitnick. The government wasn't going to let him disappear like some small-time crook. Kevin Mitnick was a hacker.

.   .   .

"Why should I talk to this Eric dude?"

"I don't know," Spiegel drawls. "All I know is he saved my ass. Came over one night with Erica and told me there was a tap on my line."

"Really?"

"Yeah, a couple weeks later, some Secret Service and Sprint guys paid me a visit."

"What else can Eric do?"

"He wiretaps, wins radio contests."

"So why should I talk to him?"

"I don't know. You're a hacker. He's a hacker. Maybe he wants to share information."

"Can you call him?" Mitnick asks.

"Hold on a minute."

Spiegel flips through his address book, and dials Eric's pager number. "It should only be a couple minutes. He usually phones back fast."

He's right.

Spiegel makes the introductions, then drops off the line to see how his girl's doing. Spiegel monitors Mitnick's call on speakerphone.

"I'm into phones, computers," Eric coolly introduces himself. "I like keeping in touch with people. I'm willing to share. Course I don't do any hacking myself."

"Same here," agrees Mitnick.

"Yeah, but I like to stay current. You know what I mean?"

"Right," answers Mitnick. "Look, I know somebody else you might want to talk to. His name is Bob."

.   .   .

Bob, Roscoe ... Lewis De Payne has a few aliases. He's Mitnick's old friend and hacker sidekick. De Payne has also been prominent in the Los Angeles phone phreaking scene, and was busted for computer fraud back in 1982. But he managed to elude the sort of criminal and public limelight heaped on his young disciple. He even had his record legally expunged. He graduated from the University of Southern California, and satisfied himself with running the mainframe computers of a large Los Angeles wholesaler.

De Payne toys with Eric for a couple of weeks, stringing him along with vague hints that he might be committing crimes. Finally, a frustrated Eric pages Mitnick again, and the elusive hacker phones Spiegel to set up another three-way call. Henry Spiegel's Hollywood phone is the electronic meeting place for Mitnick and Eric.

"Found anything good for monitoring lines?" Eric asks Mitnick.

"You know about the SCC talk and monitor feature on the 1AESS, right?" Mitnick offers.

To hackers, the SCC talk and monitor feature is considered a quick and dirty wiretap. But Mitnick knows it only works on the 1AESS Pacific Bell phone switch, makes an audible click, and requires the target to be mid-conversation to work.

"Have you heard of SAS?"

Mitnick doesn't know what Eric is talking about.

"Tell me how it works," Mitnick presses.

Eric clams up.

But he's already said too much. Eric has given Mitnick the name of SAS, a mysterious wiretapping system.

Mitnick makes a few phone calls to Pac Bell offices, pretending to be a Pac Bell employee, a tech looking for information. Hackers call this social engineering. The key is knowing the jargon, the corporate infrastructure, and human nature. Mitnick exudes confidence, and few challenge him or his requests for data. He tracks down the person he needs.

"Can you read me the copyright notice on the manual?"

"Sure, hold on. . . . You know they've gone out of business."

That doesn't stop Mitnick. He does a little more research, finds SAS's designer, and phones him up.

The engineer is excited to have someone at Pac Bell take an interest in his old masterpiece. He searches the hard drive on his PC, and finds his design notes. The engineer wants to know where he should send them.

"Here's my fax number . . ."

Mitnick laughs to himself. They never check fax numbers.

•   •   •

Three weeks pass. Mitnick figures it's time for a face-to-face encounter. The three meet at Hamburger Hamlet on Sepulveda.

De Payne and Mitnick await Eric's arrival outside in De Payne's car, scanning all two hundred channels for FBI traffic with De Payne's Radio Shack scanner. They pick up nothing.

De Payne looks much like Eric expected. Too slender, pants too tight, movements jerky, almost robotic. Mitnick is the surprise. Nothing like the 240-pound monster in the newspapers. He's dressed casually, stocky but athletic, just under six feet tall and about 180 pounds. His dense, dark hair is short, but styled. His face is handsome, his eyes almost warm. His voice emotional, even child-like at times. He seems to be always on the verge of a smile. Or could it be laughter?

Mitnick is puzzled by Eric. He looks like he's just come from a Metallica rock concert. He looks too old to be a hacker. But he's knowledgeable. He seems to know his stuff.

"We brought some toys, Eric," De Payne says with a smile. "We scanned the place. It's clean. So why don't you tell us a little about yourself, Eric?"

"Well, you've heard of Kevin Poulsen, the guy charged with espionage?"

They nod. They've seen the dramatic *Unsolved Mysteries* television episode on the hacker fugitive, and read his front-page *L.A. Times* clips. Poulsen pulled off some of the coolest hacks in cyberspace. Won Porsches and $20,000 cash prizes by taking over radio station phone lines. Messed with secret FBI and national security wiretaps. He lived underground for two years, always one step ahead of the cybercops until last April, when he was finally nabbed in a nearby Ralph's Supermarket. Poulsen, like Mitnick, is a legend, a hero to thousands of young hackers.

"We won some contests together," Eric continues. "Crashed central offices a few times a week. Poulsen could do whatever he wanted in Pac Bell's computers. . . . But, hey, enough about me. What have you guys done recently?"

Mitnick and De Payne don't have much to say.

Eric gets up suddenly.

"I gotta go to the john."

Mitnick looks. De Payne looks. Eric's left his laptop on the table, facing them.

De Payne pulls out his Opto Electronics frequency counter and waves it like a magic wand to pick up any local transmissions. The old hacker buddies are thinking the same thought. Why'd Eric leave his safe open?

But the frequency counter picks up no transmissions, no tiny microphone tucked inside the laptop, though there could be a hidden tape recorder.

"He seems like such a nice guy," volunteers Mitnick to the laptop.

"Too bad we don't have as much information as he does," bemoans De Payne.

They wink at each other, holding back their smiles as Eric saunters back.

"So why didn't you get busted with Poulsen last spring?" asks De Payne.

"They got me in Texas in June," says Eric. "I did four months on credit card and ATM stuff. I'm on probation now."

"You ever called the FBI?" Mitnick asks.

"They contacted me on the Poulsen stuff. They didn't want to know anything about Poulsen. They just wanted me to tell them about the things I'd done."

Doesn't sound like the FBI I know. When the FBI talks to me, they want to know everything.

The hackers decide it's time for a little fun. Mitnick and De Payne have been waiting to make their next move.

De Payne pops a floppy disk in Eric's laptop.

Eric's eyes widen. The protocols for SAS flash on his screen. Mitnick got the program, the blueprints. In less than three weeks after Eric's slip on the phone, Kevin Mitnick has learned more about SAS than Eric ever knew. SAS is an automated computerized test system that works on any Pac Bell switch in Southern California. He can use it to wiretap anybody's phone or data line. SAS is the ultimate hacker's tool, the power to play Big Brother whenever you want, and never leave a trail.

De Payne ejects the disk, places it in his shirt pocket, and speaks slowly to Eric. "As soon as you start producing information, we'll start producing information."

Pending
Investigation

"**H**i, Lew," Kevin greets his friend in his hangdog voice. It's January of 1992. He's talking on the phone from his dad's apartment in Calabasas, and he's got that awful pang in his gut. Kevin Mitnick trusts his instincts. He decides he better check to see if the line is being tapped.

Mitnick phones the remote Pac Bell central office in Calabasas, on Las Virgenes Street.

"You have one of our boxes there," he informs the technician.

Mitnick's launching another social engineering attack.

Mitnick listens to the tech walk down the frame and then return.

"Yeah, here it is."

"And the monitor number on that box was?"

Kevin Mitnick knows exactly what questions to ask. He knows that when Pac Bell wants to wiretap somebody they first create a new phone line, what they call a "monitor number" in the local central office. On the steel and wire frame where the phone lines run, Pac Bell connects the monitor line to the target line through a special interface box. Next, Pac Bell security personnel in Oakland phone the monitor line and enter the touchtone security code 1-2-3-4 to activate the wiretap.

And Kevin Mitnick knows some other things Pac Bell would

prefer he didn't. The taps are referred to as pen registers, or Dial Number Recorders, DNRs. All the phone numbers dialed from each tapped line print out at the Pac Bell security office in Oakland. And Mitnick is one of a handful of hackers who know the taps also transmit voice, and can also be used to eavesdrop on conversations.

Mitnick's got the monitor number. One more phone call and he figures he'll get the number of the actual wiretap.

His car radio's playing a familiar ad as he cruises with his cell phone. "This is Tom Bodette for Motel Six, and we'll leave the light on for you."

Mitnick dials Pac Bell security in San Francisco.

"Hi, this is Tom Bodette," Mitnick drawls.

Shit. I can't believe I used that name!

"We've got a box here with your name and number. I'm going to have to disconnect it," Bodette continues.

The security investigator is being helpful. And why not? She's one of the half dozen phone company professionals in California that makes sure citizens are being properly wiretapped. Intercepts. That's what Pac Bell calls them. It sounds less threatening than a wiretap.

"Do you need to do it now?" the security woman asks.

"Yeah. You ready?" primes Bodette.

"Go ahead."

"OK. Hold on a minute. I'll be right back."

This is the fun part. Mitnick cups his hand over the phone for a couple of minutes and works himself into character.

"I, HUFF, HUFF, disconnected it. HUFF, HUFF. Can you give me some help connecting it back to the frame?"

The Pac Bell security woman rattles off the LEN, the line equipment number, of the wires the box has to be tied back into.

"I don't have Cosmos handy," Bodette casually offers, mentioning the Pac Bell computer database. "What's the phone number?"

Kevin Mitnick is so smooth that the security professional doesn't even pause.

"It's 5 5 —"

Hook, line, and sinker.

.   .   .

Kevin is half right. There is a wiretap out of the local Calabasas central office, but it's on the phone of Teltec Investigations, a nearby Calabasas private detective firm. By coincidence, Mitnick's father, Alan, knows a private detective who works at the firm, a guy named Mark Kasdan. Mitnick senior invites him over, Kevin fills the detective in on what he's learned, and then Kasdan brings Kevin down to the firm's offices for a little show-and-tell.

The detectives don't believe Mitnick at first, the things he says he knows, the things he claims he can do. But as Mitnick starts to prove his encyclopedic knowledge of phones and computers, they take him seriously. The detectives confide why they think their phones are being tapped. Teltec was investigated for allegedly using stolen codes to run TRW credit reports on individuals, and the three-year statute of limitations on the case is about to expire. Perhaps, they tell Mitnick, the recent wiretap is a sign of renewed law enforcement interest.

·   ·   ·

The on-ramp light turns green, and Mitnick guns it onto the crowded 101 freeway at Sherman Oaks. His probation officer has given him permission to take the long drive to Vegas, where his mother and grandmother live, for his brother's funeral.

The death of his half brother has hit Mitnick hard. The facts are sketchy. On the evening of January 7, 1992, Adam Mitnick was found dead in Echo Park, a neighborhood notorious for gangs and drugs. They had been close. It was Adam who arrived at the gate at Lompoc when Mitnick's prison term was up. They were talking about renting an apartment together. Adam had started his own business selling miniblinds and had enrolled in college. That's what gnawed at Kevin. His brother had sworn he'd quit heroin.

To the Los Angeles police department the death of Adam Mitnick was just one of the hundreds of overdoses each year that clog its files. But Kevin Mitnick had to investigate, and before long he learned that Adam was found in the passenger seat of his own BMW, slumped against the dash.

So who had driven his half brother to Echo Park to die? Mitnick learned Adam had visited his uncle that same night, the same uncle who was addicted to heroin. Suddenly, Kevin Mitnick didn't want to know any more about how his brother ended up dead at just twenty-one. It reminded him too much of his family.

.   .   .

Mitnick's parents divorced when he was three, and he lived in a series of unmemorable apartments in the San Fernando Valley. Although Kevin saw his father rarely, he liked him and looked up to him. The Mitnick men were salesmen, smooth tongued, sharp and successful. Mitnick said his dad worked for Capitol Records, and then sold home improvement contracts. *Los Angeles Magazine* would list him as one of the most successful businesses in the San Fernando Valley, but court records told another story. Alan Mitnick filed for bankruptcy in the mid 1980s, and Los Angeles criminal filings included charges for forgery, grand theft, and battery.

Crime was no stranger to the Mitnick family. Mitnick's aunt, Chickie Leventhal, ran Chickie's Bail Bonds in Los Angeles. Mitnick's uncle worked in construction, but Southern California court files were full of civil actions filed against him. By the late 1980s his uncle's life began to unwind. There were charges for possession of controlled substances and drug paraphernalia. In 1989, he was charged with grand theft and sentenced to a year in county jail and three years probation. Incredibly he served part of his term in the same Jewish halfway house with his nephew, after Kevin's DEC conviction. But Mitnick's uncle wasn't rehabilitated. The following year he fled probation. He had at least three aliases: Jay Tenny Brooks, Richard Stewart, and William Contos. And years later he would be charged and convicted of manslaughter. During a robbery he shot and killed a man.

Kevin was often left to fend for himself. His father was more interested in Adam. His mother, Shelly Jaffe, was busy just trying to make ends meet, waitressing at a couple of Jewish delicatessens on Ventura Boulevard. Mitnick appeared eager to work, toiling as a delivery boy and kitchen helper at one of the delis, and helping out in the office of a local synagogue. When Kevin was ten or twelve, he'd push carts back into the slots at the local Safeway for Blue Chip stamps. He was proud of his Jewish faith and displayed his framed Bar Mitzvah certificate on his dresser.

But like everything else in the Mitnick household, even Kevin's faith was a bit off-kilter. Mitnick's stepfather was an active member of the radical Jewish Defense League. When Mitnick was eight or ten his stepfather would take him out into the desert near Los Angeles and let him watch while they fired automatic weapons at posters of Hitler.

Kevin was a loner, uninterested in sports and too shy for girls. At thirteen he learned how to punch out his own bus transfers, and after school he'd ride out toward San Bernardino and the desert, or down the coast to Long Beach. His grandmother was proud of Kevin for memorizing the routes and schedules. No one in the family would think to scold him for tricking the transit district out of bus fare. Kevin's little game was an ingenious system of babysitting himself, of creating a travel opportunity for a boy whose mother rarely had the time to take him anywhere.

One afternoon on the bus, Kevin met a fat boy. They'd ride together to Beverly Hills, eat junk food, and gawk at the homes of the movie stars. Soon Kevin too was fat and ate almost constantly. Bob Arkow, a bus driver, struck up a conversation with the kid on his empty bus one day. He'd noticed his T-shirt emblazoned with "CBers Do It on the Air." Mitnick told him he was into citizens band radio, and the driver asked if he'd heard about ham radio. That's all it took to get him started. Mitnick went to the ham radio outlet, picked up some books, and in no time earned his own ham radio license.

As a ham radio operator Mitnick had his own call sign, and could radio other ham operators around the world. The parallels to hacking were great. Mitnick didn't have to pay for his radio messages. His call sign was his identity, or "handle," and he was part of a worldwide community of radio enthusiasts. Though cellular phones were years off into the future, he was already mastering their basic principle — radio.

To Arkow, Mitnick was just another thirteen-year-old boy with a new toy, making on-air personal attacks on other ham radio operators. Soon, he was able to manipulate the phone system to harass people too. He began rummaging through phone company dumpsters for discarded manuals and reading Bell technical journals at the library. Just as Mitnick rode L.A.'s buses free, he could travel the long distance lines wherever and however he pleased.

Lewis De Payne discovered Mitnick one day while listening to one of his ham radio fights. They became fast friends, though De Payne was several years older than the fifteen-year-old. De Payne admired the young enthusiast's obsessive streak. Mitnick could be whoever he wanted over the radio or on the phone. He'd call a Pac Bell switching center and impersonate an angry supervisor, and if one person wouldn't give him what he needed, he'd just dial someone else.

His mother couldn't afford to buy him a personal computer so Mitnick roamed like a techno gypsy from one Radio Shack to another, slipping in a communications program disk and using the store's modem to dial any computer he wished. His teachers at Monroe High School described him as clever, until he began using its computers to hack into the files of other schools. He dropped out and was later expelled from a community college for similar pranks.

Those who crossed Mitnick did so at their own risk. He attached a hospital's $30,000 in long distance charges to the home phone bill of a ham radio enthusiast he hated. His goal was power. Mitnick had little interest in making money with his phone and burgeoning computer skills. For kicks, he tracked Susan Thunder, a prostitute who had fallen hard for De Payne, finding out where she lived and turned tricks, shutting off her phone service, forwarding her calls, and broadcasting her sex talk on ham radio. In 1981, after Mitnick and De Payne talked their way into a late-night unauthorized visit of a Pac Bell computer operations center, Thunder planned her revenge. The computers of a San Francisco leasing company nearly ground to a halt, and the operators arrived one morning to find the floor littered with printouts carrying threats and the names of Roscoe and Mitnick. It wasn't long before an investigator from the district attorney's office chased young Mitnick on the 405 freeway and handcuffed him at gunpoint. The charges were burglary, grand theft, and conspiring to commit computer fraud. Thunder testified for the prosecution and the juvenile court ordered a diagnostic psychological study of Mitnick and sentenced him to a year's probation.

By 1984, Mitnick had a job and a black Nissan with the conspicuous vanity plate "X-HACKER." But the D.A.'s office was already back on his tail, investigating allegations Mitnick was harassing people on MIT's computers and hacking into phone company computers. Mitnick's new office job was a convenient place to make his pretext calls to Pac Bell and run TRW credit checks for kicks. But the day before the D.A. served its search warrant, a man identifying himself as a Los Angeles Police Department detective called into the warrant section of the LAPD to confirm a probation violation warrant on Mitnick.

It was Mitnick, presumably, checking to see if he was wanted, and when he got the bad news, he went underground, not to resurface until the summer of 1985, after his arrest warrant expired. He enrolled at a Los Angeles technical school, the Computer Learning Center, and impressed his instructors. In 1987, he surprised everyone by dating a pretty, petite woman named Bonnie Vitello. They were soon married.

Love brought out another side of Mitnick. The impulsive hacker lost weight, danced at nightclubs, and shared romantic trips up the California coast. But Mitnick hadn't gone cold turkey. To start with, Bonnie Vitello happened to work for GTE, a phone company. Like an addict, Mitnick would periodically escape into cheap motels with a computer and modem for hacking binges, and sure enough, in 1987, he was busted again, this time for hacking into the computers of a small Santa Cruz UNIX software maker. The charge was reduced to a misdemeanor when he agreed to explain how he did it, and Mitnick was given three years probation.

He was on the verge of being hired by Security Pacific Bank, but calls from an enemy ham radio operator and an LAPD detective scuttled the job offer. Mitnick tried to get into security, and even filed a fictitious business name, Security Software Services, in Sherman Oaks in April of 1988. But by that summer, Kevin Mitnick had a new plan. He wanted to learn more about Digital Equipment Corporation's latest VMS operating system for its powerful minicomputers. He didn't just want the operating system, however, he wanted the source code, the genetic blueprint, to discover more about its vulnerabilities. With the source code, Mitnick could understand more about the complex program. He could also plant the seeds of his own future games. At the least, he'd know better where to attack. And if he was truly bent on creating mayhem, he could try to send the software back to Digital's distribution centers, implanted with his own Trojan horse programs, secret back doors to enable him to manipulate the system at will.

But once again Mitnick was caught red-handed. Lacking his own powerful computer, he'd been forced to stash his loot at the University of Southern California's computers, and, not surprisingly, the university's system administrators had noticed his bulging files. There was no evidence Kevin Mitnick planned to sell the software, modify it, or even redistribute it. But what Mitnick looked upon as simple copying, the government viewed as theft.

Kevin Mitnick was a serial hacker, and he'd given no one any reason to believe he intended to quit.

The Tap

Kevin Mitnick lifts his cell
phone to his ear on the 101
freeway, as he begins his three-hour trip to Las Vegas.

"Canoga Park SCC."

"Hi, this is Tom Bodette calling."

Why not? It worked on the security woman.

"I got a problem on a line," Bodette tells the technician at the Pac
Bell Switch and Control Center. "Here's the number, the trunk and
the TGID [trunk group identification number, the identifying number of a group of outgoing phone trunks]."

Mitnick is impersonating a Pac Bell technician, giving the perti-
nent line and trunk information to trace the switching trail of the
wiretap step by step, from the small Calabasas facility to the bustling
Sherman Oaks central office, and then to the LA 70 Tandem, one of
the main north-south phone corridors in the state.

He drives past Glendale and Alhambra, and at Ontario veers east
on Interstate 15 toward Vegas. He's finally free of the Southern California sprawl, climbing above the smog into the San Gabriel Mountains. Off to his right is Silverwood Lake and the San Bernardino
National Forest. A few minutes later the freeway sweeps back down
out of the mountains.

He's in the Mohave now, ten minutes from a lonely outpost called

Victorville. He's driven about seventy miles, but on his cell phone, he's traveled four hundred miles north, back to an Oakland switch. The one that switches all the Pac Bell wiretaps.

"I'm checking some trouble on a line," Bodette drawls, one hand on the wheel, giving the number. "Can you put it down ?" Mitnick's asking Pac Bell to knock down its own connection temporarily so he can dial in.

Mitnick's driving through Victorville when he phones the wiretap.

"WHUUUUUUUU!"

Blowing through wet lips, that's what it always sounds like to Mitnick, the thousand-cycle pulse of a line waiting for voice to activate a tap. The pulse has one purpose. When it ends, the tape recorder spins.

"WHUUUUUUUU —"

The pulse stops. The voice he hears is as familiar as his own.

Son of a bitch!

In Mitnick's ear, his own father talking!

He was right about his premonition, it just took a while to materialize. They took the wiretap off Teltec and put it on his dad's line.

It's all desert to Barstow, and Mitnick floors it, pulling in at the first gas station on the dusty outskirts of town. His cell phone won't do. He punches in the number on the pay phone.

"Lew, go to a pay phone and call me back," Mitnick snaps. "The number is . . ."

He paces back and forth in the piercing desert sun.

Finally it rings.

"Get rid of everything!"

He hangs up, dials his dad.

"Go to the Village market. Call me from the pay phone."

He hangs up, waits for the call.

"Kevin, you're getting paranoid."

"Dad, I just heard your voice on a tap. Get the fucking computer out of the house!"

.   .   .

What exactly Kevin Mitnick did next is difficult to know for certain. Messing with Pac Bell or federal wiretaps is a serious crime. But

Lewis De Payne hinted that Mitnick and he pulled off the ultimate social engineering scam. Only Mitnick or De Payne knows whether it actually happened, but there's little doubt it was and is possible. For if Mitnick could trick Pac Bell into letting him know there was a wiretap on his line, what was stopping him from moving the tap to someone else's number?

"Say if someone from security were to call the central office and tell them they need a box moved," De Payne hypothesized. " 'We put it on the wrong pair . . .' They would certainly comply. And if somehow that box were to get moved over to the next phone cable pair, it would likely sit there and no one would notice for a while. It would keep working and keep recording.

"If that happened, the powers that be wouldn't be very happy when they finally found out about it. Especially if they spent all their resources and time analyzing the calls and trying to track all the outgoing phone numbers.

"No, they wouldn't be very happy at all."

.   ■   ■

Caller ID is what Pac Bell calls it. When someone dials a Caller ID–equipped phone it works like a law enforcement trap, spitting back the number of the caller. There's only one problem. Pac Bell has never introduced the service in California.

Kevin Mitnick has. Caller ID works just perfectly on his pay phones. And why shouldn't it? The feature exists, Pac Bell just hasn't been able to gain the regulatory approval necessary to introduce Caller ID to the general public.

Mitnick and De Payne lay the trap. Eric has never given them his home telephone number: he knows they could quickly find out where he lives. Instead, when they want to reach him they have to call his beeper and leave their number. They page Eric to call a pay phone, a number the hacker's never dialed.

Eric dials the number from his apartment. The pay phone rings and rings and rings. That's all they need.

■   ■   ■

"Hi, Eric," De Payne cheerfully threatens, telling Eric he's calling from the Oakwood Apartments pay phone near the pool.

"Do you mind if we come up?"

They've already done a walkby of apartment 107b. They know the exact apartment number from the phone number they picked up with Caller ID.

Eric is shocked. He finally manages to speak.

"No. I, I never have hackers up."

"Eric, we need to talk to you about something," De Payne continues, adopting a serious tone. "We've noticed there are all of these taps on our lines."

"Look, it will take me a while to come down. I'll meet you down in the clubhouse room by the pool."

That's OK. Mitnick and De Payne have plenty of time. They wait in the two-story building at the front of the sprawling stucco complex with the burgundy and teal carpet, the big screen TV, and the two rows of overstuffed chairs. They've seen the tennis courts, the lap-swimming-length pool, the groomed professionals and students on their way to the pool-sized Jacuzzi. Yet something's wrong with the picture. What's a rocker like Eric doing in a yuppie complex like this?

Eric strolls in with his torn Levis and his teased hair. He's got the same look he wears at the strip clubs.

Eric's pissed. "I need you to respect my privacy!" he hisses. "Do not violate my privacy."

Mitnick's amused. The guy's a hacker. The guy says he wants to share information. So why get so bent over a little hack?

"There are all of these taps on our lines, Eric," De Payne says.

"What do you mean?"

"There's a tap on Kevin's line. There's a tap on my home line. There are even taps on my lines at work."

"You're sure?"

"We're sure, Eric," De Payne says. "All seventy-eight lines at my office are being tapped. That's a lot of taps, Eric."

"OK. I'll check it on Pac Bell's computers," promises Eric. "But I need you to respect my privacy."

Mitnick and De Payne already know the lines are tapped, but

they're interested by the proposal. What Eric's talking about is illegal, hacking into Pac Bell's proprietary systems, checking for wiretaps.

Mitnick and De Payne phone Eric a couple of days later on three-way.

"Eric, we wanted to let you know that we don't need your help," De Payne tells him, holding back laughter. "We've already gone in and checked. The taps *were* on our lines."

But not anymore.

.   .   .

"A Home, Not a Hotel," reads the glossy four-color Oakwood brochure:

> At Oakwood, we understand what experienced travelers miss when they are on the road. That's why we've created a comfortable, cost-effective alternative to conventional hotels: short term, fully-furnished lodgings that provide all the comforts of home. In addition to linens, housewares, TVs and maid service, your amenities package is easily customized with a VCR, stereo system, microwave oven, answering machine and a wide range of many other necessities for business or pleasure.

Mitnick phones the Oakwood Apartments offices in the Valley. He knows it's part of a massive, national chain serving over 400 cities across the country. He knows Oakwood provides short-term corporate housing for businesspeople, and is the choice "of 300 of the Fortune 500" companies. He knows Oakwood couldn't possibly be the choice of Eric and his torn jeans.

Mitnick enjoys the game, the masquerade he's about to play. Eric is pretending to be someone he isn't, so Mitnick will pretend to be an Oakwood employee to find out more about Eric. It's only fair.

Mitnick already knows the people structure of the corporation, but when he calls he apologizes, explaining he's a "new" Oakwood employee. Mitnick is friendly and easy to trust, and people just seem naturally to like him. The woman pulls the application of the current occupant of 107b.

It's no problem at all.

Mitnick scours the routine information on the rental contract: social security number, date of birth, driver's license, previous addresses. Good information, but not the critical clue Mitnick seeks. He knows Eric Heinz is renting apartment 107b and paying the phone bills under another name, Joseph Wernle. He knows this mysterious Wernle is self-employed and has provided no references. But what's this business phone number he's left? It doesn't match either of the two lines in the apartment.

．　　　．　　　．

Pac Bell helps Mitnick research the calling patterns of the inhabitant of Oakwood apartment 107b.

When Mitnick wants Pac Bell to do his research, he finds less-knowledgeable technicians. Rather than admit their ignorance, or ask a question, they'll freely issue a command on the switch for a knowledgeable superior, like Kevin Mitnick.

Take a line history block (LHB), for example, a command that generates the last number dialed on a line. Mitnick finds a technician to run the check, and it spits back the last number dialed from apartment 107b.

Three separate times Mitnick cons technicians into running LHBs.

On the fourth LHB, the number 310-477-6565 comes back. Mitnick doesn't have to dial it. The number is permanently filed in his head: Los Angeles headquarters of the FBI.

It's the proof Mitnick wanted. Eric is phoning the FBI.

Next, Mitnick researches the business number Oakwood gave him for Joseph Wernle. He learns it's a cellular number, but still there's a puzzle. Why is Eric's Pac Tel Cellular number, 213-507-7782, registered in the name of Mark Martinez?

It shouldn't take Mitnick long to find out.

"This is Mary with Pac Tel Cellular," the service rep answers cheerfully.

"Hi, this is Mark Martinez, 213-507-7782," Mitnick introduces himself. "I don't know why, but I didn't get my bill. What address did you send it to?"

"Just a minute, Mr. Martinez. . . . We sent your bill to P.O. box . . ."

"That's funny, it's the right address."

Mitnick has the postal application pulled on the P.O. box. On one level, the cover is good. From all appearances, Mr. Martinez appears to be a real estate attorney who works in Bel Aire, California. But whoever Martinez may or may not be, Kevin Mitnick deploys his social engineering tricks to trace Mr. Martinez's P.O. box to 1100 Wilshire Boulevard, FBI headquarters. Within hours, Pac Tel Cellular diligently faxes Mitnick the toll records on the FBI cellular number: calls to government agencies, the IRS, the Army, internal Bureau numbers.

The cellular tolls are the beginning of a web. Mitnick gets the bills on all the other cellular numbers. Mitnick doesn't stop. He can't.

Gotta know how I'm being screwed. Who he is. Why they're doing it.

.   ■   ■

Mitnick continues investigating Joseph Wernle. He's amazed how easy it is to investigate the FBI.

Wernle's Pennsylvania driver's license reveals he's forty, far too old to masquerade as rocker Eric Heinz. Mitnick tracks down Wernle's uncle, adopting his favorite Social Security Administration ruse.

"Hello, this is Tom Bodette with the Social Security Administration. I wonder if you could help me with a problem we're trying to clear up."

"I'll try."

"Our records seem to be confused. We think the cross reference files for your relatives may be skewed. Let's see . . . Do you know Mary Eberle?"

"That's my sister."

"Your sister? Then, who's Joseph Wernle? Doesn't Mary have a son, Joseph Wernle?"

"No, her son is Joe Ways."

"Does he live in Pennsylvania?"

"No, he lives in Southern California. He's an FBI agent."

"I apologize, I must have the wrong Wernle."

.   ■   ■

Mitnick's cracked the cover! Wernle is FBI agent Joseph Charles Ways. Mitnick runs Ways's California driver's license, learns his height, weight, date of birth, address, even the name of his wife. Once again, there's no match. The man's too short, too heavy, too married, and too old to be Eric Heinz.

But Mitnick's got the identity of an active FBI undercover agent. He's done it with hacking, with phones, and with his disarmingly friendly voice. Most of all, he's done it because he's more possessed than the System. The first page of Mitnick's file on the Bureau's operation is extraordinary, the kind of information the FBI wishes it had on the hacker. Mitnick has uncovered the real names of his pursuers and their wives, their IDs, their phones, their beepers, their contacts, their home addresses. The phone numbers and the addresses are the ammunition for Mitnick's countersurveillance, to anticipate the next moves of the agents, day by day, hour by hour.

FBI agent in charge: Joseph Charles Ways. CDL [California driver's license]: A7988424 DOB 6/16/52 FBI eyes brown, hazel (hair) ht: 5'9", 175 lbs. (805) 529-xxxx home.

False ID: Joseph Wernle. DL A0519400 DOB 8/23/52. Philadelphia PA. Mom: Mary M. Wornley. Dad: Joseph Ways. Uncle: Joseph Wornley, Sr. Uncle's sister: Mary Everly lives in P.A.

FBI business front. Alta Services. 18663 Ventura Blvd. Ste 301. Tarzana, CA 91356. (818) 345-6435/3495.

Beeper Information. Type: Motorola Bravo Plus. (310) 785-4399. Page frequency: 931.0375 Cap Code: 0806793. Mode: High-speed. POCSAG signaling method.

Special Agent Stan Ornellas: (310) 645-6606 Inglewood. Contact w/ (310) 215-xxxx. DOD Criminal Investigative service El Segundo.

The game has just begun.

Summer Con

"**D**o you want to hear the Kevin Poulsen story?" Eric Heinz blandly offers.

"Oh yeah!" clamors the crowd.

They've got handles like Bloodaxe, Signal Surfer, Gatsby, The Serpent, Stroke and Key, Republic, Slave Driver, and Drunkfux, and they've driven and flown from every corner of the nation to this dingy conference room at the Executive Inn in St. Louis, Missouri. It's a sweltering, humid afternoon, and Eric Heinz flew all the way from L.A., though this crowd knows him only by his handle, Agent Steal. It's Summer Con 1992, a conference for hackers and wannabes. Dentists do it. Lawyers do it. Accountants do it. Why not hackers? Share a few secrets of the trade. Tell a few tales of unauthorized computer access, a few intrusions into Ma Bell's switches, a little wiretapping.

"You need to move over," a squeaky voice orders.

Bloodaxe, the famed, longhaired Texas hacker, motions Steal to slide into the range of his video lens.

"But I'm so comfortable here," Agent Steal drawls, a hip bandana neatly wrapped around his forehead, his frazzled locks falling around his shoulders, one blue-jeaned leg propped up on a chair.

Bloodaxe obliges Steal. The camera jerks and focuses on Steal's artificially tanned, bored face. He's the picture of detachment.

"Poulsen's a virgin, very obsessed with hacking," begins Steal. "He takes it very seriously. Pretty much thinks he owns the phone company. He was breaking into central offices. He had his own key. He knew what time to go in when people weren't in there. . . . Some of you might have seen the story on *Unsolved Mysteries?*"

The crowd breaks into laughter. Poulsen's two *Unsolved Mysteries* TV episodes are infamous among the hacker underground. Steal delivers his second punch line.

"He was in touch with this guy that was a pimp."

He never mentions his name, but he's talking about Henry Spiegel in Hollywood.

Steal smiles knowingly and finishes. "Who I had put him in touch with."

The room erupts. Agent Steal is one cool hacker dude.

Steal quickly weaves through Poulsen's escapades, and cuts to the chase. "They [the cops] kept finding me. I mean they were like putting so much effort into it. Eventually we got the scanner frequencies and we were listening to them, basically watching them watch us."

The hackers roar.

"How I got caught I still don't know. . . . The main reason they wanted me was to get to the bottom of Poulsen because Poulsen was in the process, allegedly, of gathering top secret information, which I'm not allowed to discuss because I signed an agreement saying I wouldn't talk about it.

"Anyway . . . what they're going to charge him with, is gathering national defense related information with the intent to injure the United States. If they can prove that, he's going to get twenty years. And they don't mess around . . . on that kind of stuff. . . . Poulsen's going to be in jail for a long time."

"How come you didn't have to cut your hair?" Bloodaxe asks.

"Because I was in a federal jail."

"I'll remember that," Bloodaxe quips.

"So, let's see what else," Steal continues. "I got charged with wiretapping, computer fraud . . . interstate transporation of an automobile." Steal continues reciting his resume. He's even stolen a Porsche. To the hacker, that's Harvard with honors.

"What Porsche did you steal?" asks a teen.

"Nine forty-four Turbo."

"Gusto!" someone cries.

Encouraged by the enthusiastic response, Steal launches on a primer on car fraud. He can't resist sharing his knowledge. You establish a bank account under a fake ID, he explains, and make a small down payment. "A lot of times they just let it fold. You know they won't bother trying to get it back."

"What about the title?" asks a teen.

"You never have title. You never own the car. But what the hell. You know, if you wreck it you can buy another one."

The crack brings down the house.

"So Kevin Poulsen's trial is coming up pretty soon. . . . I anticipate the whole thing to be a big media blitzkrieg. . . ."

Bloodaxe zeroes in for one last close-up. Bloodaxe knows quite a bit about Steal. He knows he's been up for membership a couple of times in the notorious hacker gang Legion of Doom. He even knows the single word used to describe the mercenary Steal in his latest, unsuccessful nomination: "Crime."

Bloodaxe, of course, is himself a celebrated member of the Legion of Doom, and he has lots of connections in the murky world of computer hacking. When Steal was arrested in Dallas in June of 1991, word had reached Bloodaxe almost instantly, and he'd quickly dispatched a junior hacker to check the court records. There weren't any. That doesn't square with Steal's talk about being a fugitive from California, wiretapping, computer fraud, or interstate transportation of a stolen vehicle. Bloodaxe quietly spreads the word among the 1992 Summer Con attendees. Be careful of Steal. Party with him? Sure. But don't *do* anything with him, don't *say* anything.

"Dude, what are you doing saying that stuff about me?" Steal confronts Bloodaxe in the lobby.

Word's reached Steal of Bloodaxe's warning. He's pissed.

"Well, you want to explain a few things for me?"

"Dude, I was arrested! Look, man, I can't talk about anything 'cuz they made me sign a bunch of things. They were trying to get me to do all these other things and I wouldn't do it!"

Steal whips out several government forms.

"They made me sign all this stuff," Steal complains, flipping the papers so fast that Bloodaxe has no chance to read them.

"It's cool. I'm not doing anything."

Bloodaxe shrugs.

Private Eye

He drives west on Las Virgenes on the road to Malibu, past the tidy roadside apartments and million-dollar houses high on the hill, over the busy 101 freeway. Right at the gas station, into the strip mall, past the shops and the Jack In the Box. Sprints up the terra-cotta stairs and turns left to the potted palms and the white walls flooded with light from the upper windows.

Teltec Investigations. Suite 212.

"Push here. Identify yourself," the black speakerphone commands. Mitnick's got a key.

He opens one of the wood double doors and pads down the dull gray carpet, past the boxes of phones, cables, and miscellaneous junk that line the hallway. Teltec's half-dozen crowded private offices are similarly cluttered with paper-strewn desks, girly calendars, and computers.

Mitnick boots up the laptop he's linked to his scanner. He's entered his "hot list" of fifteen cellular numbers into the program: FBI agents, Pac Bell security agents, Eric Heinz; in short, the people trying to stick him back in jail. Mitnick's scanning gear isn't unique. Some of the best law enforcement agencies in the country use it to pursue drug dealers, mobsters, and other big-time criminals. Kevin Mitnick uses it to track the FBI.

Mitnick knows a cellular telephone is a radio transceiver that sends and receives. He knows that for each call, it broadcasts a mobile identification number (MIN), the phone number, and the electronic serial number (ESN), the phone's unique identification.

He knows each call bounces to the cellular site that covers that geographic region. He knows his scanner picks up the local "handshake," the "forward control channel" of each call, as the caller moves into a new cell site.

Mitnick's program constantly scans for his MIN "hot list." If the FBI makes a cellular call in an area he's monitoring, it pops automatically onto his screen. He watches the FBI's movements and monitors who they call. The agents might as well be wearing electronic dog collars.

Mitnick moved a few weeks ago, with his father's friend Mark Kasden, into the tony Malibu Canyon Apartments at 5810 Las Virgenes, just a four-minute drive to Teltec. For the first time in his life, Mitnick's finally earning a good living, enjoying luxuries he's never known. He loves water, and the resort-like complex boasts a sprawling pool and a man-made waterfall and creek — nothing at all like the ordinary apartments of his youth.

Mitnick does his detective work mostly with phones. He impersonates the target, faxes release documents with authentic signatures, says a fire burned the records. Any kind of ruse he can imagine. He tracks down bank accounts and foreign assets. Talks people into revealing wire transfers. It's a talent. In most cases, some attorney is suing somebody, and if Mitnick can dig up substantial assets, Teltec sells the information to its clients. While other detectives at Teltec waste days on cases, trying to determine someone's whereabouts, Mitnick, equipped with a laptop, a phone, and his soft, puppy voice, digs up answers in minutes or hours: tax returns, credit and employment histories, phone bills, and bank accounts.

Joseph Wernle, the undercover FBI agent renting Eric's Oakwood apartment, isn't a Teltec assignment, but Mitnick investigates him anyway. Mitnick comes up empty at Bank of America, Union Bank, and Security Pacific, but it doesn't take long. Joseph Wernle banks at Wells Fargo, the second largest bank in the state.

Great, Mitnick thinks. Wells Fargo requires just one daily code and a social security number to get a customer's private information. Mitnick phones a branch listed in a banking guide, impersonates a manager, and tricks someone into giving him the code for the day. Next, he calls Wernle's branch, and convinces the teller to read everything on Wernle's signature card: his account and social security numbers, his mother's maiden name, his business address.

Mitnick keys Wernle's account number and the last four digits of his social security number via his touchtone phone into Wells's automated banking system. He listens to the synthesized voice recite the account activity: a deposit for $5,000, checks for $3,000 and $6,000. Mitnick's already impersonated Wernle to get his phone bills. Where are the matching checks for those amounts? Why hasn't Wernle paid his Oakwood phone bill?

.   ▪   ▪

Mitnick's been having fun investigating Wernle and Eric. First, he found the apartment the feds stashed Eric in at Oakwood, then he tracked down his latest hideaway, McCadden Place, apartment #9 in Hollywood. Mitnick and De Payne are playing a high-tech game of hide and seek, and Eric isn't totally to blame for the security breakdown. The FBI agents call Eric's new phone numbers on their cell phones, which Mitnick continues to monitor. And they even continue to take out phone service under the name Joseph Wernle.

Fully aware that the feds are tapping Mitnick's phone, his boss at Teltec sees an opportunity to throw the feds a curveball. He prepares an impromptu script for the FBI, including the names and numbers of competing detective firms that might be engaged in illegal activity. What better way to level the playing field than to trick the FBI into investigating his competitors?

At the same time, Mitnick and De Payne meet with an attorney friend and play the tapes of Eric's clumsy attempts to entrap them. Just like Mitnick's boss, the attorney coaches them for their next conversation.

"Eric, I know this guy who has access to [Pac Bell] billing systems," Mitnick confides. "Can you keep this to yourself?" The guy is a detective at one of Teltec's competitors.

"I just want to make some fucking money this time!" Mitnick blurts out in another call to Eric.

The FBI shoves, Mitnick shoves back.

"We're trading stuff with Rop and Bill Squire in Holland," Mitnick and De Payne tempt Eric.

"Yeah, they can come in through their channel, and that way, it's not illegal," the hackers tell Eric. "They get the information and download it for us."

Eric's hit the jackpot! Holland's an international center of hacking. The Dutch-based hackers are notorious.

.   .   .

SAS is a powerful hacker's tool for the simple reason that it can be used to wiretap almost any phone line, and therefore let the wiretapper hear all sorts of secret conversations. Just how far Mitnick and De Payne go with the technology only they and perhaps the FBI know. But De Payne knows what you can "theoretically" do with SAS: listen to law enforcement lines and monitor how officers call in to get information. Glean their names, badge numbers, and IDs. Pick up the lingo. Who works what shift. Who to make requests to.

If Mitnick could learn the routine, he could get the same results as the real officers. With SAS someone could learn how anything works. Anything that involves a phone.

.   .   .

"There's no way they could actually be monitoring us?" the FBI agent asks Eric on the phone one day.

De Payne says he and Mitnick heard the call. He doesn't say whether it was a cellular or a regular phone call, and he doesn't say when it happened. It's not every day a couple of hackers can turn the tables and listen to the FBI. But Mitnick's puzzled by one fact. Why hasn't the government pulled the plug on SAS? Is it a setup, a game to entice Mitnick into hacking, into illegally accessing the secret Pac Bell system?

The FBI must know Eric spilled the beans on Pac Bell's wiretapping system. Why wouldn't the FBI or Pac Bell shut it down or at least spend the few thousand bucks necessary to make it secure?

Why sit by while millions of telephones in the state of California are vulnerable to massive, untraceable eavesdropping? No accountability. No audit trails. SAS is the ultimate hacker tool. And Mitnick knows as time passes, SAS will only get better. The new, Northern Telecom DMS (Digital Multiplex System) phone switches being installed by Pac Bell all over California make SAS an even more foolproof wiretapping system. On a fully digital DMS switch, SAS wiretaps make no audible click and can stay up for hours or days at a time.

Kevin knows the FBI believes he can't resist the temptation, and he feels the same way about them. If all it takes to wiretap someone illegally with SAS is a PC and a couple of phone lines, why would the FBI bother with a court order?

.   .   .

Pac Bell is wiretapping.

On July 31, 1992, John Venn of Pac Bell Security places a DNR tap on 818-880-6472, the home number of Mark Kasden and Kevin Mitnick.

At 8:09 P.M., the tap picks up Pac Bell's computer activating the Priority Ringing and Speed Dialing custom calling features for Kasden and Mitnick's line, an ordinary event except for the fact that Pac Bell has yet to offer the new features to the general public.

Over the next week, the tap picks up calls to various voice mail boxes. Calls to the voice mail of Pac Bell security investigator Lillie Creeks and the voice mail of Pac Bell investigator Darrell Santos.

On August 6, 1992, Venn connects a tape recorder to the tap, capturing the first two minutes of any subsequent call. Venn doesn't need a court order. He works for Pac Bell. He can tap whoever he wants to under Title 18 Section 2511 (2) (a) (i) and (h). Mr. Venn believes Pac Bell's property rights are in danger. That's all he needs.

On August 25, FBI Special Agent Ken McGuire meets with Venn and Terry Atchley, another veteran Pac Bell security investigator. Atchley briefs McGuire on the activity he's been monitoring since late January. Pretext social engineering calls to Pac Bell central offices to check for taps. Calling features that mysteriously appear on the home phones of Alan Mitnick and Lewis De Payne. A mysterious

Ernie from "ESAC," an internal Pac Bell division, who instructs technicians to make specific entries into Pac Bell's computers. And modem calls made from De Payne's offices into Pac Bell's computers. But it's the wiretap recordings the FBI agent wants to hear. Venn hits play, and the men listen to three calls made to Pac Bell security voice mail boxes, and three more phone calls made to a mysterious "Dave."

Atchley's sure of it. He worked the first case against Mitnick and De Payne back in 1981. The voice on the tape is one Kevin David Mitnick.

.   .   .

BEEP! BEEP! BEEP!

It's the morning of September 28, 1992. The warning bell on Kevin's scanner, programmed to pick up the local FBI agent's calls, is ringing in his office. Mitnick bursts in and scans the screen. The number, he knows that number. They're closing in on his apartment.

That's McGuire, fucking Special Agent Ken McGuire, calling a pay phone. The Village Market, right next to my apartment!

Wipe

___

The doorknob wiggles. *Why do they always have to come so early in the morning?*

"Excuse me, who's breaking in?" Mitnick yells.

"Open up! It's the FBI."

Mitnick hops out of bed, unlocks the door, and swings it open.

Mitnick stands eye to eye with a female FBI agent in her late thirties. She's surrounded by several middle-aged male FBI and law enforcement agents in suits, craning to get a better look.

Kevin Mitnick is stark naked. He takes after Marilyn. He always sleeps in the nude.

"Can I put some clothes on?"

Mitnick pulls on a pair of jeans and a T-shirt and returns to count the FBI agents, officers of the peace, and phone company security personnel. There are more than a dozen of them milling through his apartment, numbering the few rooms, sorting through his things.

"This is your second time around, Kevin," Special Agent Richard Beasely warns, sitting Mitnick down in a chair.

"Do you have a cassette recorder I could borrow for a minute?" Beasely asks.

Why don't you bring your own goddamned cassette recorder?

Mitnick hands his player to the FBI agent, who pops in a cassette.

CRACK!

Mitnick looks, and sure enough, the door on his player is broken. *I'd like to break something of his.*

The FBI agent presses play, and the law enforcement agents gather round to listen. It's a tape recording of somebody who sounds an awful lot like Kevin Mitnick, talking and listening to what sounds like Pac Bell security's voice mail.

"That's an interesting tape," Mitnick volunteers, impressed. *Amazing what the FBI can do with technology.*

"Do you have any more?" Mitnick inquires.

The FBI doesn't. And they don't appreciate Mitnick's sense of humor.

"Time is running out, Kevin," Beasely tells him in jargon that sounds straight out of a B movie. "Lewis is spilling his guts. You're gonna be left behind."

"So, are you going to arrest me?"

Mitnick knows there's no way in the world they are going to arrest him. That's not the way the FBI works. They usually get a search warrant first, gather the evidence, and then come back with an arrest warrant. That's why Mitnick's there. He wants to know the FBI's cards before they play them.

.   ▪   ▪

KNOCK, KNOCK, KNOCK.

Several minutes go by without any response. The agents are getting impatient. They know the hacker's inside, but they don't dare try a forced entry. Why won't he open the door?

"Lewis De Payne. This is Ken McGuire from the FBI," says the voice on De Payne's answering machine.

Bonnie Vitello, Mitnick's ex-wife and now De Payne's live-in girl-friend, rolls over in bed. They're both deep sleepers.

"Let us in or we'll break down the door!' shouts a voice on the landing.

KABOOM, KABOOM, KABOOM.

De Payne is expecting company. He checks his alarm clock. It's very early. Must be the FBI.

"Get dressed," he tells Vitello.

De Payne swings open the door. It's the big Hawaiian, Special Agent Stan Ornellas, a bear of a man at six foot three, well over 230 pounds, with a hand made for crushing things. Ornellas is from the FBI's old school. He talks tough; he's fond of phrases like "I think I'll go over and squeeze that little pinhead." Ornellas doesn't like De Payne. The feeling is mutual.

De Payne is enjoying every minute. The comedy, the irony of it all. The FBI, the most powerful law enforcement agency in the most technologically advanced nation on earth, has come to search his modest condo for evidence of his computer hacking. But it's De Payne who knows everything about the FBI, not the other way around. De Payne knows the numbers of the agents' cellular phones, pagers, and bank accounts, the names of their wives, their children, their friends at the FBI and the CIA, along with more mundane personal secrets the agents wouldn't want to share with the public.

"Could I read the warrant?"

Ornellas hands De Payne the document. De Payne skims down the list, ticking off the names of the numerous agents standing stiffly by as the stray cats swarm on the landing. He knows most of them: Special Agent Ken McGuire of the Los Angeles office of the FBI, and of course, Terry Atchley, the Pac Bell security agent who helped arrest De Payne and Mitnick back in 1981. Atchley's black hair stands up in an unlikely wave on his forehead, a cigarette permanently attached to his forefinger. Atchley and De Payne don't like each other either.

Atchley and the agents are thorough. Everything in the stale-smelling condominium is potential evidence: Scanners, cellular phones, modems, computers. The agents box well over a hundred computer disks, bag after bag of miscellaneous computer and electronic parts, boxes of computer manuals, and one Pacific Telesis ID card in the name of Lewis De Payne. All told, the agents fill out eight pages detailing their seizure of over a hundred boxes, bags, and single items.

When you're Kevin Mitnick's best friend and former co-conspirator, the most mundane, private possessions are potential evidence of a global computer hacking conspiracy. The FBI confiscates ordinary telephones, a business card holder, tax forms, telephone jacks, common commercial software programs, and a collection of erotic videos that includes three "Ginger" productions, *Gang Bang No. 8*, and *Mediterranean Fuckers*.

Bonnie Vitello is forced to hand over her purse to the G-men. She's not allowed to leave the sofa so she tries to do her homework for her night class.

"If you studied computer science please raise your hand," she asks in her cheery voice.

No hands go up. Computer science, it seems, is not a prerequisite to investigate computer hackers. But the agents are friendly to Bonnie. At least one of the younger agents thinks she's cute, and insists on following her to the bathroom. A couple of them even try to help her with her homework.

And McGuire tries to protect the former Mrs. Mitnick.

"We're not taking Bonnie's computer," he tells the gruff Ornellas.

Ornellas has one question for Bonnie.

"Did he ever touch your computer?"

"Yes," admits Bonnie.

"Take it!" orders Ornellas.

The questioning isn't going the way Ornellas planned.

"There's this guy, Eric. He's doing really bad stuff," De Payne tells Ornellas in a concerned tone. "He says he lives on Sepulveda but he's really living at McCadden Place."

Special Agent Stanley Ornellas doesn't want to talk about Eric. "These encrypted files on your computer. What's the password?"

"You fellows have to stop this guy Eric," De Payne hammers back, spinning the conversation in a circle. He has only one question, and one answer.

"ERIC. ERIC. ERIC."

Terry Atchley has a question for De Payne.

"Did you use SAS?"

"I'm not sure," says De Payne. "What legal definition are you using?"

"Well, we don't want to get attorneys involved," suggests an FBI agent. "They make everything much messier and complicated."

"I agree," says De Payne. "I just don't know what you mean."

Atchley tries again.

"Did you use SAS?"

"I'm not sure of your interpretation," repeats De Payne.

Ken McGuire tries Bonnie.

"Do you know what SAS is?"

"Oh, that's Swiss Airlines Systems. I fly them all the time."

McGuire smiles.

"Aha!" Ornellas exclaims. "What's this?"

The G-man has burrowed through the tea leaves in De Payne's Argentinian tea bowl.

He hold up his prize, a tiny microcassette.

The best part of the prank will be revealed in the days and weeks ahead. Soon the FBI will play De Payne's secret tape and hear its own informant, Eric Heinz, talking about how he's tapping people's phones and breaking into phone company central offices. Then, the FBI will get to the matter of De Payne's encrypted hard disk. Without the codes, the FBI may need to send the encrypted files to Washington, D.C. There the Bureau could arrange for some super-computer time to begin the tedious process of decrypting the codes. And if the Bureau spends enough time and enough money, it will peel away the first encryption mask to reveal another encrypted layer. And another and another and another.

For when you encrypt garbage upon garbage, in the end, even the FBI can only find garbage.

．　　　．　　　．

"If you aren't going to arrest me can I go to my dad's?"

"We need to search your car first."

A platoon of law enforcement agents escort Kevin Mitnick past the complex's pool and tennis courts to his car, where they subject the vehicle to a full search. Mitnick can't believe his eyes. A couple of uninvited FBI agents jump in the backseat of his car like kids eager to go for a ride.

The nerve of these guys.

Mitnick orders them out, and hops in and guns it. He screeches down Las Virgenes, and speeds onto the busy 101 freeway:

Eighty, ninety, one hundred miles an hour.

What are they going to do? Pull me over for speeding?

At his dad's place, Mitnick phones an attorney and his aunt, Chickie Leventhal, owner of Chickie's Bail Bonds.

"Don't talk to the feds," Chickie advises her nephew. An hour later, Mitnick emerges from the apartment to an audience of FBI agents.

"I'm not going to talk," he announces.

Five minutes later, once he's sure the feds have cleared out, Mitnick jumps back on the 101 freeway and peels over to Teltec's offices, checking his rear view mirror for a tail. He boots up his hard drive and scans his directory. This is what the FBI wants. This is what they'll look for in a few minutes or an hour when they arrive with their search warrant: Mitnick's secret files on the FBI.

Deleting them won't suffice. Mitnick knows that the delete command doesn't erase files, it just abandons them on the disk. Only if the computer runs out of memory will his "deleted" files be overwritten. He's got to erase the files permanently, immediately overwrite them so they can never be reconstructed.

Mitnick types the command in a burst:

wipeinfo . . .

Early Departure

Kevin Mitnick doesn't have much time. He's got one chance. Find dirt on the undercover agent the FBI sent to screw up his life.

He begins with a name and a number. But unlike most people, Eric Heinz Jr.'s social security number reveals little. No employment record, no taxes paid to the IRS, no real estate. The only useful fact he uncovers is the name of a father in San Rafael, California.

Mitnick puts his finely tuned social engineering skills to the task. "Can I speak to Eric Junior?" Mitnick asks in his friendly voice.

"There's no Eric Junior here," Eric Heinz Sr. replies.

"It's important I get in touch with him," Mitnick implores.

After an awkward silence the man finally speaks.

"He died in infancy."

A death certificate, Mitnick thinks. Gotta know where little Eric Jr. died.

"Really. Where was that?"

But it's one question too many. The man asks for a number to call back.

A minute later, Eric Heinz Sr. phones and Kevin Mitnick answers the pay phone at a restaurant on Sepulveda, his trusty sidekick,

De Payne, standing by. But the ruse fails. Eric Heinz Sr. suspects something's not right.

Mitnick pushes on with his search. He learns Eric Heinz Sr. is originally from Washington, D.C., so the hacker canvasses the death certificates of five neighboring states, looking for Eric Heinz Jr. It's not that easy, since many are closed to public inquiries. When he comes up empty-handed, he tries another tack.

Kevin Mitnick, Mr. Social Security impostor, phones Heinz Sr.'s brother.

"Are you Eric Heinz Senior?"

"No, he's my brother," the man says.

"We'll straighten that out," Mitnick says helpfully. "This is odd. We have an Eric Heinz Junior here in the database."

That's all it takes to get the brother to reveal the whole tragic story. Mrs. Heinz's ill-fated drive with her son to the 1962 Seattle World's Fair, and the terrible car accident that killed mother and son.

But Mitnick is already planning his next step. It's easy, even legal. Washington is an open state when it comes to most records. Mitnick simply applies for the death certificate of one Eric Heinz Jr., and a few weeks later, an official document arrives, proof that Eric Heinz Jr., the FBI's undercover operative, has been fraudulently assuming the identity of a two-and-a-half-year-old toddler who died three decades ago.

.   .   .

On November 6, 1992, Robert Latta, Chief Probation Officer of the Central District of California, petitions the court to issue a bench warrant with bail fixed at $25,000 in the case of the United States versus Kevin David Mitnick:

It is alleged that the above-mentioned supervised releasee has violated the terms and conditions to wit:

1. . . .[O]n August 7, 1992, Mr. Mitnick participated in the unauthorized access of Pacific Bell computers (confidential voice mail system). This was accomplished through the unauthorized use of confidential and personal passwords of Pacific Bell Telephone Company

security investigators who, along with local authorities have been investigating Mr. Mitnick's employer at the time, Teltec Investigations.

2. The offender had previously been instructed regarding the special condition prohibiting him from associating with any . . . persons known to have engaged in the illegal or unauthorized access of computers or telecommunication devices. The offender violated this condition . . . as he maintained association with one Lewis De Payne. Mr. De Payne had been convicted of violation of 182/502 Penal Code (conspiracy to commit computer fraud) on April 2, 1982 (Case No. A370979).

.   .   .

The Los Angeles U.S. Attorney's Office says once the bench warrant was issued for Kevin Mitnick he was nowhere to be found. Mitnick tells another story. He says he was home, the FBI just came a tad late.

Mitnick plans everything carefully, timing his operation to midnight, December 7, 1992, the last seconds of his federally ordered supervised release. He invites his mother to visit to tell the FBI he was there till midnight, and precisely at the zero hour they argue. That explains his sudden departure.

But mom has to wait for a while. The FBI isn't nearly so precise. A week after his parole is up, on December 15, 1992, a team of FBI agents shows up at his apartment to arrest the wily hacker. They've got a warrant, and they present it to Mitnick's mother. She's there to keep Mitnick's door from being kicked in, and to gauge how badly they want him. Mitnick's mother doesn't have much to say and the FBI turns up very little evidence: no computer, no disks, no cellular phones, no papers, no tangible leads. Just a newspaper article quoting Scott Charney, the head of the Justice Department's computer crime division, talking about the department's "deep undercover" agent.

Mitnick has underlined the words "deep undercover" and written in a name.

"ERIC."

.   .   .

It's a few minutes before 10 A.M. on Christmas Eve, and Kevin Mitnick is on the phone to the Department of Motor Vehicles' local law enforcement counter, hoping to coax them into sending a holiday fax.

Mitnick's been trying since September to get the driver's license photos of the people he figures are trying to take away his freedom. Mitnick's previous attempts failed, but something tells him today will be different. Christmas Eve is a perfect time for a social engineering attack. People are less suspicious on the holidays, more likely to let something slip. And if it fails again, what does he have to lose? The FBI already wants him. What's a few pretext calls to the DMV going to matter?

Besides, Mitnick sounds like he works in law enforcement. He knows the requester codes. Everything he says sounds authentic.

"Hold on a minute," a technician tells him. The flag on the file tells him something's unusual. On a second line, the technician phones DMV Investigator Ed Lovelace in Sacramento. This isn't just any driver's license photo.

"I've got him on the line."

"Tell him you're getting the photos. Say they're having problems with the computer in their office," Lovelace instructs the technician. "Tell him to call back in forty-five minutes to see if they're available."

Like clockwork, Mitnick phones back. Today his persistence is paying off. The pictures are ready.

"What's your fax number?" the technician asks Mitnick.

Up at DMV headquarters in Sacramento, Lovelace quickly does a reverse check on the fax number: Kinkos Copies, Studio City, 1210 Ventura Boulevard. The investigator phones Shirley Lessiak, DMV internal affairs in Van Nuys, and gives her the rundown. Lessiak phones the Kinkos manager, who in turn promises to tell them when the suspect comes in to pick up the fax. Around noon on Christmas Eve, Lessiak and three other DMV investigators arrive at the busy Kinkos on Ventura Boulevard.

Kevin Mitnick calmly walks behind the counter and picks up his fax. He's always been a self-service kind of guy. But the DMV photo isn't what Mitnick's expecting. It's a young woman, a full body shot. Some kind of joke.

What the fu —

"Hey, we want to talk to you!"

Four suits. They don't want to talk about root beer.

Mitnick walks toward them, and then tosses the papers up in the air.

The chase is on. Two of the suits clutch at the papers, and Mitnick doubles his odds. He's in the parking lot, running toward Ralph's supermarket, dashing toward the crowded holiday sidewalks. He churns his strong legs and pumps his arms. Within a minute, the footsteps fade. One DMV pursuer is overweight, the other is out of shape.

Down the sidewalk, across Ventura Boulevard into a residential neighborhood. He clambers over a wall and hits the ground running. Kevin Mitnick is in top physical condition. They don't have a chance.

Two miles from Kinkos, the hacker slows to a jog.

He peels off his sport shirt and congratulates himself on having worn shorts under his pants. He turns his shirt inside out, tears the pants off, and stashes them in a front yard. Then, he finds the nearest pay phone, and calls a cab and his friend Lewis De Payne.

Kevin Mitnick is on the run.

II.

The Garbage Man

I t's early 1992.
Ron Austin is cruising down
the Sunset Strip past the Rainbow Bar and Grill, when he sees Eric
Heinz huddled in the doorway of the club next door, dodging the
rain. It's nearly 3 A.M., as Austin pulls over and rolls down his window to say hello.

The last time Austin saw him was a few months ago at a Taco
Bell. Eric wanted him to bring his laptop and meet him there, and
Austin did just that. But then, suddenly, Eric had to go to the bathroom. Everything skidded into slow motion. The undercover cars
converged on the outdoor patio. Big Agent Stan Ornellas slammed
Austin's face against the wall, shouted, and in one quick move
pressed a gun against his temple.

Austin was blindsided. He had considered Eric a friend. When
they first met in 1989, Austin was studying economics at UCLA,
trying to go straight after being busted for hacking in 1983 with
Kevin Poulsen. But neither Austin nor Poulsen had found it easy to
quit. Poulsen took a job in Northern California for a defense contractor and seemed on the verge of a legitimate career in computers.
But Austin knew that was only half of his life. Nights Poulsen would
phone Austin from yet another Pacific Bell central office he had
sneaked into, his voice barely audible over the clatter of old electro-

mechanical telephone switching equipment. Soon Poulsen was playing Austin wiretaps and describing how they could win radio prizes. Then the inevitable happened. The police stumbled onto a storage locker Poulsen kept crammed with hacking and burglary tools. The FBI secretly readied a federal indictment, and Poulsen, fearing the worst, ducked underground.

In 1989, Eric put an ad in a Los Angeles paper looking for someone with special knowledge of the phone company. Poulsen and Austin responded, and they became an unlikely trio: Poulsen, then a famous federal fugitive profiled on *Unsolved Mysteries*; Eric, the rocker; and Austin, the economist. Poulsen wanted Eric around to join him on his nightly forays into the central offices of Los Angeles, looking for new secrets to the phone system. But he didn't trust Eric and guarded his knowledge carefully. It was Austin who found Eric's Hollywood style and fearlessness intriguing. He taught Eric the secret of SAS, the Pac Bell system that could manipulate phone lines to win radio contests or wiretap. Austin even shared a $10,000 radio prize with Eric, so the rocker could buy his girlfriend breast implants. He helped Eric secretly move when the FBI found out where he was living. And once, when Eric was traipsing through a Pac Bell central office, Austin called him on the PA system to warn him the cops were about to surround the building.

After the FBI roughed him up at Taco Bell, Austin spent a long weekend in solitary confinement and then pled guilty to wiretapping, fraudulently winning a $50,000 Porsche, and rigging a host of other L.A. radio giveaways. Austin admitted his crimes, and put up bond for the $50,000 bail, but still Austin needed to understand. He was the educated member of the gang after all. Why had Eric betrayed him?

●   ■   ●

Late tonight on the Sunset Strip, a few months after the bust, Austin can finally confront Eric. He hops out of his car and approaches. Suddenly the rocker reaches behind his back. A black shape whips forward. Austin flashes on the time Eric jammed his gun to a homeless woman's head. But it's just an innocuous Motorola flip phone.

"What's up?" says Eric coolly, as if he were expecting the chance encounter.

"You changed your hair color," offers Austin.

"No, I haven't," Eric shrugs, though he's clearly got new blond highlights.

"So why'd you turn me in?"

"They wanted to put me away for ten years," Eric begins defensively, and then becomes more combative. He doesn't need to make excuses. He was just doing his job. When the feds debriefed him he could have made it worse for Austin. Made it seem like Austin did more than he did. "I didn't like you talking with Frecia, and I didn't like the double agent game you were playing, telling Poulsen one thing and me another."

Austin can't believe Eric turned him in just because he talked to one of Eric's girls. And that line about him being a double agent? All he did was teach Eric how to hack: how to wiretap by computer and win radio prizes. Is that why Eric ratted him out?

Austin protests for a moment, but realizes he's getting nowhere. He motions to say goodbye, but Eric isn't finished. "We should talk," Eric suggests, asking Austin to give him a ride home. Eric wants to see what Austin's up to, whether he's freelancing or whether the feds sent him to check up on him.

But at his third Oakwood apartment (Mitnick's already discovered the first two) Eric shows Austin the toys the FBI has let him keep: a lineman's test set useful for wiretapping, a computer, a modem, and a thin, flat tape recorder to plant on himself. Even more surprising is some of the paraphernalia Austin recognizes from the past, notebooks Eric used to document commands to hack into Pac Bell and other computer systems.

"They're trying to get Kevin Mitnick," Eric announces, handing Austin a ham and cheese sandwich, and joking, "You're eating government ham."

Austin listens carefully as Eric describes how the FBI is footing the bill for more than just the eats.

"They've got me set up to bust hackers. They pay me cash, and they pick up the thirteen-hundred-dollar rent. They're going to let me live here awhile."

Austin gets the feeling Eric shouldn't be confiding these secrets. But could the FBI really be in business with Eric? The whole thing sounds so off the cuff, so unsupervised. Handing a guy like Eric cash, a cellular phone, his own apartment, and tools to wiretap? The FBI has to know about Eric's credit frauds, his wiretapping for a Hollywood detective, his bondage games, his gun.

"I've been talking with Mitnick," Eric brags.

.   .   .

Over the next year, Austin spots Eric on the Strip every few months. He keeps his distance, never letting Eric spot him. But in August 1993, a happenstance gives Austin an opportunity for revenge. Like Kevin Mitnick and so many other hackers, Austin has a score to settle with the double agent. One afternoon, Austin is out for a drive with a friend on Laurel Canyon Boulevard, winding up above the bright lights of Hollywood.

"There it is!" she cries, excitedly pulling over.

She's spotted the BMW she saw a few days ago on Lookout Mountain, the California Highway Patrol baseball cap still sitting on the rear dash, the expensive motorized antenna protruding from the roof. Eric's BMW. Eric had made no secret about what he was doing with the equipment. He was monitoring a DEA operation with his scanner, snapping photos of a DEA undercover plane with his telephoto lens.

At least that's the story he gave her.

As a self described "FBI Consultant" Justin [Eric's real name] had once told me that all of his rent and living expenses were paid for by the FBI. Though I was always curious what he did for the FBI I knew that the FBI would soon find that employing Justin in any capacity was a grave mistake and quickly rid themselves of his services. I began to wonder how he was supporting himself. How could he afford a BMW? I noticed that the house had an expensive directional antenna on the roof. How could he afford that, the radio equipment he'd been seen with, a car phone, telephoto camera, etc? . . . The only time in the past that he'd made any substantial amount of money was through credit card fraud or placing wiretaps and selling credit information to the private investigation firm. . . . I began to wonder about his motives for the intense interest in Drug Enforcement Agency surveillances. Could he be selling the information he obtained to those being watched by the DEA?

— Ron Austin, memo to the FBI, 1993

Four A.M. one August morning, Austin arrives at 2270 Laurel Canyon Boulevard, two hours before the Thursday morning garbage men make their regular rounds.

He doesn't look like the type who'd rummage through garbage. He's got a bit of a tan, shaggy blond hair that hangs over his penetrating, intelligent eyes, a strong, square jaw, and a straight nose. He's athletic, though his shoulders hunch and he tends to stare at the ground as he walks.

He drags the bin quietly around the corner and removes the lid. Austin slowly draws out a wad of Saran wrap, tangled with duct tape and Vaseline, remnants from Eric's latest bondage session. He's glad he's worn the gloves.

Flashlight in hand, Austin digs out bits of Eric's garbage: VIP passes for a weekly evening, "On the Rox," Eric co-hosts at a private Sunset club. There's a slick drawing of a sexy woman pursing her lips with the caption "I'm so excited I could spit." Austin smooths out the next piece of paper from the bin, a crumpled computer printout titled "G: Girls," with entries such as "Heather, met at Bar One," and "Lesa, Oriental," and notations like "Crazy Girls" and "20/20" — a couple of Hollywood strip joints. Next, there's a business card listing Eric Heinz as an "Electronic Surveillance Specialist," with expertise in "phone tap detection" and "high-tech debugging."

.   .   .

Austin comes up empty-handed the following two Thursdays, but he's persistent. On September 2, 1993, he stumbles onto a parking ticket issued just days ago for the BMW, phones the Parking Violations Bureau, and learns the car has four hundred dollars in unpaid parking tickets. The same morning he retrieves discarded collection notices for Sprint and MCI bills in the name of Joseph Wernle.

The next couple of weeks' pickings are so-so: a one-page handwritten list of sixty hijacked cable channels, nearly nine hundred dollars of prescription bills gone to collectors, and a scrap of paper that names the electronics chain The Good Guys, with an account number that Austin discovers was closed due to "fraudulent activity."

Finally, on September 23, 1993, nearly six weeks after he began his regular trash inspections, Austin finds something solid. "Top 200" reads the note, in what appears to be Eric's handwriting:

1. *L.A.P.D.*
2. *Misc P.D.*
3. *D.E.A.*
4. *F.B.I.*
5. *S.S. + Marshall*
6. *P.S.*
7. *Fire + Rescue.*
8. *Cellular.*
9. *Cordless*
10. *Spooks.*

Top 10 is more like it. Eric has programmed his scanner's memory with about ten frequencies — the FBI, the DEA, the Secret Service, and others. What surprises Austin is item six, Eric's new interest in the postal service. But the biggest clue is a single scrap of paper Austin plucks from Eric's trash October 7.

#3 G — pencil
#3 Go — pen
#3 P — Crayon
#4 — Blue Marker
#4 Go — Gold Marker
#5 — Red Marker
#5 — Gold Silver Marker
#6 — Spray Paint
AT — Ass Tounger
7-11 — feeder
Gas Station — burn

Pesos — Monopoly
PI — Dudley
PD — Bullwinkle
Scanner — TV
Boxing — Take a Walk
P# — pink slip
Cash — peanuts
The B — coin collectors
Surveillance — Nice day, means none
Encrypted Speech — Screwing
Use our Radios to chat — Whats on HBO
I am being watched — Watch a Porno Flick
You are being watched — Steak dinner
Box — Pussy
Shopping — Going to a Concert
C went bad — Sour Milk
Security — They had Friends
Key — Diamond
$100 — 1 peanut
$1,000 — 10 Peanuts
I.D. — Borrow a Tool.

Eric seems to have developed an elaborate X-rated code to discuss his crimes by radio and phone. Austin is puzzled by the first items, then kicks himself for not figuring it out faster. Credit cards, of course! American Express cards begin with the number "3" and are either "G" (green), "Go" (gold), or "P" (platinum). Visa cards begin with the number "4" and are either regular or "Go" (gold), and so on.

"Box," "Key," "$1,000," "ID," "Encrypted Speech," and "Surveillance" are all pretty clear to Austin. So are "C went bad" — credit went bad — and "Security." Austin guesses that "PI" stands for Postal Inspector, "Boxing" has something to do with rifling mailboxes, and "AT," or "Ass-Tounger," is code for an ATM, or automatic teller machine.

.   .   .

About a week later, a little after ten in the evening, Austin is strolling in the Melrose fashion district when just as he passes the trendy Nuclear Nuance nightclub he runs into Eric. Austin has calculated the coincidence. He's still working on his case against Eric, playing his own game of cat and mouse. He doesn't trust the FBI to act on the evidence he's already collected on Eric's crimes. He's going to see what else he can learn about Eric's misdeeds before he meets with Agent Stan Ornellas. Austin understands the system, and he isn't going to give the FBI a chance to protect their paid informant.

"What are you doing here?" Eric asks.

"I've got a friend who lives around the corner. What about you?"

Eric doesn't believe him for a second. More than a year ago, when Austin dropped by the Rainbow, Eric reported it to the FBI. Tonight, too, Eric knows Austin is up to something, but like their last encounter, he'll play along. He needs to gauge whether Austin's working for the feds, because this time Eric's getting back into "business."

"This is my club," Eric says. "I'm hosting Velvet Jam Night."

Austin already knows. In his pocket is the complimentary pass he plucked from Eric's trash that reads, "Live music, celebrity guests, dancing and dinner til 2 A.M.!"

"Come on in!" Eric welcomes. "I'll buy you a beer."

Austin follows Eric inside, taking in the ficus trees strung with white lights, the red carpet, the oak trim and red tufted button Naugahyde booths. Eric fits right in with his suave four-hundred-dollar olive drab Italian suit, crisp denim shirt, and Doc Marten's combat boots. He seems happy in his element. But when Austin mentions the fugitive hacker, the FBI's undercover operative's mood sours.

"Fucking Mitnick!" he grumbles. "He got ahold of the SAS designer's notes, and now he's using SAS to tap phones. He's tapping me, too."

"Really?" Austin says, wondering how Mitnick got SAS.

"You want to hear something funny?" Eric asks. "When I told Mitnick that Poulsen was a better hacker than him, he got pissed. It really seemed to offend him."

Austin asks what Mitnick looks like, and Eric tells him he's lost a lot of weight. He also says he thinks Lewis De Payne is going to be a witness for the prosecution.

"So why didn't they just bust Mitnick anyway?"

"The FBI blew the Mitnick investigation. The FBI still doesn't know how Mitnick caught wind of the bust," Eric explains. "I offered to go to Vegas at my own expense and track down Mitnick, but the FBI turned down my offer. Now the fucker pages me day and night. His favorite one is to page me with the number of the Los Angeles office of the FBI."

Eric doesn't tell Austin what else Mitnick did to him to avenge his undercover work for the FBI. The persistent calls Mitnick made to Fernando Peralta at the Hollywood office of the Social Security Administration. The investigation that suspended Eric's thousands of dollars of fraudulent social security benefits. In fact, Mitnick orchestrated the handing over of Heinz's file to the Office of Investigations for preparation of a criminal case. But there had been no arrest or prosecution of Eric Heinz on his fraud. Vickie Roberts, the OIG supervisor to whom Fernando Peralta gave the file, explained, "We would investigate anything that would involve a fraud. Whether that would be prosecuted would be up to the U.S. Attorney's [Central District] Office."

Six months have passed, and the U.S. Attorney's Office has given no sign of prosecuting Eric for social security fraud.

•   •   •

"My new hobby is listening to law enforcement surveillance on my scanners," Eric says, ticking off the names of his countersurveillance equipment.

"I'm not up to anything, you know," Eric insists. "I make enough money promoting these clubs."

Austin glances around at the uncrowded room and thinks what a far cry it is from the evenings when he and Poulsen used to meet Eric down at the Rainbow Bar and Grill, barely able to squeeze their way through the leather and lingerie girls. Austin sits on his bar stool, skeptical but expressionless, waiting for Eric to say something.

"Well, I suppose if something really big came along . . ."

•   •   •

Three evenings later, Austin parks by the garbage cans at 2270 Laurel Canyon. This time he's been invited.

"Hey, how it's going?" Eric welcomes him, and proudly displays his seven radios and two scanners. Austin is surprised Eric is showing off his stuff, but then that's like Eric. Maybe he's got something up his sleeve, too.

The phone rings. Eric picks up the handset. Silence. The same interminable silence he's come to expect the last few months. "Have fun, Kevin!" he groans, hanging up.

Eric's barely put down the phone when his pager buzzes. "It's just Mitnick," Eric explains. He says he's on Mitnick's tail, listening to the local ham radio channels for signs of the hacker, and thinking of going to Vegas to dig up leads. He asks Austin if he's interested in joining the chase. Austin isn't. He can see for himself that Mitnick hunts his pursuers with a vengeance.

Eric explains how the Mitnick investigation began. He says the FBI had a budget set aside to find Kevin Poulsen's secret computer and bust Austin. When Eric helped the FBI find the computer quickly and under budget [and set up Austin], he was hired to build a case against Mitnick.

Eric flips on a scanner. "I've got them all programmed in," he says, handing Austin his list of law enforcement frequencies.

"What have you heard on the federal frequencies?" Austin asks.

"Postal Inspector stakeouts of mail trucks," Eric replies. "People breaking into the trucks to steal mail, social security checks and stuff."

Eric's other scanner crackles with the sound of two FBI agents discussing an informant. As Austin and Eric listen, the FBI surveillance moves to the Oakwood Apartments. "The FBI moves a lot of informants there," Eric explains of his old FBI address. "When I was there I knew at least one other informant in the complex. . . . Maybe we should go have a look at these guys."

Eric opens his dresser drawer and pulls out some photos he's taken with a telephoto lens.

"FBI Organized Crime Division," Eric announces, pointing out several unmarked cars and a van with a roof vent. "See the agents?" Eric spreads out several pictures, and describes the FBI agents standing in front of a bar or restaurant. "It's where they go after surveillance."

Eric's show-and-tell continues as he pulls a SAS wiretapping manual from the closet and hands it to Austin. "I can't believe the FBI gave this back to me," Eric laughs.

"You know for a while I even had a desk in the FBI offices on Wilshire," he chuckles. "There are a lot of things I know that the FBI would rather I didn't."

.   .   .

The phone rings again. "Have fun, Kevin!"

And again. This time it's a friend. Eric talks for a couple of minutes.

"Mitnick just paged my friend with Frecia's number!" Eric moans. "I don't even talk to Frecia anymore! How did Mitnick get that number?"

Austin shrugs. Doesn't Eric know it's hacker justice? "Aren't you worried that Poulsen might also harass you when he gets out of jail?"

"I'll just drop out," Eric says. "He won't find me."

Austin is silent.

"So," Eric says, smiling. "Do you really expect me to believe that you were just walking by the club on Friday?"

I asked Justin [Eric] if he knew why the private investigators he worked for . . . were never charged with wiretapping. . . . He said, "What makes you think that they might not still get charged?" I asked Justin if he'd ever spoke [sic] with . . . [a former partner in the detective agency]. He said that he'd met him at the [detective's] office and spoke with him a few times there. I asked Justin if he was aware that [the detective] was [with] the FBI in Los Angeles. . . .
— Ron Austin, memo to the FBI, 1993

Fresh Air

ctober 22, 1993.

Eric slumps in his chair at the large oak table in the U.S. Attorney's conference room on the eleventh floor of the Federal Building, drained from last night's kinky games with the stripper from the Seventh Veil. Next to Eric sits his court-appointed attorney, Morton Boren, and standing in the room are the two FBI agents Eric knows by first name. But it's Special Agent Stan Ornellas who commands attention, his thick arms crossed, his 230-pound torso immobile, his face a dark mask. The FBI agent waits a long, calculated time before he narrows his fierce eyes on Eric.

"I told you not to fuck with me."

Eric knows better than to respond. He's in trouble, that much is painfully obvious. The sudden request for a meeting, the suggestion that he bring his attorney, the early hour . . .

One single sheet of white paper sits on the big oak table. The paper is upside down, facing the seat the Assistant U.S. Attorney will occupy, but Eric can still make out a portion of it. It looks like a list of federal law enforcement frequencies — the FBI, the DEA, the ATF — the same radio frequencies he showed Austin.

The door opens.

"Sorry I'm late," apologizes Assistant U.S. Attorney David Schindler, breezing in and taking his chair.

Schindler is everything Eric Heinz isn't, from his neatly trimmed curly black hair to his crisply starched white dress shirt and elegant, understated suit. Polite, orderly, and boyishly handsome, Schindler is a rising star in the powerhouse Los Angeles U.S. Attorney's Office. Only one person stands between David Schindler and the top slot.

"Justin."

Eric hates that name. His given name.

"I know you've been up to some things lately, doing counter-surveillance," Schindler begins. "Why are you listening to ATF, FBI, and DEA frequencies?"

Eric says nothing.

"Are you gearing up for something, Justin?"

"It's a hobby," Eric shrugs.

Schindler lowers his voice. "Are you using other people's credit cards?"

"In what context?"

"What the hell do you think you're doing, Eric?" Ornellas yells.

What can Schindler say? He's the Assistant U.S. Attorney who offered Eric the golden parachute: rat on Austin and Poulsen, build a case against Kevin Mitnick, and walk. Schindler helped create this longhaired Hollywood monster sitting across the table. Thanks to Schindler and Stan Ornellas, Eric now knows how the FBI works, how it does surveillance, how it tracks phone records, how it targets hackers just like, well, himself.

"How is this going to make us look, Justin?" asks Schindler. "We put so much time and effort into you."

"Can I talk to my attorney in private?" Eric asks.

Eric and Morton Boren are buzzed out by the receptionist behind the bulletproof Plexiglas. They ride the elevators down to the fourth-floor snack bar. Eric buys a Coke and his attorney picks up a coffee.

"Looks like he's going to charge you on the credit card stuff," Boren tells Eric. "You've probably blown your cooperation agreement, too."

They walk down two more flights to the attorneys' lounge on the second floor. Around the corner are the red padded leather doors of

Courtroom 6, the courtroom of Eric's judge, Stephen V. Wilson. Boren ducks into the attorneys' lounge to telephone Schindler and tell him they'll be right back.

But Eric needs some fresh air, a walk. Four steps to the metal door under the red cylindrical art deco exit sign. Hand on the brass railing and down the twenty-three marble steps, straight past the entrance lobby metal detectors.

Eleven flights up, Assistant U.S. attorney David Schindler and Special Agents Stan Ornellas and Ken McGuire await the return of their man.

The three U.S. Marshals don't even notice Eric as he steps out the front door.

.   .   .

Later that morning, the clerk in U.S. District Court Judge Wilson's court announces the three cases. They all begin with the same heading: The United States of America versus Justin Tanner Petersen.

"Good morning, Your Honor. David Schindler on behalf of the government. Thank you for making yourself available on such short notice."

"Good morning, Your Honor. Morton Boren on behalf of Justin Petersen, who is not present."

Not for want of looking. When Eric failed to return to the U.S. Attorney's conference room, Special Agent Stan Ornellas paged Ron Austin, asking for help. But not even Austin had any ideas about how to find him. So Schindler had no choice. He had to admit in federal court that the star informant for the Justice Department's secret war on hackers, the principal witness in the case against Kevin Mitnick, had flown the coop.

"This is an emergency application by the government to revoke the defendant's bond," Judge Wilson says. "What is the situation, Mr. Schindler?"

"Your Honor, this morning we asked for a meeting with Mr. Petersen and his counsel because the government was made aware this week that certain allegations had been made that Mr. Petersen had been engaged in additional criminal conduct while on bail. . . . We asked Mr. Petersen . . . whether or not he was in fact engaged in additional activities, specifically credit card fraud. . . .

"Mr. Petersen repeated that yes, in fact he had used other people's credit cards, and at that point the meeting was terminated to allow . . . Mr. Boren and his client to confer, and his client has apparently fled.

"The government believes . . . it's inappropriate for Mr. Petersen to be out on bail given those circumstances."

"What was the underlying charge?" asks Judge Wilson.

"There were multiple underlying charges, Your Honor . . . transferred from Texas, that were credit-card fraud related. . . . There were additional computer hacking related charges here in the Central District involving Mr. Petersen's accessing federal interest computers. . . ."

"Is this the young man who had part of his leg amputated?" asks Judge Wilson, who has been previously briefed about Petersen.

"Yes, Your Honor."

"I remember reading a report, because he was scheduled for sentencing this Monday, and that was continued."

"Correct," agrees Schindler.

"So I am familiar with the defendant. He did have a fairly significant background. . . . The defendant entered pleas to these charges?"

"Yes, Your Honor."

". . . And then by mutual agreement, the sentencing was put off, I take it, for the purpose of seeing if the defendant wanted to help himself by cooperating in some way?"

"Yes, Your Honor."

"And then the government," continues the judge, "on its own, uncovered the fact that since he had pled guilty, he was continuing to violate the law; is that right?"

"Yes, Your Honor."

Well, sort of. Schindler and the FBI had a little help. Austin had typed up weekly memos to Special Agent Ornellas, and prepared a meticulous, fifty-page fact- and photograph-filled brief for the FBI. All on his own initiative and free of charge.

". . . I think this defendant is most unreliable," Judge Wilson concludes. "Clever, but unreliable. So, therefore, I am revoking his bond forthwith, and setting bail at one hundred thousand dollars. A bench warrant is ordered forthwith."

The Other Half

The time is 1:15 P.M., January 3, 1994. The phone rings in my attic office.

"Hello," he says coolly. He doesn't have to say his name. I've heard his voice before, and besides, he makes abundantly clear who's on the line.

It's Eric Heinz, the FBI's undercover man, the hacker who sent Kevin Mitnick on the run. Eric is a fugitive now, too. Maybe that's what happens when you double-cross hackers.

Eric is phoning because I've been nosing around on his Hollywood turf, interviewing people who know all sorts of things about his colorful life. Last September, I wrote "The Last Hacker," an article about Kevin Poulsen for the *Los Angeles Times Magazine*. Eric phoned me then, masquerading as his own friend, telling me what an amazing hacker he is. The last few weeks I've started researching a book on the same subject. Eric's calling me now to figure out my angle, to see how I might portray him.

His phone voice is distant and measured, nothing like other hackers I've spoken to. And Eric isn't just a hacker. He's also a Don Juan, with tips for aspiring pickup artists. "There's something about long hair for tittie dancers," Eric muses. "You can't pick up tittie dancers without long hair.

"My exploits aren't all that uncommon. It's a way of life in the rock-and-roll scene. I'm at around six hundred. That's not dates. That's *physical intercourse.*"

I don't think I've even gone to dinner with six hundred different people.

I change the subject to hacking.

"How much time are you looking at?"

"I'm probably looking at three to five years. I'm not coming in. They're probably looking at charging me with the original and additional time. Unless they want to get ugly and charge me with espionage. . . ."

■   ■   ■

Eric pines for the good ole days, when he was Agent Steal, undercover operative for the FBI, living in an all-expenses-paid Oakwood apartment.

"I had plans for a big sting operation. . . . I could have done so much for them. This could have been the biggest hacker sting ever. I had ideas that would have been a bug light to hackers."

"So what went wrong?"

"Schindler is such an anal retentive fuck," Eric blasts the Assistant U.S. Attorney he embarrassed by fleeing from his office a couple of months ago. "With Schindler you can't just go gung ho. Everything has got to be taped, everything's got to be by the book. I would have been setting up bulletin boards, all kinds of things."

"What did you do with Mitnick?"

"I built a whole case on Mitnick. He's a fugitive because of me. I contacted him through Spiegel [the Hollywood pimp]. He and De Payne and I talked together. We met at a restaurant. The FBI was watching."

"What did Mitnick want?"

"His motive was information. I knew things that he didn't. I had access to the biggest, baddest system. The thing that let us win the radio prizes."

Eric's referring to SAS, the untraceable wiretapping system Eric told Mitnick about.

"So what went wrong?"

"The Bureau is so lax. I told them Mitnick would find out about me. He found out that I had built a case on him. Right before the feds were going to move, he took off."

.   .   .

In late February of 1994, my search to understand the hacker underground takes me to Los Angeles. I talk to a detective, a pimp, strippers, a Pac Bell security man, a federal prosecutor, and yes, hackers. But there's still one hacker I haven't talked to.

The freeway abruptly ends, throwing me onto a four-lane avenue of rundown businesses and homes. I find 5502 Dobbs, but I'm early so I park and go into the only open shop I can find. The sparse goods on the dusty shelves look like holdovers from the sixties: white bread, Twinkies, SOS pads. The main attraction is the wall of glass-front refrigerator cases stocked with beer and wine. I buy a juice from the cashier behind the large bulletproof Plexiglas cage. This is East L.A., home of Lewis De Payne, longtime friend and associate of Kevin Mitnick.

I walk by the ragged patches of grass and up the concrete steps. The large, brown stucco apartment complex looks cheaply built but shows few visible signs of the recent, devastating Northridge earthquake. Stray cats swarm on the landing. "FBI," says a joke note pinned on the door. I knock.

De Payne opens. He smiles.

Short, black slicked hair. Darting eyes. Glasses. He grabs a saucer of milk and places it on the landing, scooping up one feline in his arms as it tries to sneak inside. More than half a dozen cats scurry for the milk like a pack of giant rats. De Payne's movements are jerky, slightly robotic. He's slender, his tight pants accentuating his awkward body.

"Make yourself comfortable, Jon," he welcomes, pointing to a sagging couch. His words, like his walk, seem mechanical.

I edge past a long coffee table stacked with cellular phones, half-opened boxes of miscellaneous electronics, technical manuals, and papers.

I look around: the average two-bedroom unit, the bare walls in need of a paint job. There's an aquarium, a small bookcase, a telephone mounted on the wall next to the small kitchen. And the pervasive stench of cat pee.

"Excuse me," De Payne says politely. He stands next to the telephone and dials, watching me while his fingers snap over the keys like a blind pianist. He's giving a silent performance. I figure he's checking his voice mail.

We chat about the smooth-talking Beverly Hills detective I met earlier this afternoon who told me about his star contract employee, Eric Heinz.

"The detective wasn't easy to find, and he likes it that way," I tell De Payne. "It took me a couple of months to track him down."

As I speak, De Payne punches keys on his cell phone. Again, he says nothing. Then he repeats a Los Angeles phone number to me. The detective's number.

But the detective isn't in the phone book.

"How'd you do that?" I ask, amazed.

De Payne grins.

.   .   .

De Payne and I pull into a parking lot somewhere in Los Angeles a half hour later. The glassed entryway is lined with green plants and Astroturf. The interior is brightly lit, clean, an American theme.

De Payne flirts with the pleasant, blond waitress.

"If you were having dinner what would you order?" He smiles, focusing all his attention on the waitress. Just as in his phone routine, De Payne doesn't need to look at the menu.

She mentions her favorite.

"What would you have to drink?" De Payne continues.

"Maybe a glass of Chardonnay," she suggests, returning his smile.

He's actually getting somewhere, I think, as she leaves with our orders.

"It's all just acting, Jon." De Payne shrugs. "It's all just acting."

By the time she serves our entrees, De Payne has entered her name, food and drink preferences, and days off into his old-fashioned little black book.

"She seems nice," I offer.

"It's just practice, Jon. Just practice."

.   .   .

It's midnight. We're sitting on the worn carpet in De Payne's living room, rummaging through a shoe box of old cassettes from his answering machine. De Payne's searching for a recording of an oath he made with Mitnick a decade and a half ago.

"Kevin has talent," De Payne declares reverently, popping the tapes in and out of an old cassette player. "The most accurate definition of Kevin is a sociopath. He'll pursue his obsession without consideration of anything. They're never going to find Kevin," De Payne insists. "They're never going to find him."

De Payne plays a recording of his pickup artist guru, Ross Jeffries. NLP is what De Payne calls it, Neurolinguistic Programming. I have no idea what NLP really means, but I know what it means for De Payne. It's what he just performed on the waitress. It's the ultimate hack, talking women into going to bed with a computer nerd.

De Payne hands me a copy of the pickup artist's catalog, advertising Jeffries's *Speed Seduction* home study course, plus *The Slut Report, Secrets of a Marathon Lover*, and *How to Be the Jerk Women Love*.

De Payne keeps shuffling through cassettes, searching for Mitnick's pledge.

"This is it!" he finally exclaims, pressing play.

The tape crackles, and then booms with the boisterous voice of an excited, sixteen-year-old Kevin Mitnick.

"The agreement states that every number we get — except GIRLS, only girls on party lines that are not well known — everything else goes between us. Whatever we get. And no number one crap. Everything and there it is!"

"OK. Date it!" orders a subdued, then nineteen-year-old Lewis De Payne.

"What's the date?" wonders a spacy Mitnick.

"April —" begins Lewis.

"It's April, around April twentieth," guesses Mitnick.

"Eighteenth, 1979," corrects a perturbed Lewis.

"Nineteen seventy-nine, at the twentieth century —" gushes Mitnick.

Lewis cuts him short. "Yeah, OK."

.   .   .

A month passes. I return to L.A. for more interviews. I acquire a copy of the SAS manual, the secret wiretapping system that Eric tipped Mitnick off to. I interview David Schindler, the Assistant U.S. Attorney, in his eleventh-floor office at the Federal Building. The very week I am in Los Angeles, March 21 through 26, the FBI mistakenly grabs a fat kid and a longhair at a Chicago computer conference, thinking it's captured Mitnick and Agent Steal in one lucky sweep. But the twenty-three-year-old Jewish kid's prints don't match Mitnick's, and when the FBI asks the longhair to pull up his trouser legs, they see he's got two healthy legs. Meanwhile, my *L.A. Times* article and proposed book on Kevin Poulsen has been optioned for a movie. This doesn't hurt my efforts to dig deeper into the Mitnick story. In Los Angeles, the prospect of a movie means far more than a book to hackers and feds.

De Payne and I are dining at his favorite restaurant. It's March 23, 1994. The blond waitress greets him by his first name.

"So the feds were looking into what Kevin was doing?" I ask.

De Payne tells me the feds were worried Mitnick might turn into a star detective and start invading people's privacy on a large scale. Mitnick was working for a detective firm that had been busted for illegally running TRW reports on people. And Mitnick was performing very well for them. De Payne says he could find people or assets in a couple of hours while other detectives would spin their wheels for days.

"Did they want Eric to build a case against Kevin and his company [Teltec]?" I ask. "Or was it mainly just to build a case against Kevin?"

"Kevin," De Payne answers. "But you know, don't forget me. They didn't seem to like me either for some reason."

De Payne's remark doesn't strike me as odd at all — for a hacker. He wants to be recognized as a hacker, wanted as a hacker, even if that means attention from the FBI.

.   .   .

The waitress serves us the apple pie she'd like to eat with Lew. I decide it's time to make a leap. We've broken bread together, listened to Ross Jeffries Speed Seduction tapes, and joked about Eric. Time to get serious.

"What happens if someone wants to speak by phone to Kevin?" I carefully inquire.

De Payne considers my request for a moment.

"So if you were to speak to Kevin, what would you say to him?"

"Well, you know Eric's started calling me. I figure we know someone in common."

De Payne gets up and walks to a pay phone by the bathroom. I bite into my slice of pie.

Five minutes later, De Payne returns, a distracted look on his face.

"We'll have to sit here for a while, Jon. We may have to sit here for a half an hour."

And so we wait for Kevin Mitnick to phone.

Career Counseling

The phone startles me, and I stumble out of bed to pick up the portable. It's Eric again, calling at about four in the morning on Thursday, the last day of March, 1994.

"Be very careful about what you hear about my current activities, because I am in the process of disinformation," Eric threatens in a calm, even tone. "Everything that you hear about my whereabouts or activities may not be true."

Eric may be a fugitive on the run, but when it comes to his story, he's in total control. He pauses a moment and then coolly orders, "Stand by. There's some movement here. . . ."

Have they already trapped and traced the call? Is the FBI moving in for the bust? Should I hang up?

"It was nothing," Eric deadpans a few seconds later.

I've climbed the steep steps to my cluttered attic office, switched on the lamp, and booted up my Macintosh. I'm in my pajamas.

"So how badly do the feds want you?"

"I think they don't care. Schindler probably does, but I think he realizes he's got a can of worms on his hands if he finds me. I'm one of the few defendants that has ever had extensive personal phone calls with Schindler. We've been very much on a first-name basis for some time. It makes him very nervous now that I'm out here."

.   .   .

Eric makes his smooth, Hollywood sales pitch.

"You have the opportunity right now to buy the complete rights to my story," Eric pours it on. "Right now, every penny counts. The more money I have, the more free I feel to spend money on security measures."

I mention that Phillip Lamond, one of Eric's Hollywood rock-and-roll pals, told me he was living the high life.

"I'm doing fine, but I don't like taking chances. I'm not a greedy person. There's a lot of things I could do to make a lot of money if I really wanted to stick my balls on the line.

"HELLOOOO! If you touch the FUCKIN' car I will KILL you!"

The line is silent. When Eric returns a few seconds later, he doesn't explain his outburst. Some poor schmuck must have gotten too close to Eric's wheels.

The incident doesn't faze Eric. He's moving in for the closer, like the pitchman on a late-night TV offer.

"This offer is only going to be available for about thirty days. After that it's not going to be a concern to me. Money in my pocket right now will help me. I'm talking about cash within about thirty days."

I don't say anything.

"It is very risky for me to be talking to you at all," Eric says. "Not to mention the information, but the mere phone call itself. I think we're OK at this point. After spending forty-five minutes on the phone with you, nothing happened.

"Have you talked with the FBI?" Eric probes.

"No."

"So how did he [Phillip Lamond] give you the impression that I was doing OK?"

"He said you were driving a BMW and seemed to have plenty of money."

"Phillip has such a big mouth. If I was a killer, I'd fuckin' BLOW his brains out."

.   .   .

Five thousand dollars cash, that's what the cyberfugitive wants. In return, I'd get one hundred percent access. Meet him in person while he's on the run, be granted unlimited interviews, receive a copy of his memoirs, and get phone numbers of his friends. When I mention that this sounds an awful lot like aiding and abetting a fugitive, Eric casually contradicts everything he's just said, and calmly assures me I would certainly not be giving him money to flee. He, like Mitnick, is practiced in the art of social engineering. Eric's trying to con me.

"Can you hold on a second?" Eric asks.

"Sure."

I wait a couple of minutes, long enough to start thinking about how cold I am.

"Sorry to keep you waiting," Eric jokes, imitating an operator. "How may I process your call?"

Eric's slightly out of breath, but he's jazzed. "You'll never believe what I just did!

"There was this air compressor that kept going off every ten seconds. I walked over to this fenced-in area. I broke into it, shut the valves off, turned the pressure way down, and pulled this pin and released the pressure, and it blew up in my face!"

Suddenly Eric is serious.

"If I came in right now it would be three to five. I don't see the point. It's not going to teach me any lessons.

"If you dropped a hundred dollars on the floor, I would pick it up and hand it back to you. But if you're the federal government and you dropped a thousand dollars, or you're stupid, I'm going to take advantage of it."

How did Eric come to have this cynical worldview? He talks reluctantly about his upbringing in an upper-middle-class suburb of Washington, D.C. His father was a chiropractor, fond of auto racing, his mother an accountant. "Dad's got a couple mil, mom's got maybe a mil invested."

They divorced when Eric was twelve.

"I was an unwelcome child. That's caused a lot of problems in my life. I know it's kind of stupid to blame your childhood for your problems, but there's no question in my mind we are a product of our —

"Hang on a second!" he interrupts his own monologue. The seconds turn into minutes.

"That was pretty scary," Eric returns, sounding shaken. "I was at this bar with like two thousand people and now like the parking lot is empty, and it's almost spooky. I've got to call this girl real quick, and I'll call you back."

.   .   .

I rush down the stairs to pull on a jacket. We've been talking for nearly two hours and the last half hour I've spent shivering in my chair. I check a clock. It's about a quarter till six. The sun will rise in less than an hour.

Ten minutes pass. I pick up on the first ring. Eric's voice is changed.

"There are so many things I have yet to experience, places I need to be," Eric says, suddenly melancholy. "I want to leave something behind. I really feel I have a positive influence to leave. I really feel I can make up for what I've taken and I just don't feel I deserve to go to jail. Granted, life's not fair, and there are a lot of really good people that are suffering. But that just makes me want to do what I can with my life."

Eric Heinz, cyberpunk, worrying about the fate of the downtrodden masses? I don't believe him for a second. I change the subject to a topic Eric is more qualified to comment on.

"What's the difference between hacking a radio station and an individual?"

"I think I am a bit more karmic in my beliefs. It's just a conscience thing. I would feel grief if I were to cause somebody great grief just for my mere profit. Because money, although I like it, is not that important."

.   .   .

Eric's telling me how he and Kevin Poulsen investigated the Pac Bell security man bent on capturing them. "Actually it was really ironic because Poulsen and Mitnick both are the same way."

"Investigating the investigators?" I ask.

"Yes. It's something we were using to attempt to catch Mitnick at one point. We started making it look like he might get caught. Or things were heating up on his investigation, and he'd start taking risks to find out what's going on, whereas normally he would be very stealthful and very careful."

"Why do you think Mitnick had to know?"

"One of the reasons you become a computer hacker, and this is a very important point that you should know, is because you want control. You want to know what's going on in your life. You want to be able to control your life."

"Is that important to you?"

"To me? I think it is to a lot of people that are involved in computer hacking. They feel kind of helpless in a weird way. They do this to compensate," Eric explains.

"What does hacking do for you?"

"Knowledge is power. I just like to know as much as I can. It makes me feel more comfortable. It intrigues me —"

"I don't see you as the typical computer nerd. You have a whole other life —"

"A lot of hackers aren't nerds."

"What is it about hacking that appeals to you?"

"It's the control, the adrenaline, the knowledge, the having what you're not supposed to have."

.   .   .

Eric's in control now, shooting questions back at me.

"Do you consider yourself to be living vicariously through these subjects you're studying?"

It's a fair question. What is getting me out of bed at four in the morning to listen to the musings of a wanted cyberpunk? I suspect it's because there's something distinctly American about hackers. We invented hackers, just like we invented cowboys and gunfighters and gangsters, and if they aren't part of freedom and democracy, they sure seem to come with the territory. Listening to the confessions of Eric in the middle of the night is like talking to the Sundance Kid as the posse moves in. Eric's a marked man, and there's something compelling about hearing a desperate man's story.

Eric has another question.

"What would you recommend for me to do with my life?"

What would I recommend? I haven't read the federal statutes. Does career counseling a cyberfugitive land you a charge of aiding and abetting? "Well, you're talented, intelligent. There must be plenty of jobs you could get."

"I don't want to be stuck in a life where I have to work for a living."

"What about detective work?"

"It's still work," Eric reminds me, irritated at my lack of understanding. "I don't want to have to work. I don't want to have to do something that I don't really enjoy."

Eric sighs. "I would rather be a criminal."

Three-Way

"**T**ake a walk," teases the woman in a sexy voice at about 10 P.M. on May 19, 1994.

I don't know who it is, but I can guess. It's probably Bonnie Vitello, the former Mrs. Mitnick and current girlfriend of Lewis De Payne.

This is the only way Kevin Mitnick will talk. De Payne phoned a month ago and asked for the last four digits of a pay phone near my house. Then, a couple of weeks later, I gave De Payne the pay phone's prefix.

"OK," I say to Mitnick's ex and hang up. I pull on my down jacket and ski cap and jog down the deserted neighborhood street. The local public library is empty except for the lonely buzz of the janitor vacuuming behind the locked glass doors. I pace across the bricks, warm in my ski gear, catching my breath.

The phone rings. I let it ring again. A man's voice greets me. And then another.

"Hello."

"Hello."

It's Mitnick. And De Payne. They sound like they're in the same room.

Within the first minute I pick up enough clues to have a pretty good hunch where De Payne is. He's doesn't seem to be driving, walking, or leaning on a pay phone. He must be at 5502 Dobbs

Street, lounging on his couch, in front of the table crammed with electronics gear and cellular phones. There's probably a cat on his lap and another curling its tail around his ankles. I imagine Bonnie Vitello getting something to drink in the kitchen.

De Payne is playing telephone chaperone for Kevin Mitnick, cyberfugitive. In any other world, this would be considered strange. Mitnick is, after all, on the run largely because he violated his parole by associating with De Payne. Why would he rely on De Payne to set up a three-way chat line with a journalist?

Wouldn't the FBI be trapping De Payne's line?

But I'm looking at this from the wrong angle. De Payne and Mitnick must be talking over cell phones. Surely they're employing ingenious methods to befuddle the feds. Surely they're doing it because the feds would never believe they would be so bold. Surely they're doing it because they can't resist thumbing their noses at the FBI.

The odd couple raises an even more basic question. De Payne is the guy who stole Mitnick's wife and helped plunge Mitnick into cyberspace exile. Why are they still friends?

．　　　．　　　．

Why is Mitnick talking to me? Information. It's what feeds hackers. On one level it's crazy for a wanted fugitive to be talking to a journalist, but I'm the only journalist who has talked at length to Mitnick's nemesis, Eric Heinz. Mitnick can't resist knowing more about his enemy, even if I tell him little more than Eric's fondness for wrapping women in cellophane. And, of course, he may be talking to me for another reason. I had a big story in the *L.A. Times,* and I've got a movie option. Most hackers can't resist talking to the media.

De Payne brags about how he toyed with Eric and the FBI, but he quickly tires of the conversation. He fades in and out, tossing an occasional barb.

"Why'd you get involved with Eric at all?" I ask Mitnick. "Why didn't you just walk away?"

"He had so much information. It was the first time I'd encountered somebody that knew more than me."

Mitnick launches into a forty-five-minute description of how he figured out Eric was working for the feds, and how the FBI bungled its investigation. His voice surprises me. One minute he's got a puppy dog's warmth and enthusiasm, the next he flares angrily. He sounds a decade younger than his thirty years: animated, intensely emotional, naive, trusting, human, and nearly always on the verge of raucous laughter. Mitnick's grammar is off, he confuses tenses, and he has the attention span of a kid. Mitnick doesn't sound like a genius, and he doesn't sound evil.

"Who else do you think was wiretapping with SAS?" I ask Mitnick about Pac Bell's secret eavesdropping system.

"Probably the Bureau [FBI] was using it," Mitnick guesses. "They knew Eric was using it."

"Why would the Bureau use it?"

"They could wiretap without court orders. This is all speculation, of course, but it's interesting they didn't shut it [SAS] down. They did nothing to block it."

What an allegation! The FBI and Pac Bell won't talk, but Pac Bell does acknowledge the system exists.

"Do you have any evidence the FBI was using it to illegally wiretap?"

"My battery's running low. I could patch out anytime," Mitnick warns. "Who knows. If they thought I had access to it, they'd believe I was using it," Mitnick snarls. "I feel the same way about them. . . ."

"SHHHHHHHHHHHHH!" Mitnick's call patches out.

·   ·   ·

I pace in front of the library, still bundled in my down parka and ski cap. I've been staring at the phone for the last ten minutes, trying to will it to life. The janitor is long gone and the stacks are dark, except for the yellow glow cast by the sodium streetlight. It's getting colder, and I'm wishing I'd worn my long johns.

BRRRRINNNNNNG!

"Hi, Kevin."

Mitnick's put off by my greeting.

"Do me a favor," he snaps in a cold tone. "Don't call me that."

Mitnick's in a funk, and when he's upset he talks about how he's been screwed by journalists. Mitnick's a stuck record that way. He's sore that a movie deal based on *Cyberpunk,* a book partly written about Mitnick and De Payne, is about to die. Mitnick says the movie option is up June 8, 1994.

"I had a deal, a three-year option for five thousand dollars," the hacker fumes. "They want me to extend the option for no money. What do you think of that?"

"It doesn't sound like a very good deal."

Mitnick fills me in on the story behind *Cyberpunk*. He'd just finished eight months in solitary confinement and another four months in a federal prison when the authors began interviewing people for the book. Mitnick knew the book's authors were getting a six-figure advance, so he wanted to be paid for an interview. He figured he deserved it.

"So why'd you keep investigating Eric?" I change the subject.

"I wanted to know how I was being screwed. Who Eric was. Why they were doing it." Mitnick steams. "How I could discredit him if he were to come to court to testify."

"Why do you think they targeted you?"

"My probation was ending. They obviously picked me. Scott Charney, the head of the [Justice Department's] Computer Crime Division, maybe he was delegating, maybe he wanted some major convictions."

"So when did you take off?"

"My supervision was up on December seventh, so on December eighth I was legally free. I left. It's none of anyone's business where I went!" Mitnick spits out the words. "So far as I'm concerned I completed my parole. They made a mistake. I abided by all the conditions. Fuck them! Goodbye."

The call patches out. The time is a quarter to one in the morning. I pace for five, ten, fifteen minutes, just to be sure, staring at the silver and black pay phone.

.   .   .

"Hulloo," I mumble, groggy. It's pitch dark. My wife's asleep. I was too, a few seconds ago.

"Sorry to call so late, Jon, but this is the best time."

I'm half asleep, but I recognize the metallic monotone of Lewis De Payne's voice.

Kevin Mitnick operates on a different schedule, and I can't be choosy about when he's in the mood to chat. It's closing in on midnight, the last day of May 1994, twelve days since my first call from Mitnick. I pull on some long underwear. Summer may be approaching, but in Northern California it's still chilly this time of night.

Mitnick laments how hard it was for him to go straight.

"When he [Eric] called, I was unemployed at the time. I had a tough time getting a job. I had to tell them about my past. How easy is it to get a job when you have to say, 'Hey, I'm a criminal. Can I have a job?' "

"My probation officer would call and say, 'Does he have access to cash?' I can't understand how people on probation can ever get a job."

Mitnick talks briefly about his futile attempts to find work in Vegas, and then he hits that scratch in his record. He's talking to a journalist. Bad memories come back.

"I don't want you to paint me as an evil personality," he steams. "It's just not true. Katie [Hafner] said, 'Talk to me or else.' I knew she was going to be well paid for the book. All I wanted was five thousand dollars for an interview."

Katie Hafner and her former husband, John Markoff of the *New York Times*, are coauthors of the book *Cyberpunk*. I've read the book, and it's not hard to understand why Mitnick isn't terribly fond of it. The book chronicled hackers who spied for the KGB and the son of a National Security Agency code breaker who crippled the Internet with a terrifying computer worm. But the authors portrayed Mitnick more harshly than perhaps any other hacker in a section entitled "Kevin: The Dark Side Hacker."

"I'm not half as vindictive as Katie makes me out to be," Mitnick insists. "The book makes it out like my whole life was harassing people!"

■   ■   ■

Talking to Kevin Mitnick is like channel surfing. He skips from topic to topic, sometimes interrupting himself midsentence. But nearly everything he says is intriguing, especially when you consider he's wanted by the FBI.

Suddenly, Kevin Mitnick is giving me a primer on how Pac Bell wiretaps people like, well, Kevin Mitnick.

"When they want to wiretap somebody, Pac Bell calls the people in the [company's] dial group number assignment and says they need a number. They are given a phone number and a LEN [line equipment number].

"On the frame, there's a wire, let's say the number is 555-1212. They'll get you a line, put a half tap on your line. On the frame they put a special box they can dial from their security room in San Francisco.

"The phone line up there [in San Francisco] is carrying a conversation on the line. They place a DNR up there [a dial number recorder, a simple device that prints out all the numbers dialed from a phone]. But nothing prevents them from listening to your calls."

It's sort of like John Dillinger giving a lecture on bank security.

"It's scary. If Pac Bell wants to, if they believe you're up to no good, say you subscribe to 2600 [a phone hacker 'zine], they can monitor your line. Wiretap your line! And Pac Bell doesn't need a court order."

This sounds implausible, but Mitnick rattles off the federal statute. He's memorized this, too, just like the numerous phone numbers he's recited within the last hour.

"Title 18, Section 3142, The Wiretap Act. There's a clause that says any telephone service producer who believes his services are being fraudulently used may wiretap the suspect without a warrant."

Kevin Mitnick is right. I look up the statute and it's just as he says. Pac Bell or any other phone company in the nation can legally wiretap citizens without any government approval.

.   .   .

"Are you sure it was a full implementation of DES?" Mitnick probes.

Mitnick is asking about rumors that the FBI enlisted a Cray Supercomputer to crack Kevin Poulsen's Defense Encryption Standard–encrypted computer files. Poulsen says it happened. He double-encrypted his files, and the government cracked the encryption, a feat next to impossible. If true, it's the first evidence that the government's code-cracking powers are greater than it's publicly acknowledged.

"Yeah. Supposedly the files were encrypted two to three times," I say.

"Wow!" Mitnick exclaims, his voice jumping a few octaves. "They spent some money on Poulsen!"

Mitnick muses about which of the FBI top guns might currently have him in their sights.

"I'd be interested if Jim Settle was involved," Mitnick wonders out loud. "Or Hal Hendershot."

Harold Hendershot is the FBI's Supervisory Special Agent, Economic Crimes, Financial Crimes Section. He coordinates major computer crime investigations. Settle, too, has been a major FBI computer crime investigator, but he's just retired.

Then Mitnick surprises me. He starts chattering about a letter to Attorney General Janet Reno that De Payne's attorney, Richard Sherman, has written, a letter that I am told will blame the FBI and Assistant U.S. Attorney David Schindler for Eric's transgressions. It's a letter sure to enrage the very FBI agents who are trying to capture Mitnick.

Dillinger would never have dreamed of this. Nor would Capone.

Mitnick chuckles. "I'd love to see Schindler's face when the judge asks him about Eric."

I don't get it. De Payne hires a lawyer to enrage the FBI and shove Kevin Mitnick higher up the FBI's Most Wanted list. And Mitnick thinks it's funny?

De Payne hasn't said anything for over half an hour. Maybe he's snuggling in bed with Mitnick's ex.

It's risky, but I've been waiting all night to ask this question.

"What do you think about De Payne doing all this?"

"Lew has a tendency to always get attorneys involved. That's just the way he is," Mitnick explains, sounding ambivalent. "Lew is the one person since 1981 they have not been able to get."

Dear Janet

Somewhere on the planet, Kevin Mitnick is laughing.

My fax beeps, and I walk over to see the threatening letter to Janet Reno that Mitnick warned was in the works.

I have to smile. They're actually doing it, accusing the federal government of committing crimes. It's revenge. It's the ultimate hack. It's yet another De Payne–Mitnick full-court prank. Charges of illegal activity by FBI agents. Allegations that a U.S. attorney deceived a federal judge about his knowledge of Eric's continuing crimes. The fugitive hacker and his prankster friend are fighting back, attacking their enemies for their handling of hacker double agent Justin Petersen, aka Eric Heinz.

Law Offices of Richard G. Sherman
May 19, 1994

The Honorable Janet Reno
Attorney General of the United States
Department of Justice
10th & Constitution Ave. N.W. Room 4400
Washington D.C. 20530

RE: *Illegal Activities by Certain Special Agents of the Federal Bureau of Investigation.*

Dear Madam Attorney General:

It has come to my attention that Federal Bureau of Investigation Special Agents Stanley E. Ornellas, Kenneth G. McGuire III, and Joseph C. Ways . . . have engaged, individually and jointly, in a course of conduct which is illegal and contrary to Bureau policy in their handling of an informant working under their direction and control. . . .

. . . On or about October 31, 1991, the Texas prosecution against Petersen was transferred to the Central District of California pursuant to Rule 20 of the F.R. Crim.P. and sealed as Petersen was then cooperating with the government and it was alleged that his life might be in danger. . . . Indeed, there was substantial danger, however, it was to the general public and not Petersen.

. . . Justin T. Petersen obtained, illegally, several . . . Driver Licences under various fictitious names. . . . He then filed a false claim with and started receiving disability benefits from the Hollywood Social Security office under the name of Eric Heinz Jr., who was then deceased, claiming that he was disabled due to having a missing hand.

. . . DMV [Department of Motor Vehicles] investigators ran Eric's various aliases through their computers. This triggered automatic notification to the FBI that someone had requested information through the computer regarding their informant Justin Petersen. As a result, the FBI called the DMV investigators to ascertain if they had a legitimate reason to run their informant. The FBI was made aware of Eric's state crimes. SSA [Social Security Administration] investigators attempted to ascertain from the FBI the whereabouts of Eric, so that they could question and arrest him. The FBI agents "handling" Petersen refused to provide any information to the requesting law enforcement officers. . . .

I laugh at the sheer audacity of the letter, and the potentially damaging facts that De Payne and Sherman choose to leave out. Mitnick's relentless and possibly illegal ploys to unmask Petersen's undercover identity. His hounding of Social Security officers to investigate and terminate Petersen's bogus social security benefits.

But as I continue reading, I see that De Payne's attorney is not content with blasting the FBI and the U.S. Attorney's Office for protecting Eric so that he could continue his life of crime. Sherman goes on to claim that more than just botching its undercover operation, the U.S. government permitted Eric to wiretap illegally.

> Placing such a system . . . in the hands of law enforcement, would be an invitation to catastrophe . . . the SAS computer . . . represents one of the greatest dangers to the civil liberties of U.S. citizens. . . . It is a computer system which allows someone . . . to literally take over any phone in the United States.

> Allowing the FBI to share such information with a common informant like Eric, who can then pass it on to others, makes the former catastrophe pale by comparison. . . . It is hard to believe that such an adventure would be approved by any responsible Justice Department Official.

> To obtain his release from detention in Texas and allow Petersen to remain at liberty given his background, criminal record, and criminal activity, confounds me. He is one of the most dangerous techno-criminals in the United States. No information, telephone conversation, or data transmission is safe so long as he is at liberty and free to teach others his craft. . . . Why did all of this occur? . . . What was so unique about this informant that the FBI would ignore his background, and criminal activity, while acting as their informant, cause them to conceal him from state law enforcement officers, and deceive a Federal District Judge? . . .

> *Yours Truly,*
>
> *Richard G. Sherman*
>
> *cc: Hon. Louis Freeh*
> *Hon. Nora Manella*
> *SAC Charlie Parsons*
> *Clerk, Hon. Stephen V. Wilson*

The lengthy letter with numerous exhibits doesn't suggest the government's motive, but the implication is clear. Only one prize could be sufficient to warrant Petersen's alleged dangers to the public and national security.

The chance to capture Kevin Mitnick.

.   .   .

My wife cups her hand over the portable phone.

"It's John Markoff of the *New York Times*."

The call was bound to come sooner or later. Though I've been researching my book about Poulsen for months, only in the last few weeks have I been interviewing Kevin Mitnick. Reporters don't take kindly to others nosing around their subjects, and Markoff, *Cyberpunk* coauthor and recognized cyberspace journalist, routinely scoops the competition on high-tech stories.

But still, I'm surprised Markoff is phoning me at home on a Saturday. He's only called me once in the last six years or so, and I barely know him. We first met in the summer of 1987 when, as an editor at a San Francisco computer magazine, I contracted him to write a story. At the time, he was a respected high-tech reporter for the *San Francisco Examiner*. He, too, had gotten his start with technology magazines.

We had met for lunch in a bistro across from the old offices of *Rolling Stone* magazine. Tall, with a curly mop of dark hair and thick glasses, Markoff struck me as confident yet modest. He lacked the usual hard-boiled cynicism of most newspaper reporters. The story was about a new Sun Microsystems computer, and I wanted to hire Markoff for his contacts. Over lunch, he discussed the new, secret UNIX computer Sun was planning to introduce. I was impressed. Markoff had the contacts of an insider, and the technical expertise of an engineer. But what most impressed me was his demeanor. He had an ease about him, an earnestness that was appealing. It was easy to see why people would confide in him.

The next week Markoff turned in a good, technical piece. Our paths didn't cross again for nearly three years, until early 1990 in Syracuse, New York, when we both attended the trial of the Internet worm hacker, Robert Tappan Morris. I was writing a feature article on the case; Markoff was covering the trial for the *New York Times.* His then wife, Katie Hafner, was there to cover the event for the book they told me they were writing together, *Cyberpunk.* Markoff had broken the story on the front page of the *Times,* when Robert Morris Sr., a personal friend of his and one of the National Security Agency's most talented code breakers, helped tip off Markoff that it was his son who had unleashed the Internet worm.

We spoke briefly during the trial, and the evening of Morris's conviction we shared a cab back to the Sheraton. Markoff's wife called me during the summer of 1991, asking if she could use some of the material in my Morris article in *Cyberpunk.* Hafner phoned again in early 1992, asking for advice on promoting the recently completed book. I offered my suggestions, and in the book's preface the couple thanked me for my assistance.

.   .   .

It's a Saturday afternoon, June 1994.

John Markoff launches into conversation with no mention of the four and a half years that have elapsed since we last spoke. He's all business. Markoff has heard that Mitnick social engineered a copy of the source code for a cellular phone made by Qualcomm, a company in San Diego. He's hot on his trail. Source code is the most fundamental level of software — the actual instructions that make computers perform specific tasks. When you buy a regular program like Microsoft Word, you don't get source code, you get a program that has been built — compiled — for commercial use.

If indeed Mitnick's got the source code to the program that drives Qualcomm's phone, he could command the phone to do things not intended for the general public's use.

"He [Mitnick] talked to six people in the company," Markoff claims. "It was his style. The stuff ended up on CompuServe."

If true that would mean Qualcomm's proprietary cellular software ended up publicly available on the Internet.

"What's the software good for?" I ask.

"You can clone a phone with it."

In other words, the source code, or base software, would enable a hacker to hijack the serial number and other identifying information of other people's cellular phones, thereby sticking them with the bills.

"Why do you think Mitnick's doing it?"

Markoff doesn't seem to know, and admits he's "never found a profit motive" behind Mitnick's hacking.

Markoff has a copy of the Janet Reno letter claiming FBI misconduct and tells me he's heard Agent Steal pursued Mitnick and "he [Eric] was dirty." He plans to fly down to visit De Payne's attorney in Los Angeles soon, but he isn't impressed by the government's wayward undercover operative.

Markoff thinks Kevin Mitnick is by far the superior hacker.

■   ■   ■

"Have you talked to Kevin?" Markoff continues.

"I'm talking to lots of hackers," I venture.

"How do you think I might get in touch with Kevin?"

"Well, you know he's still close with De Payne."

"I've thought about trying to catch Kevin," the *New York Times* reporter jokes before saying goodbye. "But I guess that wouldn't be politically correct." (Markoff later denied saying this, even in jest.)

Press Tactics

It's Independence Day 1994. I wander down to the curb, pick up the *Times,* and strip off the blue plastic wrapper.

There he is, staring back at me from the front page of the *New York Times,* the fugitive I've been talking with down at the local pay phone. It's the same old menacing picture of Kevin Mitnick.

CYBERSPACE'S MOST WANTED: HACKER ELUDES F.B.I. PURSUIT

By John Markoff

He did it! He actually managed to get Kevin Mitnick on the front page. I scan the article looking for the breaking news that catapulted this old story to the premier spot. But there's no hot lead, no mention of a victim company or individual, no promise of an imminent capture. There are plenty of allegations, but the only solid charge against Mitnick appears to be a probation violation, generally not the sort of stuff that lands a year-and-a-half-old fugitive case on the front page of the *New York Times.*

The story reads like a feature article, beginning with the rehash of an old myth Markoff helped propagate in *Cyberpunk.* Markoff must know the NORAD War Games tale is nothing more than a story told by one of Mitnick's cohorts famous for his fictional accounts.

I flip to the inside page and read about a Mitnick hacking rampage that Markoff claims could threaten the "future of cellular telephone networks." When I finish the story, I look for a source for Mitnick's alleged crimes, or a sign that someone other than Markoff believes Mitnick threatens the future. But I can't even find a reference to the possibility of a grand jury indictment, and there's not a single quote from an Assistant U.S. Attorney, FBI agent, or Justice Department spokesman.

I slowly notice items missing from the fifteen-hundred-word article. Like the word "hacker," the term chosen by the *Times*'s headline writers. Markoff never calls Mitnick a hacker. He uses phrases like "computer programmer run amok" and derogatory terms like "grifter," and "criminal." He's right in a sense. Mitnick definitely has the skills of a grifter. But Markoff himself acknowleges in his article that Mitnick doesn't appear to have a profit motive. Why then does he call him a grifter? Grifting is about conning people out of money.

And what about Justin Petersen (aka Eric Heinz)? The government's informant isn't even mentioned. Why is Markoff ignoring Petersen's role in entrapping Mitnick and sending him on the run? Several paragraphs recount decade-old Mitnick myths, yet Petersen's involvement is timely and newsworthy. Why is there no reference to the Janet Reno letter alleging FBI misconduct? Markoff had a copy of if. If Markoff thinks the Reno letter is off base, why doesn't he take the opportunity to debunk it?

Combining technical wizardry with the ages-old guile of a grifter, Kevin Mitnick is a computer programmer run amok. And law enforcement officials cannot seem to catch up with him.

. . . Now one of the nation's most wanted computer criminals, Mr. Mitnick is suspected of stealing software and data from more than a half dozen leading cellular telephone manufacturers. . . .

As a teen-ager he used a computer and a modem to break into a North American Air Defense Command computer, foreshadowing the 1983 movie "War Games.". . .

Mr. Mitnick is now a suspect in the theft of software that companies plan to use for everything from handling billing information to determining the location of a caller to scrambling wireless phone calls to keep them private. Such a breach could compromise the security of future cellular telephone networks. . . . Last year, while a fugitive, he managed to gain control of a phone system in California that allowed him to wiretap the F.B.I. agents who were searching for him.

. . . F. B. I. and Justice Department officials said they were still uncertain of his motives and did not have absolute proof that he was behind the attacks on cellular phone companies. . . .

In July and early August, numerous Los Angeles newspaper stories pour out of my fax with their version of events. Stories about Mitnick and stories about Justin Petersen, aka Eric Heinz. The difference between the *New York Times*'s and the Los Angeles papers' coverage is striking. The *Los Angeles Times* and the *Los Angeles Daily News* report several aspects of the story, making tentative connections between Petersen's alleged FBI undercover work and the investigation of Kevin Mitnick. I don't doubt De Payne and Mitnick helped spur the stories, both by initiating the Janet Reno letter and, on De Payne's part, by actually phoning the *Daily News*. But either way Petersen's role is part of the picture. In short, in sharp contrast to Markoff's article, the Los Angeles papers raise as many questions about the government's conduct as they do about hackers.

Los Angeles Times, July 31, 1994

HACKER IN HIDING: DIGITAL DESPERADO WHO CLAIMS TO HAVE WORKED FOR THE FBI IS NOW BEING SOUGHT BY THE AGENCY

By John Johnson
First there was the Condor, then Dark Dante. The latest computer hacker to hit the cyberspace most wanted list is Agent Steal, a slender, good-looking rogue partial to Porsches and BMWs who bragged that he worked undercover for the FBI catching other hackers.

. . . Ironically, by running he has consigned himself to the same secretive life as Kevin Mitnick, the former North Hills man who is one of the nation's most infamous hackers, and whom Petersen allegedly bragged of helping to set up for an FBI bust. . . .

. . . But was he really working as a government informant? . . . The FBI refused to talk about Petersen directly. But J. Michael Gibbons, a bureau computer crime expert, expressed doubts. . . .

"It's not safe. Across the board, hackers cannot be trusted to work — they play both sides against the middle." The agents "could have had him in the office," Gibbons said. "They probably debriefed him at length. Send him out to do things? I doubt it."

Los Angeles Daily News, July 31, 1994

FORMER FBI INFORMANT A FUGITIVE
AFTER HELPING TRACK FELLOW HACKERS

Keith Stone — Computer outlaw Justin Tanner Petersen and prosecutors cut a deal: The Los Angeles nightclub promoter known in the computer world as "Agent Steal" would work for the government in exchange for freedom.

. . . Now FBI agents are searching for their rogue informant — scouring computer conventions and nightclubs for a man they say can change his identity and fill his pockets with cash just by pushing a few buttons.

Two weeks ago, the U.S. Department of Justice announced it had found no proof of criminal wrongdoing in the government's handling of Petersen, but the case was referred to the FBI's Office of Professional Responsibility for more investigation.

Pushing the investigation is Santa Monica attorney Richard G. Sherman, who contends the FBI used Petersen as an informant while knowing he was breaking the law. . . . "How can you let a man like this run loose who had a record he had — who had the criminal problems he had?" Sherman said.

"They don't want to find this guy because then they are really in trouble. Why? Because he will tell what he was doing for them," Sherman said.

Assistant U.S. Attorney David Schindler ... disputed Sherman's core allegation — that the government knowingly allowed Petersen to break the law.

"He describes this nefarious plot by the Justice Department and FBI to run around the city and do wrong things — and this is patently wrong," Schindler said.

... De Payne and Sherman insist that Petersen knew how to manipulate Pacific Bell computers to create false records to try and implicate De Payne and Mitnick.

Seattle

Kevin Pazaski gets a call the afternoon of July 27, 1994. He's sitting in his cramped, windowless, eight-foot-square office by Yarrow Bay in Kirkland, Washington, a phone pressed to his ear. The customer service rep is puzzled. A new account is complaining about several hundred dollars of unauthorized charges on his bill. And he hasn't made a single call.

Could Pazaski look into it?

Pazaski is a fraud analyst with CellularOne. He looks like the marathon runner he is: broad chest, trim waist, early thirties. He wears jeans, a sport shirt, and athletic shoes to work. His duties keep him active, tracking cases in Washington, Colorado, Utah, and Alaska and helping cops with subpoenas for criminals using cell phones. Pazaski views his job in old-fashioned terms. He helps nail the pirates of the cellular phone revolution. He calls them Clone Jockeys, Call Sell Operators, and Skip Jackers, but to him they're all the same. Criminals swiping cellular phone time.

Cellular phone fraud always has one common component. The perpetrator uses someone else's legitimate number, their electronic serial number, to bill calls. Pazaski's job is to find out who's actually swiped the ESN, and perhaps, how they did it.

Pazaski scans the billing statement. The first call is from Eugene,

Oregon, on June 27, 1994, 1:16 P.M. A call to information. Pazaski knows the pattern. A phone hacker dials information to test his clone job before making calls.

The investigator scans the remaining calls made the afternoon of June 27, calls from Oregon — Albany, Salem, Portland. Pazaski knows the route. The phone hacker was heading north on the I-5. At 3:52 P.M., in Portland, the phone hacker made his last call of the afternoon, to Las Vegas.

Pazaski dials the number on the bill.

"SHHHHHHHHHHHHHHHHHHHH!"

Modem breath. The phone hacker's jacking into a modem in Vegas.

Weird, Pazaski thinks. He walks down the hall to Information Services, and asks a techie to try the same number. But all he gets is the prompt of some anonymous, online computer system. The techie would need a password to get in, a password he hasn't a clue how to crack.

The calls continue. By 6:07 P.M. on June 27, the phone hacker was in Seattle. The next morning, June 28, the hacker dialed at 11:13 A.M. It's the last call on the Oregon-based pirated cellular number.

Customer service alerts Pazaski to a new pirated number that sprang to life June 28 at 11:29 A.M. — calls to taxi cabs, the local Metro bus line, and an alternative Seattle movie theater, the Seven Gables. But most of the numbers are dead ends, modem numbers or calls to roamer access numbers.

A roamer access number works as a bridge to phone a mobile cellular customer who has left his or her area code. First you dial one of the roamer numbers in the cellular subscriber's general area, say Los Angeles, then you dial their full cellular number.

The hacker is dialing roamers so often that Pazaski wonders whether he's using them for another reason. When you dial a roamer it's the only number that shows up on a bill. There's no trace of the person actually called. Roamers are a great way to mask long distance calls.

The investigator begins to form a sketchy profile of the pirate: no car, frugal, a movie buff. But Pazaski has no idea where he gets his ESNs. Maybe he's got a scanner and he's listening to calls and picking up ESNs? Maybe he's hacking ESNs with a computer? Maybe he's social engineering?

Pazaski can only guess.

The Well

The first week of August, Ron Austin phones with strange news. While talking with De Payne, Mitnick's pal, totally out of context, dropped phrases like "roller blading," and mentioned how Austin had met me at the airport. De Payne never explained these provocative non sequiturs, and Austin never asked. He got the message.

We both know at least two ways Mitnick and De Payne could have gotten the information. The FBI, via its informant Eric Heinz, helped supply De Payne and Mitnick with SAS. But while I don't doubt Mitnick and De Payne's wiretapping abilities, I figure the second possibility is far more likely. Cracking into someone else's e-mail, for Kevin Mitnick, at least, would be child's play.

I think back over my e-mail exchanges with Austin. I mentioned roller blading in a recent message, and about a week ago, on one of my L.A. research trips, Austin met me at the airport. We discussed the airport arrangements both in e-mail and on the phone, but we never talked about roller blading on the phone.

That settles it in my mind. Mitnick and De Payne have cracked my Internet gateway, the Well, and are reading my e-mail. The question is what can I do?

.　　　　.　　　　.

"The Well," welcomes a young, hip female voice.

Calling the Well isn't like calling any other Internet provider. The men and women who answer the phones and work the computers have a hippy, sixties look and attitude. I know because I've driven from my home to visit their nearby offices in Sausalito, California. It's not a big operation, but it's become a trendy Internet club, frequented by a close-knit community of upscale ex-hippy libertarians, liberals, Greatful Dead fans, technophiles, and journalists. The cognoscenti have e-mail addresses there, people like Mitch Kapor, the founder of Lotus, and the privacy group the Electronic Frontier Foundation. Markoff, too, has a Well address.

"Technical support, please," I ask. In a few seconds a friendly young man picks up the line.

"Hi, how can I help you?"

"Somebody's reading my e-mail," I tell the technical support person.

"How do you know?"

"Well, I'm sending e-mail to somebody, and this third person knows everything."

"OK," responds the tech support person calmly. "Did you give someone else your password and just forget it?"

"I don't think you understand," I say, growing impatient. "A hacker is reading my e-mail on the Well."

"Who is this hacker?"

"I don't know," I say truthfully. I don't know if it's De Payne or Mitnick who is reading my e-mail. For all I know they could have put somebody else up to it. Besides, does it really matter who's hacking the Well? The point is the Well isn't secure, and my mail is an open book.

"Do you change your password frequently?" the Well tech asks.

"What?" I say, amazed he's asking this question. "No, I don't."

"Well, you know that could be the problem."

"Look, I don't think you get it! There's a hacker on the Well. He's probably got root. Do you understand what I'm saying?"

"Yes."

"Well, if you've got root on the Well you don't need passwords. You can read anybody's e-mail."

Root access is like having the master key to the building. You have complete control of the computer. You can change any password, read any file, write to any file, erase everything stored on the computer. Users are at the mercy of a hacker who has root access.

"That's not possible," the Well technician tells me.

"What's not possible?" I interject. Hackers know it's been done countless times before. It's easy for a skilled hacker to get root access on the Well and nearly every other Internet provider.

But the Well technician refuses to accept this possibility.

"It's not possible for a hacker to get root on the Well," he says stubbornly.

Maybe for an average hacker. But for Kevin Mitnick it's a walk in the park.

The Hunt

Two or three times a day, Ron Austin slowly drives past the Los Angeles Federal Building looking for the gold BMW with the Texas plates.

He figures it's the least he can do since his trashing treasure hunts sent Eric on the run. Special Agent Stan Ornellas phoned recently and told him the Bureau had decided Eric's escapade had gone on long enough. Austin suggested Ornellas talk to Phillip Lamond, Eric's former partner in the nightclub business, and sure enough the tip worked. Lamond gave the agent a description of Eric's car. A little more legwork and Ornellas had the name of a stripper Eric was seeing, recent snapshots of the couple from a jealous boyfriend, and an address, incredibly, just a stone's throw from FBI headquarters.

But this Saturday, Austin is taking a day off from his surveillance to drive his girlfriend to Tower Video on Sunset to pick up some new CDs. He turns off the boulevard, down the hill to the parking lot, and there it is, Eric's gold BMW, parked in front of the Viper Room.

Austin drops off his girlfriend and returns to take a closer look. No dent like the FBI described, and no license plate, just a dealer's temporary. But the handicap plaque seals it. Austin jots down the number.

"FBI," answers the voice at Headquarters.

"Yeah, could you transfer me to Special Agent Tepper?"

"I've spotted Eric's BMW," Austin tells the agent. Tepper phones Ornellas and the FBI agent hops in his Crown Victoria and burns up the 405 freeway.

Austin walks back to his car, keeping the BMW in view.

What's this? The valet's strolling toward the car.

Shit! Austin thinks. Eric's leaving!

The valet tosses a brown lunch bag in the gold BMW, his BMW. Austin confronts him just to be sure.

"I'm sorry," Austin sheepishly calls Ornellas a minute later.

"Don't be sorry," replies the special agent, a few minutes away on his car phone. "We want to know anytime you see anything like this."

.   .   .

"We've heard Eric's been hanging out at Gecko's," Ornellas tells Austin on the phone several days later. "Ever heard of it?"

"No," Austin replies. "Where is it?"

The agent gives Austin the Huntington Beach address of the night-club, and declares matter-of-factly, "We'll be there Sunday evening."

"Fine, I'll be there too," says the hacker.

Around ten o'clock on the appointed night, Austin pulls into the multilevel parking lot across from Gecko's and spots Ornellas's Crown Victoria.

"Hi, how you doing?" greets Ornellas, getting out of the big American car.

Ornellas is dressed as he always is when he doesn't have to visit a courtroom or an Assistant U.S. Attorney: short-sleeve shirt, blue jeans, and tennis shoes. His partner is a perfect match; big, with a New York accent, maybe Italian.

Austin shakes both men's hands, but he's nervous. The conspicuous Crown Victoria is in clear view of the club.

"Aren't you afraid Eric's going to see you here?"

"Well, how do you expect us to see him?" shrugs Ornellas. "Why don't we get in back?"

Austin hops in, and listens with amusement to the FBI agent's running commentary on the shapely female arrivals. It's not just the locker room cop talk. It's the friendliness of Ornellas. Who'd believe he once banged Austin's head against a wall?

"Does that guy look like he's limping?" wonders the other agent.

"Nope," says Ornellas.

"Hey that looks like him!"

"No," Ornellas deadpans from the backseat. "That's a girl."

.   .   .

Lewis De Payne is on the phone. It's August 17, 1994.

He tells me a *London Observer* reporter flew all the way from England for a story about Mitnick. De Payne wouldn't talk, and neither would Mitnick's ex-wife, Bonnie Vitello, until the reporter paid her a hundred dollars.

But that's not why De Payne is calling.

"A new piece of information has come to my attention," De Payne proudly declares. "We've got several of Eric's phone bills with telephone calls to computers he was illegally accessing at Pac Bell and the DMV [Department of Motor Vehicles] under the Joseph Wernle name."

De Payne is alleging that Eric was illegally hacking while working as an undercover FBI agent, implying that the FBI had to know about it. And he's claiming that he's got the evidence.

"The neat part about it," De Payne continues, sounding giddy, "is the FBI wasn't paying the bills. They let them go to collection!"

I know at least part of the story is true. I've got copies of overdue Joseph Wernle Sprint and MCI phone bills, too. Excited, De Payne tells me he's informed Sprint that Special Agent Ken McGuire of the FBI ordered the now delinquent service. "Now McGuire's started giving them excuses," De Payne laughs. "He says he's taking care of it."

One more prank that's sure to put Mitnick on the hot seat.

.   .   .

I tell De Payne that somebody's hacked into my e-mail account, and he chuckles at the Well technician's suggestion that I change my password. Changing a password won't stop a clever hacker like

Kevin Mitnick. Certainly not if the hacker has root capabilities over the whole Well system.

"Have you tried putting a dead bolt lock on your door and bars on your windows?" De Payne mocks.

"I hadn't thought of that."

"I can set you up with good PGP [Pretty Good Privacy, an encryption program]," De Payne says with a laugh. "If you're having problems, you might receive some help online."

This is an eavesdropper's inside joke, gleaned from further intrusions into my e-mail. Austin has been encouraging me to encrypt my e-mail to him for months, but I struggled with the cumbersome technology and the stigma attached to encryption. What many hackers and technophiles fail to realize, of course, is that if you encrypt your mail, you're waving a red flag for the government and the NSA.

"So why is the Well so insecure?" I ask half of the duo I suspect of reading my e-mail.

"The problem is the UNIX platform," De Payne declares matter-of-factly, explaining that the Well, like most Internet providers, has minimal security.

"I'm on Netcom, which is also a UNIX system. Half a year ago, I didn't use it for three months. I forgot my password. I called them and they said, 'What's your name?' They set my password to so and so."

De Payne is implying that he could have been anyone, and Netcom might have been handing over his password to a total stranger.

I try one more time to broach the subject of De Payne and Mitnick's apparent eavesdropping. "The Well didn't seem to believe it was possible to hack my e-mail."

De Payne pauses and his voice slows. It's as if he's whispering in my ear.

"Tell me, Jon, do you feel violated?"

This isn't what I expected, but I decide to play it out. "Well, yes, actually, a little."

"Do you feel female?"

I'm silent.

"It's the same feeling of electronic rape that a lot of companies are complaining about," De Payne continues. "I wish some reporter would write about these companies that are being electronically sodomized."

He's irritated.

"I think the whole thing is academic. These companies complaining. Kathleen Carson of the FBI comparing someone [Mitnick] to a child molester. Why not just say they're being sodomized?"

.   ■   .

A six-inch stack of customer bills with bad charges sits next to Kevin Pazaski's PC. Summer is nearly over and the investigator is still spinning his wheels. Customers stuck with thousands of dollars of unauthorized calls. Thousands of dollars of calls CellularOne can't collect on.

Finally he tracks a clue, a call to a local modem. Pazaski's friend in Information Systems tells him it's an Internet access port. The systems guy traces it to Netcom in San Jose, California.

Pazaski drives his gray Subaru over to 45th Street in Seattle and parks in front of the two-story mall and movie theater, the marquee listing the summer hits. It doesn't look right, he thinks, but that's the address the systems guy gave him.

Pazaski takes the elevator up through the glassed atrium and walks the corridors trying to find the Netcom suite. Finally, the investigator spots a Netcom plaque on a locked door. Pazaski doesn't get it. Where is everybody? He asks somebody in a neighboring office.

"It's just a relay station for the Internet," explains the man to a disappointed Pazaski. "They rent space all over the country."

Data Thief

I think he is out of touch with reality. I think he lies very much and is not sure when he is lying.

—DONALD PETERSEN,
Eric's father, *Los Angeles Daily News*

Eric has been hacking up a storm, cramming two-by-three spiral mini-notepads with swiped log-ins for TRW and notes of his latest scheme. He keeps meticulous "to do" lists: "Plan . . . Spread rumors . . . Get U-haul . . . Call Mom . . . Bring hand gun." Notes about places to stay, eight different women in Los Angeles alone. And personal tips to his girlfriends, such as, "Don't hate me because I'm beautiful."

Eric is planning one last big score. If he can get away with it, and he sees no reason why he can't, he'll leave the country for good.

He plans his heist in a letter to his co-conspirator, and signs it XRAY. They've committed plenty of small-time crimes before. Why not one big job for the road?

OK . . . You need $7,000 to open an account. I'm kinda short on cash. We should both have money. The name of the system is Mellon Bank. I checked Lexus. Either it hasn't been done or banks aren't saying. . . . I'll get a telenet [tap] up and running soon. . . . You need two sets of log ins and passwords and I have them. . . .

After we've done the transfer we'll want to buy some time to get the money out of the bank. . . .

I could:

>   A. *Cut the lines.*
>
>   B. *Phone in a bomb threat.*
>
>   C. *Burn down the bank.*

I'll see you in the Rivierra.

XRAY

·   ·   ·

"I'm back in L.A. for a week," Eric awakens me after midnight on August 9. "Nobody knows where I am. I mean nobody. I'm just afraid somebody's going to see me and have read the articles and drop a dime on me. So I'm extremely careful while I'm back here in L.A. I won't go to any clubs here at all."

Is Eric nuts? De Payne and Mitnick have just made certain that L.A.'s two biggest newspapers have broadcast his height, weight, hair colors, haunts, and aliases to hundreds of thousands of Los Angelinos. L.A. is the last place Eric should be.

"Do you miss the Hollywood scene?"

"I'm just really hoping that this is going to blow over."

But the wind isn't blowing in his direction. Eric Heinz, Agent Steal, or Justin Petersen — take your pick — is suddenly a cyber-celebrity, a notorious rogue, and the FBI, which so far hasn't made much of an effort to hunt Eric, now has a very good reason to capture their man in the computer underground. Eric has become a public liability for the Bureau, and the only way to clean up the FBI operation gone sour is to put Eric behind bars.

"I think the whole thing with De Payne pushing this story is ridiculous," Eric fumes. "He's making all this smoke so the government might say, 'We don't want to fuck with that can of worms.' Then again it might piss them off and blow up in his face."

"Don't you think De Payne and Mitnick figure it's hacker justice?" I venture. "You messed with them. They mess back."

"I was just doing my job. Perhaps you should explain it to them. It really wasn't anything personal. I was hired, and I did my job. But you know, that's the mentality of a typical hacker."

"Mitnick seems to think the FBI entrapped him," I offer.

"Well, he's guilty," Eric snaps. "We didn't entrap him. I think he's into hacking. I think he wants to know information."

Not money? Not crime? Just information. Is Eric right? Is this the real reason the FBI considers Mitnick dangerous?

"He may not have been doing anything at the time that we called him," Eric continues, unwittingly making a possible argument for entrapment. "But as soon as Mitnick knew that I had something that he wanted, they [Mitnick and De Payne] were all over me. They wanted to share information.

"What really blows me away is how does the FBI *know* what Mitnick is doing?" Eric wonders. "When the Bureau came to me, I asked the agents, 'What's Mitnick been doing?' [They said,] 'We don't want to talk about it, but we're pretty sure he's been up to something.'

"You know, *how* do they *know?*" Eric asks me.

It's an intriguing question. I've looked at the court records and they give no hint of any legal investigation by the FBI or Pacific Bell before they sent Eric undercover in late 1991. Did the FBI really know Mitnick was hacking in the fall of 1991, a full year before his probation was finished? Or did they just assume Mitnick would be unable to resist their temptations?

"Is it the analogy that De Payne gave?" Eric continues. "That once somebody has the key to everything, every time something is opened they think it's the person who has the keys?"

Suddenly, police sirens scream on Eric's end. "Hold on a second!" Eric orders.

"Is there a problem?" I ask nervously.

But Eric's cool. He knows cop stuff. He doesn't respond for several seconds. "Nope. I don't think they're going to come and get me on a code three."

I don't know what a code three is, but Eric isn't the slightest bit worried.

"Hey, there are trailer people living in this parking lot," he remarks with amusement, the sirens sounding like the cops are closing in. Eric is in a philosophical frame of mind.

"The Bureau really pissed me off. They weren't very thorough. They were very slow at doing things.

"In a lot of ways I feel like the victim," Eric laments. "The government didn't give me the protection to stay clear of Mitnick that I asked for. Therefore, Mitnick found out who I was and he fucked up my benefits.

"When I got thrown out of the Oakwoods after eight months of living there, the government gave me one week's notice. That's it! One week's notice!"

.   .   .

Eric jokes about his surroundings. "I'm in one of those parking lots you have to pay to sit in, and this guy's cleaning it up and turning the lights off. I just offered him a beer."

Eric's pulled a chair up to the pay phone and made himself comfortable. He sounds slightly tipsy. He's talking about how the FBI outfitted him for his undercover Mitnick mission.

"The FBI gave me two computers, two phone lines, two modems, a cell phone, a pager, a test set, and recording equipment. They gave me a Nagra miniature tape recorder. They had these special tapes, and these wires that you put on your chest, the classic tape recorder that FBI informants wear.

" 'This is yours, keep it,' they told me. I taped it into a void in my leg and to my chest. Being a sound engineer, I modified it. I put the microphones on my shoulders. That way, when I was at a loud bar, when someone was yelling into my ear, I'd pick it up on my shoulder."

"We had Mitnick admitting to using SAS and cell phone fraud. He said his phone was chipped [cloned]. Lewis was very proud to rub it in my face that just by me barely mentioning SAS he was able to completely access it and get all the information on it."

Eric pauses and then reflects on the dangerous opportunity that he and the FBI created. "I'd really hate to see some other hackers get ahold of that stuff."

.   .   .

"I'm asking your personal advice," Eric demands in a serious tone. "Would it do me any good to make it clear to all the newspapers out there that if my picture gets published it will cost them money?"

"No," I respond without thinking.

"I'm saying this as a *threat*," Eric continues. "In other words, I will *fuck* with them. Do you think that would stop them from printing my picture?"

"It would probably get your picture on the front page."

"It obviously hasn't worked with Mitnick," Eric concurs. "He's fucked with everybody and he's still getting his picture published."

Suddenly Eric's tone mellows. "I'm very safe right now, but I do eventually want to get back to having a life. I can put it on hold for a while, maybe a year. I have money now."

No wonder Eric's in such a friendly mood.

"How'd you get money?"

"I don't want to talk about it. It was necessary. I have to do these things to stay free. That's one of the biggest hurdles that a fugitive has, not having enough money to do the things you need to do."

At this time I have no idea whether Eric is bullshitting me or not. But five weeks later I will learn that at the time of our August conversation he was in the final stages of hacking into a Southern California bank and electronically transferring $150,000. And he did move the money.

.   .   .

"It's starting to rain," Eric announces.

"It doesn't rain down there," I remind him.

"Maybe I'm not down here," Eric teases.

"Now I know you're somewhere in the country where it's raining."

"Yeah," Eric mutters.

"There are probably only one or two places in the country where it's raining," I continue.

"You've got like three minutes," Eric warns. "My sunroof's open and it's raining."

"Hey, remember you mentioned you would try to send a copy of your memoirs?" I quicky add. "The part the FBI didn't confiscate?"

It's 4:40 A.M. We've been talking more than four hours. Now that he's in the money, Eric's feeling magnanimous. He's stopped asking to be paid for his story; he's happy to keep chatting.

"Yeah," Eric says before hanging up. "I'll see what I can do."

■　　　■　　　■

Five days later, a big file bobs up in my Well account. Eighty pages of Eric's life of kinky sex and crime.

Data Thief

ONE OF AMERICA'S TOP COMPUTER HACKERS REVEALS ALL.

I download the file and read about Eric's self-described addiction to sex, his hundreds of female "victims," his illegal wiretapping of hookers and Playboy Playmates, his check-kiting schemes and gun-toting coke dealer buddy. But Eric also reflects on another obsession, the one that's drawn him into the web with Mitnick, De Payne, Austin, and the FBI. "Many of today's top programmers . . . at one time considered themselves hackers," writes the wanted fugitive. ". . . And now it's illegal? Or is it? Where do we draw the line?"

Natural Born Killers

The night at Gecko's in Huntington Beach didn't pan out, but Special Agent Ornellas has been pounding the pavement, paying a visit to the Rainbow Bar and Grill, making the rounds of Eric's Hollywood buddies, even driving out to the house of some guy who bore an uncanny resemblance to the hacker. He told the FBI agent a convoluted tale that began with the accidental shotgun blast that tore off his leg a few months ago. Eric befriended him, and then suddenly a girl named Lisa who stripped at the Seventh Veil appeared one day at his house. She was Eric's girl, but she quickly made her new acquaintance her second one-legged conquest.

Suspecting a con, the guy with the missing leg started tapping his own phone. Sure enough, he caught Eric secretly talking to Lisa, planning some $2 million heist. When his birth certificate and driver's license disappeared, the amputee started to worry where he might fit in.

. . .

The time is about 1 A.M., Monday morning, August 29, 1994.

Ron Austin steps out of the late show of Oliver Stone's *Natural Born Killers* at the AMC Century City 14 near the UCLA campus. He drops off his girlfriend and drives the few blocks to the address

Stan Ornellas gave him across from the towering white Federal Building on Wilshire Boulevard. Could Eric really be that bold? Could he really be sleeping with a stripper across from the Los Angeles headquarters of the FBI?

Austin cruises the 10900 block of Ashton Street in his girlfriend's black convertible Toyota Celica. The hacker slows as he approaches the sports car. The gold BMW's rear end hangs out five feet in the street, as if the driver had been drunk, or in a very big hurry.

Austin hits the brake, and then quickly eases off. Don't blow it, he thinks. Keep rolling. Eric might be watching from a window.

He glances back and reads the plate.

Texas!

"BVX29R . . . BVX29R . . . BVX29R," Austin repeats the sequence over and over. At the top of the next block, he pulls over, scribbles the plate number on a scrap of paper, then guns it, running three red lights to the nearby UCLA university police station.

"Can I get a patrol car?" Austin blurts out to the student dispatcher.

"Why?"

"There's a federal fugitive on Ashton Street," Austin hurriedly explains. "I need a patrol car to watch the building until the FBI arrives."

The dispatcher radios for a patrol car, while Austin dashes out to a pay phone, dials Ornellas's pager, and waits for his call. "So what's going on?" an amazingly alert Ornellas asks a minute later. The agent's been sleeping with his beeper by his pillow.

"I spotted him."

"You pretty sure?"

"I'm sure," Austin tells Ornellas. "It's in front of the apartment. Gold BMW Texas plates."

"Does it have a dent in the door?"

"I don't know. I'm trying to get the UCPD cops to watch the car."

"OK. I'll be there in a minute."

.   .   .

"What's this guy's name?" questions the UCLA cop from his patrol car window.

"Justin Petersen," answers Austin.

"What's he wanted for?"

"Computer crimes. He's a fugitive."

"And your name?"

"Ron Austin."

The hacker hands the skeptical cop his driver's license, and watches his own license run for any possible criminal record. This is taking way too long, Austin thinks. Eric could be history any minute.

"Can we go?"

Finally, the cop returns Austin's license and radios another cop. Three minutes later they finally take off.

The two patrol cars wait for every green light, slowly tailing Austin's car. Austin breathes a sigh of relief as they drive past the gold BMW. But one patrol car cruises by the apartment a second time with its lights out. Austin worries. If Eric's looking out the window he's gotta see this.

Seconds later, the big Crown Victoria pulls up with Ornellas and Tepper. Austin hops out and approaches Tepper on the passenger side.

"Why don't you get in back?"

Austin's barely in when Ornellas starts pumping him.

"What do they know?"

Austin shrugs. "They don't really know anything."

"Did you tell the cops not to run him?"

"No," Austin admits, realizing his blunder. Maybe Eric's got his scanner, maybe he's already heard them run his record.

Ornellas hops out to talk to the UCLA cops.

"So what's the plate?" Tepper asks Austin.

The agent phones the FBI in Dallas on his Motorola flip phone to run the license number. Ornellas waves his FBI badge at the cops, and the two squad cars slowly drive off.

"Did they run him?" asks Tepper.

"Yeah," grumbles Ornellas.

Eric's BMW is parked only a few short steps from the front door of the stripper's apartment. The Crown Victoria is about a block and a half back. Austin isn't sure the agents are close enough.

"If Eric makes it to his car before you're there, you'll have a chase on your hands."

"Good point," agrees Ornellas. "Why don't we move in closer?"

Austin gets out, and the Crown Victoria slowly circles the block, stopping about five car lengths behind the BMW.

Austin walks back to his Celica, settles in, and waits. Even if Eric is onto the surveillance, he's bound to come out sooner or later, and Austin knows there's only one way out. Just to be prepared, on an earlier trip he checked to make sure there was no back exit. The minutes tick by. The night is pleasantly warm, but Austin resists the temptation to open his window. He slouches comfortably, his eyes just above the dash. He flips the dial and listens to talk radio. He watches the car clock. It's 2:35 A.M, forty-five minutes with no sign of Eric. Austin makes a decision. If Eric doesn't come out by three, he's going home to catch some sleep. Five minutes pass, ten.

A crack of light flashes from the FBI agent's car.

"ERIC!!!!!" yells one of the agents.

A figure hesitates by the BMW and then dashes across the street. If he makes it across the parking lot, Austin thinks, he'll be on Wilshire, and he's got a chance. Austin starts up his car, and screeches around the block.

But the looming figure of Stan Ornellas topples Eric in the bushes. Ornellas sticks a knee in Eric's back, cuffs him, and jerks him up by his collar.

Eric isn't surprised the powerful agent took him down. Why, the hacker even feels a small twinge of guilt. Ornellas, after all, was Eric's control, the agent who groomed him for his undercover work, joked with him, and once picked him up from a hundred-dollar appointment with his hair stylist. Eric always wanted to work undercover for the FBI, and now he feels a wave of remorse over having failed so completely as a snitch. Why not say something stupid so Ornellas can just pop him one and get it out of his system?

"So how'd you catch me?" snaps Eric.

But Special Agent Ornellas won't be drawn in. He's a professional. "Shut up, you piece of shit!"

Cut Off

Los Angeles Daily News, August 30, 1994

COMPUTER CRIMINAL CAUGHT AFTER 10 MONTHS ON THE RUN

Keith Stone — Convicted computer criminal Justin Tanner Petersen was captured Monday in Los Angeles, 10 months after federal authorities said they discovered he had begun living a dual life as their informant and an outlaw hacker.

Monday's arrest ends Petersen's run from the same FBI agents with whom he had once struck a deal: to remain free on bond in exchange for pleading guilty to several computer crimes and helping the FBI with other hacker cases.

. . . The FBI paid his rent and utilities and gave him $200 a week for spending money and medical insurance. . . . Another computer hacker Petersen said he helped the FBI gather information on was Kevin Mitnick. . . .

Eventually, Petersen said, the FBI stopped supporting him so he turned to his nightclubs for income. But when that began to fail, he returned to hacking for profit.

"I was stuck out on a limb. I was almost out on the street. My club was costing me money because it was a new club," he said. "So I did what I had to do. I am not a greedy person."

. . .

"Hi, Jon."

It's Kevin Mitnick, sounding chipper at 8 A.M. Tuesday, September 6, 1994. I'm a little surprised by the early call since we haven't spoken in three months. There wasn't the usual warning call from De Payne, and the morning hour is out of character. But I figured Mitnick would phone sooner or later to rejoice in Eric's recent misfortune.

"How's it going?"

"It's going good," Mitnick says breezily. "Other than my problems."

"Something new?"

"No, just the *New York Times* story," Mitnick says, his voice suddenly flat. He doesn't have to tell me which one. By his tone I know he's talking about Markoff's front-page article featuring Mitnick's photo.

"So why do you think it appeared?"

"He was pressured by the powers that be to do that."

Editors? The government? Intelligence agencies? I ask Mitnick who he means, but either he doesn't have an answer, or he doesn't want to tell me.

"What do you think of Eric getting caught?"

"I think the slimeball deserved it," Mitnick says gleefully. "His little game paid off. I think he exactly parallels Aldrich Ames [the treasonous CIA spy who sentenced to death over a dozen of his fellow spies by revealing their identities to the KGB]. He'd sell out anybody. He calls the *Los Angeles Daily News* and says he has no choice but to do credit card fraud because the government didn't pay him enough. Like somebody fucking owes him a living."

"You don't think that's right, credit card fraud?"

"He's got a different philosophy. That's the line I wouldn't cross."

"What did you think of the *New York Times* article?"

"It's media sensationalism. You oughta see the thing in the U.K. Somebody actually gave an interview to a British newspaper that separates the myth from the man."

Mitnick's referring to himself, of course.

"Really?" I ask, surprised.

"It's in the magazine section of the *London Observer*. It's mainly about one person."

"I'll have to get a copy. So what are you doing these days?"

"Right now?" Mitnick asks, irked. "I'm not going to tell you what I'm doing."

"I'm sorry. I don't need to know what you're doing."

"Look, it's nothing personal," Mitnick assures me, his voice calm again. "Someday, we can talk."

.   .   .

The next day, the afternoon of September 7, Mitnick is not his usual friendly self. He's worried.

"I'm curious. I hear you got a call from Schindler?" he ventures.

Schindler is the Assistant U.S. Attorney who allegedly paid Eric cash to hunt Mitnick.

"Yeah," I answer, wondering how he knows.

Mitnick's voice is echoing strangely.

"You sound like Zeus."

"It's a computer room and it echoes," Mitnick brushes me off, clearly agitated. "I'm trying to find out what transpired on your part. It's kind of weird for Schindler to just call you up."

"Yeah, I think what happened was he called me the first of July."

"Before the article?" Mitnick asks, referring to the July 4 *Times* story.

"No, I had called Schindler because there was going to be a settlement in Poulsen's trial, and he called back, and before saying anything, he immediately put on his tough guy voice and said, 'When was the last time you heard from Eric and Mitnick?' "

"You could have said, 'What makes you think I even talked to someone?' and prodded him for information." Mitnick sighs at my clumsiness. "I guess you weren't in the frame of mind. Do they know what we talk about?"

"No."

"Well, my contact is going to stop tonight," Mitnick says coldly.

I'm stunned. "What did you say?" I ask.

"I said all the contact will be stopping this evening."

"Uh-huh."

"With everybody. So I wanted to find out what transpired. I wanted to talk to you directly to find out what you would say."

"BUZZZZZ."

"Can you hold on?" Mitnick asks.

Could that be Mitnick's pager?

Mitnick comes back a few seconds later. It's my last chance.

"Let me just quickly ask you. What's the message Eric sends? The way he was groomed and allowed to do certain things. What kind of message does that send about the government?"

"I think it's a normal procedure for the government," Mitnick says matter-of-factly. "If they wanna snag a big drug dealer, they'll let all the little ones do illegal things, and basically have a blind eye to their activities. But from what I've heard he [Eric] had the manuals for SAS in his house. The government actually gave them back. There would be only one purpose for the government to give him those manuals back. To use the equipment."

Mitnick sounds cocky, like he's got a card up his sleeve. "I believe there's a lot to learn from Eric, if he ever talks."

"What do you mean there's a lot to learn from him?"

"About what activities they condoned, and what work he did for them. I'm sure he knows and the government knows. *I* don't know and *you* don't know.

"He's complaining the government wasn't giving him enough cash to be a stool pigeon, and that's why he had to do credit card fraud. Why couldn't the guy just get a job?" Mitnick bristles. "He has the attitude he doesn't have to work. That's what separates me from him. I would never snag someone's credit card and do that type of shit, unless it would be a phone card or something like that. I must admit I did that type of thing *in the past;* I did that five years ago and more."

Five years just happens to be the statute of limitations on most federal crimes. Is this the cyberfugitive's standard disclaimer, the small print at the bottom of the computer screen? Does Kevin Mitnick really think I believe that everything he did happened at least five years ago?

"I kind of used it as a way to mask my location," Mitnick continues. "But as far as actually ordering equipment or getting cash from people's cards, that was a line I didn't cross."

"That's a line you don't cross?"

"No. And I don't think Eric had a problem with that because I don't think he's a true hacker. I think he just used computers to do high-tech burglary. Maybe he started off as one, and thought that it could be a profitable business and turned into a thief. I don't know."

Kevin Mitnick, the most wanted man in cyberspace, is defining the line between a high-tech criminal and a true computer hacker. Mitnick says he doesn't hack for money. It's knowledge he wants, tricks that can make him a master wizard.

"With DEC [Digital Equipment Corporation], all I did was take it [the company's latest source code to its VMS operating system] to learn and figure out the holes in it. There was no ulterior motive to wreak havoc or anything. I kind of justified to myself that's OK because I'm not going to sit there and sell it.

"I kind of in my own mind picture it as, hey, going to a video store and getting a copy of *Jurassic Park,* and making a copy of it. Their copy is still intact and untouched and unharmed. I have a copy of it. I'm not going to invite people over and charge them admission to watch the film, yet I have it for my own viewing.

"That's how I saw my type of stuff, and that's how I still see it. The government totally convinced the public that, 'No, he deprived the other person!' Instead of my analogy, it's like they say, 'He went into Lucasfilms and took *Jurassic Park* and nobody got to see it but him, and he made a mint by selling it to Paramount.' There's two different sets of laws, you know what I'm saying?"

Few people get busted for making a single copy of *Jurassic Park,* or, for that matter, a single copy of Microsoft Windows. But then the programs Mitnick supposedly copied aren't anything like videos or commercial software. If they are for sale, they'd be worth hundreds of thousands, if not millions, of dollars. And those that aren't for sale are considered proprietary, part of a corporation's closely guarded assets.

Second, the odds are Mitnick first had to hack into the target computer before he made his copy. Title 18, 1030, of the United States Code, "Fraud and related activity in connection with computers," defines computer crime broadly as "knowingly access[ing] a computer without authorization." Just about any computer that isn't your own is off limits. That includes corporate computers or those operated by any United States agency, or any with "financial record[s]" or a "federal interest."

The statutes provide additional penalties for damaging computer files or trafficking in passwords or access codes for computers. 1029 describes "access device" frauds, and defines an access device as "any card, plate, code account number . . . that can be used . . . to obtain money, goods, services or any other thing of value. . . ." In other words, anything from cloning cellular phones to using stolen credit or telephone cards, or computer passwords.

The government could conceivably charge Mitnick with a host of 1029 and 1030 violations for cloning phones and hacking into computers. What's much less clear are the ultimate penalties. And the value of the software Mitnick may have copied is anyone's guess. In his earlier DEC case, the government initially claimed his copying and hacking caused a $4 million loss, only to later reduce the figure to a modest $160,000.

One thing's for certain. It's easy for the government to grossly exaggerate the software loss caused by hackers. The law doesn't require accuracy. The sentencing guidelines state in Title 18, 2F1.1. Section 8, that "the loss need not be determined with precision. . . ." Nor does it matter whether Mitnick has any plans to profit by illicitly copying software. The guidelines suggest an "upward departure" or longer sentence may be warranted if "a primary objective of the fraud was non-monetary. . . ."

Hackers without a financial motive are considered the most threatening.

.   .   .

"Why do you think they've tried to make you into this incredible —"

"Bad guy? Monster?

"Because it's easier to do anything they want with you if they make sure the public has that view. Then no one gives a shit.

"On the other hand, I don't consider the acts that I'm accused of being heinous. There's no money I've stolen. Nobody made a profit."

"Acts that you're accused of?" I repeat.

"Things that I'm accused of that they mention in the papers [copying the source code for cellular phone service, wiretapping FBI agents, and attempting to social engineer DMV officials], I'm not commenting one way or another. I'm just saying, if they were true or not, I don't think it's public enemy number one material."

"Is the software something you could turn around and sell?"

"What they're claiming is if someone had that software he could modify the software so they could fuck with the ESN and then they could turn around and sell that technology to dope dealers that wanna make calls that aren't trackable.

"But that's a hypothesis," Mitnick quickly adds.

He pauses, organizing his thoughts. Then Mitnick's voice changes.

". . . Tonight is my cutoff night. I'd be happy to talk to you later or something, so if you wanna grab a number that I can call you at, like outside —"

"I've got one," I interrupt Mitnick, grabbing the library pay phone number I've jotted down just for this occasion.

"Should I give it to you?" I ask.

"Yeah, hold on."

"It's 388-XXXX."

"OK. This is what I'd like to do," Mitnick begins, telling me he'll call at 8 P.M. "On the way to that pay phone, get another pay phone number that works. You'll tell me the other one and I'll call you on the other [second] one. Do you understand?"

I think so. It sounds like something a spy would do. Or a cyberpunk.

"Uh-huh," I say. "So you will call —"

"At that pay phone," Mitnick confirms. "If I don't reach you, I'll call you at home at ten o'clock. OK?"

Last Call

The phone rings and I wonder who could be calling so late. Suddenly it hits me. I forgot to go to the pay phone!

"What happened?" Mitnick presses. He sounds angry, suspicious.

"I'm sorry, I screwed up. I'll be there in five minutes," I assure him, hoping I haven't blown it.

I throw on my jacket, grab my notepad, pen, and battery-powered book light, and shout goodbye to my wife as I run out the door.

Five minutes later I'm pacing in front of the library pay phone. BRRRRINNNNNG!

I grab the phone as fast as I can.

"Hello," Mitnick greets me in a pleasant voice.

"OK," I say. "Ready for step two?"

"Yup."

"The last two digits are ten," I say cryptically, referring to the two numbers that differ at the next pay phone.

"The last two digits are ten," Mitnick repeats. "How long will it take you?"

"Five minutes."

I run two hundred yards to the Pac Bell phone on the corner, flip open my notepad, and switch on my book light. To my right lies a small park in a grove of redwoods. Across the street stands an old fix-it shop and an elementary school. The phone stands alone on a pole, protected with a metal shroud, the lines disappearing overhead into the trees.

The phone rings. I grab the handset, tuck my down jacket under my rear, and sit cross-legged on the cold sidewalk.

"How are things going?"

"Things are not good," Mitnick says with a sigh. "No, things are not good at all."

"What's up?"

"Just stress, a lot of stress. The British had this guy who wanted to interview me. I figured he had some cash. He paid Bonnie a hundred dollars. I thought they might want to interview the main man for five hundred. I asked him what he wanted to write. I trust the British. Americans are afraid to alienate their DOJ [Department of Justice] contacts. They'll never write the truth because it will put their contacts in an unsavory light."

He's right, to a degree. Newspaper reporters depend on lots of inside government sources, and Department of Justice contacts are jealously guarded. If a reporter is going to burn a bridge it's likely to be a criminal, not a DOJ, source.

"What's the story about?" I ask.

"He said he wanted to know me as a person. They're [the government] painting me as Carlos the Jackal. They're trying to turn me into this guy who raped and murdered Polly Klass."

"At first I enjoyed the attention. When I was sixteen, back in 1979, I thought it was cute. Now I think of my future. I'd like to have a house. I'd like to have a wife. My future looks like the movie *No Way Out*."

"How's that?"

"It's a bad, bad situation. I'm an asshole for calling you. There's no reason I should talk to you or anybody else. It's stupid."

Mitnick's right. He shouldn't talk to anybody if he doesn't want to get caught.

"What can you do?"

"I'm willing to go for double what I did before — two years — and then I'm willing to do the Peace Corps or charity for five years, where I can be productive. I'd be willing to do that. Do something where society wins. But you can't approach these people this way.

"I'm no angel, but all of the evil stuff they say about me isn't true. The Security Pacific News wire [a phony business wire release saying the bank lost hundreds of millions of dollars]? I doubt it happened. And if it did happen it wasn't me. Why should I lie to you?

"NORAD [hacking into the computers of the North American Defense Command]? That was because of Rhoades," Mitnick claims, sticking the blame for the rumored incident on an old hacker associate who he says framed him.

"I think it hurts you when you don't talk [to the press]," Mitnick concedes. "Anyone can say anything. They can turn you into a monster."

.   .   .

Mitnick offers me an analogy to put what he's done in perspective, to explain how he believes the government has overblown his crimes.

"If I went into Ralph's Supermarket and took a forty-nine-cent Bic pen, would they say I stole something they spent four million to develop and three million to market, and therefore the penalty will be seven million and they will have to hire three new security guards to watch the pens?

"It's crazy," he fumes. "They charge the hacker with the time it takes to make security better."

I ask Mitnick what the government thinks he's done.

"The last five years I have no comment," he says flatly.

But Mitnick's got plenty to say about the old charges he's already done time for.

"On the U.S. Leasing case they said I purposely erased a disk. I did social engineer passwords and they got circulated, but Susan [Thunder] wiped out the disk. She put 'Fuck You' on the computer. She put my name there. Bob Ewen [an investigator] said, 'We caught you, you put your name there.' Susan would do anything to get back at us [Mitnick and De Payne].

"With DEC, suddenly they're talking about interstate transport of stolen goods. There was no intent to profit from selling it. They charge me with their development costs, for the time to figure out what I did, the damage I might have caused."

I try to drag Mitnick back to the present.

"So why are they targeting you now?"

"The government is scared. They go on a tangent. They think this guy is dangerous because of what he might do."

Sometimes Mitnick refers to himself as "somebody" or "this guy." Sometimes he forgets the mask.

"My supervision was ending. They had an inkling I might be continuing my hobby. Either Eric on his own suggested this or he was told to seek me out."

"Why you?" I ask.

"They prefer to go after somebody already painted with a bad history. They'd prefer to use a scapegoat rather than somebody new."

Mitnick's getting emotional. Suddenly, he starts telling me he wishes it had never happened, that he'd never set eyes on a computer. It's the closest he's gotten to telling me about his past, his childhood.

"If I could go back in a time machine, I'd be the kid in school who did good in sports, had a good social life, played baseball, football, and didn't know anything about computers. If I had the chance to do it over again that's what I'd do.

"I was fat and overweight. What else did I have to turn to but computers? I never got along with kids my age. They were into smoking pot and drinking. I wasn't into it. I was not happy as a kid.

"My hobby when I was thirteen was riding buses for free. I went to terminals and saw they would discard transfers at the end of the day and leave them in the garbage. I'd punch out my own transfers and go everywhere. It was pretty sad. I'd be gone the whole day. One day I set up a trip that was going to take me until eleven P.M. to get home.

"I met this bus driver who'd let me on free. He became my big brother. I'd spend days after school going to San Bernardino or Long Beach. I did this till I was sixteen. I started putting on weight when I met this kid who was the son of another bus driver. We'd get the maps to the movie stars and ride together to Beverly Hills. He'd eat twenty times a day. That's when I started getting fat.

"I hung out at Radio Shack. I had a CB radio. My family couldn't afford to buy me a computer."

.   .   .

Maybe Kevin Mitnick misses his lost childhood and wishes he could change, but he still loves to hack. He's just finished telling me how he wishes he'd never seen a computer. Now he's telling me why he can't resist the temptation.

"People who use computers are very trusting, very easy to manipulate. I know the computer systems of the world are not as safe as they think," Mitnick proclaims proudly. "Information is not safe. Only military computers are secure."

Kevin Mitnick worships technology.

"I believe it's fascinating, the marvel of communications and technology. A little palmtop that can store masses of data or do intense calculations. The ability to walk down the street and talk to someone at the other end of the world.

"I have the ability to find anybody I want to find. I'm very good at what I want to do. I was teaching PIs. They were amazed. High-tech PI firms aren't what they're cracked up to be. They go and pay somebody off at the DMV, or at the IRS. They grease the palm. I do it with a laptop and a cell phone."

Mitnick's revved up, jumping from thought to thought.

"It's been a unique learning experience. My philosophy, it's hard to explain. It's like a high-tech game, figuring out how to crack a computer. How to actually outwit opponents. I have one overseas."

Suddenly Mitnick's depressed. Maybe the thought of his opponent just reminded him he's a wanted man.

"It's a big game, but I could end up in the can. They're saying I'm John Dillinger, that I'm terrible, that it's shocking that I could get this awesome power. They can get away with whatever they want. It's like Saudi Arabian law."

"Why do you think the government is taking it so seriously?" I ask.

"They're afraid because the technology is new. They [the FBI] are not up on it. They are used to old-fashioned, stick 'em up crime. This is something new, something they can be violated with. They're scared of the new technology. They've convinced the public they are in great danger."

Suddenly, Mitnick's other half speaks up. I've almost forgotten De Payne is on the line. He's hardly said a word.

"The people who are experts, the security people, they look like fools when some kid can do something," De Payne mocks. "That puts it in perspective."

A kid like De Payne or Mitnick, I wonder?

De Payne continues with a story about how he pranked some security people years ago, but I steer the conversation back to Mitnick.

"So do you think you're a criminal?"

"No, I don't like to think of myself as a criminal. But if the technology laws are like Singapore, where it's illegal to chew gum . . ." Mitnick sighs. "I guess I'm a criminal.

"I'm the type who's a master safecracker. I'd read your will, your diary, put it back, not take the money, shut the safe, and do it so you never knew I was there. I'd do it because it's neat, because it's a challenge. I love the game.

"I guess you could paint me as the alcoholic. Five years ago, that's all I looked forward to, even in my marriage. I put my hacking above my work, my time with my wife, anything. At the time I knew I had this drive to do it, but I didn't think about it."

"What was the attraction?"

"The high. To beat the System. It's scary not knowing why you do something, but I didn't want to do anything else. I'm trapped. There's no escape."

.   .   .

I've been wanting to ask Kevin Mitnick this question for a long time.

"What is a hacker?"

"A computer hacker? It's a person who can figure out ways of bypassing security. Whatever way you get in, using technology upon the System, hardware bugs, tricks. That's what I consider to be a hacker. It's not being a super programmer. Most super programmers are not good hackers.

"It takes a mind-set, trying to think of every possible way to get in, watching your back all the time. You pick the easiest path in. If all it takes is a phone call, rather than a wiretap, then you take the quickest way in."

Mitnick uses the games he played with Eric and the FBI as an example.

"We told Eric bullshit. We told him we were planning to check a DNR [a phone tap] in a Calabasas Central office. We told him we'd picked the lock. We were playing Eric as a mark, we fed him with bullshit."

"Eric says you told him that you just wanted to 'make some fucking money this time.' "

"I could have said that to play him, but look at my actions versus the words. I could have pulled off scams. Credit card fraud is easy. You get access to a credit agency, you get someone's maiden name, change the address, switch the phone number to voice mail. I could do that, but that's being a thief. It's not a challenge.

"But if you're asking might I go in and get a copy of Microsoft Windows? I would do that. Would I take a hundred dollars someone left in their top drawer? No."

"So how is Eric different?"

"Eric is Aldrich Ames," Mitnick bristles. "If Eric wants a Porsche he'd sell out fucking anybody to get his Porsche."

"The government knows Eric's motives. They understand him. They don't understand Poulsen. They don't understand me —"

De Payne interrupts: "Someone with no monetary gain they don't understand."

.   .   .

"What's the hardest thing about being a fugitive?"

"Not being able to call friends and family," Mitnick complains. "I can't be myself. When I go outside the door, I have to believe I'm another person or I'll goof up. Once outside I'm in the twilight zone. I have to be a different person. It's terrible. I'd like to sort the mess out. I don't consider it fun. I have friends, but I can count them on my left hand."

But then, it does have an upside.

"It's interesting to be undercover," Mitnick reflects. "It's like being in a movie, like being a CIA operative. Being so good that if somebody calls your real name you don't turn around.

"Now I'm changing again."

"What do you mean?"

Mitnick's heard his face will be beamed to millions of television screens from coast to coast on the network program *America's Most Wanted.*

"I have to prepare for the worst. I have to change everything I do."

.   .   .

The police car cruises down the quiet, tree-lined suburban street a third time. This time the black and white stops.

"Are you OK?" asks the local cop, leaning toward his open window.

It's long past midnight. My book light died a half hour ago. I'm scribbling by the dim yellow glow of the street lamp. My rear is numb from sitting on the cold concrete, my legs stiff.

"Just fine, Officer!" I shout. "Just fine!"

"You've been there a couple of hours," the clean-shaven cop observes.

"Yes, Officer. Thanks very much," I say politely.

The cop shakes his head and drives on. Ordinary cops aren't used to people having two-hour midnight pay phone calls.

"What's going on?" Mitnick asks.

"A cop was questioning me," I tell Mitnick and he laughs.

.   .   .

Kevin Mitnick is replaying his conspiracy theory.

"The government controls the press. They didn't want Eric in public view. They're interested in the old story. As soon as they put that out — the Markoff *New York Times* story — we [Mitnick and De Payne] decided, let's make what the government is doing public. Suddenly Eric was facing stories in the *L.A. Times.* The boys in Washington didn't like that."

"Why do you think Markoff wrote the *New York Times* story about you?"

I don't tell Mitnick, but Markoff's article has jolted the FBI into suddenly making his parole violation a high-priority case. Ken McGuire of the FBI has started calling his hacker informants in Los Angeles, digging for information about Mitnick. Ironically, some of the first files provided to McGuire are De Payne's Internet posts in which he mocked the FBI.

"Markoff's a pawn. He was asked to do it. A cellular company said a hack [against its computers] sounded like the character [Mitnick] in his book. They asked him to keep their name out of it."

Mitnick doesn't name the company but it sounds like Qualcomm, the San Diego cellular phone company Markoff mentioned to me in his call back in June.

The conversation drifts. I ask about the rumor I've heard that Mitnick ran into Susan Thunder just before he went on the run.

"Yeah, I confided in Susan. I met her at the Stardust, at Saint Henry's Chinese Restaurant. I told her, hey I've got this guy named Eric, I think he's a rat. Would she keep it to herself? Susan was going to visit Eric. She was going to seduce him and look for his real ID while he was asleep. I thought to myself, this is crazy. Eric would never sleep with this woman.

"She had these crazy plans of seduction. She's the type of gal I'm embarrassed to be around, her ass is so big. And here I was fat myself. I would see her about once a month. She was interested in listening to vice squad frequencies for professional [call girl] reasons. She offered me a job handing out handbills."

I've met Thunder in Vegas too, heard her imaginative fictions and seen the handbills; nude color photos of Thunder herself, with erotic names like Sweet Serena, Voluptuous Valerie, Victoria, or Mandy, and captions like, "Share your secret fantasies and fetishes with me tonight. . . . Motorcycle Mama will ride your machine. . . ."

"What would you say to young kids thinking about getting into hacking?"

"Don't make the same mistakes I did. Hacking might look exciting at the beginning, but when you look back on it, you only have one life to live."

.   .   .

Mitnick's battery dies and his call patches out. I gather my notepad and dead book light and stand up, but before I walk away the phone rings.

"I'd like to figure a way out of my predicament," Mitnick continues, telling me about his plan to get a job, save twenty thousand dollars for an attorney, and then go public. But surprisingly he can't find an attorney that wants his case. Mitnick doesn't understand the lack of interest in his predicament. He doesn't believe he's committed any serious crimes. He's an old-fashioned hacker. He's in it for the knowledge, the thrill.

"It's the challenge," he says. Mitnick copies software to "learn and study." If he bills phone calls to other people, he does it only for "the security of the call."

But Mitnick partially contradicts himself. He doesn't pay for his phone calls and invades people's privacy because he *can* do it, because he figures if the information river is already running, why shouldn't he enjoy the waters?

"The bus goes down the street anyway. In my mind, they've built the service. It's like the people who hijack cable TV. I don't think I'm invading anyone's privacy. Everybody's open game for that. The government invades your privacy every day. I just like to have the same ability the government does."

Besides, Mitnick says he can be trusted to use discretion. "The only time I would tap phone calls is if someone is trying to hurt me. Only in the case of watching a rat."

•   ■   ■

Life on the run may be taking its toll on Mitnick, but he's far from ready to turn himself in.

"It's better to live the way I am. I have to get used to it. It's serious. It's not like the movies. One flub and it's over."

"How do you prepare yourself?"

"I think of a past I'd like to live, a place I'd like to have grown up. It's living a lie. I'd like to see what drives me, why I have this passion. I'd like to go to a therapist."

"Why don't you?"

"If I did it might happen like this. The therapist might be talking to his wife about it at dinner. His kid, who's checking out the Internet, might hear something. And the next thing you know I'd be busted."

.   .   .

"What do you think of these articles De Payne is encouraging?"

"I didn't call the papers. Lewis did. I tell him to stop, but he doesn't listen. Is this guy really my friend? Sometimes I wonder. He has nothing to lose. I keep telling him to shut up, but he won't stop. I'm not happy with him."

With De Payne asleep, I ask Mitnick about his ex-wife, Bonnie Vitello, currently dating De Payne.

"I was obsessed with trying to figure out why she left me. I was restricted [during probation] to the Jewish Community Center. I knew she had bought an answering machine at Radio Shack for a hundred dollars. I called up the store and asked what answering machine they sell with a beeper. They said they had one for a hundred and one for one seventy-five. I decided to sound out the machine for a hundred. I told them I'd lost my beeper, and asked if they could look at the machine. It's got a,b,c,d tones." Mitnick then describes how he social engineered the store into playing all the tones that worked on Bonnie's machine.

"So I called Bonnie. It [the recording of the beeper] worked on the second one. I had a feeling there was another guy. I hear Bonnie's voice, " 'Hello, it's me, good morning!'

"Why is she talking to her own machine, I think? Then, I hear him say, 'How do you turn this thing off?' That really bummed me out. I was devastated that she left me. Then she moved in with Lewis. I've always wondered whether she was with him while I was in jail. That's not a cool thing. I've always wondered."

Mitnick's stories of his ex-wife moving in with his best friend bring back memories of prison. "I did eight months in MDC [Metropolitan Detention Center in downtown Los Angeles]. Solitary was a hellhole. They said I was too dangerous to be near a phone. They let me out one hour a day. You're shackled when they take you to the shower. It's like the movies. They treat you like an animal. One day is hell. Imagine eight months. They fuck people.

"At Lompoc [a federal detention facility north of Santa Barbara] I did time with the Barry Minkow people [famous for the ZZZ Best carpet-cleaning scam that rocked Wall Street in the late 1980s].

"I spoke to Boesky at Lompoc. Me and Ivan were waiting for the phones. He went to get coffee. He puts his quarter in the vending machine and returns.

" 'Hey, Ivan, I wouldn't drink that.'

" 'Why?'

"Then, he sees the cockroach floating around in his cup.

" 'Hey, Ivan, I'll teach you computers, if you'll teach me stocks.'

"Ivan said, 'No.'

"Then he asked me how much money I made hacking.

"I told Ivan, 'Nothing. I didn't do it for money.'

"He looked at me like I was an idiot."

About a quarter to two in the morning Mitnick's battery dies again, and I'm sitting on the concrete listening to static after three hours of conversation. I gather my dead book light and notepad and walk home.

Overseas

The second week in September I get an electronic copy of the *London Observer* Kevin Mitnick profile. Appearing in the Sunday, September 4, "Style" section of one of London's biggest newspapers, the six-thousand-word article is the longest to date on Mitnick and certainly the most sympathetic. Unlike the U.S. press, the English newspaper discusses what it calls the "paranoia" surrounding Mitnick's case.

TO CATCH A HACKER

By John Sweeney

There is only one word which can describe the reaction of the American judiciary and prison system to Kevin, a white-collar 'criminal' who had caused no physical injury and had not enriched himself: paranoia. Reading the transcripts from the People v Mitnick court case, it is clear that no one in authority understood how a heavily overweight techno-nerd, as the papers defined Kevin, had hacked into the nation's most secret computer databases. . . .

That Kevin had not damaged . . . anything in his travels through cyberspace was not taken into account; that he had trespassed into areas where he should not go was enough to condemn him in their eyes as an outlaw.

.   .   .

Not only is Mitnick's case spawning articles overseas; the FBI believes he's committing international crimes. Los Angeles Special Agent Kathleen Carson, one of the primary FBI agents on the Mitnick case, is corresponding with Neil Clift, Mitnick's overseas "opponent," an expert in security on Digital Equipment's VAX computers. Carson has taken a profound interest in Mitnick's case. De Payne managed to be the third party on one of her private phone calls with an informant, and he didn't like it when Carson compared his friend to a child molester.

So being a prankster, De Payne was pleased when the FBI agent confided to the informant her fondness for hot tubs. De Payne immediately started appending his e-mail with the postscript "Kathleen 'Hot Tub' Carson." The taunt fit nicely with his usual host of damning statements allegedly made by FBI agents, Pac Bell security investigators, and other enemies.

Meanwhile, Carson, at least in her letter to Neil Clift, hardly sounds confident of the FBI's abilities, describing herself and the FBI as virtually helpless in tracking Mitnick.

U.S. Department of Justice
Federal Bureau of Investigation
11000 Wilshire Boulevard #1700
Los Angeles, CA 90024
September 22, 1994

Mr. Neil Clift
Loughborough University

Dear Neil:

It must be quite frustrating to sit over there and wonder if the FBI or British law enforcement authorities are ever going to do anything and catch our "friend", KDM. I can only assure you that every little piece of information concerning Kevin which finds its way into my hands is aggressively pursued.

In fact, I just verified the information you provided. . . . It certainly appears this computer system has been accessed and compromised by Kevin. Our dilemma, however, is that the "NYX" system administrator is not as helpful to law enforcement as you have been; and we are somewhat limited in our pursuit of watching the account by the American legal procedures.

I wanted to let you know in this letter how much your cooperation with the FBI has been appreciated. Any telephonic contact made to you by Kevin is very important — at least to me.

. . . I can report that you (and only you) are the one concrete connection we have to Kevin outside the world of computers. I do not believe we will ever be able to find him via his telephone traces, telnet or ftp connections, and/or other technological methods. It is only through personal (or, in your case, telephonic) exchanges with Kevin that we gain more insight as to his activities and plans. Your assistance is crucial to this investigation.

. . . I can only assure you, once again, that your efforts in the Kevin "chase" are appreciated. . . . [I]f you choose to continue your cooperation with the FBI by providing me with information about discussions with Kevin, I promise that, one day, all the little pieces of data filtered to me from around the world will fall into place and lead to a computer terminal where I will find Kevin and promptly place him in handcuffs. . . .

Thanks again, Neil.

Sincerely yours,

Kathleen Carson
Special Agent
Federal Bureau of Investigation

.   .   .

"The guy looks pretty stationary in the university district," Kevin Pazaski says, tracing his finger across the printouts of phone numbers and cell sites called by the phone hacker. It's the first week of October, 1994, two months since Pazaski began his investigation, and the phone hacker's still swiping calls.

The redheaded fellow sitting next to Pazaski nods. The printouts show ninety-two calls made in a mere day and a half. Nearly all originate from cell site four, sector C, the university district. The redhead is Todd Young, a bounty hunter roving the cyberspace plain. He looks a bit like David Caruso, and like the movie star, rarely smiles. He's just thirty-three, but then everybody in his business is young. Six years with US West Cellular, three as a security manager. He served on the Cellular Telecommunications Industry Association Fraud Task Force.

The last couple of years, Young's headed up the investigative arm of the Guidry Group, a security consulting and investigations firm headquartered near Houston. He's coordinated investigations in Los Angeles, Phoenix, Houston, Wyoming, and Mexico and helped arrest fifteen suspected cell phone hackers running call-selling operations.

Recently he was hired by a Southern California high-tech corporation to do a background check on aliases and former addresses of relatives and friends of Kevin Mitnick, but the investigation led nowhere, and Young quickly forgot about it. Young often has to juggle several investigations in different states. He's a new breed, a cybercop for hire, trained in basic surveillance and all the latest gizmos and gadgets. A thousand dollars a day. That's his price.

Pazaski's bosses figure it's a small price to pay. Pazaski's already estimated what the hacker's costing CellularOne. He pulls it up on his screen for Young.

Mobile #	Dates Cloned Calls	Approx Losses
419-3006	June 28–July 2, 1994	$1,030
601-3020	July 2–July 5	$ 700
219-2460	July 5	$ 150
419-3588	July 12–July 19	$1,500
419-3013	July 19–July 22	$ 600
419-3005	July 22–July 29	$1,030
619-6353	July 29–July 31	$ 600
419-4081	August 6–August 17	$1,900
979-1536	August 20–August 23	$ 60
619-0105	August 24–August 25	$ 730
	Total	$8,300

Roughly $250 dollars of airtime a day, and the calls keep racking up. And that's just the stuff Pazaski has sorted out. Yet the truth is CellularOne's actual losses are intangible. The phone hacker isn't running up bills on stolen credit cards, he's pilfering airtime. CellularOne's losses are mostly service and time related. But those losses are real. When they're selling a service, they can't have their customers being inconvenienced.

Young isn't worried. So a phone hacker pirated a dozen or so ESNs in the span of a few weeks. ESN skipping, jumping from one serial number to another, doesn't fool Young. Pazaski has done his gumshoe work, found the patterns, the familiar numbers that show up on different bills: modem numbers, information calls, out of state or international numbers. Young knows they're dealing with an operating range of one or two primary cell sites. A couple of square miles.

Besides, crime is crime, even in cyberspace. Cell phone hackers make basic mistakes, like making too many calls from the same place. Young figures the technology tricks them into thinking they're invisible. But he knows what they don't. To a skilled, persistent investigator, every pirated call is a footprint.

Pazaski shows Young a list of the phone hacker's most frequently called numbers.

Number Called	Findings When Number Called
303-756-0322	Voice mail system (Denver, CO)
303-758-0101	Modem tones (Denver, CO)
206-547-5992	Modem tones (Seattle Internet access line)
312-380-0340	Modem tones
213-718-7626	LA cellular roamer access number
702-791-5177	Modem tones (Las Vegas, NV)
303-757-8901	Modem tones (Denver, CO)
702-734-9807	Modem tones (Las Vegas, NV)
206-346-6000	US West Network Operations Center, Seattle
503-242-7910	US West Communications Equipment Office, Portland

Young considers what the calls to Denver, Vegas, and L.A show. The phone hacker's dialing modems, changing MINs [mobile identification numbers] every few days, racking up several hundred if not thousands of dollars of calls on each before moving on.

Today he has a new MIN. How does Pazaski deduce the new MIN is pirated? He runs searches on the patterns, checking the billing records. The hacker always calls the same voice mail box and modem in Denver, the same Seattle Internet access line. The calls to US West's operations and communications offices are also suspicious. Generally, only employees or vendors would call those numbers.

Pazaski lays the photocopy of the area map on his desk, and Young pencils in the boundary of the university cell site. They figure they're looking at about a hundred thousand people. One needle in a hundred thousand straws of hay.

The bounty hunter is cool, unsmiling. A grand, he figures. Just a day's work.

Skip Jacker

Todd Young pulls his dark green Jeep Cherokee up in front of the glass office building by Yarrow Bay in Kirkland, Washington. The time is a little after 1 P.M. on October 7, a sunny, unusually warm fall day in the Pacific Northwest.

Circled map in hand, they drive west toward the University of Washington. They pass brick university buildings, a bike path crowded with roller bladers and cyclists, and pull into a parking lot in the shadow of Husky Stadium.

Pazaski takes the wheel and the bounty hunter readies his equipment. Young sticks the small Doppler Systems directional display unit on the velcro swatch glued to his dash. Red pinhead LEDs on the six-inch plastic box indicate north, south, east, and west. Lodged behind the front seat sits a bulky green metal ICOM 7000 receiver tuned to 824–849 megahertz, the frequency cellular calls transmit on. The receiver is wired to the cigarette lighter, a cable connecting it to the Doppler display. A black metallic dish with four rubber nipple-shaped antennae sprouts from the roof.

Young boots up the Toshiba that sits in his lap. Cellscope 2000 is the name of the whole elaborate setup. It cost about $15,000 when Young bought it a couple of years ago. Only employees of cellular carriers and cops can legally own Cellscopes. And licensed bounty hunters, too.

Radio Direction Finding, or RDFing, is what the pros call it, tracing cellular radio transmissions back to their origin. The trick is to get close enough to the caller to pick up what's known as the reverse voice channel, the weaker portion of the call, which is transmitted from the cell phone to the nearby cell site. The Doppler antenna and display work like radar, with the added advantage that the Doppler helps filter out signals bouncing off buildings or walls to provide a more accurate reading. When the Cellscope locks onto a call, one of the sixteen LEDs lights up, showing the direction of the suspect.

Cellular phones transmit at 600 milliwatts, but within a very short distance the signal weakens dramatically. Decibel strength readings on the Toshiba estimate the proximity of the caller. Signal readings of -100 dBm are weak, just one tenth of a billionth of a milliwatt, or over a thousand feet away, while -40 dBm is one ten thousandth of a million milliwatts, less than a hundred feet away.

But technical as the setup sounds, Young is as comfortable with his tracking rig as a cop with his trusty 38. After forty hours of formal training on the Cellscope and another three hundred hours in the field tracking cell phone hackers and call-selling operations, he knows his equipment.

At 2 P.M. the cybercops fuel up at the Quality Food Center in the University Village Plaza. Two Snapples, some chips, and a couple of hot jalapeño bagels. Pazaski punches a number into his cell phone and slowly walks around the Jeep to make certain the Cellscope's accurately reading his direction. Young watches Pazaski's test call light up his directional display, the LEDs mirroring Pazaski's progress around the Jeep.

"Good enough!" Young declares after one revolution.

Pazaski hops back in and rattles off the MINs he suspects the hacker is pirating while Young taps them into the laptop's memory.

"419-3006."

"Next."

"601-3020."

"Next."

"219-2460."

The Jeep leaves the campus shopping center, and skirts the northern border of the university, going west on 45th Street. Young knows from experience that the radio signals in a particular cell site never travel identical distances on any two different days. Wet or humid weather can impede the signals and create inaccurate readings. The investigators need to know the exact radio coverage for the hacker's suspected territory. As Pazaski drives, Young hits the F7 function key on his laptop and his scanner automatically searches for the strongest channel. Pazaski drives the first loop quickly, Young calling out the borders.

The boundaries set, they circle again just to be sure. The results are clear. The heart of the cell site, the best place to trap the phone hacker's calls, is the center of the bustling university area.

Trap readied, the investigators park in front of the Washington Alumni House at the corner of 15th Avenue and 45th Street and watch the stream of students, punks, and homeless.

Finger on the cursor key, the bounty hunter bounces through the static of the twenty-odd channels. Once in a while, he catches a conversation, checks the MIN to make sure it's not the target, hits the cursor key, and moves on. Modem breath is what he wants to hear.

Pazaski drives north of the campus, and parks at University Way and 55th Street NE. The engine idles, powering the Cellscope gear. Time creeps by. Young watches a couple of kids dealing dope. A gang of twelve- or thirteen-year-olds shuffles past the Jeep, eyeing the blue-white glow illuminating the Jeep's interior, and the strange antenna protruding from the roof.

It's a little after 5:30 P.M, and still they've heard nothing. Young knows they're in the right place. It's gotta be somewhere in these six square blocks. He switches the scanner to automatic trap mode, and listens as it skips from channel to channel. When it traps one of the preprogrammed MINs the laptop should scream.

Maybe a change in location would help. Pazaski sticks the Jeep in gear, turns left on 55th Street NE, then right on Ravenna Avenue, past the 1920s-style bungalows and under the elevated I-5 freeway, west of the campus. They pass a bar and Pazaski jokes that they should call it quits and have a beer.

But Young doesn't look up from the laptop. Pazaski downshifts and drives up a steep residential street, circles the block, then parks on 6th Avenue NE amid the tidy bungalows and well-manicured lawns. They're looking southeast over the crowded I-5 freeway to the houses and apartment buildings of the university district. A pretty, old, brick church steeple dominates the view. The hundred feet of elevation should improve reception.

"eeeeeeEEEEEEEEEE!" the laptop screams.

"It's him!" Young yells. "We've got him!"

The call data pops up in a window in the upper right corner of the laptop's screen.

MIN 206-619-0086,
ESN: XXXXXXXX
Dialed: 303-756-1116

It's a voice call. Some guy chuckling about computers to a friend in Denver. Some guy wondering if he's been detected. It's the right ESN, the right MIN, the right profile. They've gotta be listening to their Skip Jacker.

"Coming from three o'clock!" Young shouts, the red LED locked dead on the tall steeple of the distant church.

6:23 P.M., flashes the laptop.

Pazaski spins a U-turn, up one block to 5th Avenue NE, and roars back down to Ravenna. Young's eyes are fixed on the dash-mounted display.

The signal could terminate any second.

"We gotta get over there!" Young yells. "We can't lose the call!"

Pazaski speeds up to the light at 56th Avenue NE and Roosevelt Way, past the bar, and slows to a crawl at the intersection below the broad concrete freeway. It's the evening commute and traffic is snarled.

Green, yellow.

"Damn it! Damn it!" Pazaski shouts. Six cars between them and the light.

He's less than a quarter mile away. Seconds, if Pazaski could just get through the light. What an irony, he thinks. They've got the Skip Jacker's signal, but they're stuck in traffic.

"Damn!" Young yells, pounding the dashboard as the light turns. But the phone hacker just keeps laughing, oblivious to their surveillance. Young listens incredulously as he jokes about what sounds like plans for computer sabotage. Revenge against people he used to work with.

"These guys are electronic terrorists!" Young shouts.

He kicks himself for not bringing a tape recorder. At least then he could have recorded his voice. They sound as if they might hang up any second. The guy in Denver's shopping for a cellular phone, and mentions a local price plan of forty dollars a month.

"Why don't you try the same 'free' service I'm already using?" jokes the phone hacker.

"I want to keep a low profile," replies Denver.

If we can just get through this light, thinks Pazaski.

Green. Yes!

The Jeep roars south on Roosevelt Way, past Dante's Cocktails, Paul's Auto Upholstery, and a neighborhood library.

Meanwhile, Denver is talking about the Hotel Gregorio near US West Cellular. Young knows exactly where they're talking about. He worked in Denver. The bounty hunter picks up more snippets of conversation. Talk about generating reports and printouts for someone at his work. Talk about renaming some "test" file.

"If Elaine is gone, they'll never figure it out," boasts Denver.

"We'll really fuck them up!" laughs Seattle.

The red LED glows to the northeast.

"Damn it! Damn it! Damn it!" Young mutters, as they miss another light.

South on Roosevelt Way. Young glances down at the Toshiba. The decibel readings bounce. Getting closer.

"Left here!" Young orders, eyes glued to the display as they approach 50th Street NE.

"Left here. OK. Drive, drive, drive."

The decibel readings jump again at Brooklyn Avenue.

"Left here!" Young shouts. "OK, slow down a little."

They cruise by a beautiful old picturesque school, and then a three-story brick and wood apartment building on the left. The signal jumps to -60dBm, the red LED blinking at nine o'clock.

This is it, Young thinks. "Keep going!"

Time to frame up the target location.

Pazaski circles to a narrow alley behind the apartment building. Like a Geiger counter, the Cellscope leaves no doubt: -65dBm reads the laptop, the LED pointing at the back of the building. This is the place.

A voice is still coming over the ICOM 7000 receiver. Seattle is laughing about the damage he's about to do.

Cocky son of a bitch, Pazaski thinks. He thinks it's some kind of joke.

Dusk is falling as Pazaski pulls up by a fire hydrant in front of 5227 Brooklyn Avenue. Check out the mailboxes first, Young thinks. Cross the street casually and take down the names.

A bank of brass mailboxes. Unit one, a blue typed label, Brian Merrill.

"Ha, ha, ha."

The Skip Jacker's familiar belly laugh booms through the basement apartment wall.

Amazing, Young thinks. He takes a couple more steps, and presses his ear against the large wooden door.

"Ha, ha, ha. . . Yeah, I've got the records."

Young sprints back to the Jeep. "Kevin, you're not going to believe this! That was the voice on the call."

They run back together. This time, Pazaski crouches below the peephole.

"The password is . . . "

Pazaski's eyes widen and he gestures toward the door, silently mouthing the words.

"That's him!"

Back at the Jeep, the Cellscope grabs a one-minute call at 6:44 P.M. and another at 6:45. Young walks behind the Jeep, quickly jotting down a physical description on his palm: two white buildings separated by concrete stairs and paths. Metal frame windows. Suspect apartment subground, ochre brick facing, two street-facing windows, curtains drawn.

"Jingle, jingle, jingle."

Couldn't be, Young thinks, glancing up.

The Skip Jacker! He's locking the white door to unit one. He's built, pushing two hundred pounds, wavy, shoulder-length hair, mustache, silver-rim glasses, a dark leather jacket and faded jeans. He's carrying a purple and black athletic bag.

They can't grab him because they're not cops, and they don't want to risk spooking him. But that doesn't stop them from trailing him.

Young ducks behind a van, watching until the phone hacker walks a safe distance down the street. Young hops back in the Jeep and Pazaski pulls a U-turn and trails him.

Hands in his pockets, head slightly bent, the phone hacker crosses 50th Street NE, passes Burger King, and walks into Safeway.

Pazaski veers into the Burger King parking lot. They need a solid physical description. And Young is worried he may already have been spotted.

Pazaski jumps out and brushes past the homeless in front of the Safeway. He grabs two bottles of Arizona Iced Tea and a bunch of bananas, and then casually falls behind the phone hacker in the checkout line. The hacker's face is in profile. He has no idea he's being watched. Tall, Pazaski thinks. Glasses, pretty buffed, not too heavy, not bad looking. Not at all what he'd expected. He's buying a large bottle of Evian water.

Pazaski pays for his bananas and drinks and returns to the Jeep.

"Todd, he's a normal guy," Pazaski tells Young. "He bought a bottle of water. No porno mags, nothing unusual."

But the phone hacker is walking briskly, passing Burger King, turning away from his apartment. He walks toward the evening melting pot of students, workers, and street people, and then he's gone.

Suitcase

I t's Saturday night, and the electronic surf is up.

Todd Young is back, alone, sitting in his Jeep, down the street from Merrill's apartment. He locks onto Merrill dialing a familiar L.A. cellular roamer access number.

The Skip Jacker is chatting about computers with someone who sounds like his father. He's getting emotional. He wants to talk to his grandfather.

"He's not going to talk to you 'cuz you're a fugitive."

"I know, I know! What am I gonna do?" groans the Skip Jacker.

Is this guy wanted? Young wonders. Is Merrill some big-time cybercrook?

Todd Young is driven now. Brian Merrill is somebody big, he can feel it. He bangs out a ten-page affidavit over the weekend and faxes it on Monday to the Seattle Police Department and, on a long shot, to the local office of the Secret Service.

But the local police and Secret Service don't share his enthusiasm. Frustrated, Young phones a cop he knows at the nearby King County PD.

"We want to do it," the cop tells him. "But it's outside our jurisdiction. Try John Lewitt in Seattle."

Young dials the cop in the Seattle PD Fraud and Explosives

Division, and Detective Lewitt says he'll get right back to him. But a few hours later Lewitt too calls with bad news. His boss says the case isn't big enough. It's the same story with the Secret Service. Special Agent Tom Molitor with the local office is interested, but the U.S. Attorney in Seattle isn't.

A ten-thousand-dollar fraud isn't worth their time.

.   .   .

Eight days have passed since Young first tracked Merrill. He's still trying to get the cops to act, but nobody seems to want the cybercrook.

On Saturday, October 15, around 5:30 P.M, Young methodically loads up his family Jeep with his receiver, directional finder, laptop, and Doppler antennae. Young wants to get into the guy's head, find out what he does on the weekend. He tells his puzzled wife they're going to the university district. They'll make it a date. A little cybersurveillance, dinner, and a movie.

"He lives right there," Young announces fifteen minutes later, proudly pointing to the basement unit.

Young parks at his usual spot by the elementary school on Brooklyn at about 6 P.M. Twelve minutes later, he traps a call. An unfamiliar MIN flashes on his screen, but Young knows it's him: the call is to one of Merrill's familiar L.A. cellular roamer access lines. Four minutes later, the Skip Jacker dials L.A. again.

At 6:24 P.M., the Skip Jacker emerges from his apartment and Young scribbles in a notebook that he's wearing the same clothes as before. He and his wife watch as Merrill pulls a cell phone from its black case, dials, and places it to his ear. The call flashes on Young's laptop:

MIN: 206-310-4335
ESN: XXXXXXXX
Dialing: 303-757-2227

Young wants to tail him. His wife has other ideas.

"What about that movie you promised me?"

The couple drive to the small, alternative movie theater in time to catch the seven o'clock show. For dinner, they grab a little pasta at the nearby Italian restaurant with the opera singers. But their after-dinner entertainment is back on Brooklyn Street. Young parks in the school lot. It's the late show, starring Brian Merrill, at about 10:30 P.M.

"So what has this guy done?" Mrs. Young asks her husband.

Young runs down the little he knows about Brian Merrill, and Mrs. Young is anything but impressed.

"Why do you even bother?" she asks. "He seems so small-time."

"He's bigger than you think," Young tells her. "This guy's on the brink of what's possible."

"SHHHHHHHHHHHHH!"

Mrs. Young turns to her husband. "What's that noise?"

"That's him," he says with a smile. "He's dialing a modem."

Time passes. To Mrs. Young, the modem tone sounds soft, invisible, like a breeze.

"Is he still on?"

"Yeah," he answers.

And then, suddenly, nothing.

"There he is!" Young says.

Out on the street, the now familiar Brian Merrill, a cell phone against his ear. The time is 10:50 P.M. He's making another call.

> MIN: 206-310-4335
> ESN: XXXXXXXX
> Dialing: 303-757-2227

Young knows this number. It's a voice line in Denver.

Young and his wife trail slowly in the Jeep, pass Merrill at the Burger King, and pull into the Jack In the Box lot.

But the Skip Jacker takes an unexpected turn and walks straight toward the couple. Young snaps the laptop shut and shoves the Doppler directional finder down on the floor.

"Quick, give me a kiss," Young whispers.

Oblivious, Brian Merrill strides by.

"Where do you think he's going?" Mrs. Young asks, pressed against her husband.

Seconds later, the couple follow on foot, half a block behind. Young drags his wife into a doorway when they seem a little too close for comfort, but they don't have long to wait to find out where he's going. The Skip Jacker's human; the Skip Jacker needs food. On this Saturday night, a couple of minutes before 11 o'clock, he walks into Taco Bell.

"Keep walking!" Young urges his wife.

She wants a closer look. It's only natural. But Young tugs her across the street, into a covered construction walk. They watch.

The Skip Jacker waits in line, orders, sits down, and eats, alone. Young turns to his wife. "This guy doesn't have much of a social life."

A pattern? Mrs. Young wonders. He walked to the fast food joint as if he'd done it dozens of times.

The bounty hunter thinks about what he's seeing. Fast food, no sign of a car, an ordinary basement apartment. Whatever this Skip Jacker is doing, he's not getting rich by ripping off cellular calls.

Suddenly, he leaves Taco Bell and turns to the right, onto Brooklyn.

Young and his wife hop back in the Jeep and tail him. The Skip Jacker snaps out his cellular. The L.A. roamer number pops up on Young's laptop. This time, the call doesn't go through.

They keep following, approaching the Skip Jacker's block. He's less than a hundred feet away.

"What does he look like to you?" Young asks.

"He's got curly hair, glasses," his wife says.

The Skip Jacker turns and stops. He stares right through Mrs. Young.

"This guy's got the make on us," she whispers.

.   ■   .

Kevin Mitnick is on the phone laughing uncontrollably.

It's Sunday evening, October 22. My wife and I just finished watching 60 Minutes. But Kevin Mitnick's got some real news. Mitnick's just hacked a hacker.

"We didn't get everything," Mitnick chuckles. "But we got the stuff on the Oki phones."

The Oki is a cellular phone popular with hackers because of its easy programmability. In other words, it can be hacked.

The victim is Mark Lottor, codefendant and former roommate of Kevin Poulsen. (Charges against Lottor will be dismissed in 1996.)

"Lewis called him first," Mitnick explains excitedly. "He called him on his cellular phone, on Mark's [Lottor's] phone, and said, 'Can I look at something on your machine?'" Mitnick chortles. "Lottor was belligerent. He was getting perturbed."

How does Mitnick think people should react when De Payne demands they open up their computer files?

"I figured he would be smart. I did a full investigation on him. I spent a day of research in case he might use personal names or personal information for certain directories. I knew his parents, his girlfriend. . . ."

Mitnick isn't kidding. He's a dedicated hacker. When he picks a target, he's thorough.

"His girlfriend's into art history. I looked at her account. It contained her feelings about Mark. . . ."

I try not to listen to the personal details. Lottor isn't just a name to me, I've interviewed him in person several times, eaten dinner with him, been to the condo where he keeps his impressive computers and cellular phones.

"Lottor had his own Ethernet network tied to the Net," Mitnick continues, describing the technical details of his hack. "Lottor runs the provider. I narrowed it down, how his Ethernet connection works, everything."

Mitnick chuckles. "Someone got in there seven times in a space of a week —

"Could I see a menu, please?"

Without a pause, Mitnick's talking to somebody else.

"Sure," bubbles a waitress. I try but can't identify an accent.

"That's my suitcase there," Mitnick says protectively.

Suitcase? Are the feds onto Mitnick's new location? Or does he always bring his suitcase, perhaps with his laptop and a scanner for countersurveillance?

"So then I phoned Lottor direct," Mitnick continues with his story. "And he started getting belligerent, giving me false information."

Attitude. Mitnick phones a hacker under federal indictment and orders him to hand over his computer files — or else. Mitnick has no mercy.

"The guy [Lottor] is a hacker just like me," Mitnick rationalizes. "He's not an innocent person. He's cracked Pac Bell. He's a hacker, he hates authority. I'm just having fun with the guy. He's making money, selling his Oki 900 program.

"I was interested to see if he reverse engineered the whole thing. Man, he did!"

Mitnick still hasn't fully explained what Lottor's Oki software and interface device does, but Lottor himself has told me it enables hackers or cops to put people under surveillance. Hooked up to a HP Palmtop or other small PC, Lottor's souped up Oki can follow a cellular call in progress, picking up each handoff as the caller moves through the cellular network. The phone can also be used to intercept and eavesdrop on those very same calls. In other words, it's a mobile, low-cost, illegal countersurveillance and eavesdropping system.

But that's just the part Lottor and his associates offer for sale. What Mitnick wants is Lottor's reverse engineering of the phone's basic operations. One reason he's switching to the Oki phone is because it can transmit data at a fast 14.4 KBs (kilobytes per second), more than ten times faster than the cellular phone he's been using. But if Lottor has truly reverse engineered the phone, it means Mitnick may be able to program it to do whatever he wishes. Maybe he wants to program other people's ESNs into its memory to make free cellular calls? Or perhaps he wants to add a security routine so if the phone falls into federal hands the ESNs are automatically erased?

.   ■   ■

Mitnick orders. "Yeah, I'd like a Garden Burger, fries, and a large Diet Coke."

Kevin Mitnick is in an American burger joint with his suitcase, complaining about how hard it is for a cyberfugitive to find a good attorney.

"Even Shapiro working with Simpson, he's asked for more money. These attorneys don't care. I don't know if anybody has defended a case that might take multiple jurisdictions: Finland, the United Kingdom, Japan. A lot of countries want my ass. Somebody did Nokia mobile phones in Finland. Somebody got into their computers. They're out for blood. Man, I need another planet," Mitnick sighs.

"Maybe I should go to France, join the French Foreign Legion," Mitnick considers, then thinks twice about the wild idea. "They send you into covert missions. That would be a problem. I'm not going to look into mine fields."

"So where are you thinking of going?"

"Brazil. Argentina. I can't tell you what I'm thinking!"

The Raid

█ van Orton, a fortyish, red-haired prosecuting attorney in the King County, Washington, Prosecutor's fraud division, sits on a stool and peers down at his 486 PC, its screen oddly recessed into an architect's drafting table. Behind him sits a 286 PC that answers his phone, and a CD-ROM PC. There's a worn leather sofa, and a delicately carved armoire with the half dozen suits, shirts, and ties he wears for the few days he must appear in court. Boxes of documents clutter his office.

Todd Young of the Guidry Group is on the line. It's the morning of October 26. Nineteen days have passed since Young first found the Skip Jacker, and Orton listens carefully to the familiar political Ping-Pong game. Young and his client, CellularOne, have run out of places to turn. It's a story the prosecutor has heard before. Orton's the guy people call when the cops tell them to get lost.

After hanging up, Orton walks down the hall to his boss. Orton could care less about CellularOne billing losses. What intrigues the prosecutor is the idea that criminals can disguise their cellular calls. His gut tells him that soon all kinds of fraud will revolve around cell phones.

"Somebody's out cloning phones," Orton tells his boss, filling him in on the bureaucratic wrangling. The Secret Service isn't interested because the case doesn't meet its $25,000 threshold. Seattle PD declined because they felt the Secret Service was trying to pass along its "garbage." But Orton's boss doesn't care about the politics. He tells Orton to change Seattle PD's mind.

.   .   .

Superior Court Judge Larry Jordan sits in his chambers and scans the records of pirated calls, and the lengthy, precise description of the suspect and his residence at 5227 Brooklyn Avenue. Ivan Orton, Todd Young, Kevin Pazaski, and Detective John Lewitt of the Seattle Police Department look on expectantly. Jordan flips to the last page of the affidavit for a search warrant and signs on the line marked "Judge."

It's Thursday, October 27, 1994, about 1 P.M., and Ivan Orton is making things happen. He's convinced Seattle PD to execute the search, and now they've got a signed search warrant. But still, they're running out of time. Young is leaving the country on Friday to teach a cellular fraud seminar in London. If they don't execute the search fast, the Skip Jacker might split Seattle for good.

Detective Lewitt returns to his office at the Public Safety building in downtown Seattle, logs onto a terminal, enters his ID code, and taps in the name: Brian Merrill.

10/27/94 13:11:14 FROM ACCESS — DATABASE ID: DOL
FOR UNIT: RTW8
D. WASPD00W8.OLN/MERRIBD080559
NO COMPUTER RECORD FOUND.

Nothing. Lewitt pages down the screen.

** NO WACIC WANTED, MISSING OR RESTRAINING
ORDER RECORDS FOUND **CHECKING NCIC
***DOC LOCATOR FILE HAS BEEN CHECKED ***
NO RECORD FOUND
QW.WASPD00W8.MERRILL, BRIAN D.080559
102794-130955

The detective keeps checking. Only one Brian Merrill is even close. The hair color is off, the 1959 birthdate is a little too old, but it's all he's got. Lewitt does another search. Could it be the same Merrill? Lewitt's unsure. He pulls up the arrest record, a juvenile charge.

Maybe it's the Brian Merrill they're looking for. Maybe it isn't.

.   .   .

Sergeant Ken Crow of Seattle PD, a trim forty-nine-year old with a prominent nose, points to his hastily drawn diagram on the white board. He's mapped out 5227 Brooklyn. Red felt pen for the building, blue for the front and side streets and the alley behind. Black X's mark the agents and cops positioned south on 47th, in the alley, and sprinkled through the building. Crow hands out the photos Lewitt snapped half an hour ago, views of the alley, the main street and the stairs.

Todd Young glances around the crowded north precinct conference room in amazement. He figured they'd round up a couple of cops for the 6 P.M. briefing. But four Secret Service agents? And that's just the feds! Young is surrounded by the entire Seattle PD fraud unit: one captain, two sergeants, three detectives, two uniformed Seattle PD officers for backup, and one detective specially trained to take down computers. Fifteen troops all told, counting Young and Pazaski.

Brian Merrill is about to be seriously outgunned.

"Todd, you want to give us a physical make on this guy?" Crow asks.

"He's a white male," Young begins. "Long, wavy brown hair, about five ten, two hundred pounds. He's always worn this dark brown or black leather jacket and blue jeans."

"When can we expect him to be on the air?"

"After six P.M.," Young replies.

Crow lays out the raid strategy. "OK, I'm going to divide everybody up into teams.

"Remember," reminds Crow. "We ran him and we didn't get anything conclusive. We've got no prior history. We don't know who we're dealing with."

"John, you want to give us the layout?"

Detective John Moore, a seasoned, grumpy cop in his late forties, stands up. "I did a slow drive by before coming over," drawls the cop, wearing his usual deadpan face. "There aren't many cars out in front, and there's no sign of activity. The suspect's apartment is on the street level. There's only one way in or out. We don't have to worry about going down a hallway with multiple units. It's a fairly easy unit to secure."

"Here's the plan!" barks Crow. "Molitor and Lewitt, you guys go first to the door and knock as a ruse to make sure he's controlled."

.   .   .

The Secret Service agents and cops mill about Burger King near the white bomb squad van and the Dodge Aries compacts, chowing down on burgers or tacos from Merrill's favorite Taco Bell. Everyone's dressed in standard Seattle garb, blue jeans, flannel shirts, down jackets. Crow sips his coffee and watches his breath steam in the cold evening air.

It's 1900 hours.

"This guy could walk right by and we wouldn't even know it!" Detective Linda Patrick jokes to Lewitt. None of the other cops are worried. How could they be spotted? There's only one manned squad car in the lot.

"It's too goddamned cold to be out chitchatting," grumbles Crow, climbing back into the warm blue vinyl of his metallic blue Dodge Aries.

Meanwhile across from 5227 Brooklyn, Young sits in his Jeep and taps the cursor key, bouncing between channels, listening for modem breath. The lights are on in Merrill's apartment, but Young hears nothing. Pazaski was afraid this might happen. Every fifteen minutes Crow's voice crackles over the police radio the cops loaned them for the raid.

"Any activity?"

"No," Pazaski says. "No activity."

Young keeps surfing. More than an hour with nothing.

"Damn it!" Pazaski swears. "They're going to go in anyway." Crow's voice crackles over the police radio.

"We're going in."

"I'd like to wait a little longer, till he's on the air," argues Young.

"No," Crow orders. "We're going in."

Detective John Lewitt and Special Agent Thomas Molitor carefully approach the door and knock, and knock and knock.

"Police! Open up! Police! Open up!"

The time is 2100 hours.

Agent Molitor kicks the door. It won't budge. Detective Lewitt kicks the door. Nothing.

"Linda, you wanna try a kick?"

Patrick, all five foot two inches of her, gives the door a few kicks. Another cop kicks it a few times.

Nothing.

Lewitt suggests they try to break it with a team kick. Another Secret Service agent joins them, and they lean back against the door, placing the soles of their shoes near the door frame.

"One, two, three," Lewitt counts.

KICK!

The door jamb splinters.

"Police!" Lewitt and Molitor shout, waving their guns. They're wearing bulletproof vests just in case.

Is he gone? Lewitt wonders, surprised at how sparsely the apartment is furnished. But why would Merrill leave the lights on?

Crow stakes out the musty living room. Two worn couches, a police scanner on a table, a workout bag by the front door, and a mountain bike in the corner. A Toshiba laptop sits on a Formica table in the cramped, windowless kitchen. They fan out, waving guns in case he's hiding. The place smells damp, the air stale. Neon green linoleum tiles curl from the bathroom floor. A thick layer of mold covers the ceiling over the apricot-colored tub. The bedroom is claustrophobic, with faded olive indoor-outdoor carpet. The closet is nearly empty.

Brian Merrill is nowhere to be found.

Detectives Patrick and Moore snap photos of the depressing scene.

"We've given up our whole night for THIS?" Crow grouses.

Lewitt pulls out his supply box stuffed with clipboards, sandwich-

and garbage-sized plastic bags, black marker pens and labels, and flattened boxes. They stick the little yellow labels on each piece of evidence, numbering and photographing the items. But Lewitt doesn't see much of interest besides the laptop and scanner, some papers, perhaps, a battery charger, cellular phone parts, a couple of antennae, a few computer disks, a cheap porn mag, and an envelope from some company called Netcom.

"Hey, look at this," Patrick cries, dragging a set of brown martial arts Chaco sticks out from under the bed. Minutes later, Patrick is flipping through hospital bills they found from a nearby Virginia Mason clinic. It appears Merrill's got some kind of stomach problem.

"It's getting to him. This guy's sweating it," she says to a Secret Service agent. "He's probably getting ulcers over this stuff."

Young and Pazaski are invited in to take a look around. Pazaski is struck by what a guy's pad it is. Hardly anything personal. He notices a Vegas hat decorated with slot machine coins, and a *New York Times* article with a big picture of a fat, mean-looking guy with glasses, and a big headline,

CYBERSPACE'S MOST WANTED: HACKER ELUDES F.B.I. PURSUIT

The Seattle PD crime lab van pulls up in front and the cops and special agents methodically load up the evidence. Meanwhile, Todd Young paces back and forth on Brooklyn, hoping to catch sight of Merrill before he's frightened off by the late-night circus.

A little after 10 P.M., David Drew, the tall, thirty-ish apartment manager, shows up. He chats for a while with the cops, and tells Lewitt what he knows. Merrill rented the place on the first of July, always paid his rent in cash, was polite, and kept to himself. Drew could hear Merrill logging onto his computer at all hours of the night, and late one night, he had to ask him to turn down his heavy metal music. Lewitt thanks him, completes the nine-page search warrant inventory, and leaves a copy on Merrill's kitchen table at about 10:30 P.M. The front door hangs off its hinges, wide open.

Young and Pazaski sit in the Jeep and watch the evidence van and the last undercover Dodge Aries drive off, headed for Orton's

downtown Seattle office. They debate sticking around a couple
more hours in case Merrill returns.

"We can't just jump the guy if he shows up," Young shrugs.
They're not cops.

The bounty hunter flips off his scanner and turns to Pazaski.

"Hell. If they're not gonna stay, we're not going to stay."

.   .   .

KNOCK, KNOCK, KNOCK.

What do the cops want now, David Drew thinks, rousing himself
from bed.

He opens the door. It's Brian Merrill. He's agitated.

"Did you let somebody into my apartment?"

"No," says Drew. "But they did."

"Who's *they???*"

"The police, Brian. There's a search warrant on your kitchen
table."

"Oh, shit!" mutters Merrill.

"They left a phone number you're supposed to call."

"Thanks," Merrill offers, turning away.

"Good luck, Brian."

Brian Merrill doesn't turn to say goodbye. He walks to the narrow alley behind the building and disappears into the darkness.

It's midnight in Seattle and once again Kevin Mitnick has nar-
rowly escaped capture.

III.

"**M**y technique is the best," chimes the male, cockney, almost computerized voice on Tsutomu Shimomura's voice mail on December 27, 1994.

"Damn you. I know sendmail technique . . .

"Don't you know who I am? Me and my friends, we'll kill you." A second voice comes on the line.

"Hey, boss, my kung fu is really good."

Three days later, December 30, 1994, a second message will be left.

"Your technique will be defeated. Your technique is no good. . . ."

.　　　.　　　.

An unusual piece of e-mail pops into my Well account a couple of days after Christmas.

To: jlittman@Well.sf.ca.us
From: articles@playboy.com (Peter Moore)
Subject: Kevin Mitnick

I've been talking with John Markoff of the NYT about a Kevin Mitnick profile we at Playboy would like to do, covering Mitnick's fugitive years. He tossed the ball to you. Do you think there's stuff there for a good profile/cyber-whodunit? Is it possible to find Mitnick right now? Are you interested? . . .

.   .   .

"Hey."

Kevin Mitnick is not in the holiday spirit. He sounds sullen, downbeat. It's nearly noon, the day before New Year's Eve, just an hour after I agreed by telephone to write a story about him for *Playboy* magazine.

The calls from Mitnick have continued the last couple months. Just days after he evaded capture in Seattle in late October, Mitnick phoned with the story that he'd been burglarized and lost everything, his computers, his phones, his clothes, his gold. By then I knew that De Payne had received a frantic SOS call from Mitnick after the raid. Mitnick then phoned one of the officers, pretending to be part of the investigation, and social engineered information about his near capture. I just didn't know it had happened in Seattle.

My most recent Mitnick call was right before Christmas. He was in a cheery mood. He congratulated me on the birth of my daughter, offered to teach her to hack one day, then apologized for the comment. But today he's down in the dumps.

"Hi. I guess you heard the news?" I venture cautiously, knowing Mitnick's uncanny sleuthing skills.

"Yeah. Well, when I saw my name there I figured I better call you."

Mitnick's still regularly hacking my e-mail, and why shouldn't he? Neither the Well nor I can protect it. It's almost like we're old acquaintances. It's just that Mitnick does most of the acquainting.

"I think it would be more interesting if you did a story on Petersen," Mitnick begins in his most persuasive tone. "If you put my name in the media, they'll start looking for me."

"Who will?"

"Markoff and his buddy in San Diego," Mitnick says matter-of-factly.

"Who's that?"

"Tsutomu Shimomura — he's a spook for Los Alamos Labs."

"Who does he work for? Which initials?"

Mitnick pauses. "I better not say."

"Just one of the initials?" I try.

Mitnick ignores my probing. "I looked at your mailbox. I read it. I thought, *shit,* I got to call you! So what are you planning on writing, what kind of story?"

"They want me to write a story about you. I think it could be interesting. *Playboy*'s got a lot of readers. It's a pretty big forum."

"It's a *big* fucking forum!" Mitnick booms. "You know more information than anybody. It's scary thinking all the information might be used against me. I *trusted* you. The stuff with Mark Lottor could put me in a bad position."

"How?"

"I know how they twist things. I don't want to give them *anything.* I'm not asking you to lie, I'm just asking you to leave stuff out."

Mitnick's voice has an edge I've never heard before. He's not threatening me, but. . . .

"I'm too much of a trusting person," Mitnick groans, his voice cycling like a record on the wrong speed. "They are going to be scanning you on Sprint and MCI — oh *fuck!*

"I don't know how you feel about it, whether you give a shit. I don't want you to put anything in that would lead them to me. I should have taken Settle's [a former FBI agent] advice and disconnected from the past.

"I haven't lied to you. I don't know if you owe me something, but I'm scared. I'm hoping you would help me out. I didn't ask for shit from you. Lewis said you seemed like an all right guy. Like you wouldn't fuck me over. I said, OK, I'd talk to you."

"Look, they've given me a few months to do this," I say, reassuring Mitnick that I'm not going to rush something out and repeat the old rumors. "What I want to do is get the facts straight."

"All those accusations Markoff put in the book," Mitnick stammers. "Anything bad that happened was attributed to me."

"What things weren't true?"

"NORAD. I don't think it's possible," Mitnick says.

"So how'd you get the bad reputation?"

"I victimized some people when I was sixteen or seventeen, but after I was twenty I grew out of it."

Really? I think. What about when you hacked Mark Lottor for his Oki phone software?

"I'm tired of fighting it. Something happened to the probation officer's phone, and right away it's a fact. It's brought up in all my cases. Everybody thinks I'm such a bad person because when I was seventeen I used to fuck with the ham radio guys . . .

"Lewis would fuck with them and I'd antagonize them. We'd work as a team. Lew would go find private information, then I would say stuff like, 'How's Betty doing?' Personal information. It was a game, it was a *fucking game*."

"Tell me about the Security Pacific incident," I prod Mitnick. "The one where they said you put out the false release, saying they lost hundreds of millions of dollars."

"I was legally hired by Security Pacific Bank. It was in writing. They even sent around a notice saying, 'Please welcome Kevin Mitnick aboard. . . .'

"My fucking luck, one of the ham radio operators worked for the bank. He contacted the bank [and sabotaged Mitnick's hiring]. Somebody apparently did a news wire that said they lost four hundred million dollars. I didn't do it. If somebody had actually called the bank they might have found out the truth. I don't even think it happened.

"It's the tip of the iceberg. I'm not innocent, but I'm also not evil.

"I'm afraid to be back in the light. All this is intertwined, the Poulsen case, my case, the Petersen link. I'm just really not excited about it. I'm not going to fuck with your phones, I have no plans to screw anybody."

I'm feeling a little uneasy.

"So what do you plan to write?"

"You read the e-mail," I remind the eavesdropper. "*Playboy* wanted a story about you. Markoff turned them down and suggested me. If they didn't assign it to me, they'd assign it to someone else."

Mitnick pauses, his voice calmer. "I guess I'd rather have you do it than someone else."

The Many Faces of Kevin Mitnick

April 1989

April 1989

April 1991

February 1992

Courtesy Reba Vartanian

1992

WANTED
BY U.S. MARSHALS

NOTICE TO ARRESTING AGENCY: Before arrest, validate warrant through National Crime Information Center (NCIC).

United States Marshals Service NCIC entry number: (NIC/ W721460021).

NAME: .... MITNICK, KEVIN DAVID

AKS (S): .... MITNIK, KEVIN DAVID
MERRILL, BRIAN ALLEN

DESCRIPTION:

Sex: .... MALE
Race: .... WHITE
Place of Birth: .... VAN NUYS, CALIFORNIA
Date(s) of Birth: 08/06/63; 10/18/70
Height: .... 5'11"
Weight: 190
Eyes: .... BLUE
Hair: .... BROWN
Skintone: .... LIGHT
Scars, Marks, Tattoos: .... NONE KNOWN
Social Security Number (s): 550-39-5695
NCIC Fingerprint Classification: ... DOPM20PM13DIPM19PM09

ADDRESS AND LOCALE: KNOWN TO RESIDE IN THE SAN FERNANDO VALLEY AREA OF CALIFORNIA AND LAS VEGAS, NEVADA

WANTED FOR: VIOLATION OF SUPERVISED RELEASE
ORIGINAL CHARGES: POSSESSION UNAUTHORIZED ACCESS DEVICE; COMPUTER FRAUD
Warrant Issued: CENTRAL DISTRICT OF CALIFORNIA
Warrant Number: 9312-1112-0154-C

DATE WARRANT ISSUED: NOVEMBER 10, 1992

MISCELLANEOUS INFORMATION: SUBJECT SUFFERS FROM A WEIGHT PROBLEM AND MAY HAVE EXPERIENCED WEIGHT GAIN OR WEIGHT LOSS
VEHICLE/TAG INFORMATION: NONE KNOWN OFTEN USES PUBLIC TRANSPORTATION

If arrested or whereabouts known, notify the local United States Marshals Office, (Telephone: 213-894-2485).

If no answer, call United States Marshals Service Communications Center in McLean Virginia.
Telephone (800)336-0102: (24 hour telephone contact) NLETS access code is VAUSMOOOO.

Form USM -132
(Rev. 3/2/82)

PRIOR EDITIONS ARE OBSOLETE AND NOT TO BE USED

November 1992

February 17, 1995. Mitnick shackled in Raleigh, North Carolina.

Hackers and Friends

Kevin Poulsen, aka Dark Dante

Henry Spiegel

Ron Austin with his father

Wild Bill

Erica

Videotape image of
Justin Petersen, aka
Eric Heinz or Agent
Steal, working
undercover for the
FBI at a 1992
hacker conference.

Courtesy Erik Bloodaxe

The Trackers

Shimomura in North Carolina

Shimomura's equipment

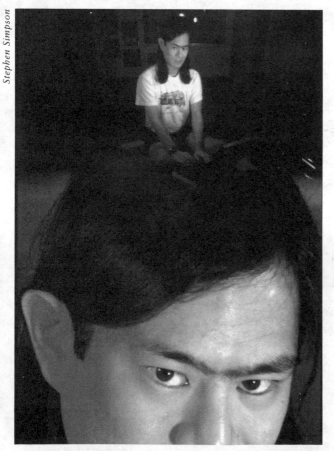

Tsutomu Shimomura, John Markoff of the *New York Times*, former San Francisco Assistant U.S. Attorney Kent Walker, and Joe Orsak and Jim Murphy of Sprint Cellular.

Shimomura in the Media

Kent Walker

John Markoff

Joe Orsak

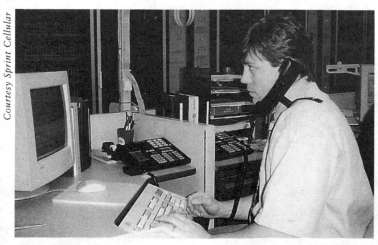

Jim Murphy

The Unknown Hunters

Kevin Pazaski

Todd Young

Young's Cellscope

Todd Young, a cellular fraud gumshoe, and Kevin Pazaski of CellularOne in Seattle, found Kevin Mitnick in a few hours and kept his basement apartment under surveillance for two weeks. Federal authorities rejected the cellular fraud case as insignificant.

Mitnick's apartment in Seattle

I figure I might as well ask my subject for some ideas on where to start researching. "Who do you think I could call to check out some of these old myths, like the NORAD hack, or the Security Pacific release?"

". . . All the different people in the ham radio world. The Underground. 435 [a ham radio group]. My old teacher, John Christ, lives in Lake Tahoe. There's this guy, Steven Shalita. We weren't friends. His parents live on 7833 Cantaloupe Street. There's Irv Rubin. He's like the head of the JDL [Jewish Defense League]. My old teacher liked me, Larry Gehr. He worked at the Computer Learning Center in Downy, Los Angeles."

This is what's amazing about Kevin Mitnick. His openness, his seeming naïveté, his incredible memory. He's rattling off a list of real people who know him, real people who may convey an uncensored image.

"What about Lewis?"

"Lewis has this Internet group. He *loves* to antagonize people. It's his hobby. I did too. Then, I actually turned around and tried to be friends with these people. I got back on the 435, and I said, 'I was an asshole, but now I'd rather be your friend.'

"Everybody was shocked, but after that I never had to pay for breakfast. It actually worked."

Kevin Mitnick even describes his transformation into a nice guy as a hack, a con, a social engineering job.

"When was this?"

"Ninety or '91," Mitnick recalls. "Most of them love me. Try Tony Cardenas. His call sign is WB6ID. He lives in Cerritos."

"You've got a pretty good memory."

"I know. Let's see, there's Bob Arkow, a Highway Patrol radio engineer. He works in the Hollywood office."

"What's his call sign?"

"WA6HMC."

"How'd you meet him?"

"He was a bus driver. I met him and he turned me on to ham radio.

"Then there's this guy Ed Jules," Mitnick continues. "When I was a kid, he used to jam my radio frequency. So I found a local hospital and anytime they had a long distance call I attached the bill to Ed. I think it was *thirty thousand dollars!*" Mitnick chuckles like a naughty boy. "Is that *bad?*"

"Why'd you do it?"

"He was fucking with me over the air. . . . I just went to the L.A. switch. All the billing is done at the actual switch. It's the most direct way. It takes effect immediately.

"The old stuff, the Rhode Island directory stuff," Mitnick continues, describing another of his infamous hacks, when he and his friends hacked into a telephone switch and intercepted people calling directory assistance. "They'd ask for somebody and we'd say, 'Is that person black or white?'

"I consider them pranks, like the stuff you hear about at Cal Tech, where they'll take someone's car, take it apart, and put it back together. Or they'll rewire the scoreboard at the Rose Bowl. They do the same thing and the government doesn't care."

.   .   .

"I'm *always* successful. A guy asked me recently, 'Can you *really* do this?' I *can!*"

Mitnick's voice is bouncing with emotion.

"I three-wayed us to an office. I got *everybody's* password. *Six* people's passwords!" Mitnick chuckles. "I was laughing."

"What was the office?"

"It was a phone company office. I did them all in a row — I'm very good at convincing people."

"When did you do this?" I ask.

"Two weeks ago."

I can't believe Mitnick's just told me of another one of his recent hacks. I try to not let it show in my voice.

"Who was this guy?"

"It's a new friend."

"He has no idea who you are?" I ask.

"*Nooooooooo* idea!"

.   .   .

The call ends a few minutes later. It's been a bizarre few days. In my mind, I play back the sequence of events.

First, John Markoff, the reporter who put Kevin Mitnick on the front page of the *New York Times,* recommends me to write a story in *Playboy.* Then, the assignment editor at *Playboy,* probably thinking it's the cool thing to do with a cyberspace story, doesn't phone me or write me a letter — he e-mails me. A couple of days later I agree to write the story, and within the hour, this electronic fugitive reads my e-mail and phones me up.

I can see why Mitnick's angry. Plastering his photo in *Playboy* for millions of Americans may impress the hacker's friends, but it's only likely to make it easier for him to get caught. Sure, he knew I was going to write about him in a book. But an article in *Playboy?* Well, that could be out a lot faster, in just a few months. And it might pressure the FBI to step up its efforts.

January 8, 1995

Mitnick phones me again at home on Sunday afternoon, January 8. A little over a week has passed, and he seems to have resigned himself to the prospect of my *Playboy* story, and decided that he might as well cooperate. Mitnick seems suddenly lax on security, not bothering to call me at a pay phone, talking far longer than the few minutes he once told me was all he dared on a line that might be trapped. But I don't bring up the subject. It's none of my business. Only once, last spring, when I put my initial request through to De Payne, have I asked Mitnick to phone me.

I tell him I'm thinking of interviewing a host of players: Mitnick's hacker associates, the old detective agency he worked for in L.A., and the cellular companies he's allegedly hacked. He tells me they may have their own agendas. Mitnick says the detective firm is trying to talk him "into meeting so they can pay me big money on a big case to entrap me. I believe they got scared or something turned them completely because they were afraid for their own skins."

The story about one of the alleged cellular victims is more complicated. "One of the companies accusing me of stealing their cellular software — I saw it on electronic mail, on the Net, so it's no big secret — one of them is Qualcomm out of San Diego. I guess they got hit by a social engineering attack. Somebody called them up and I don't know exactly the details of what was done.

"And so one of the guys there knows Markoff pretty well. And when this whole thing came down, he called Markoff and told Markoff about it because he read the *Cyberpunk* book and the method of attack was exactly like my MO. He called Markoff and then Markoff started his own investigation and that's how the whole thing leaped off."

"Who really was doing the social engineering at Qualcomm?" I ask.

"I'm not going to talk about anything more about that," Mitnick snaps. "I'm just showing you how Markoff got notified, because that's in the last five years."

Why the five-year disclaimer? Did Mitnick have something to do with the Qualcomm attack?

"Now, were they also claiming that something happened in Silicon Valley?" I fish.

"*What* company in Silicon Valley???" Mitnick screeches.

"I don't know."

"I know Qualcomm is one of them because in Tsutomu Shimomura's mail somebody sent him a fucking message that I just saw that says something like, 'I wonder what so and so is up to.' Talking about me. And, 'I'm wondering if he's enjoying the source he stole from Qualcomm.' Something like that. So I go, uh-oh. The son of a bitch, you know, accusing me of stuff. You know, I've already been tried and convicted in their eyes."

What's Mitnick been up to? Has he or one of his cohorts been into Shimomura's e-mail? How could a self-taught hacker like Mitnick break the security of a world-class NSA hacker?

"What about in foreign companies?" I continue. "Is there anything I should look at there?"

"What Neil told me is that Nokia, the biggest cellular manufacturing firm in Europe, their office of federal investigations has been contacting Neil because they're sure that I'd gotten into their systems as well."

"Do you know who that person would be?"

"No. But Neil does. He told me his name but I didn't write it down. It wasn't like I was going to call the guy."

188 THE FUGITIVE GAME

"So when you say 'office of federal investigators,' that's like their FBI?"

"Yeah. Neil told me that they want somebody's ass *really* bad. And they're trying to get the help of a whole bunch of other countries, like the UK and the USA."

"Why would they be trying to get the help of the UK?"

"Apparently after I contacted him [Neil], he contacted all the authorities and the Finland authorities found out I was talking to him in the UK, so they were trying to get the UK's help to find me. He still thinks I'm in the UK right now."

"He knows you're after him!" I joke.

"He's disillusioned," Mitnick says derisively. "The only thing I wanted from him is his bugs and I got them. I *got* what I wanted."

"His what? His bugs?"

"His security holes. This guy has a great talent for finding security holes within the VAX [Digital Equipment Corporation] operating system. And instead of figuring them out myself, I knew he had a whole shitload of them and I successfully got them from him and he was very angry." Mitnick has intercepted Clift's e-mail by electronically impersonating DEC.

"Why was he discovering them?"

"That's what he does for a hobby. He breaks security on VAXs. Figures out the security flaws. Where do bank robbers go? The bank. Well, the holes were with Neil. Where are the UNIX [security] holes? There's three people in the world, well four, that have the UNIX holes. . . ."

. . .

A few minutes later Mitnick says good night for the evening. It was a relatively short call, but I learned quite a bit, especially that parting insight into Mitnick's method.

By his own admisssion, Kevin Mitnick's been swiping security bugs from a talented security expert in England, Neil Clift. He's figured out a shortcut, and isn't that what smart people do? Why read the book if you can steal the Cliff Notes?

Mitnick just swipes the best work from the world's top security experts. It's brazen, it's direct; his goal, after all, isn't to be the world's best programmer. That's for the drones at Microsoft. Mit-nick wants information. And if he's clever enough to target who has the secrets, why plod through the drudgery of the original work?

As usual, Mitnick isn't entirely consistent when it comes to his predicament. He's got a love-hate relationship with his crimes. He panicked when I mentioned rumors that the investigation might spread to Silicon Valley, but then he volunteered that he's apparently the subject of an international manhunt that includes Finland and the United Kingdom. And I thought I heard a little tinge of pride when Mitnick blurted out "they want somebody's ass *really* bad."

But Mitnick's most fascinating disclosure was about the e-mail of the guy from Japan. If Tsutomu Shimomura's a spook for the NSA, as Mitnick claims, how in the world could Mitnick pickpocket his e-mail?

January 17, 1995

Late the morning of Tuesday, January 17, I drive over the Golden Gate Bridge toward the beautiful pastel houses of San Francisco. I've invited John Markoff to lunch to thank him for recommending me for the *Playboy* magazine article.

I meet him at his choice high-rise office. From his desk, Markoff's got an executive view of the San Francisco skyline and the bay. In the five years since we last saw one another, like the best of his generation, he's ridden the high-technology wave to the top.

"Goodfellow suggested a dim sum place," I say, knowing this will intrigue him. Geoffrey Goodfellow is one of Markoff's best sources, an innovator in cellular phones and radio, and a former employee of SRI International who has held high security clearances. The night before, on Martin Luther King Day, I interviewed Goodfellow about Kevin Poulsen. "We had dinner and he said he always eats at the dim sum place when he meets you."

"He's a character," Markoff chuckles about the outspoken Goodfellow, and then agrees with his recommendation. As we walk toward Chinatown, I ask Markoff about his upcoming story on Microsoft's troubled version of Word for the Macintosh. It's well known that Markoff is about to publish a piece on the flawed program, and it's just as well known that Bill Gates himself fears what he may write.

"They really screwed it up!" Markoff exclaims, relishing his role as spoiler to the world's most powerful corporation.

As I pour us some tea, I ask Markoff if he's read a recent hacker book by a *Time* magazine reporter. He did, and he hated it. "He's a phony," Markoff dismisses the featured hacker, and then lashes into the book. For John Markoff, there's only one hacker story worth telling.

Markoff eagerly recounts a few of Mitnick's exploits, chuckling at his most outrageous hacks. We agree that his escapades make for good copy, and I thank him again for his recent recommendation. He shrugs it off. He says he passed on the story because he couldn't figure out what to write. With Mitnick on the run, and no end to his fugitive days in sight, the story had no ending. "So how are you going to tell the story?"

We've been chatting for a good half hour by now. Markoff is smooth and confident. He has sources in the Justice Department and intelligence agencies. If I want some of Markoff's information, I have to share some of mine. That's how journalism works.

Mitnick warned me Markoff has a vendetta, but I haven't bought into his conspiracy theory. Sure, Markoff is obsessed with Mitnick, but he's also a journalist. That's his job. I figure he's already sensed I've had some telephone contact with Mitnick.

"I'd like to tell you something, but I can only tell you if you promise to tell no one. Not the FBI. Not anyone."

"I don't talk to the FBI," Markoff says, agreeing to my conditions.

"Mitnick phoned me a few times last spring," I say, watching Markoff's reaction. "He placed the calls through an elaborate series of people and pay phones. He told me a lot. Then, the calls just stopped."

Markoff's face lights up. He's impressed and intrigued, and he quickly asks more about Mitnick. He's not grilling me. This is, after all, just a friendly chat. I tell him nothing that might be a clue to Mitnick's methods or whereabouts. Instead, I talk more about De Payne. I'm curious to know if Markoff suspects that De Payne may have played some role in some of the hacks for which Mitnick is ultimately blamed. And I warn Markoff that De Payne threatened to slander his ex-wife with personal secrets uncovered through his hacking.

Markoff appreciates the confidence, and seems to agree with my theory about De Payne. Just as I'd hoped, he begins to reveal more. He tells me of an extraordinary deal he cut with Qualcomm, the alleged cellular phone company victim. Franklin Antonio, Qualcomm's head of engineering, told Markoff that he and his employees would only reveal the full story if the *Times* reporter agreed to two conditions. First, that he not publish the company's name. Markoff would later say he agreed not to use the name in an article that he was preparing at the time. Second, that Markoff fly to San Diego and give an hour talk on computer security to the company's employees.

"That was kind of weird," Markoff admits, going on to describe how he flew to San Diego to lecture the employees on how to protect against the Kevin Mitnicks of the world.

The story strikes me as odd. Executives routinely ask reporters to keep their company's name out of a story, though it's not necessarily a fair demand when the same company is accusing an individual of a crime. But trading a security lecture for the inside scoop?

I take another bite of dim sum and Markoff pops out another surprise.

"I've thought about trying to catch Mitnick," Markoff grins. "But I guess that wouldn't be politically correct."

He's almost laughing when he says it, and I almost laugh too. Markoff said the same thing to me last summer just before he catapulted Mitnick onto the front page of the *Times*. I didn't take it seriously then, and I don't take it seriously now.

Markoff's in a good mood, and somehow the topic shifts to Mark Lottor, the indicted hacker and former roommate of Poulsen. Lottor is a cell phone hacker, says Markoff. And a damn good one. Then he smiles. "I wrote a story for *Wired* magazine about cell phone hacking," adding he was careful to use pseudonyms to protect the identity of the story's two principal subjects.

"Mark was one of the people in the article," Markoff confides, enjoying the game. "The other was . . ."

But Markoff changes his mind at the last second, and decides he can't tell me. After all, his article revealed illicit, if not downright illegal acts. That's OK. I've already got a pretty good idea who he's talking about, and I've never even read the article.

We finish our dim sum, and I ask for the check. I reach for my wallet, but it's not there. I rifle my jacket pockets, and nervously glance around the floor. How embarrassing! I take this guy out to lunch to thank him, and now I can't pick up the tab. But Markoff's magnanimous about it. He flips a corporate American Express card on the check. "Don't worry about it," the *Times* reporter assures me. "I'm sure Arthur Sulzburger can cover it."

While we wait, Markoff says he's impressed by my ability to get Kevin Mitnick to call and talk. Mitnick is one of the few prize sources he's missing.

"Do you ever work with anyone else?" Markoff asks.

"Sure," I say, even though it's never actually worked out for me.

"Would you be interested in freelancing pieces with me for the *Times?*"

"Sure."

We're back on the bustling streets below Chinatown, strolling toward the commanding Embarcadero Center towers. Markoff's excited about his idea.

"You know," Markoff says to me as he steps off the curb, "a book on Mitnick's life as a fugitive would be an incredible story."

.   .   .

We're back in the *New York Times* San Francisco bureau in front of John Markoff's big-screen Macintosh. He's pulled up an impressive file on Mitnick, and is graciously letting me jot down a few names: Deputy Cunningham, the U.S. Marshal in Los Angeles tracking Mitnick, and Neil Clift, the computer security expert in England who alerted the FBI to a Mitnick call that they tried, but failed, to trace back to its origin.

It's nearly two in the afternoon. I thank Markoff for the lunch and the contact names and numbers, and as he walks me to the door, I offer him some information in return. "I think Mitnick may be hacking into that secret e-mail account you have with that guy in San Diego."

Markoff looks at me oddly and shrugs off the suggestion. My information is wrong, he says. He [Markoff] doesn't have an account on Tsutomu Shimomura's computer.

That's funny, I think. That's not what Mitnick said.

Morning,
January 19, 1995

t's just two days after my lunch with Markoff and eleven days since my last call from Mitnick. De Payne phoned the previous Friday, and knew all about my assignment with *Playboy*. He asked when the magazine article would be published, and I told him not for several months.

"Oh, good!" he replied stiffly. "That will give us plenty of time to sabotage your efforts."

Apparently, he meant it, because De Payne or somebody else has already begun to play games. Somebody phoned *Playboy*, asked to be paid for a Mitnick interview, and left a call back number that turned out to be disconnected.

At about a quarter to eleven in the morning Mitnick phones.

"I understand somebody's been calling *Playboy* and masquerading as my relatives."

"Who do you think it was?"

"I don't want to say, because he's my *friend*."

"You think he's your friend or you *thought* he was your friend?"

"It's my friend. He's a hoaxter. I don't have time for games!" Mitnick snaps. "I didn't have anything to do with it!

"Hey, I have bad news, man. I don't think I'm gonna be calling you much anymore. The reason is something came out in *U.S. News*

& World Report — a big article on policing cyberspace — and they plaster my name in there as being America's most wanted computer criminal. And a bunch of bullshit claiming I did millions of dollars' worth of damage — *millions,* right?"

Mitnick's pager suddenly blares and he starts cussing. I tell Mitnick that while I was talking to my editor at *Playboy* his phone went dead.

Mitnick breaks into a chuckle. "I think you should phone *Playboy* and say, 'You better *pay* this guy!' "

Then, he's suddenly miffed again. "See, that's the same *fucking thing* that happened to the probation officer. Her phone went dead one day and just because they know me, everyone thinks I have all the time in the world to sit all day —"

"You give me your word? No way?"

"No way! Why would *I* make the phone go *dead?* That would blow my cover. I'd listen and keep my mouth shut so I could negotiate better, right? Because I'd know what the other party's thinking. I wouldn't blow my own cover. That's stupidity! That's exactly the sort of shit that I'm being blamed for.

"Do me a favor. Find out if there's millions of dollars' worth . . . [if] I'm responsible for millions of dollars of losses. Do me a favor and figure that out for me."

All of a sudden, Mitnick sounds panicked. There's an urgency in his voice I've never heard before.

"Hey, listen Jon. Let me call you right back, OK? I gotta go."

.   .   .

He phones back an hour later, still agitated.

"What happened?"

"It was an emergency," Mitnick explains.

"Really?"

"Yeah," Mitnick groans. "Things are *not* good."

It's not going to cheer him up, but I've used the last hour to think about the trouble he may be in. I have no idea what damages the government may be claiming. But my sources have told me that Mitnick's hit a number of companies for the source code to their products, and the FBI even called them together for a meeting to warn them Mitnick was on the loose.

"I've heard Motorola in Arizona," I start. "That's the latest claim I've heard."

"That they got *hit?*" Mitnick asks, incredulous.

"Yeah."

"It's supposedly me, now?" he moans.

"That's the rumor I've heard. Unsubstantiated. Another is a Canadian company, Novatel."

"Oh, that's the kind of cellular phone I have," Mitnick muses, enjoying the irony. "How about that? They got hit?"

"Yeah. So the four I've heard so far are Motorola, Novatel, Nokia, and Qualcomm."

"They claimed over half a dozen," Mitnick adds. "You know Markoff exaggerates. I *never* believe what I read. What are they claiming?"

"I heard they [the FBI] actually had a meeting and warned them [the cell phone companies] that you're out here coming to get them."

"*Wait* a minute! All the cell companies in the world got together?"

"I've heard there was a meeting with our government and some of these companies, and I don't know whether they held up a big dart board–sized picture of you —"

"That's pretty goddamn *serious!* That's *not* funny!" But Mitnick can't resist a joke. "How come they didn't invite me to the meeting?"

"And I guess some of these people claimed to have tapes of you talking."

"That would be interesting," Mitnick ponders.

"And there's supposed to be some investigation in Finland."

"That's Nokia," Mitnick volunteers. "Neil Clift told me. Somebody, he thinks it was me, actually called these people up, had them send a tape, and he wouldn't say where, but they went to deliver the tapes and like an hour later, they got a phone call saying, 'I see your car's in the parking lot —' "

"In other words," I say, "he knew the drop wasn't going to work." But I've missed the point entirely. It was just another prank. Mitnick or somebody else set up law enforcement to watch them chase after a false alarm.

"The whole idea was to fuck with them," Mitnick says, sounding impatient. "It wasn't even to get anything. Do you *see* what I'm saying? In other words, doing it so *sloppy* that you'd know they'd catch on to it. Then when they think they're gonna get their man, they get egg in their face.

"Neil says that's just like me. But if you wanna know the truth, it's more like *other* people."

"Have you tried asking this other person to not do this stuff?" I ask.

"Yeah," Mitnick confides. "I kinda asked the person to stop attracting more attention. I'm already in enough problems. But this person *loves* it, really *loves* it."

"I'm amazed because I was just told something today. I didn't realize he still lives with your ex."

"*No*, he *doesn't!* My ex doesn't live with him anymore."

"But you weren't happy about that to begin with?"

"No! I wasn't happy when, hell, I figured it out.

"We were kinda dating again, and I went to use her bathroom upstairs and I saw the phone bill laying right there on the counter. She was calling Lewis's number hundreds of times. And she never even told me she was talking to Lewis! So I was furious because I didn't know what was going on when I was in Lompoc."

"How long was that after leaving Lompoc?"

"Oh, within five or six months. After I found out, she admitted, 'Oh yes, me and Lewis are dating, blah-blah-blah.' A few months later she moved in with him. I was like bummed at first. Then Lewis said, 'If you ever wanna talk about it with me, you're welcome to.' I just never brought up the subject."

Kevin Mitnick can seemingly hack any computer on the planet, terrify governments, the military, and intelligence agencies. But he can't stand up for himself. He can't tell Lewis De Payne to get lost.

"Obviously, you and Bonnie were very close when you went through Lompoc, the stuff before and then this."

"*Yeah,*" he admits, his voice small. "It was rough. The only reason she's not with me today is she predicted that I'd be in trouble again."

"She predicted it?"

"Yeah! She said that if there was any chance that it could happen again that she couldn't go through that pain again. Just the possibility scared the hell out of her. That's what she told me. I don't know if it was genuine or not."

Life on the run is clearly getting to Mitnick. He's flipping between nostalgia, self-pity, and rage at the world. Cryptically, he explains why he cut short our conversation earlier this morning. Someone's clerical mistake has put him at risk again, and he will have to start all over again with a new job and identity.

"Just one incompetent fool just today fucked me around so bad. I made one request which any normal person would have handled normally, but the person was so stupid and they fucked up so bad that now it's costing me a lot. It's costing me like three grand because I just had to relinquish some —" Mitnick stammers. "For example, let's say a car. Like a person fucks up so bad because they were so stupid, not out of any suspicion, you know, just because they're an *imbecile*. I can't really elaborate. Just put it this way. It fucked up my *whole world*. I was safe and happy. Now I have to —"

"That was just earlier this morning, when you said things aren't going well?"

"There could have been a link established and I can't take a chance of that even happening, so I just have to —"

"Just an innocent, just a bureaucratic thing?" I probe.

"Not bureaucratic. Not a DMV employee. An *idiot* just fucked up my *whole world*! My new world, which is gonna change again anyway. If I told you, you would laugh, but it's things like that that could fuck me up. Things like that if I don't know about it before they happen, could be *disastrous*."

•   •   •

The conversation shifts to Mitnick's overseas opponent, Neil Clift.

"He thinks I'm *evil*," Mitnick says.

I quote Clift talking about Mitnick: " 'Technically, he's not incredible, but he's a very bright guy.' He said, 'The way he told me he does it [social engineering] is he pretends he's an actor in a film and plays it out in advance and becomes that character.' "

"That's *right!*" Mitnick says enthusiastically. "I practice it and it's to the point where I psych myself out that the story I'm portraying is real, so even *I* believe it. So that's how I'm so convincing."

"His [Clift's] girlfriend said he was playing with fire, that he got a kick out of talking to you."

Mitnick sounds almost sentimental. "The only reason I stopped is because I thought it was too risky because he kept calling them [the FBI] every time I called him."

"How did you know?"

"I did a fishing expedition," Mitnick explains. "I said, 'Neil, I'm really getting pissed off! Every time I call you you're telling these people. I wanna know why.'

"The first thing he said was, 'How'd you know?'

" 'Well, *idiot!* I didn't know. You just told me, right?' "

I continue. "He said that you told him you had an advanced degree."

"Economics."

"Economics. A master's?"

"No, just a bachelor's. That's enough," Mitnick snaps, the irritation racheting up in his voice. "That had something to do with this *idiot!*"

"Pardon?" Mitnick seems on the verge of revealing what his fake degree had to do with today's close call, but he says nothing more about it.

"But how do you get a bachelor's?"

"Oh, I can't tell you," Mitnick says coyly. "Four years of *grueling* work!"

"Did it take two hours or twenty hours or three days?"

"All it takes is getting access to the right computer and accessing the database in any college in the world," Mitnick says matter-of-factly. "So figure it out!"

"So it might have taken ten minutes?"

"Yeah, it might have. But actually, when I get in — you gotta look around, see how things are set up."

"Then it's probably more like an hour or two?" I ask.

"I dunno. I hate to reduce it to things," Mitnick jokes gleefully. "I went to school!"

.   .   .

"Do you play chess?" Mitnick asks.

"No."

"You have to look six moves ahead. Because some *idiot* in human resources fucked up, something could come of it. There is a twenty percent chance of trouble," Mitnick pauses for emphasis. "Twenty percent is too high in my business."

"So you don't work in computers?"

"Come on!" Mitnick shouts. "No programming, no systems. But I can create a background of my choosing and it would be verifiable. The only way you verify someone is by writing a letter or by calling a phone. Think of the possibilities. It's pretty easy."

Mitnick could hack into a university computer and create a courseload of specific classes, grades, and a degree, then, just in case he might be detected, forward calls or faxes to one of his lines so he could be his own reference.

"I'd love to get a job with the U.S. Marshals!" Mitnick cries, his voice revving. "I know a flaw that could be discovered, a way to discover people in the witness protection system. A way to discover their identity. It would only take me two days of computer time to find *everybody* under that program. There *is* a way. And no one told me about it either."

.   .   .

The conversation drifts from topic to topic, the hours gliding into the middle of the day. I'm hungry, but Mitnick's feeding me with information. He's lonely, isolated, and just needs someone to talk to. He tells me how simple it is for a fugitive to get lost in New York, how he managed to get an official-sounding AT&T recording of "Thank you for using Kevin Mitnick!" for kicks, and how he can't trust anybody, not even his own mother and father. Today, there's little background noise. Mitnick doesn't sound like he's at work. Could he be at his apartment?

"Which are the most secure systems out there?" I ask the world's most feared hacker. "Are any of them secure?"

"If you're on the Internet, you're in trouble."

"OK. What about CompuServe?"

"No."

"America Online?"

"No."

"But they told me they're secure."

"Why don't you call the Well?" Mitnick snips sarcastically. "You know the Well is secure. Use the Well. You don't like people reading your mail, do you?" Mitnick chuckles. "Why don't you just say, 'Hey, don't read my mail!' "

I ignore the taunt, and ask more about Internet security. "It's funny because one of the larger Internet providers told me, 'No, only those smaller providers have problems. We're perfectly secure. And if you wanna be extra secure, we just won't list you in the directory!' "

"Maybe you should go with Netcom," Mitnick snickers.

It's an inside joke. Netcom is the Internet provider Lewis De Payne uses, and one of Mitnick's many personal cyberspace playgrounds. De Payne told me the government ordered a wiretap on his own Netcom account. So how did De Payne find out? He phoned up Netcom and asked them.

"You don't feel this fear out there?" I ask. "What do you think could be done?"

"I don't know if it's real or not. I guess it's real, because who am I to say how someone else feels? But I think fear is played upon a lot, too."

.   .   .

"Who do you consider to be the cell phone experts in the country?"

"The best cell phone company is Motorola."

"So would the expert be the head of a particular division?"

"Yeah, but they're a victim. . . . You want to get someone that knows a lot. . . . I found out the guy that actually helped Mark Lottor break the Oki phone code was Tsutomu Shimomura, an NSA spook."

"He broke it?"

"They worked on it together, but Mark has no idea that I know it was Tsutomu."

This rings a bell. Something Markoff told me . . .

"You probably read *Wired* magazine, right?" I ask. "They had an article about cell phone hackers and I wonder if that might be Mark? It was written by Markoff."

"He [Markoff] only knows what he's told, and Shimomura is one of his friends, and Shimomura believed I tried to social engineer him once. . . ."

Markoff is a friend of Shimomura? That's news to me, as is this claim that Mitnick tried to social engineer Shimomura. What was he looking for?

"How do you know Shimomura broke it for Mark [Lottor]?"

"I know they worked on the code together. Someone told me that Shimomura has a copy of the broken Oki phone code on his workstation in San Diego. I just heard that through the grapevine," Mitnick states.

"So they broke the Oki phone code together?"

"Yeah. They worked on reverse engineering the Oki phone code together."

"And you heard this from —"

"I know it for one hundred percent positive fact."

"How do you know it one hundred percent —"

"Because this person's very trustworthy."

"And they did this, like, a year ago?"

"Yeah. They've been doing it for like the past couple years, and Mark has been sending Shimomura [code]. Mark modifies the firmware [the memory chips that hold the phone's basic workings]. So you can do things like change your ESN and scan and he has a directory. And apparently he downloads a copy of all he's working on to Shimomura's machine. And apparently, Shimomura wrote the disassembler for Mark that Mark uses. The 8051. He wrote that disassembler."

"The 8051 disassembler?"

"Yep!" Mitnick chimes. "For the 8051 processor . . . and they've worked on it together. So you have a government employee hack[ing] with Lottor, the ex-roommate of the superhacker Poulsen. Boy, I'll bet you can sensationalize something with that, huh?"

Mitnick is saying that Shimomura translated the machine code of the Oki's 8051 chip into understandable assembly language —

words and commands that might enable Lottor and others to decipher and then modify the phone's basic operation. Lottor later confirmed that Shimomura did write the 8051 disassembler.

"It's kind of interesting. What would be the benefit to Shimomura?"

"I don't know."

"Do you know how I can find Shimomura?"

"He doesn't know me personally," Mitnick replies, defensive. "He's a spook. I think he works for the NSA."

Markoff told me the same basic story at lunch. That Shimomura works for the intelligence agency.

"What's the company he's with in San Diego?"

"UCSD," Mitnick answers.

"And he's definitely a smart guy?"

"I would think so."

•   •   •

"How much time do you think this Shimomura spent talking to Lottor or working on this stuff?"

"Oh — a year or two."

"So he would have spent weeks on it?"

"Oh yeah!" Mitnick chuckles. "He's been a busy beaver there."

"And Shimomura, of course, knows all about Lottor's problems with the other arm of his employer?" I'm referring to the federal hacking indictment against Lottor and Kevin Poulsen.

"Yeah! Interesting, huh?"

"But who is Shimomura's official employer?"

"I dunno. He's easy to get ahold of. Hold on, I'll get his number for you. Where's my file?"

"You mentioned Los Alamos," I continue, trying to draw out more information, "but is that Shimomura's official or unofficial employer?"

"Hold on a minute. Where's his file? Hold on a second. Here's my Shimomura file, it's right next to my Littman file!" Mitnick teases. "Where's his phone number? Oh, here it is!"

He's probably just kidding, but it does make me wonder. What does Kevin Mitnick really know about my private life? "So how much do you know about me? You must know a little about me, right?"

"Just what you tell me," Mitnick says.

"Honest to God?"

"I just know what you have told me, seriously. OK, here's his phone number. I don't know if it's listed or not, 619 area code, 259-65XX. And his work number is 619-534-50XX."

Mitnick's got Shimomura's home number. And something tells me it's not listed in the phone book.

"OK. Thanks."

"You want his mom's number?"

"You've got his mom's number?"

"Yeah. But I'm sure he's not gonna be at his mom's house."

I don't ask for Shimomura's mother's number.

"OK, I'll take it that you don't know anything about me. You don't know that I've got a . . ."

"As far as I know, you could be a federal agent," Mitnick drones in a flat, emotionless voice. "That's interesting," Mitnick muses. "I think I found his [Shimomura's] beeper number. I don't know if it's his beeper number. Should we call it?"

"No. I don't wanna spook a spook," I say nervously. "It's probably not a good idea. He's one person I wouldn't want to mess with. He probably has friends."

Mitnick's not listening. He's still reading his secret files.

"Here's Mark Lottor's cell phone number. That's interesting!"

.   .   .

The hacker has put on a pretty impressive display. In a couple of minutes, Mitnick has offered evidence that he can invade nearly anyone's privacy, even the privacy of a world-renowned government hacker. He's also provided me with the perfect setup for my question about fear and privacy in the information age.

"The average Joe would think that you do this all the time — that you know everything about everybody. And somebody you knew from a past life said, 'Do you know what you're getting into? You and your friend [De Payne] will make my life miserable for years and years.' How do you respond to that?"

"I have to know who you're talking about," Mitnick says carefully. "That's the problem."

What Mitnick is really saying is he wants to know which of his enemies issued this warning.

"I can't tell you," I tell Mitnick. "But when people say things like that, I think it has to do with our modern world. If somebody wants to cause problems for somebody, they can obviously do it remotely from thousands of miles away in an untraceable fashion. You're not breaking somebody's leg or physically hurting them, but you can certainly irritate them and cost them some time and even money. It costs money to fix phones that are disconnected or accounts that are closed."

"Accounts that are closed," Mitnick repeats, his voice pitching higher. "Yes, it does!"

"It does."

"Houses that get moved!" Mitnick whoops. "You go on vacation and when you get back, all you have is an empty lot!"

Mitnick can't stop laughing. I am too, but listening to Mitnick in stitches, I can't help but wonder if he's ever actually pulled off this incredible prank. I ask him.

"My other friend would do it in a second if he had the capability. He would do it in a second! I can say the word "go" and there would be like twenty people he would do it to. That's cold. I would never do that. Some people he messes with, I approve of. Some I just say, 'Ah, have fun at it.' Who am I to judge?"

"What do you think about the fear out there that our world has changed?"

"Yeah . . . That's why they're instilling fear of the unknown. That's why they're scared of me. Not because of what I've done, but because I have the capability to wreak havoc."

Afternoon,
January 19, 1995

I try to make sense of Mitnick's rambling calls: his anger at *U.S. News & World Report* for dubbing him the world's most wanted hacker, his sudden declaration that it's gotten too dangerous to phone me, and then, what sounded like a crisis. That was strange, talking to Mitnick at the very moment he learned his freedom may be in jeopardy.

I also heard more proof of something I've long suspected, a tight web of betrayal and denial that binds Lewis De Payne and Kevin Mitnick. Why won't the world's most feared hacker confront his old friend? At first, I chalked it up to to denial, but it's more than that. De Payne must know too many of Mitnick's crimes, including ones the authorities haven't caught on to. Perhaps Mitnick won't confront De Payne because he doesn't trust him.

To the public, Mitnick's a dark wizard of high tech, toying with the FBI and major corporations. But the Mitnick I know is also a lonely fugitive looking for somebody to talk to. Mitnick clearly doesn't know what's good for him. He keeps confiding in an old friend who gets his kicks out of putting him at greater risk, and now he's taking another leap of faith, talking to me, a journalist. Mitnick is no genius, but to me, that only heightens the dangers he symbolizes. If Kevin Mitnick can threaten the information superhighway, then what does that say about who else may be threatening our electronic world?

Just now Mitnick boasted he could hack the federal witness protection program. If I were a former mob guy in the program and Kevin Mitnick hacked for the Mafia, I wouldn't feel too safe right now. It's a system, like any other system, and Kevin Mitnick understands how computers and people work. Mitnick's told me that the security claims of nearly every major Internet provider are an illusion. I know firsthand that at least part of that claim is true. Why might not Mitnick and other hackers be capable of far greater intrusions?

Still, I can't take anything Mitnick says at face value. He flaunts his social engineering abilities, and there's no reason I shouldn't be a prime target. He's constantly trying to diminish his crimes and exaggerate those of his enemies. But while I think Mitnick's a greater danger to the public than he would have me believe, I suspect there's some truth to what he says about his enemies. This morning, he hinted that his NSA hacker nemesis isn't one of the good guys. Mitnick claims Shimomura helped write the OKI phone code that Mitnick swiped from Lottor last fall. He's linking Shimomura to Lottor, a hacker under federal indictment.

But why would Shimomura flirt with the law and collaborate with an indicted hacker? And how does Mitnick know so much about Shimomura? Like his work number, his home number, his mom's number.

What other Shimomura secrets does Kevin Mitnick have up his sleeve?

·   ·   ·

The phone rings again, as it often does around 1:30 P.M. any day except Sunday. It's the time hackers in jail are in the mood to chat.

Today, the automated Sprint operator is offering a collect call from Kevin Poulsen at Mitnick's old haunt, the Los Angeles Metropolitan Detention Center. Poulsen's working on his fourth year behind bars, and he's still facing another federal case. He sounds optimistic, and frankly I don't understand. Because he's been awaiting trial, Poulsen's never enjoyed a federal camp like the Ivan

Boeskys and Michael Milkens of the 1980s. Kevin Poulsen's four years in the 1990s have been hard time. He hasn't studied anything, worked on a degree, or picked up a hobby. He smokes, reads a lot, and beats everyone at Ping-Pong and chess. He has no plans because he can't survive inside dreaming about the future when he doesn't know if he's got one.

The light is already fading outside when the phone rings again. "Sorry," says Mitnick, as if there hadn't been a two-hour gap in our conversation. "I had to reroute my communications. I'm going to have to give two weeks' notice just because of someone's *stupidity!*"

If this is true, Mitnick is a remarkable hacker. Not only does he work for a living when he's a fugitive, but he gives two weeks' notice like a responsible employee.

"So before we got cut off, I said I guess you don't like me reading your mail."

I say nothing.

"You're asking me about privacy? The only way to obtain privacy is PGP [Pretty Good Privacy, a publicly available, powerful, non-government form of encryption]. But you better not use PGP on the host, you better use it on your home system. All these idiots! They put their workstations on the Internet, and then they run their PGP software on their UNIX box, right, and I just backdoor PGP, so it stores their pass phrase somewhere."

Mitnick is saying that many people are just asking for hackers on the Internet to backdoor their copies of PGP and swipe their secret PGP keys. He's right. If they simply kept their PGP software and keys on a machine not connected to the Internet, their encrypted files would be a lot safer.

"What's that crunching sound on the line? What are you snacking on?

"Caviar!" Mitnick declares with flourish.

"I'm eating caviar crunches and running your credit report."

I ignore the comment. "Let me ask you this —"

"If you don't write a *good* article, you're going to be *history*."

I laugh. Mitnick laughs. Did he just threaten me?

"I'm just kidding," Mitnick quickly adds, becoming serious. "I don't want to influence the way you write your story."

"If somebody wanted to protect themselves from cyberspace intrusions, what would you suggest they do?"

"Where people get hurt is their money," Mitnick says with authority. "If you hurt their credit profile, it's a bitch to straighten out. A way to protect yourself? It's hard if they mess with your credit."

"You mean I couldn't call up TRW [the national credit reporting company] and say, 'I write about hackers, and who knows, one of them might not like me one day?' "

"They're [TRW] secure, *very* secure," Mitnick snickers. "You can call TRW up and ask them how to run credit reports and they don't even ask who you are."

I laugh.

"You don't believe me," Mitnick snaps.

"No, I *do* believe you! What about your bank account?"

"The bank is vulnerable. I remember somebody who worked at a private investigation company," Mitnick recalls, referring obliquely to himself. "They used to track down accounts. The clients would give them paperwork, say a lease on property. Then you'd get a bank in Canada that wouldn't tell you anything. So then this person went to the Xerox machine with a letter of release. He photocopied the person's signature onto the letter of release and faxed it. This guy accepted the signed letter from this person, saying, 'Please release my bank records.' It worked like a charm," Mitnick chuckles. "If they accept it over electronic media you're in trouble. . . ."

Mitnick's reliving the excitement, talking faster.

"They can send letters to your mortgage company that say 'Fuck you.' They can send letters to your creditors, letters to all your business relationships, saying, 'You're fucked. I'm *not* paying you.' All these creditors start doing foreclosures. You can imagine the *headaches*. Everything is phone, mail, or signature."

"What about somebody trying to get access to funds in Bank of America?"

"That's where they're worried," Mitnick says, never revealing exactly who *they* are. "I was going to work in wholesale banking. I would have been in charge of securing their wholesale banking networking. An executive let me look through their manuals." He laughs heartily. "I think they thought that was a mistake."

Mitnick flushes the toilet.

"Who was that?" I ask, referring to the bank executive.

"Sandy. One of the past presidents of information security, Security Pacific."

Now I can hear Mitnick tapping away on his keyboard.

"You're logging in while we're speaking. You're multiprocessing?"

"I'm reading your e-mail," Mitnick teases.

"It's probably pretty boring today. So what were you going to do at the bank?"

"I was going to be writing policies, I was learning about banking security systems."

"So you would eventually have been doing security?"

"They were hiring me into the information security department as a security analyst. I told Lenny [an old accomplice] if I get the job I'm not going to hack anymore. I met the president, Ed, the president of the area," Mitnick recalls nostalgically. "Three interviews. Then, she [Sandy, the president of information security] called me."

Mitnick, half laughing, mimicks how the bank vice president asked him if he had ever "dug in anyone's garbage cans." Mitnick says he joked that was only when he was "looking for food." An hour later personnel called and told him his references didn't check out.

The incident happened years ago, but Mitnick's bitterness makes it sound like yesterday. "Lewis was one of the references, but they were all legit. On the application I marked 'never convicted.' I was not convicted in the Santa Cruz case! All the juvenile stuff was sealed. I didn't lie! It was sealed. When it is sealed you can legally answer no."

.   .   .

"So what can I do to protect my credit? Can I ask TRW to do anything?"

"There's a service. It's called "Protect My Friend Service," Mitnick chuckles. "You pay me a certain fee per month and I make sure nobody causes you problems."

"Is this the Capone program?"

"Yeah. It's a new program. It was developed throughout the years to protect stores and stuff, and now we're going into the computer age."

Mitnick can't stop laughing. I can't either.

"I think you really need this service!" Mitnick howls.

"So what sort of services are provided?"

Mitnick catches himself, holding back the laughter. "Don't print *that* shit because someone's actually going to believe it!"

"There's nothing I can do, huh?" I say. "I can't call up TRW —"

"Protect it? No. It's already protected," Mitnick says facetiously.

"What would have to happen for there to be better protection for the average —"

"The CEOs of these companies to get fucked *themselves*," Mitnick thunders. "Somebody that counts. But you can install the best security system there is and someone can find a way through. There is no way. Just make it harder, so they go to the next guy.

"Seriously, if you wrote anything bad . . . I don't want to prejudice you in any way." Mitnick reassures me. "I would never attack you. *Unless* . . ."

"Unless?"

Mitnick's voice is icy. "Unless you set me up so that I'd make calls and everything."

"I don't play that game."

"And you're working for the government, coaxing me to call you."

"I don't play that."

"I don't think you're doing it. I don't wanna taint your story. I don't have enough time to mess with people because my own life is too messed up," Mitnick grumbles.

This is supposed to put me at ease? Kevin Mitnick won't hack me because he doesn't have the time.

"But somebody else does," I counter, thinking about his alter ego.

"I have a friend, all right. You know those little flyer cards that come in the mail?" Mitnick begins, absorbed in his story. "You fill it out and you get junk mail? This guy, I swear to God, spent a week just printing out labels [with the address of a person he disliked] and sticking them on these cards. So their mailboxes at work, home, their parents' house, were just *flooded* — flooded with mail of companies sending *mail, mail, mail.* Like on the Internet, you know how you could flood someone's mailbox?"

"The same thing?"

"The same thing. Talking about so much mail that it would be work to find out where your real mail is. They could make this junk mail look like a pay to the order of your name. You would open that up, right? I mean this guy is dedicated."

"On the Net, he's known as —?"

"Yeah, he's using my name. My name is trouble. If he puts my name in lights, he has nothing to lose. I don't dislike him at all. I'm just saying it's worked its way out over the years so a lot of the shit he's done, people think I've done.

"He'll say, 'This guy on Netcom, I want to know where he works and how much he made for the last five years, and if he's married and how much is in his bank.'

"I'll say, 'OK, I'll run that one, too.' So he uses that ammunition to fuck with people."

"What do you feel about that?"

"They think it's him. I don't care. It's not *my* battle. It's *nothing.* You're not releasing somebody's *personal* diary. You worked at Apple Computers and you made 22,406 dollars and 12 cents."

So this is how Mitnick justifies his role in De Payne's campaign of info harassment. If Mitnick can get information, he figures it's not really personal. I'm not surprised by the amoral techno logic. Hackers don't get to be hackers by worrying about rules or by respecting privacy.

"Then he likes to project, 'This is what I'm telling you. Can you imagine if I know *this* how much I *really* know?'" Mitnick continues, amused. "In other words, bluffing. That way, people get scared of him. When people are scared of you, that's *power.*"

"You think it's a power thing for him?"

"The power over somebody?" Mitnick considers. "I think so. He likes to watch people get unglued when he can tell them all about them, personal shit. I'm the one that obtains the information for him, though, and he just uses it."

"Do you think it's wrong?"

"No, I don't see anything wrong with it! I don't see anything wrong with him doing it. I could care less! It's not really hurting anyone. He's just agitating people. It's not like he's giving people's credit card numbers out and people are gonna get financially hurt. It's like walking in a bar and saying, 'Fuck you!' "

"It's just without fists."

"Yeah, right. What are you gonna do?" Mitnick laughs haughtily. "Turn off your computer?"

.   .   .

Mitnick doesn't read many books, but he loves movies.

"The one I like is *Three Days of the Condor*," I say.

Mitnick sounds suspicious. "That's supposed to be my favorite film, remember?"

"It's a good film," I say.

"And then the fucking media twisted it around," Mitnick booms. " 'Oh! This is *really* the reason why he picked the Condor. Because condor is a *vulture* and he's a vulture.' "

"What did you like about the movie?"

"Well, the technical stuff, and he plays a slick guy. He was able to get himself out of a bind when the powers that be had something hanging over his head. They wanted him killed."

"The powers that be weren't good guys."

"No, they were evil government bureaucrats."

"Evil CIA factions, actually."

"Yeah, CIA within the CIA. That's one thing I never try to do is get in the military computers because if you find out something you're not supposed to know, I don't think they would have any problem killing you.

"That's why I'm surprised Poulsen actually went into that shit because that's something I have the capability of doing but I wouldn't even *cross* that boundary because when you start fucking the military, they take that *real* serious. . . ."

Night,
January 19, 1995

It's about 5:30 P.M. when Mitnick hangs up to answer his pager. I haven't been outside all day, and night is already falling. All the talking has given me a big appetite.

The phone starts ringing again. Something tells me it's Mitnick.

"You want some calamari?" I greet the caller.

"Yeah," Mitnick says.

"With tomato sauce? A few mushrooms?"

"That sounds good. Hey, did you ever eat in Chicago in a place called Gino's Eats?" Mitnick asks.

"No."

"It's on Michigan Avenue. The best pizza I've ever had. I was actually there about two days ago on business."

"Really?"

It's the first time Mitnick has hinted at his whereabouts. It seems too spontaneous to be a test. But then who knows.

"Yeah," says Mitnick.

"It must be freezing there!"

"Dude, I was walking down the street and the wind — I never felt such cold wind in my life. My head felt so cold that, oh man, it's hard to describe that wind."

So Kevin Mitnick was in the Windy City just two days ago. Or he's playing with me and anyone who happens to be listening in.

.　　　.　　　.

"Do you cook?"

"Nah. I go out to eat all the time. 'Cuz I'm always traveling."

Another hint. Does Mitnick's job keep him on the road or is this just his life as a cyberfugitive?

"Do you date women that cook?"

"Yeah. This one gal was into making Thai food, and I really like Thai food."

"So I'm gonna ask you another silly question since you're a world-famous cyberperson. What do you look for in a woman?"

"Well, that's a new one," Mitnick chuckles. "I like her to be pretty, number one. And have a pretty good mind. Someone you could actually talk with. You know, I wouldn't date someone like the blond in *Married with Children*." Mitnick laughs again.

"Somebody that would stick by me through thick and thin. But I'm kinda a hard guy to stick by.

"I like 'em to be *really* beautiful. I mean I wouldn't date any big two-hundred-pound gal. She wouldn't turn me on. You know how *we* are. We go by looks."

"You mean the male species?"

"Yeah. We go by looks, number one."

"How about women?"

"I think they do it by feelings. Like Bonnie. I was really fat and ugly. And you know, we got together and she was pretty beautiful, so . . ."

"What was it like for you to have a beautiful woman attracted to you?"

"It made me feel good," Mitnick brightens, then sighs at the memory. "She was always on me to lose weight and stuff, to get into exercise. I was too busy with my hacking. I mean this overconsuming hobby kinda screwed up my life."

"Some people have tried to portray you as not having the normal sides of your life that most people have —"

"I'm like everybody else," Mitnick cuts in angrily.

"As a cyberman, how do you find women?"

"Well, I send them messages on their computer screens," Mitnick jokes.

"Do you tell them, 'I'm the most famous hacker in the world'?"

The idea annoys Mitnick. "No. I don't tell them anything about that. Hold on a second. I'm looking for a battery pack. Hold on a second. Doo, doo, doo. Where did it go?"

I can hear Mitnick tromping around in what must be his apartment. He sounds like a big, oafish guy. That's what I'm imagining anyway.

"Hope I didn't lose one of my eighty-dollar battery packs," he grumbles.

Everything has a price to Mitnick. Probably because money means freedom. Probably because he's never made much of it.

"OK. Sorry about that," Mitnick apologizes for the interruption. The battery's still lost.

"So you see someone in a supermarket and you —"

Mitnick laughs. "I just say, 'Hey, I'm the greatest lay and the greatest hacker in the world.' "

"What more could you ask for?" I joke.

"Yeah. Well, I'm not a Don Juan. I just meet 'em and if I'm interested get their phone number. Like there's one gal I met but she was only nineteen."

"And how'd you meet her?"

"Actually, waiting for a doctor. I said, 'Hi,' and, of course, they ask 'What do you do for a living', and I tell them I'm a private investigator. You tell 'em that, and they're 'Oh, I always wanted to do that. Can you find out anything on me?'

" 'What do you want me to find out? I can find out all I want about you from you just telling me.' They laugh. You always get 'em to laugh," Mitnick explains. "It's a numbers game. You know, you're gonna get one for every ten you ask out, pretty much."

"This is what's interesting. Your public image is a nerd," I counter.

"Of course I wear my pocket protector," Mitnick stresses in a serious tone.

"And you would never think that you ever talked to ten women your whole life, right?"

"Well, they don't know me," Mitnick angrily snaps. "Markoff doesn't know me. I wouldn't even talk to the guy."

·   ·   ·

"So you talked to this woman in the doctor's office."

"She was pretty young was the problem, really. You can tell if someone's interested 'cuz, you know, body language. It's all in the game. You gotta strike something with the person. Then you start out as friends and go on dates and take it from there. I don't have a script. It's not like I'm doing a social engineering attack."

The computer arena is another matter.

"I sometimes do social engineering if it's a hack attack," Mitnick begins, switching to his favorite pursuit. "I'll just be driving in the car and think, hey, I wonder if they'll fall for it? I'll just pick up the phone and just do it. Just take no thinking or no planning. I mean, some of the most *interesting* places have been looked into that way. It's like I'll call this division and see if there's an idiot there and blah-blah-blah."

By now, we've talked long enough for me to know that "idiot" is one of Mitnick's favorite words. An idiot is a mark, someone fooled by one of Mitnick's cons, and he spits out the word with a mixture of contempt and glee.

"I'm in the car and I'm getting all this information, and I'm thinking, 'Could you hold on a second?' " Mitnick chuckles. "I've gotta pull over near a gas station and get a pen. So the guy thinks I'm in some executive office instead of a piece of shit car going down the road. He has no idea! If he only knew!"

"And who are you when this happens?"

"Could be *anybody*," Mitnick sidesteps. "It depends on what I'm doing."

"Is that fun to be anybody?"

"Yeah, pretty cool," he confides.

"So you've got a cute girl and things are fine but —"

"I can't tell her anything about who I really am. Rule number one, trust no one. It's like that poster of the Puppetmasters, you know, *trust no one*. I always think about that and it's true."

"What do you feel then when you start to feel close to someone but you know you're in this bind?"

"Well, I just put it out of my mind that I'm in the bind and psych myself out like it's not there. And it doesn't exist and therefore there's nothing to talk about 'cuz no problem exists.

"So I can settle down and get married, but [first] I'd break my ties with everybody for a couple years to make sure I'm safe. 'Cuz I'd hate to get married, and all of a sudden everything comes down and she's all pissed off 'cuz I lied. But you know I can't trust anybody. I'll never ever tell my spouse who I am."

"Even if you broke the ties before?"

"I can't," Mitnick insists. "I can't, 'cuz you can't trust 'em. You can't trust anybody."

"Even if you decided this is the woman to spend the rest of your life with?"

"No. A wife is not like your mother or your father or your grandmother or your grandfather. A wife could always come and go. Family, your parents, never come and go. "

.   ■   ■

"Trust no one," Mitnick utters like a mantra.

"Do you think that's the world we're headed toward?"

"No. It's my world. It's an unfortunate world, but it's better than being in jail. Why would I have to ever bring it up? What's important is the future. Shoot, we're only here a maximum seventy, eighty years, and I'm thirty-one. Who wants to spend it in custody with a bunch of assholes? It doesn't do me any good. What are they gonna do, keep you off the streets so you can't hack for a while?"

This is what Eric said a few weeks before he was captured.

"Have you ever wondered why they can't figure out a way to take people with your talents and supervise you and have you fix things?"

"I dunno," Mitnick mumbles, dubious of the idea. "I think they tried that with Poulsen, didn't they?"

"Almost but not quite."

"I thought he was damn lucky to get a job with SRI [SRI International, a think tank and defense contractor in Menlo Park, California]. If I got a job at that bank [Security Pacific], I wouldn't be here now. I'd probably be rich. I'd probably be driving my Mercedes on the 405 [freeway]."

Mitnick starts to say good night. "I just wanted to let you know about that *U.S. News & World Report*."

"This week's edition?"

"Yep. I'm walking by the newsstand and there's this big badge and it says 'Cybercop.' I start going *whoa!* A new movie! And then I read it's an article on Internet security and how these companies on the Internet had better watch themselves. . . . It said the worst guy in the world is blah-blah-blah," Mitnick recalls.

"Well, at least you're at the top of your profession."

"Yeah. I mean I'd like to be rich and be famous one day. It's not nice to be infamous, but to be famous would be nice," Mitnick reflects. "I've made my mark in history. Now I need the money to go with it."

.   ■   ■

"Here's an Italian place! I think I'll eat here," Mitnick exclaims, sounding like he's driving past a restaurant. "I hope it's not too expensive."

"I didn't even hear the car."

"HONK!"

"You hear the horn?" Mitnick chuckles like a kid. "It's a real car."

"Why's the connection so good?"

" 'Cuz I have it routed. No, I dunno. I guess the high bills I pay on my cellular phone, I deserve a good connection."

"You're gonna love this," I tell Mitnick. "I was just talking to this guy . . . he doesn't like hackers, and he told me, in China, if you have someone else's ESN, guess what the penalty is?"

"Death," Mitnick replies.

■   ■   ■

"I had to go on business like six months ago, flying to D.C.," Mitnick begins, his voice bubbling with excitement. "So I actually went on the White House tour."

"You're kidding?"

"No! Could you imagine, all these Secret Service agents?" Mitnick chuckles at the irony. One of the Secret Service's jobs is to catch hackers. "They're in uniforms. It's weird they're not in like suits."

"So Cyberman goes to the —"

"The White House, dude."

"I wanted to get some pictures taken, but I decided that was a bad idea.

"They didn't have much security," Mitnick observes. "Little did they know I was there to get into WhiteHouse.gov," Mitnick chortles, referring to Clinton's Internet site address. " 'Hello, I just wanna see the computer room, guys.' "

"They're on the Net, right?"

"WhiteHouse.gov. That's one that's secure," Mitnick deadpans. "I'm just kidding. Any computer is insecure unless you're military."

.   .   .

A day in the life of a cyberfugitive. Five hours of conversation in a single day, his moods as fleeting as his erratic cellular calls, so much time that I feel as if I've been following him around. The long calls provide clues, too; that is if they aren't just misinformation. Hints that Mitnick recently visited Chicago and, incredibly, the White House. More than anything, the calls convince me Mitnick is on edge. He told me in the morning he wouldn't be calling anymore now that his name had been plastered in *U.S. News & World Report* as the nation's most wanted hacker. But instead of silence, the warning spawned an endless verbal stream of consciousness.

Talking to Mitnick is like trying to tell when a double agent is telling the truth. And his parting comment about military computers being secure just makes me wonder. Is he telling me they aren't safe? That he's hacked military computers, too?

The hacker's given me no reason to believe anything is off-limits. Mitnick doesn't see anything wrong with invading people's privacy because he doesn't see computer information as private. He's blind to his key role in De Payne's harassment program. Does Kevin Mitnick have a conscience? I'm really not sure. He sees himself in almost mechanical terms. Mitnick just supplies the information, he doesn't *do* anything. I remember the anger and denial in his voice when I confronted him about his role in the harassment.

Now I have a different theory about Kevin Mitnick and Lewis De Payne. Perhaps, in the pop psychology of the nineties, they're co-dependents. The hacker doesn't tell his friend to get lost because on the anonymous Internet they're electronically linked, two sides of the same schizophrenic.

A network version of Dr. Jekyll and Mr. Hyde.

Morning,
January 20, 1995

"**S**o apparently some guy broke into his workstation."

Kevin Mitnick's on the phone, chuckling, telling me about what sounds like the hacker break-in of the year. Somebody's hacked the home computer of Tsutomu Shimomura, the Internet security expert Mitnick is convinced is an NSA spook bent on putting him behind bars.

It's the morning of January 20, 1995. And you won't find this news in the papers.

"He's pretty upset," Mitnick chortles. "They're actually putting out a big CERT advisory."

"A CERT advisory?" CERT is the Computer Emergency Response Team, a federally funded team of computer security experts, headquartered at Carnegie Mellon University.

Mitnick's beside himself, his voice the same high-pitched frenzy as after he'd hacked Shimomura's friend, Mark Lottor. But this time Mitnick describes himself as just a spectator.

"That means they actually held a press conference because the way he was attacked was so sophisticated that no way could anyone on the Internet protect themselves," Mitnick says with what sounds like pride.

This is strange. There hasn't been a report of a press conference. Who or what could Mitnick be talking about?

"But no one knows about the CERT advisory yet," he advises. "It won't be released until tomorrow. So he's not a happy camper."

This doesn't add up. CERT never releases advance information of its security advisories. Even when it e-mails international CERT groups it encrypts the messages. So how could Mitnick have found out in advance? By snooping on Shimomura's e-mail, or Markoff's? Or wiretapping their phone calls?

"What was so sophisticated about it?"

"They did it through a TCP/IP prediction packet attack."

"A TCP/IP prediction packet attack?" I ask, not having the slightest idea what he's talking about.

"Each packet has a sequence number," Mitnick explains, slowing down for my benefit. "If you can predict the sequence number, there's a way to impersonate a packet coming from any host. You have the packet look like it's coming from your internal network or a trusted host.

"The person [intruder] realized that he was being logged. In other words that he [Shimomura] was logging all his [the intruder's] TCP/IP traffic through a TCP/IP dump, but he [the intruder] didn't realize until recently that he [Shimomura] was e-mailing out to another site all his logs on a constant interval. And that's how he [Shimomura] was able to determine how the attack occurred."

Mitnick seems to know a lot about the intricate details of the attack.

"You say they had a press conference, what, this morning?"

I can hear a car honking in the background. Mitnick sounds like he's outside.

"I don't know," Mitnick replies vaguely. "Within the last few days."

But there was no CERT press conference. Could he be talking about a "private" press briefing?

.   .   .

Three days later, on January 23, Shimomura will describe the attack in a widely distributed public Internet post. IP source address spoofing and TCP/IP sequence number prediction are the technical terms Shimomura uses to describe it, much like Mitnick's description. But his analysis is extremely technical, and even some UNIX security experts find it tough going.

That same day, about 2 P.M., CERT will blast out an advisory to its international mailing list of 12,000 Internet sites in the United States, Germany, Australia, the United Kingdom, Japan, and other countries. The vaguely worded report is much less specific than Mitnick's one-minute explanation on the telephone. Most likely, CERT is trying to provide enough detail so Internet sites can protect themselves against future attacks without providing so much detail that it could encourage copycat attacks.

On one level, the hack is simple, a clever strike at a basic weakness of the Internet. Computers on the Internet are often programmed to trust other computers. The Internet was created to share information, and the attack on Shimomura, just like the Robert Morris Internet Worm attack seven years before, exploits that trust.

The Internet has its own way of sending e-mail or files. Messages or files are split into smaller digital chunks or packets, each with its own envelope and address. When each message is sent, it's like a flock of birds that migrates to a planned location and reunites as a flock at the destination. Computers on the Internet often act like great flocks of birds that trust one another too. And all it takes is one enemy bird to infiltrate the flock.

.   .   .

On Christmas Day 1994 the attack begins.

First, the intruder breaks into a California Internet site that bears the cryptic name toad.com. Working from this machine, the intruder issues seven commands to see who's logged on to Shimomura's workstation, and if he's sharing files with other machines. Finger is one of the common UNIX commands the intruder uses to probe Shimomura's machine. As a security professional Shimomura should have disabled the feature. Finger is so commonly used by hackers to begin attacks that 75 percent of Internet sites, or about 15 million of the more than 20 million Internet users, block its function to increase security.

The intruder's making judgment calls on the fly about which

commands will help him uncover which machines Shimomura's workstation might trust. He works fast. In six minutes he deduces the pattern of trust between Shimomura's UNIX workstation and an unknown Internet server.

Then the automatic spoofing attack begins. It will all be over in sixteen seconds. The prediction packet attack program fires off a flurry of packets to busy out the trusted Internet server so it can't respond. Next, the program sends twenty more packets to Shimomura's UNIX workstation.

The program is looking for a pattern in the initial sequence numbers — the numbers used to acknowledge receipt of data during communications. The program deciphers the returned packets by subtracting each sequence number from the previous one. It notes that each new initial sequence number has grown by exactly 128,000. The program has unlocked the sequence number key.

Shimomura's machine has to be idle for the attack to succeed. New Internet connections would change the initial sequence number and make it more difficult to predict the key. That's why the hacker attacks on Christmas Day.

The attack program sends packets that appear to be coming from the trusted machine. The packet's return or source address is the trusted machine's Internet address. Shimomura's workstation sends a packet back to the trusted machine with its initial sequence number. But flooded by the earlier flurry of packets, the trusted server is still trying to handle the earlier traffic. It's tangled up.

Taking advantage of the gagged server, the attacking program sends a fake acknowledgment. It looks real because it's got the source address of the trusted server, and the correct initial sequence number. Shimomura's workstation is duped. It believes it's communicating with a trusted server.

Now the attacking program tells Shimomura's obedient workstation to trust everyone. It issues the simple UNIX "Echo" command to instruct Shimomura's workstation to trust the entire Internet. At that point, Shimomura's personal and government files are open game to the world. It's more than a humiliating blow to the security expert. By making Shimomura's machine accessible from any Internet site, the intruder has masked his own location. He can return from anywhere.

The hacker can't believe his good luck. The attack is only successful because Shimomura has not disabled the "R" commands, three basic commands that allow users to remotely log-in or execute programs without a password. Tens of thousands of security-conscious Internet sites, representing well over a million users, routinely block access to the R commands to avoid its well publicized abuse by hackers.

It takes a few keystrokes and about thirty seconds to shut off the R commands on an Internet server. You don't even have to turn off the machine.

Why didn't Shimomura do it?

.   ■   ■

Mitnick laughs. "He's [Shimomura's] not happy. I have nothing to do with it. I'm just telling you what I hear through the grapevine."

"Who do you think might have done it?" I ask the likely suspect. "How did he figure it out himself?"

"He [Shimomura] realized that somebody had edited his wrapper log, which shows incoming connections. Somebody actually modified those logs, and then he was able to reconstruct what happened through these logs that were mailed to another site unbeknownst to the intruder."

Mitnick's actually telling me the evidence Shimomura collected to figure out the attack. The wrapper is supposed to control connections to Shimomura's server and log all connection attempts. It failed to protect Shimomura but still it logged the hacker's spoofed connection, and a copy of the log was e-mailed off-site.

"So you were asking me if there's a secure e-mail site?" Mitnick continues, his voice suddenly hard. "My answer is no. This guy in my estimation is the brightest in security on the whole Internet. He blows people like Neil Clift away. I have a lot of respect for this guy. 'Cuz I know a lot about him. He doesn't know anything about me, hopefully, but he's good."

"On the Internet, he's one of the best in the world."

"So if this guy isn't safe, what does that mean?" I ask.

"I dunno. Go back to manual systems," Mitnick jokes. "Instead of Excel, you should go back to paper."

.   .   .

Mitnick doesn't want to talk anymore about the attack on Shimomura, but he will tell me about the girl he met at a diner last night.

"I actually sat down. The first thing that gal asked me, 'Oh can I use your phone?' I go, 'No, but you can talk to me.' She had like the ring through the nose. I don't think that's a turn-on. That's like the new generation. I guess I'm an older guy now."

"Maybe you are."

"I don't see myself as older. I still feel like I'm seventeen or eighteen. I don't feel like I'm thirty."

"Well, I got that article you told me about. 'Cybercop.' "

" 'Armed with laptops and modems,' Mitnick jokes, pretending to be quoting from the story. "What're they gonna do? Chase down the wires? It's ridiculous! It should be a movie. You know, 'Cybercop.' . . . At least what they said about me was short, but I didn't like it."

"They didn't name many people but they decided to name you."

"See, that's what bugs me. Why didn't they at least talk about Poulsen. He blows me away according to everybody, so talk about him."

"Or your other friend, Justin."

"Yeah. This asshole [Justin Petersen] is trying to snuff money from a bank through a computer and it's like he's OK. Maybe that's what I shoulda done is go into that business.

"If you do it for fun and you get zero off of it, it's big news, I guess." Mitnick sighs. "Who knows? I think I stepped on the wrong people's toes, and I think that certain individuals are personally not happy with me. They're gonna do everything in their power to put my name in lights 'cuz they want harm to come.

"I gotta get going 'cuz I gotta get to the airport," Mitnick says hurriedly.

Mitnick's getting on a plane? Is this for real, or just another test to see if I'm working for the feds, to see if this tidbit pops up later through some channel in his information superhighway?

"Are you gonna be in the air for an hour or —"

"I can't tell you where I'm going or how long I'm gonna be in the air."

"More than ten minutes?"

"I hope it's more than ten minutes!"

"Do you fly coach or first class?"

"Coach. Well, most of the time coach. I don't like to fly."

"Do you take any precautions?"

"Yeah I bring a fuckin' parachute!" Mitnick snarls. "What precautions can I take? Yeah. Here I have my flotation cushion. So when we crash in Pitttsburgh, I'll be able to float in the goddamn lake," he says sarcastically. "There's no precaution. You're basically saying to the pilot, 'You have my life!' "

"No. I meant, you said once you stay away from the big airports, like JFK."

"Well, that's not really true. I was just joking. Because I can't. My job — I'm required to go places, and I can't say to my boss, 'Hey, I can't go through a major airport because somebody might recognize me.'. . ."

.   .   .

Mitnick hangs up a few minutes later, and I sit at my desk, stunned at what he's told me.

Mitnick sounded giddy. And why not? His enemy has been publicly humiliated, stung by a novel, sophisticated attack. It's as if Professor Moriarty has struck Sherlock Holmes.

Right after Christmas when Mitnick asked me about my *Playboy* article he warned me Markoff and Shimomura would plot his capture. Did Mitnick opt for a preemptive strike? And if so, what was the prize, what secrets did the NSA hacker's machine hold that might now be part of Kevin Mitnick's bag of tricks?

Night,
January 20, 1995

"**I**IS ANYTHING SAFE IN CYBER-SPACE?" *U.S. News & World Report* warns the world on the stunning cover of its January 23 issue, which shows a silver cop badge engraved, "CYBER POLICE, CYBERSPACE PATROL, POL · NET." The feature article spotlights one of the dilemmas of computer crime fighting: namely, that in trying to catch the Kevin Mitnicks of the world, cybercops may erode basic constitutional rights.

POLICING CYBERSPACE

Cops want more power to fight cybercriminals. As their technobattle escalates, what will happen to American traditions of privacy and property?

"The day is coming very fast," says FLETC (Federal Law Enforcement Training Center] director Charles Rinkevich, "when every cop will be issued a badge, a gun and a laptop."

Adding a high-speed modem, cellular phone, cryptography textbooks and bulletproof vest to that arsenal might also be prudent because "crime involving high technology is going to go off the boards," predicts FBI Special Agent William Tafoya, who created the bureau's home page on the Internet. . . . "It won't be long before the bad guys out-strip our ability to keep up with them."

. . . The FBI says that Kevin Mitnick, currently America's most wanted computer criminal, has stolen software from cellular-phone companies, caused millions of dollars in damage to computer operations and boldy tapped FBI agents' calls.

.   .   .

"I'm not going to be able to call you anymore but I wanted to tell you something first."

It's nearly nine on Friday night, just hours since "America's most wanted computer criminal" checked in to laugh about Shimomura being hacked. But now Mitnick's agitated. Something's up. I've never heard him talk this way before.

"I just saw this movie, *Murder in the First*. It's about this guy that stole five bucks and they put him in Alcatraz for five years and started beating him. Finally he went nuts and killed somebody. It's with Christian Slater.

"It parallels my case. Here I am a computer hacker. Not that I ever went to Alcatraz. But at MDC they put me in this room with a dim light, a bed and a toilet. Six by nine foot. They let me out forty-five minutes a day for fresh air. The rest of the day I was in the part where they send you if you've assaulted a prisoner or killed somebody. Legally you're not supposed to be there more than a certain number of days. They do it to me for eight months. I wonder if that has anything to do with how I think about them. I was in this fucking room for eight months. They used the telephone as an excuse. 'We can't let him near a phone. He might launch missiles.'

"I was in there eight fucking months!" Mitnick shouts indignantly. "I don't think you can comprehend. Go into your bathroom and put in a fifty-watt bulb. Try to stay there for an hour."

Mitnick describes the daily rituals of his imprisonment. "They'd shackle my legs and arms. Two guards would escort me, unshackle me, and let me shower. A minute shower. Then shackle me back and take me back to the cell. I can see it for a few days. But eight months?

Go into the bathroom and put up a fifty-watt bulb and see if you go stir crazy."

"What time of the day did you go outside for the forty-five minute —"

"Whenever the guard wanted. It was like a big patio all caged in. Eight North. Up on the eighth floor. One time they put me in with one of these Cuban guys. I say, 'Why are you in the hold area?' He said, 'I have a three-man hold order. They can't move me without three officers. I killed two officers already.' "

Mitnick yells. "They put me with this Cuban who *killed* guys! What the fuck are they doing *that* for? Locking me up with that guy! This guy, who knows, maybe he'll kill somebody for kicks.

"It was fucking *torture*. You're just in there with yourself. I mean you're locked in your cell twenty-three out of twenty-four hours. That's the worst punishment they could do. It was fucking torture, man. It was hard to describe. I mean here it is, what is it, six, seven years later and I'm still pissed."

"Was there ever anybody else you talked to about this?"

"I never talked to anybody about it. They don't give a shit! They say, 'Oh, it's over.' But it's mental goddamn *torture* and I'll never forgive the U.S. government for it, ever! I'm not saying that I'm gonna get even or something like that, so don't read that into it. But I'll never forgive them for that shit.

"It was the judge's order. My attorney brought it up to the judge on several occasions in court, and know what her comment was? That is where *he belongs*. And this is one of the most liberal judges in the L.A. area, right? That's where he belongs. I remember those words exactly. It's like, you know, they show me no mercy, so why should I show them any? *No fuckin' mercy, man!*"

Later, I phone the Metropolitan Detention Center in Los Angeles, the federal jail where Mitnick did eight months of solitary, to check out his story.

"There's very limited information that we would have," the warden's executive assistant tells me, suggesting I call Lompoc. "If the inmate had a discipline problem, all that information would be contained in the central file."

Officials at Lompoc are also of little help, except to explain that as far as the Federal Bureau of Prisons is concerned, "lock down" or "solitary confinement" doesn't exist: "The terms we use in the Federal Bureau of Prisons are 'administrative detention' and 'disciplinary segregation.'"

Finally, I find someone at the Washington, D.C., office of the FBP. I spell Mitnick's name, and she brings up his file on the bureau's computer system.

"Oh, there he is. His registrar number was 89950-012. He came to Terminal Island as a presentencing admission on December 9, 1988. Then he was transferred to MDC LA on December 12, 1988, and remained there as a holdover until August 12, 1989."

"Was he in administrative detention?"

"No," answers the official definitively. "He was on a regular unit."

"I was told he didn't receive the same treatment as other inmates."

"It doesn't look that way. There was only one episode, but if that's the reason why he was there or in any kind of different housing, you're gonna have to go through FOIA [Freedom of Information Act] for that because I couldn't tell you that if I wanted to."

But she tells me anyway.

"It looks like he was just in regular units except for maybe two weeks, that's about it, from April 26, '89, till May 10. That was the only case where there was anything special about his housing. The rest of the time it looks like he was just in regular units."

Interesting. As far as the Federal Bureau of Prisons' computers are concerned, Kevin Mitnick's eight months of solitary confinement was only a two-week stint. But in fact Kevin Mitnick's version is true. Newspaper articles, one book, Mitnick's attorney, and statements by the judge in his case confirm that, indeed, the hacker was held in solitary confinement for the bulk of his incarceration.

.   .   .

I ask Mitnick about the *U.S. News & World Report* article that has elevated him to the status of America's most wanted hacker. "They're repeating these same allegations that haven't been proven."

"Well, now they're kinda quoting it as factual," Mitnick says, amazed. "Usually they say 'Well so and so is suspected of XYZ.' Now it's 'So and so did XYZ. We just can't find him.' "

Mitnick's right. There's no proof of the allegations in the *U.S. News & World Report* story. Not even any sources. It's as if John Markoff's allegations in the *New York Times* have become undisputed fact.

"Who knows," Mitnick harps on his old conspiracy angle. "Maybe the director of some bureau didn't like a lot of the adverse publicity with the Justin [Petersen] case. And then I'm sure Lewis's attorney aggravating over the whole case didn't help me one single bit."

But wasn't Mitnick initially excited by the prospect of the Janet Reno letter? Wasn't he happy to put Eric and David Schindler, the Assistant U.S. Attorney, in the hot seat?

"Were you upset about that?"

"Well, he [De Payne] was so excited about it 'cuz he was hoping to cause the agents trouble. You know, get them suspended. Look at the Waco case, look at the CIA, look at all those officers that shoulda been disciplined and yet they're getting promoted. It's like they're *untouchable*. They're above the law. So I knew that it was a waste of time."

.   .   .

"So you said you probably can't call me for a while," I change the subject, referring to our Friday morning conversation, when Mitnick said he was getting on a plane.

"Yeah. It's just temporary. And it's too risky 'cuz I think your line could be tapped. I'd like to talk to you, if you could come up with an alternate way I can communicate with you, like through PGP [encryption] on the Internet. But you're gonna have to get PGP working. You'd actually have to invest the time and get some secure communication."

"And I'm also gonna have to keep PGP at home as opposed to the host?" I ask the hacker who's been hacking into my e-mail.

"You don't leave it on the Well," Mitnick scolds. "No. You keep it on your Mac. I know it's a pain in the ass, you know, it's just too risky. I spend too much time on the phone with you. It's too easy to get the city I'm in, and then they can drive around to certain places, maybe ask if I've been there."

This is news to me. Is Mitnick getting sloppy, not disguising the origin of his calls?

"You know I went to a movie. And maybe if they track the call to this city, so they go to every fuckin' theater and show my pictures, maybe they'll get lucky. There's a hundred ways to get caught. A genius can think of fifty of them. Get my point?

"I don't wanna go back into solitary confinement because I guarantee you one hundred percent they'd do it again. . . . 'This guy can start World War Three! Or he could whistle the launch codes'. . . and I'll get the same judge and she'll say, 'Oh, that's where you belong!'

"My attorney went to the Ninth Circuit about the bail. They said I was too dangerous to get bail . . . that I was a threat to the community. Yet, if you read the law . . . it said . . . the judge may determine that the defendant is a threat to the community and may hold the defendant in detention. But it was only if these four specific factors were true.

"The first was if you received the death penalty or life imprisonment. . . . The second case was if it was a drug offense that carried ten or more years. The third case was if it was your third conviction for a felony and the prior two felonies were crimes of violence. And the fourth thing was treason, espionage.

"So, my case did not meet those four criteria in plain, simple English. I pointed it out to my attorney. All he did to me was shrug his shoulders. Like what the fuck."

.   ▪   ▪

I ask Mitnick what the feds think about him.

"Who knows?" Mitnick sighs. "I don't know what they're thinking. . . . As much as I would like to predict their movements, they'd like to predict mine. Believe me."

"They know for instance that your weight has fluctuated a lot."

"They don't know what I look like now. I could be two hundred ten pounds or I could be a Stairmaster Joe. I could have a beard and a mustache. Or I could be a redhead or a blond. You don't know. And they don't know."

"You could have glasses or—"

"I could have contacts. I could have a limp," Mitnick continues, his anger easing. He's intrigued. He's talking about one of his passions. "The way people walk is the number one way to recognize somebody. Did you know that? You put something in your shoe that hurts. There's a whole book on it, *How to Disguise Yourself* or *A Hundred Ways to Disguise Yourself.*"

"So another life change?"

"No. I'm not changing," Mitnick says, his voice weary. "You're confused about what I'm doing. I have to look for new employment soon. I'm not gonna quit until I find something new 'cuz I can't afford to quit and not have the income. But somebody's screwup could come back to haunt me later through the tax man. That's all I'm gonna tell you. It's because of some idiot's procedural clerical error. You gotta look at everything. You gotta look at the taxes.

"Like I said, any genius can think of fifty ways to get caught. I'm no genius, so say I can think of twenty-five."

"How smart are you?"

"I dunno. I never took an IQ test. I think I'm just average."

"Why are you so good at what you do?"

" 'Cuz I have passion for it."

"Where does that come from?"

"I dunno, I guess the heart. I just have passion for it. I don't think I'm any smarter than the next guy. If I was a supergenius, I wouldn't be in this mess."

Mitnick laughs. "I'd be driving my Mercedes to my penthouse in Manhattan."

"Or in Switzerland," I joke.

"All right, dude. Well, you take care."

Saturday afternoon, January 21, I drive to the local multi-plex and sit among the empty seats and watch *Murder in the First.* The movie stinks, but it captures the brutality of prison life. And it makes me think about what I'm doing. I'm treating Mitnick's predicament as a story, a way to practice my craft, make a living, and perhaps even enjoy myself. But Mitnick's emotional call last night jarred me. He challenged me to sit in my bathroom, with a fifty-watt bulb, to stay there for an hour and imagine what it must be like day after endless day. I didn't try it, not even for an hour.

His anger surprised me. But then Kevin Mitnick isn't some kid who did his time in a comfy Club Fed like a lot of white-collar criminals of the 1980s. Kevin Mitnick didn't successfully pocket millions of dollars. He pranked who knows how many people and illegally copied a big corporation's software. He got what he considers torture as his punishment. Mitnick was punished because of what he represented, and, I suspect, because he couldn't afford the kind of lawyers that work for the likes of Michael Milken and Ivan Boesky.

But I'm not convinced of the great conspiracy Mitnick keeps harping on. I think Mitnick is cyberspace enemy number one for simpler reasons. Because he or De Payne keep pranking the FBI. Because either the Justice Department or the Assistant U.S. Attorney in California decided he would make a great scapegoat for a much bigger problem they can't control. And because hacker horror stories sell newspapers.

I don't know if the government truly believes Mitnick is dangerous. The FBI and the U.S. Attorney have not publicly commented on his alleged new crimes. The only new crime on the books is a minor probation violation caused by Mitnick's continued association with De Payne and his alleged unauthorized listening to Pac Bell Security's voice mail.

Finding victims of his hacks that will talk is not easy. Qualcomm, the cellular phone company in San Diego that told Markoff about the alleged copying of its software, with the understanding he would not publish its name, declines to comment. Only individuals are willing to comment on the dangerousness of Kevin Mitnick, individuals like Neil Clift, in England, who sells software security bugs he finds in his spare time to the Digital Equipment Corporation:

> . . . He [Mitnick] said he admired me and wanted to do what I do. He wanted me to help him learn a bit about the operating system. What books to read. What chapters. I don't see any harm in that. If he could actually find the problems himself, he wouldn't be interested in using them. . . .
>
> Kevin's a bit too clever for me. He's always probing. He asked a question and put an answer together with an answer he got previously. . . . I never know whether he likes me or just wants information. He got quite nasty at times. . . . He kept calling me stupid. . . . He'd take things from me and say that's OK, because I don't make any money at them. . . .
>
> I got a kick out of talking to him. He was very interesting. . . . If he calls again, I'll always talk to him. If I get a chance to put him away, I'll do that as well.

Clift, who actively helped the FBI attempt to trace Mitnick's calls to England, is a perfect example of why Kevin Mitnick remains an enigma. He is one of the few people who will admit to being victimized by Kevin Mitnick, yet he describes the hacker's "crimes" as a search for knowledge, a search he willingly assisted.

Maybe Mitnick's right to think the press hasn't given him a fair shake. Judging from the *U.S. News & World Report* article he has a good argument. He hasn't been indicted, he hasn't even been accused of a crime by a law enforcement official, much less convicted. But in the press his alleged crimes are now fact.

Still, I know Mitnick has investigated his investigators, and likely helped himself to whatever software he pleases. My sources have told me Mitnick has been messing with the FBI agents on his case and has copied cellular software from major manufacturers. So far nobody will go on the record with these allegations, or even speculate on the significance of these alleged crimes. But that didn't stop the *New York Times* or *U.S. News & World Report*. Both publications printed allegations without naming any government officials. The reporters just said Mitnick was a suspect or flatly stated he'd committed the crimes. They apparently had no sources willing to go on the record.

With all this bad press, I'm not surprised that Mitnick is worrying about the prospect of returning to solitary confinement. He was more careful yesterday, his calls brief, in sharp contrast to our marathon conversations earlier in the week. It makes sense. Mitnick knew he was going to be hopping on a plane, and figured even if the feds were tapping my phone line, he'd be long gone before they could find him.

That is, if he was telling the truth.

.   ▪   ▪

It's Monday morning, January 23, three days after Kevin Mitnick phoned and chuckled that the great cybersamurai had been humbled, that Tsutomu Shimomura's computer had been hacked. I get up, stumble down the front steps, and pull the folded paper from the shiny blue plastic bag.

Here it is, on the front page of the *New York Times*.

DATA NETWORK IS FOUND OPEN TO NEW THREAT

By John Markoff

San Francisco, Jan. 22 — A Federal computer security agency has discovered that unknown intruders have developed a new way to break into computer systems, and the agency plans on Monday to advise users how to guard against the problem.

The new form of attack leaves many of the 20 million government, business, university and home computers on the global Internet vulnerable to eavesdropping and theft. . . .

The first known attack using the new technique took place on Dec. 25 against the computer of a well-known computer security expert at the San Diego Supercomputer Center. An unknown individual or group took over his computer for more than a day and electronically stole a large number of security programs. . . .

The flaw, which has been known as a theoretical possibility to computer experts for more than a decade, but has never been demonstrated before, is creating alarm among security experts now because of the series of break-ins and attacks in recent weeks.

The weakness . . . previously reported in technical papers by AT&T researchers, was detailed in a talk given by Tsutomu Shimomura . . . at a California computer security seminar. . . .

I read on, amazed at the parallels to the story Mitnick told me last week. The attack is described as brilliant and novel, and there's a reference to CERT, the federal security agency Mitnick told me about, as well as the security talk Mitnick said Shimomura gave on the subject. The *Times* story describes the attack itself slightly differently. Markoff describes it as Internet Protocol Spoofing, while Mitnick dubbed it a TCP/IP prediction packet attack. Markoff terms it "masquerading," while Mitnick described it as "impersonating a friendly host."

I don't have any doubt. It's the same hack. But who was the hacker?

Why didn't Mitnick tell me earlier of the Christmas Day attack on Shimomura? Perhaps because he didn't know about it earlier. Or perhaps because he wanted a cover for his advance knowledge, something like CERT's planned public announcement. If the latter was true it provided a convenient pretext. How could I know for certain whether or not Mitnick had merely intercepted news of the federal Computer Emergency Response Team's plans?

But then I think back. If Mitnick hadn't played a role in the hack why was he so pleased by Shimomura's predicament? Would he be so gleeful if he had simply been a spectator to some rival hacker's feat? Would his voice be tinged with pride?

And as I reread Markoff's article, it's easy to understand why Mitnick may have been proud. The hack threatens the future of the Internet, the privacy of millions of individuals, and the security of millions of dollars of emerging cybercommerce, at least according to the *New York Times.* By describing the hack as an obscure theoretical "flaw" never before demonstrated, Markoff's *Times* story treats the feat almost as an original work of art.

The unknown mystery hacker is by implication a master burglar who has single-handedly lifted a masterpiece from the Louvre. Shimomura, the master of security, was stripped of his premier Internet security programs and tools. But Markoff implies that every business and every individual may be at risk. The sky — cyberspace itself —is falling. And if there are any nonbelievers, Markoff quotes James Settle, the same retired FBI agent he quoted in his last front page *Times* hacker story, who has these four words of warning: "Essentially everyone is vulnerable."

.   .   .

It's dark when Mitnick phones, and I tell him the Federal Bureau of Prisons' official line: as far as the government is concerned, the hacker's eight months of solitary never happened. Mitnick isn't surprised. He's accustomed to nobody believing his story. And then he makes an extraordinary offer. Mitnick suggests sending me a release in his name with his fingerprint to help me learn the facts of his case.

"So, I was thinking of getting you a fingerprint card with an FOI release," Mitnick says. "Lets you take care of requesting all the releases you want. It's me doing the release and I think it has more power than you doing it."

I tell him I appreciate the offer, but I don't see why it should be hard to determine whether he really did eight months in solitary.

Mitnick disagrees. He thinks the government will misrepresent the facts of his case. "What do they care? They have one mad motherfucker out here and they don't care because I'm a bad guy in their eyes anyway. They don't give a shit. I didn't like that treatment. That's one of the reasons I'm out here like this, because I know they would do it again."

I tell Mitnick I saw the movie *Murder in the First*.

"Yeah," Mitnick sighs. "The hole in Alcatraz wasn't like the hole at MDC. But it's still the same. You're still in a locked little room, you get forty-five minutes of fresh air. They shackle you everywhere you go. . . . It's where the snitches are. They go into administrative detention because they'll get killed."

"So this was a portion of Eight North that was for administrative detention?"

"No. They didn't have a section for it. The whole floor was lockdown."

"OK, but how could the Federal Bureau of Prisons change this fact?"

"I don't have to sit here and prove it!" Mitnick snaps, nearly shouting. "Maybe they had a new law or something that says that you can't hold anyone for a certain period of time and then they fixed the computers so they can't get blamed."

.   .   .

Mitnick suddenly flips channels on me, momentarily shutting out his solitary-confinement flashbacks, to tell me about a crime he could have easily committed. Is this Mitnick's anger too? Hints about the damage he could do if he really wanted to be a criminal?

"You know who I met there were the guys who did the big ATM fraud, Scott Koenig and Mark Koenig. They're the guys that masterminded — he [Scott] worked for GTE Federal systems and they used the Star system — they mastered the network, so he actually told me exactly how he pulled it off."

By now, I know Mitnick well enough to anticipate what's coming. Mitnick's going to give me a primer on how to make millions in ATM fraud, and then tell me he, as a true hacker, would never dream of committing such a crime. "Apparently, they had these Itala encryption boxes. When an ATM is used, this Itala box contains a master encryption key. It encrypts the session key, sends it down to the ATM, then the ATM decrypts it with its session key. Then it takes that key and it encrypts the user's account number and PIN and all that shit, sends it back over the landline, and then the Itala box has the session key, it decrypts it, uses the master key, and comes back to the plain text pin, right?"

Sure, I got it.

"And what he realized was those *idiots* on the Plus system — the crux of the security is this Itala box which holds the master key. Well, apparently, it was set up to default zero through nine, a through f. They took it out of the box, set it up, and never set the key. So he was able to decrypt all the traffic going over the Net."

"It was on the *default?*" I say, incredulous GTE wouldn't have bothered to set unique keys for its encryption.

"Yeah, they left it on the default. Like you take something out of the box, your answering machines are usually zero, zero, zero. Well, that's what those idiots did. You know, they had all these account numbers and PINs. So then he borrowed one of those things that burn the information on the mag [magnetic] strip. He took one home and took his tape and cards and made thousands of clones of people's accounts and the PINs. He wrote the PIN on each card.

"So like one three-day weekend his plot was to go around and have his friends and him take all the money they can over the three-day holiday, right? So one of his girlfriend's friends snitched, told the Secret Service what's going on. They busted him before they did it and [he was sentenced], like, four years for the attempt.

"That was totally criminal," declares the most wanted man in cyberspace. "That's not hacking, you know."

·   ■   ■

I think back to the copy of the *New York Times* I picked up on my front step a few hours ago, and wonder, how did Markoff get this dry security story on the front page of the *Times?*

News. That's what makes something a front-page story, and the news that made the IP Spoof hack a page-one story is danger. Danger to the Internet's 20 million users, and danger to its future as a vehicle of commerce. But of course, it's only a new danger if those users were previously safe. That's not what Kevin Mitnick and all the other hackers I talk to say. It's not what countless articles in newspapers and magazines say. It's not even what John Markoff used to say. Every cyberspace journalist worth his memory chips knows security on the Internet is an illusion, and always has been.

The Internet is about as safe as a convenience store in East L.A. on Saturday night.

January 29, 1995

It's Super Bowl Sunday, a couple of hours before kickoff, and though I'm not a big football fan, I plan on watching the San Francisco 49ers demolish the San Diego Chargers.

I pick up the phone, thinking it's my friend, the one who's supposed to bring the guacamole, but instead it's Kevin Mitnick. It's been six days since his last call.

"I'm walking along the beach here relaxing," Mitnick bubbles, sounding euphoric.

"On the *beach*? You're kidding. Are you really on the beach?"

"Yeah. So, I'll let you go because you're watching the —" Mitnick begins.

"No. I'm not watching the game. It hasn't started yet."

"I know. That reminds me. I've gotta get to where my friends are because they're gonna want to watch it."

Amazing. Mitnick's just told me he's on a beach, and he's got friends too. I thought Mitnick couldn't trust anybody.

"The game isn't for two hours. What do the waves look like?"

"I can't tell you, but you could listen to them," Mitnick quips. "Hey! Did you hear about that little UPI release? Now the U.S. Marshals have released a [plea for] public help thing. This was Tuesday. They just said all this shit. That I got into NORAD, that I have done all these terrible things, and that I'm always one step ahead of them and now they need the public's help."

"Did they name the marshal?"

"Yeah, it was the bull dike that keeps harassing my family and keeps getting referred to attorneys. Kathleen Cunningham. I dunno. I don't have much luck with Kathleens these days," Mitnick mopes.

Mitnick is being hunted by not only Kathleen Cunningham of the U.S. Marshals office in Los Angeles, but Kathleen Carson of the FBI.

"Did you see the thing in the *New York Times* yesterday?"

"No."

I can't believe Mitnick missed it. Yesterday the *Times* led its business section with a long feature.

"Let me read you a few things," I tell Mitnick. "The title is, 'Taking a Computer Crime to Heart.' It's by Markoff, and it's got a big picture of Shimomura. And it says, 'Added motivation for a detective. He was the victim.'

"I'll read you the lead, 'It was as if the thieves, to prove their prowess, had burglarized a locksmith. Which is why Tsutomu Shimomura, the keeper of the keys in this case, is taking the break-in as a personal affront —' "

Mitnick bursts out laughing.

— " 'and why he considers solving the crime a matter of honor,' " I finish.

"This guy's an idiot because he actually believes —" Mitnick stammers, catching himself. "I mean you've got to take into account he's dealing with hackers. The grapevine believes this person who left the message on his voice mail is the one that did the hacking. I don't have any idea, of course."

Is Mitnick implying that the person who left the voice mail message was not the person who hacked Shimomura?

"There was an amusing message left on his voice mail?"

"They [the grapevine] said it's on the Internet, they actually have an audio file on the Internet, which anybody can get —"

"OK, let me read you more of the *Times* story, '. . . more than anything, Shimomura wants to help the government catch the crooks. And while he acknowledges that the thieves were clever, Mr. Shimomura has also uncovered signs of ineptitude that he says will be the intruder's eventual undoing. "Looks like the ankle biters have learned to read technical manuals," he said derisively. "Somebody should teach them some manners." ' "

Mitnick chuckles.

" 'Mr. Shimomura . . . was not home on Christmas Day because he was on his way to the Sierra Nevada where he spends most of the winter as a self-described ski bum. He says all the more reason he derides the geeks who have nothing better to do on Christmas than to sit at a computer and pry into his electronic life.' "

"He doesn't sound too happy."

I keep reading. " ' "Gentlemen are not supposed to read each other's mail," he said.' "

"Oh well," Mitnick chuckles, struggling to contain his laughter. "He was an idiot to keep stuff online."

"Uh-huh, and I heard a rumor he had GIF [graphic] files and stuff. Have you heard this rumor?"

Mitnick laughs. "I have no comment."

Maybe Mitnick really did do it.

"The story ends with him saying he's working on a software filter to make it impossible for an outsider to gain entry to his system. . . . ' "The ankle biters," he warned, "will test it at their peril." ' "

Mitnick's amused. "He sounds like he's taking it personally. I'm surprised Markoff wrote it," Mitnick chuckles. "It sounds like the guy is out to protect his Japanese honor. He's been had, like you see in the old karate movies."

Mitnick does his best kung fu master imitation. "You dishonored my family. You will die! I'll meet you . . . and we fight to the death."

Mitnick sounds like he's doubling over with laughter.

"But he's good," Mitnick cautions, no longer laughing, his voice suddenly contemplative. "I'm surprised, especially him being a spook and everything, that he would take it public."

.   .   .

"The U.S. Marshals are seeking public assistance. I wonder what egged them on at this time? It's the same time this shit went out — it sounds like a weird coincidence. When did the *New York Times* [January 23 data threat] story on Shimomura come out?"

"Monday," I say.

"And this comes out on Tuesday? That's kinda weird, wouldn't you say?" Mitnick asks.

"It sounds like quite a coincidence." Markoff writes a story saying Shimomura is going to catch a mysterious, unnamed intruder, and the next day, the U.S. Marshal issues a bulletin asking the public's help in capturing Mitnick.

"I wonder if I'm a suspect. I hope not," Mitnick stammers. "I wouldn't do . . . that, you know. I'm not that technically minded, you know. I hope they don't think it's me. I just think it's quite funny."

"It doesn't mention any agents involved in the case," I comment, referring back to Markoff's profile of Shimomura. "It says here there's no monetary loss."

"Oh, I guess they'll have some trillions of dollars of monetary loss, because they ruined his [Shimomura's] ski vacation," Mitnick says, chuckling, as he launches into one of his familiar antigovernment rants. "So now the government has to account for this guy's ski vacation that was lost so they're gonna have to finance a new ski vacation."

I can hear wind blowing in the background, or is it the waves?

"They might as well send him to fuckin' Calgary because that's where the best skiing is. . . ."

Has Mitnick been in Canada?

.   .   .

I return to Markoff's profile of Shimomura. "They mention other known victims. Loyola University of Chicago, the University of Rochester, and Drexel University."

"Rochester was involved in the Shimomura attack," Mitnick explains as if it were obvious. "That's apparently where attacks originated, or files were transferred to . . ." Mitnick continues, giving more detailed information than the article. "And another system called toad.com was run by one of the founders of Sun."

Mitnick seems to know more about the attack than the *New York Times.*

"So what are they talking about when they're talking about Loyola?"

"I don't know," Mitnick says. "I guess they were attacked using the TCP/IP packet sequence prediction as well."

"What about Drexel?"

"Yeah, same thing, Drexel, I believe. You know, the only ones I'd heard about was Rochester and Shimomura. I haven't heard about Loyola or Drexel —"

Mitnick's voice fades out suddenly. Is he telling the truth or pretending that he didn't do it, that he just knows of Rochester, the site revealed in Markoff's original article? Or is he revealing a more tantalizing possibility? That there may have been other people involved in the attack on Shimomura.

.   .   .

"Mr. Jon," Kevin Mitnick welcomes me hours later and we chat briefly about the Super Bowl. He enjoyed the commercials, particularly the one with the computerized frogs croaking "Bud-weis-er" in sequence.

I can hear the first rumblings of a Mitnick belly laugh. "I was thinking of getting in the P link [one of AT&T's satellite phone links] and sending, "Hi, Shimomura, die with honor [broadcasting it worldwide to hundreds of millions of Super Bowl viewers]."

Then, suddenly, Mitnick is pissed. "I read that shit [Markoff's *Times* profile of Shimomura]. He said now he considers it a matter of honor. . . . Remember I told you that Markoff has an [e-mail] account on Shimomura's system? He thinks all his mail is unreadable?"

Weeks ago, Mitnick mentioned Markoff corresponded by e-mail with Shimomura through a secret account on one of the security expert's San Diego computers. Why would a *New York Times* reporter have an account on an NSA hacker's computer? Why would Markoff want to keep his account on Shimomura's computer a secret? And wouldn't that mean that Shimomura could read Markoff's e-mail?

"So in other words, it wasn't just this guy's [Shimomura's] stuff [that was stolen], it was Markoff's stuff?"

"Markoff — well I guess anybody that had an account on Shimomura's computer."

"Other people too?" I fish.

"I don't know. I didn't do it," Mitnick answers.

"Did you hear about what your friend did?"

"No."

"He was on [alt.] 2600 [the Usenet newsgroup started by *2600* magazine] and after this happened to Shimomura, he sent a little message to 2600. He said what a fool Shimomura was, and that Shimomura sounded like one of these guys who learned security by listening to 2600 and that if he was such a great security man, why was it so easy for him to lose everything?"

"Shimomura is not the *idiot!*" Mitnick shrieks. "He's very smart."

Mitnick's tone shocks me. It's almost as if the hacker is defending Shimomura's honor.

"But Lewis likes antagonizing everybody," I say. "You know that."

"Maybe he can't get any feedback from Shimomura himself," Mitnick sighs. "That's probably it. Well, fine. Maybe Shimomura will think it's him."

.   .   .

It was strange to be the first to read Mitnick the *New York Times* profile of Shimomura, especially when it was such an obvious attempt to provoke the intruder and craft a public persona for Shimomura, a virtual unknown until last week. But it's easy to see why Shimomura suddenly merits star treatment in the *New York Times*. He's challenged Darth Vadar. He's vowed revenge against the very unnamed intruder who has embarrassed him on his home turf.

I wonder too about the coincidence Mitnick mentioned. Markoff first wrote of the attack on Shimomura on January 23. Then the U.S. Marshals issued a release calling for the public's help in capturing Kevin Mitnick, without ever mentioning Markoff's article. But Mitnick's question makes me think of something missing in yesterday's Shimomura profile. Why didn't Markoff's lengthy article at least speculate on the identity of Shimomura's attacker?

Why didn't the reporter mention Kevin Mitnick? He's been bold enough to make accusations without naming government sources before. Last summer he didn't hesitate to accuse Mitnick of crimes.

Is it all a question of timing?

Maybe it's because Markoff isn't ready to uncover the mystery his touted samurai has pledged he'll solve. Maybe it's because the reporter doesn't want to alert his journalistic competition to the plot's final twist.

"Stop! Cyberthief!"

TECHNOLOGY: DON'T BE ALARMED, BUT THE LAW CAN'T COPE
WITH COMPUTER CRIME.

The *Newsweek* headline blares above a photo illustration of a gun-toting burglar hoisting a bag of loot over his shoulder with what looks like a wall of microchips in the background. It's the usual overblown warning about the dangers of cybercrime, but the last paragraph has an interesting revelation,

> . . . Last week brought word that high-tech crooks have developed a new way of "spoofing" their way into even well defended computers. . . . The target was Tsutomu Shimomura. . . . At least one thief succeeded in stealing a number of sophisticated programs, some potentially useful in unscrambling cellular-telephone codes. Shimomura fears they could be used to break into yet more computers — not for fun, as most hackers do, but for financial gain. . . .

The cellular phone reference surprises me. Markoff never mentioned cellular phones in his recent Shimomura article. It's the first clue that Mitnick might be involved, since Markoff's front-page article last summer broadcast Mitnick's obsession with cellular phones. But there's a more important question. What are programs "useful in unscrambling cellular telephone codes" doing on Shimomura's computer?

I flip the page to "The Greatest Hits of Hacking," photos of six of the most famous hackers of all time, Mitnick, Poulsen, Morris, and others.

But that's just part of *Newsweek*'s hacker coverage for the week. On the facing page is an article by Steven Levy, the author of *Hackers*. It's the photo that catches my eye, an inspired, superimposed cybermontage, a giant close-up of Shimomura's intense face glowing with magenta and fluorescent green light. Above his flowing black locks floats a miniature ghost of the warrior in Buddha pose, hands poised on the keyboard, and at his side, what looks like the sword of a samurai.

Levy shares the opinion of his friends, Markoff and Shimomura. In his column he writes,

> ... Shimomura doesn't resemble your typical cybercop. With his shoulder-length hair, wraparound sunglasses and rollerblades, he's as creative in building and maintaining security as dark-side hackers are in breaking it. Cracking Shimomura's machine is like murdering Columbo's wife, a crime fueled more by chutzpah than cold profit. ...

.   .   .

It's a little after 8:30 A.M., Wednesday, February 1. Things are happening fast. Yesterday the *Los Angeles Times Magazine* asked me to write a cover story on Shimomura. Today, I'm talking with the Assistant U.S. Attorney in San Francisco heading up the Poulsen case, trying to get a sense of whether the government is going to try the hacker on espionage. My call waiting beeps.

"Rob, I'm sorry," I say. "Can you hold on for a minute?"

"No problem, Jon."

"Hey," Mitnick greets me.

"Hey, can you hold on a second? I just need to get rid of this other call."

"Sure."

"Hey, Rob, I'm sorry. Can I give you a call back?"

What an amusing way to start the day, putting a federal prosecutor on hold to talk to the world's most wanted computer hacker.

"Well, did you see that article in *Newsweek*?" I ask Mitnick, having dropped the prosecutor off the line. "The reporter brought up cellular stuff in Shimomura's stuff. Who told him [the reporter] that?"

"I dunno."

"Shimomura is not supposed to be involved in cellular." I'm talking about illicit cellular activity.

"I told you what he was doing. He was working with Mark Lottor."

"Why is a guy who is supposed to be a security expert —"

"Because he was doing it himself!" Mitnick shouts. "He was planning his own fun. Of course he'll lie. I don't know if he might have another purpose."

"They point out this [IP spoofing] was first discovered by Robert Morris. Did you know that? In 1985?"

"Well, the guy that actually discovered TCP/IP packet prediction — You might wanna call Steve Bellovin at AT&T."

"He's the one who wrote the 1989 paper?"

"Yeah. From his research and his paper, there might be references to where he researched that information."

Kevin Mitnick sounds like a professsor. What other criminal would be providing the historical precedents for a crime in which he's the prime suspect?

"Shimomura claims he could fix it," I say.

"They don't even have the theory right. I mean Shimomura himself couldn't code the program to do it with what he knows now."

So Kevin Mitnick knows precisely how the spoof is coded, and that Tsutomu Shimomura remains in the dark?

"There's some intricacies he doesn't know. He knows the theory, but to actually put the thing into practice — to code the code that does the work — there's changes that have to be accounted for."

"To do it or to protect against it?"

"To actually do the attack. He doesn't have it down perfectly correct."

How could Mitnick know this level of detail? How could he know what Shimomura knows and doesn't know?

"And if he doesn't have the code down he can't protect against it?" I ask.

"No, he could protect against it, but if he wanted to code the attack himself ... Apparently he's pissed off about something that was taken that allows some type of spoofing attacks, too. Now there is some other mail which someone told me about, and one thing he didn't want to get out."

Mitnick is hinting that Shimomura had his own spoof attack software. And that maybe Shimomura let something dangerous get out.

.   .   .

"But I still don't understand why Shimomura didn't try to protect himself a month ago or a year ago."

"Because he probably didn't think someone would launch that type of attack. He underestimated his opposition. It's like the White House isn't going to protect against a nuclear warhead coming down on top of it because they don't expect that to happen. It's the unexpected, and the unexpected works sometimes pretty well. He knew that the attack was possible. The theory was out there for a while. Nobody else went to the trouble of coding it because it was tedious and it was theory."

"How many man-hours could it possibly take to do this?"

"I dunno. Maybe two weeks."

Markoff claimed last summer in his front page *Times* article that Mitnick was an average programmer. But if Mitnick didn't write the program, who did?

"And so, just in pure coding, that's a fair amount of time. It's not a trivial hack."

"I can't really estimate because I'm not a C-programmer. So, I would just be speculating. . . ."

.   .   .

Mitnick returns to a topic he's already touched on. He's not surprised that Shimomura has managed to portray his failure to protect his home computer into a noble act. It's an irony the press has missed. Shimomura's a hero instead of a goat.

"Of course!" Mitnick exclaims. "He's a spook!"

But Kevin Mitnick, at least, believes Shimomura isn't quite the white knight portrayed by the press. "I mean why was he working with Mark Lottor in developing patches to the Oki firmware that allows people to do ESN changes via the [cellular phone] keypads? What legitimate need would someone have to change their ESN on the keypad?"

I can't think of one. Hackers generally alter the firmware of cellular phones so they can ESN skip — stick other people with their cellular phone bills — or perform countersurveillance on the feds who are trying to nab them. But it's a fine line. It's not strictly illegal to alter the workings of a cellular phone. It depends what you do with it.

"So he's a hacker." Mitnick groans at the irony. "The guy's a hacker. Maybe a cellular phone person was interested in what code he had and that's why he was attacked."

Mitnick just described himself. Or dozens of other hackers.

"Another possibility," I venture, hoping to get a response, "is that Shimomura's spook employers want him to do these hacker things. They want him to know all about changing ESNs."

"I don't know what his motive is. I don't know the man at all. Alls I know is he's very technical and he's very good at what he does. He's in the top five."

"What makes Shimomura so good?"

"When someone penetrates his system he knows what to look for. When you compile a program, it uses external files and libraries. This is the type of guy that would look at the access times of the files to try to figure out what type of program somebody was compiling. The guy's sharp."

On UNIX systems it's possible to tell the last time a file was read. Mitnick's guessing that Shimomura could determine the type of application that was compiled (converted into the computer's most basic machine language) by examining the date stamps in certain system directories. He's also acknowledging he knows that the intruder compiled a program while he was on Shimomura's machine.

Once again, Kevin Mitnick seems to have an amazing amount of detail on how Shimomura analyzes an attack.

"He's just very good at — well, he's a spook. What do you expect? This is only what I hear in the grapevine."

It must be a very well connected grapevine. Talking with Mitnick is maddening. There are so many variables. Is he telling me the truth, what he thinks is the truth, or just trying to con me? Perhaps Mitnick's telling me the truth because he's proud of himself and he's a crazy megalomaniac. After all, he's protecting himself legally by saying he didn't do it. Or maybe he's giving me misinformation so that our phone conversation or anything I may tell someone else or write will prove him innocent because his description is flawed.

On the other hand, if he didn't do the hack, there are still more variables. He may have even watched the hack, and he's giving me straight information while still providing himself with an alibi. Or he could have watched the hack, like other hackers, and even though he knows how it's done, he's feeding me wrong information to protect his ally.

Finally, there's some small chance Mitnick may actually be telling it straight. He really had nothing to do with it, and he's just passing on hearsay because he's so delighted with the outcome. It's hard to know for certain. The best I can do is get him to answer questions that can be confirmed by other sources. I return to the puzzle.

"But does the grapevine say he's primarily a spook?"

"Unknown. He's good in security and he consults with companies like Trusted Information Systems, the people that develop Internet fire walls, and a lot of people in D.C. and the Virginia area."

Trusted Information — the name strikes a bell. Markoff quoted someone from Trusted Information in his front-page "Data Threat" article.

"Where is Trusted Information?"

"Oh, in Maryland, 301 area code. Baltimore, I believe."

"What are some of the Virginia companies Shimomura works with?"

"I just have the phone numbers," Mitnick reveals casually. "I haven't called them yet to see."

"I'd be interested, because obviously in Virginia there's a high concentration of —"

"Intelligence," Mitnick says. "I'm not sure if he [Shimomura] calls the NSA or something, but I know he does consulting for them."

"Obviously, if they're intelligent, he's not calling them [the NSA]. He's just calling Trusted Information or some other company."

"Right. I don't think he's trying to hide the fact that he works for the intelligence community. Maybe — did you ever think of the big picture? Maybe the reason he didn't want . . ." Mitnick stops and pauses. "Maybe the government uses this code to break into domestic systems or foreign systems so they can look at other people's stuff in the intelligence community and they don't want things fixed. Did you ever think of that?"

.   .   .

"So I can only guess about this," I venture, " but I'm guessing he was paid by the NSA or another agency to hack this stuff out —"

"It's all speculative," Mitnick cuts me off. "I'm not interested in what the government's up to in that respect. Then they consider you a real threat. In my pranks I always stayed out of that type of [intelligence computer systems]. I don't want to know. You know what I'm saying?"

I quickly shift gears to ask him about the other big clue the intruder left behind. "The *Newsweek* story mentioned ' "Don't you know who I am?" he asked in a faux British accent.' "

"Yeah. The voice mail that he [Shimomura] got. Maybe that's the guy that did it," Mitnick offers unenthusiastically. "Who knows?"

"Any guesses who might have made that phone call?"

"No."

.   .   .

"Hi. Sorry about that," Mitnick greets me in a new call, the last one having faded out several minutes before. "I wanted you to talk to your people at *Playboy*," he jokes. "I think they could come out with a good pictorial. We could have like a scene called 'Cyberpumping.' You could have me in there with some gorgeous redhead."

Mitnick really is tired of living on the run.

"Cyberpumping? How would the layout go?"

"I'm imagining that now," he pauses for dramatic effect. "It would not have my face. My back, the back of my head. *Playboy's* pretty conservative. That's the unfortunate thing."

"Why a redhead?"

"Oh, I like redheads!"

"Intelligent?"

"Hey! I saw this one: me and a couple of friends of mine were at a titty bar, and there was this one there, man, that blew me away. My favorite trick is folding up the dollar bill between my teeth and then having them grab it with their big tits. Hey! If you ever go to Vegas, my favorite hangout is . . ."

.   .   .

"BEEP!"

It's my line again.

"Can I just get rid of this call? I'm sorry."

"Yeah. I know, you gotta beep somebody."

"I swear to god, just two seconds."

It's John Markoff. I ask if I can give him a call right back.

"OK. Sorry," I say, returning to the hacker.

"Yeah," Mitnick replies, suspicious.

"I got beeped. You know how it is."

"Why don't you just call Shimomura himself?" Mitnick presses. "I gave you his phone number."

.   .   .

"Sorry about that," Mitnick apologizes a few minutes later when he phones back after yet another of his calls patched out.

"That's OK," I say. "Bad connections this morning. Now we got some — do you hear that noise?"

Mitnick sounds like he's in a giant beehive. Where in the world is he?

"Yeah. It's because I'm in a room that has that noise."

"I won't ask any questions," I kid him.

"A disc drive spinning," Mitnick jokes.

But his good humor doesn't last long. He's complaining again about *Newsweek* putting his name "way in lights" when he says he hasn't done anything new.

"Maybe they think I did Shimomura, you know. They're bringing up cellular involved in it. Who knows?

"I know you can find out the inference here by calling your friend John Markoff because Markoff is friends with Shimomura. Why don't you just dial Markoff up and say, 'Hey, Markoff, what's the scoop?' "

A couple of minutes later, as if on cue, my call waiting beeps again.

"Could you hold on just one second? My beeper's going off again," I kid him.

"Looks like they got half of the trace done," Mitnick jokes.

It's John Markoff again. I apologize, and ask once again if I can call him back. He tells me not to worry about it, jokes we'll probably play telephone tag a couple more times, and asks me to call him back when I've got a chance.

"It didn't work," I say, returning to Mitnick.

"They couldn't get it? They didn't give you the number I'm at?"

"They tried."

"411-625 —?" Mitnick begins, deliberately leaving off the end of the number.

"First they thought it was Cleveland. Then they thought it was Detroit," I joke.

"Shit! That's close. If you ever go to Detroit, they have a great thing called Saunders hot fudge."

First strippers, and now fudge.

"Where in Detroit?"

"It's everywhere. They even have it in the markets. Put it this way. In the last month, I had a hot fudge Saunders sundae and it was out of this world!"

.   .   .

Mitnick starts joking about what he might do to Shimomura. With what he calls a beeper's "cap code" — the beeper's equivalent of a cellular phone's electronic serial number — and the radio frequency, he says he could clone Shimomura's beeper and get beeped simultaneously when Shimomura does.

"I have his beeper number. I could see who's paging his ass," Mitnick chortles. "You could really fuck up someone's social plans. Call the person. And when they beep, you call back."

Mitnick chuckles as he makes a pretend call to Shimomura, demonstrating how easily he could lead the security expert astray. Then Mitnick gets serious again.

"You know what Tsutomu's doing?" Mitnick asks. He always calls Shimomura by his first name in a familiar, friendly tone. "I hear he's working for the Air Force, working on a design to do strategic attacks on enemy foreign computer systems. He's a hacker for the government."

.   .   .

"You know this picture in *Newsweek*?" I tell Mitnick. "It has this little picture of Shimomura on top of his own head."

Mitnick's surprised.

"Shimo has a picture in *Newsweek* too? 'Cuz, I just went into the store and just saw my picture. I didn't even buy it, I didn't even want to waste my money."

"It has a huge color picture of Shimo."

"Really?"

"With a little picture of himself sitting on top of his own head —"

"He's going to make a lot of money off of this 'cuz everybody's going to want to talk to this guy!"

"You gotta just browse through it," I interrupt. "Next to the keyboard, I swear it looks like there is a samurai sword."

"I'm sure he'd like to chop some people's heads off." Mitnick chortles, and then pauses. "No, look at it. It's perfect, man. I'm the scapegoat. There's someone to blame it on for a matter of honor.

"Imagine having an advertisement in *Newsweek* fucking magazine! Do you know how many people are going to be calling this guy? 'Hey, I'm with blah-blah-blah company, come talk to me.'

"This doesn't hurt Tsutomu at all. Alls it does is makes him much more in the public eye, and much more chance to make money. I wonder if I should just become a real criminal and start doing this for a lot of cash. Because I'm going to get the same punishment either way.

"What do I have to lose? It's so fucking easy. I don't know, it's just hard crossing that boundary for me. You know, my personal values."

.   .   .

Sometime after noon, the long rambling series of cellular phone calls from Mitnick winds to a close. I grab a quick bite to eat, and then call back Markoff. He hasn't phoned me half a dozen times in my whole life. Why would he suddenly phone me twice in the space of an hour?

The secretary says he's on another call, but Markoff quickly jumps on the line. He thanks me for calling back, and then asks me if some guy named Angel Santana has phoned me.

I don't know who or what he's talking about.

"He's with Star Productions in Vegas," Markoff continues. "He's almost been driven out of business. His calls were routed to his competitors. He's sending his girls to rooms and finding other girls are there first."

Markoff believes Mitnick did this humorous hack years ago for a prostitute that Markoff profiled in *Cyberpunk*. But something tells me the *New York Times* isn't calling just to tell me about Angel. Why not ask John Markoff about the real reason he called me twice this morning?

So I ask him about the Shimomura *Newsweek* story, and the odd reference to cellular phones. He comes back with a stunning revelation.

"Somebody hit a different Tsutomu machine last summer and the NSA was pissed," Markoff tells me. "They freaked out. There's no question about it."

Why didn't he mention this in his *New York Times* stories? Why create the false appearance Shimomura was first hacked Christmas Day?

"But it was a different machine?" I ask.

"Am I being interviewed here?"

It strikes me as an odd question. Markoff was the one who called me twice in the space of an hour. Who's interviewing whom?

"Let's get on the same wavelength," Markoff suggests. "I'm glad to share this stuff with you, but I want to know where it's going to show up. 'Cuz I'm pretty close to Shimo and it's an issue for me."

Before I can respond, he starts talking about Shimomura again.

"I wrote that profile of Tsutomu because after I mentioned him in the bottom of my story ["Data Threat"] I basically outed him and a million reporters were all over him."

"He wasn't happy about that?"

"No, Tsutomu *loves* it," Markoff says. "He's playing his own games.

"I'll tell you it's unclear what was taken [referring to the Christmas hack], and point two, I can send you a public posting by an Air Force information warfare guy who described what was taken and their assessment of the damage.

"And there are lots of little snips of code that a brilliant hacker could probably use. But Tsutomu's mind works in very cryptic ways. It's not clear that without Tsutomu you're going to be able to do anything with it.

"Now in this break-in I don't actually think a lot of stuff was taken."

This break-in? Just how many times was Shimomura hacked before Christmas?

But I ask a different question. "Why would an Air Force guy post something?"

"Oh, Tsutomu," Markoff casually replies. "He produced a lot of software for the Air Force."

"Where would he post this?"

"Oh, to a mailing list. A lot of people were concerned about what was taken from his [Shimomura's] machine. What they [the hacker] got was a lot of his electronic mail. Some of it's kind of embarrassing. [But] I don't think people are going to find new ways to attack the network based on this particular attack.

"There is another issue," Markoff cautions in a serious tone.

"Tsutomu is a very sharp guy, and it is not impossible that that was a bait machine, which is why I stayed away from the issue."

Is Markoff implying Shimomura, a rumored NSA spy, laid a trap? And what about Markoff's *New York Times* articles? Were they part of the trap, too?

"Think about it for a second," Markoff pauses dramatically. "And you get into this wilderness-of-mirrors kind of world. And a lot of people that are writing don't know everything, and I don't know everything.

"I've been protecting him [Shimomura] for five years. I get the profile and the [Wall Street] Journal is on him. They don't know how close he is to the military. It would make perfect sense. Who knows what's in the code? The guy is in the counterintelligence business."

.   .   .

I feel uncomfortable. Markoff has revealed incredible information to me about Shimomura, just hours after the Los Angeles Times Magazine has asked me to do a cover story on the cybersleuth himself. I'm tempted to write the story, but I'm overcommitted.

The next day I phone Markoff to tell him about the L.A. Times offer. Obviously that paper competes with the New York Times. It's hard for me to reach him, and when I finally do, in contrast to yesterday's generosity, he seems gruff and angry.

When I tell him about the L.A. Times story proposal and say I'm probably not going to do it, he responds with sarcasm. "Don't worry about it," he says. "I already knew about it."

I puzzle over these two conversations and wonder why, if Markoff thought I was about to write a newspaper story on Shimomura, he would share his astonishing inside information.

The only source I have that Markoff wants is Mitnick. Was he trading Shimomura for Mitnick?

.   .   .

"Hey, I got that magazine!"

It's Mitnick talking about Newsweek, just a couple of hours after my conversation with Markoff.

"I'm going to get a blowup of that picture and make it a Tsutomu dartboard. Yeah, hitting the sword will be the bull's-eye," Mitnick chuckles.

.   .   .

So far, John Markoff is my only source that Shimomura has recently been compromised at least twice to the dismay of his NSA handlers.

But without any prompting, Mitnick confirms the story. He knows a hacker who "did" Tsutomu. The way Mitnick tells it, hackers have been "doing" Shimomura for some time.

"A guy named Chris" — Nug is his handle — "did Tsutomu last year," Mitnick reveals in a chatty tone. "He used a different technique. He did it about a year ago."

"Where did you hear this?"

"On IRC." IRC is the Internet Relay Channel, a kind of chat line for hackers and Netaphiles.

"[Chris] likes to brag about his feats," Mitnick continues. "He's a teenager. He started dumping Tsutomu's files on IRC. A lot of people log [capture and record] IRC. I hear he did it last year. He got into another [Tsutomu] box."

Interesting. Not one but two Shimomura computers have been compromised, and his files dumped on the Internet for all to see. So much for Shimomura's great security.

"Some guys from the [military] brass went to San Diego. There was a big security hole. Someone who took his shit might be able to reconstruct some of the stuff he's working on."

Mitnick seems to be recounting Markoff's tale about Shimomura being hacked last year and chastised by the NSA. Could this be the motivation behind Shimomura's public pledge to solve the crime "as a matter of honor"? Is he trying to save face with U.S. military intelligence?

"Where'd you hear this?"

"It was a post [an Internet message posted publicly to a newsgroup that follows a particular interest, in this case probably security]. I could dig up the post."

Could this be the post Markoff mentioned?

Suddenly I hear voices in the background.

"Where are you?"

"I'm in a magazine shop."

Mitnick's searching for articles about himself.

"I think the NSA is a crock. Everybody knows about them," Mitnick banters, as he peruses the titles. "They are not as covert as they think," he says, pausing. "What I'm saying is I'm sure there are other agencies we don't know about."

"Did you ever read *The Puzzle Palace?*" I ask, mentioning the bestseller on the intelligence agency.

"Yeah. I'm very interested in cryptography. I always wanted to get a job with the NSA," Mitnick says. "I even called the NSA once. Hey, I wonder if they [the NSA] fingerprint? You know there are ways to change your fingerprint. They look at each print and come up with a hash. You can take a soldering iron. Look at your thumb. See the wedges and the loops? You can take a soldering iron and kind of burn yourself."

.   .   .

The last two days have been confusing.

The Shimomura attack has become national news, springing from the front pages of the *New York Times* to the pages of *Newsweek.* Meanwhile, no one has connected Kevin Mitnick to the break-ins. Indeed, the only article even to mention Mitnick was the U.S. Marshals' plea for help the day after Markoff's page-one story, and that never hinted at any connection between the hacker and the security man.

I have no direct evidence Mitnick executed the attack, but I do know that Mitnick knows a tremendous amount about Shimomura. He says Shimomura had hacker's software with which he could avoid cellular charges. He says Shimomura was hacked last year and the military was angry. And that last claim John Markoff has confirmed.

But the most fascinating thing was Mitnick's declaration that Shimomura was "working for the Air Force, working on a design to do strategic attacks on enemy foreign computer systems." An outlandish claim coming from a hacker, but John Markoff had said that Shimomura produced software for the Air Force.

Perhaps the untold story is as Kevin Mitnick hypothesized, that the "government uses this code to look at other people's stuff in the intelligence community and they don't want things fixed." No one may ever know, but I'm wondering what software drew the intruder to Tsutomu Shimomura's machine, and what might have been its ultimate purpose.

Sunday evening I e-mail myself at the Well. The only problem is I don't remember sending the message, let alone writing it.

Date: Sun, Feb 5 1995 20:25:24
From: Jon Littman
To: jlittman

Tsutomu and I discussed this attack in depth, over dinner . . . Tsutomu Shimomura and I were on the system vulnerabilities session of the conference referenced in the article — and it was his system that was attacked. We discussed, privately, the attack at length. The 'tools' that were stolen are far less significant than might be expected for three reasons:

(1) this attack, in an even more elementary form, was launched, successfully, on his system last summer and most of the tools were originally pilfered then — not now.
(2) the tools were mere snippets of code that require the original code architect to string them together and compile and execute.
(3) the crackers don't necessarily need sophisticated tools, and will be loath to use pilfered, and very complicated (i.e. easily attributed)

ones if they're intelligent, because if caught intruding it will also be evidence they broke into a research system in San Diego. . . .

AF testing has verified that 50% of the systems on the net, within the .af.mil domain, are vulnerable to penetration with the simplest techniques. On 80% of those 50% my team can get root . . . [with] simple techniques. Although the IP spoofing is interesting let's work the math . . . data indicates that sendmail is still wide open on most systems, even if you prevent IP spoofing sendmail is still vulnerable. This is important because you'll have stopped one IP spoofer, but 95 other crackers will have snatched the code you built using sendmail . . . We need to identify the top ten problems, and proactively prevent them. I know, metrically, what the Air Force's top ten are and we are working on the short term solution.

. . . IP spoofing is bad, but . . . our systems (yours and mine) are vulnerable to the most elementary attacks and as long as that stands, the exotic ones should be counted but not obsessed over.

. . . Often times I'm reluctant to post anything . . . It just seemed like everyone was thinking the same thing I was so I decided to 'share'. . .

Kevin

**** *Hey john, Kevin is a good name :-)*

Capt Kevin J. Ziese   ziese@chaos.csap.af.mil
Chief, Countermeasures Development   1-210-377-0477 Voice
AF Information Warfare Center   1-210-377-1326 Fax
1100 NW Loop 410, Suite 607   1-800-217-0570 Pager
San Antonio, Texas 78213

•   •   •

On Monday morning, I don't even read this bizarre piece of e-mail. In fact, it's not until Tuesday, when I'm browsing through a host of new messages in my Well account, that it finally hits me.

I reread the header — "From: Jon Littman, To: jlittman." How weird! Someone inside the Well sent me this message, as if I'd typed and sent it myself. It's not hard to figure out who's the likely suspect. But just in case I'm not sure, Mitnick has added a footnote to the newsgroup post noting the first name he has in common with the Air Force captain.

This must be the post Mitnick referred to a few days ago on the Shimomura attack. And the post Markoff referred to. From what I can tell, it's a post to an Internet security newsgroup.

I'm impressed. It's not every day I read something written by an Air Force captain in Information Warfare. And Captain Ziese has some insightful observations that expand on Mitnick and Markoff's comments. First, the big attack on Shimomura wasn't really this Christmas but "last summer." Second, "most of the tools were originally pilfered then — not now. " Third, the tools taken in the new attack were "far less significant." And fourth, half the Internet is vulnerable to attack through "simple techniques."

In other words, the Christmas Day hack was a media creation and the Internet is swiss cheese. IP spoofing may be an interesting attack method, but according to this Air Force captain most of the Internet's doors can be pried open with the technical equivalent of a screwdriver.

.   ▪   ▪

"Have you heard anything?"

It's John Markoff on the phone, the afternoon of Wednesday, February 8. "You probably have quite a bit more information than I do," I say.

"I don't know," Markoff sighs. He's obsessed with finding out who broke into Shimomura's machine.

"It gets quite murky. I don't even know if it's Kevin I'm onto. I'm into a real heavy paranoia stage. Hang on for a second. . . ."

Is Markoff saying that he thinks Mitnick didn't do the Christmas Day hack?

"Sorry," Markoff comes back on the phone. He sounds flustered, confused, not at all the cool journalist I'm accustomed to.

"Well, I don't know. I'm sort of running around and I don't know where to run . . . " Markoff frets, and then, suddenly, is back in control. "If you had to guess where Kevin was in the country, where would you guess?"

"Guess what city he's in?" I ask, already knowing from my sources that Markoff's been telling people Denver.

"Yeah."

"I'd say he's probably not in Seattle."

Markoff agrees that's unlikely.

"I don't know, maybe somewhere in the central U.S.?"

Markoff brushes off my ambiguous reply. "What about his MO?" Markoff asks without missing a beat. "Do you think he now feels secure 'cuz he's using cell phones?"

.   .   .

"I think there might be a city," Markoff offers. "Before he was reasonably clever. He sort of worked through switches, and you couldn't really tell anything.

"But now I don't know if it's [Mitnick] at all," he groans. "Another voice mail message was left on Tsutomu's machine berating him for putting his voice on the Net."

"His voice on the Net?"

"Tsutomu posted the [voice] tapes to [the Internet]," Markoff explains. "You can go listen to them."

"Who berated him?"

"Unknown. But it sounded like the same guy."

"The same synthesized voice?"

"No, it was a different synthesized voice, a Japanese thing. 'Grasshopper, son, you make mistake.' It was very funny actually."

.   .   .

Mitnick phones the following afternoon, Thursday, February 9, saying he knows I've sent my assistant to meet with Kathleen Cunningham, the U.S. Marshal in Los Angeles. He sounds cocky, full of himself, the same way he sounded after he hacked Lottor. The same way he sounded after he told me about the break-in to Shimomura's machine.

"How do you know everything?" I ask, stunned.

"Well I keep tabs on them as much as they like to keep tabs on me. That way I can predict their next move. You would be surprised."

"Well, I guess I shouldn't be anymore. It's pretty impressive."

"Yes," Mitnick agrees. "Kathleen Cunningham."

"You're amazing. How do you know?"

"I can't say, 'cuz then you'd be obligated to tell them because of the way it's done, because then you'd be an accessory after the fact."

What does Mitnick know? The only time I ever discussed my assistant's upcoming meeting with the marshal was on the telephone.

I've got news that I figure will surprise him. "I was asked to write a story for the *L.A. Times* about Shimomura but I turned it down."

"Oh, about Shimomura?"

"Yeah. They wanted me to do a cover story."

"Well, I think it's great. It helps me out in a way. It puts him in the media."

"A strange thing happened. The *L.A. Times* called me at four-thirty P.M. one day, right, and asked me to do it."

"Hold on!" Mitnick jokes. "Did you say four-thirty?

"Yeah."

"Oh, I had it at a different time — never mind. I'm just kidding," Mitnick chuckles. "I just had to fuck with your head! I better be quiet, because you're going to start to believe it and start to be like one of these other paranoid people out there."

What about Mitnick knowing about this U.S. Marshal meeting before it happens? Shouldn't that make me a tad paranoid?

"What did make me paranoid is the next day I get a call from John Markoff. He's calling and offering me all this stuff."

"Did you ever see the movie *Puppetmaster?*"

"No."

"It's where these aliens seat themselves on the neck of the humans and actually take them over, their mind and body. Well, I picture a big FBI alien sitting on the back of Markoff. He's a puppet, that's my nickname for him. Puppetmaster."

Mitnick is on his Markoff conspiracy tirade again. I ignore it and continue.

I tell Mitnick that when Markoff called me he already knew I'd been offered the *L.A. Times* assignment.

"Yeah, 'cuz they probably have a wiretap on your phone line and they're probably taking the info I'm telling you. That's all I can make of it. Did you ever admit to Markoff that I talked to you?"

"I did slip at one point."

"Did you tell him the frequency that we talk?"

"No. I told him he had to swear — he had to swear he would tell nobody. I said, 'You have to swear you don't tell the FBI or anybody like that.' "

"I'm surprised there haven't been marshals at your place," Mitnick wonders. "I mean, relatives [of mine] have been visited that I haven't talked to in years."

"He did say one thing that made me think that he is trying to get you captured."

"Oh, hell yes! I know that! I don't know why. I never have done anything to harm him. When they [Markoff and Hafner] wanted to talk to me about writing their book, I said, 'How much money are we talking,' and they said nothing. I said, 'Sorry. I'm not going to spend my time when you guys are making six figures.'

"I don't know why I've been talking to you. I think it's because I like you. It's weird, 'cuz you're going to write what you write. I'm not making a fucking dime from talking to you. I'm risking my ass talking to you. I must be nuts."

I chuckle, but Mitnick doesn't think it's funny.

"No, seriously. I mean something eggs me on to talk to you. You've got a sense of humor. I enjoy talking to you. That's bad for me. I wish you were more of an *asshole!*"

Coming from Kevin Mitnick this is a compliment. Or a con.

"Markoff clearly knows it's [the Shimomura IP Spoof attack] not me. See, the media is interested in this Internet shit. They've got Shimomura on the front page. I know the marshal is trying to get me put on the front page as the cause for it all. 'If we put him away there will be no more computer crime.'

"Markoff was the whole cause of the whole thing. I wonder if he is on some payroll. Do you personally know why he has such an interest in me? Did I piss him off in some fashion? I want to nail his motivation."

●　　　●　　　●

"Nobody can figure out why they [the Marshals] went public with that information," I say, asking Mitnick why they revealed he was nearly captured in Seattle. "Because that's not what the FBI usually does."

"No, because if you go public with it, that makes the other person [Mitnick] know that you know. And it makes the other person change all their methods."

"How many people are involved in your case?

"Maybe a total of five, six."

"That many?" I say, surprised. "Who else besides the two in L.A.?"

"You got Ken. You got Kathleen," Mitnick runs down the list as if he's naming his bowling team. "You got their technical people. Then you have U.S. Marshal people. Then you never know if you have any people in other states."

.   .   .

I ask Mitnick about his hobbies and he clams up. He says the feds find people by their habits and hobbies.

"Remember where everything fucked up?" Mitnick cryptically refers to that "idiot's" error that cost him his last job. "That all has to do with the Sleepless thing [Mitnick is cryptically referring to his near capture in Seattle by alluding to the movie *Sleepless in Seattle*.]. When the connection [Mitnick's identification] was made there were techniques and methods that had to be completely redrawn from scratch." He says little more, except to hint that he's completely reinvented himself, down to the food he eats.

"I'm not going to say it's going to go one way or another. I'm not that confident. All I can say is, hey, I gave it my best shot. If it goes in my direction, great. I accomplished something. And if it doesn't go in my direction at least I know I tried."

"And what have you accomplished?"

"Living my life the way I want to live it."

"Is there something else, too? The feat itself?"

"No, no. I don't consider this a game anymore."

.   .   .

Perhaps. But it's clear he's still playing. Mitnick jokes about his new "degree" not quite being ready, chuckling that it takes sixty days for the paperwork to come through. Somehow in his mind it's all right because he says he's in it for the thrill.

"Take a game, say I play a Nintendo game all the time. My line of thinking, whether it's corrupt or not."

"Right."

"I know there's like a back way of winning the game. So I break into Nintendo, and I steal the source to the game, figure out how it works, don't pass it to anyone, don't keep it. There's no money in it, there's no evil intent. Well, I consider that a game.

"Now on the other hand if I took that and sold it to Mattel . . . [Some of the] stuff I've done, I could have made lots of money."

Now we're getting somewhere. Mitnick's finally talking about how he could hack his first million. That is, if he were just a cybercriminal, and not a dedicated hacker.

"Theoretically what could one make money with?"

"Information," Mitnick says weightily. "Insider trading."

Ivan Boesky, listen up.

"Let's say I wanted to make lots of money. Like right now I can get out of this fucking bind that I am in right now. Alls you've got to do is become a real criminal. Infiltrating companies that do leveraged buyouts and stocks and mergers. Obtain this information, create a new identity, and do stock trades. Something that's not going to be so high profile that the Securities and Exchange Commission steps in. Like fifty k here and fifty k there."

"A lot of money," I say.

"Become another Ivan Boesky. That's easy. I can do it tomorrow, but that's where I don't cross the line. But if somebody wanted to do that, the key would be infiltrating the companies that do the leveraged buyouts. As the guy said in *Sneakers,* it all comes down to the ones and zeroes."

"So all you need to do is infiltrate the leverage buyout companies?"

"The buyout companies," Mitnick repeats. "The attorneys that do the buyouts."

"Which is probably easier?"

"You know they're not secure, " Mitnick says. "Like for instance, I hate saying names."

"Well, I'll say a name like Lehman Brothers or —"

"Shearson Lehman. So you just basically attack those companies, and I'm good enough, I can basically get in anywhere I choose. Like now if I was a real desperado that's what I'd be doing."

"Right," I say with a touch of disbelief in my voice.

Mitnick doesn't like my tone. "You know that I'm not bullshitting you!" Mitnick snaps.

"Right. You just target somebody who has —"

"The information," Mitnick intones.

"Information." It's one of the hacker's favorite words, right after "idiot."

"There's always got to be one center that's more secure than the other," Mitnick continues, sounding professional. "They are just about to do a leverage [buyout] and the value of the company's going to double in the next week. So you buy ten k [of stock] and it's worth twenty k."

"Right, and then you sell."

"As long as you don't buy a hundred thousand dollars," Mitnick advises. "Maybe [you] establish a credit profile under it and then you take that cash. You launder it. You deposit it in your real account under your other identity in different increments. So in other words you wouldn't take five grand out of that bank and the same day deposit five grand in your other bank.

"They have certain trip levels that notify the IRS. With the new database the government's going to do on America, they're going to keep track of everyone's banking finances. So you take out two thousand dollars, and a few days later make another two-thousand-dollar deposit."

"Big Brother doesn't watch if it's under two thousand dollars?"

"Twenty-five hundred is the trip level," Mitnick explains. "Ten thousand is the big trip level, but banks also notify at twenty-five hundred. They actually have a database which keeps track of all these transactions — that's how they catch big drug traffickers."

"They do this on everybody?"

"What's the big deal? So it takes four times as long. It's basically free money," Mitnick says, suddenly wondering why he just told me this. "You're going to write this in *Playboy* like this is like my next avenue of accomplishment. I'm telling you if I was a real thief I wouldn't be toying around with cellular shit. 'Cuz there's no money in it!"

It makes sense. Petersen wasn't anywhere near the hacker Mitnick is, and he hacked out a $150,000 wire transfer. Imagine what crimes Mitnick could commit if he put his mind to it.

"Zero," Mitnick continues. "What, so I'm going to modify a cellular phone and sell it to somebody so that person can go turn me in? If you're going to commit a crime, do it where there's no witnesses. And that's in this insider shit."

"What're the other theoretical methods that could be used?"

"Besides wiretapping?" the hacker asks.

"Yeah."

"There's many different ways of wiretapping: social engineering, outside penetration, computers can be broken into. If they're on the Internet [they] might as well have a welcome mat. Hold on a second, OK?"

Mitnick puts on his jacket and says he's going to see if there's a restaurant nearby. His stomach has been bothering him all day.

"Why are they so interested in me?" Mitnick ponders. "I guess maybe one of these companies that got hit, they either think it was me — or they must have a lot of pull."

"Uh-huh."

"Because I'm just curious why Markoff is so interested. It's like he's a federal agent. That's why he's a Puppetmaster. Markoff is participating like he's a victim. For whatever reason, maybe he feels it's his civic duty."

A little after 4:30 P.M. on Sunday, I retrieve my messages. The first one arrived just minutes after I left on Saturday afternoon for an overnight trip. It was Markoff, sounding upbeat, asking me to return his call.

Before I have much of a chance to wonder why the *New York Times* reporter needs me to call him back on a Saturday, the phone rings. It's Kevin Mitnick, talking about his nemesis, John Markoff. Mitnick says his "grapevine" has been telling him that Markoff has been busily interviewing people over the weekend.

"The people I talked to that he [Markoff] placed calls to are surprised because he usually never calls," Mitnick tells me. "Maybe there's an article coming out."

"What kind of people was he calling?" I ask.

"Hackers," Mitnick says.

"These are people he doesn't call often?"

"And Shimomura," Mitnick adds. "And people like that."

How does Mitnick know Markoff is calling Shimomura? He won't say, other than to refer to his ubiquitous grapevine. I can see how Mitnick knows Markoff's calling hackers. But Shimomura? Has he hacked Shimomura's voice mail? Is he on the switch, checking the records? Or could he actually be wiretapping Shimomura's line with SAS?

"He's trying to get Shimomura to work against me," Mitnick continues.

"BEEP!"

It's my call waiting. Tonight I'm not in the mood to pick up. But for days afterward I'll wonder who was trying to call.

"I don't think he [Shimomura] has a bone to pick with me because I've never attacked him. I know a lot that goes on because I have links to the underground. They trust me because they know I'm not gonna be an informant because of the status I'm in. So I'm learning about all that's going on. Who's doing what. It's great. That's how come I have *all* the information."

Is Mitnick planting his alibi with me?

"You talk to some of the young kids?" I ask.

"No. They're not trustworthy. I trust the inactive hackers that associate with the active ones that are overseas," Mitnick explains.

"Like ones in the Netherlands?" I guess.

"Like ones overseas. Out of the U.S. territories, because if the Bureau [FBI] comes to them, they just tell 'em to go fuck off."

The rumor is that Mitnick associates with an Israeli hacker.

•   •   •

"You're sure that they [the FBI] know that we're talking?" I ask Mitnick.

"I believe they do. I haven't verified it, but I have a good gut feeling."

"But you're still able to be careful?"

"Right. Well, the actual area I'm in is temporary. I'm not living here, so if they actually tracked it down, the city I'm calling from, which is plausible, it doesn't matter because I'm not gonna be here."

"And that's as far as they can go?"

"Yeah. They can get it down to the cell site, which is within a quarter mile from where I physically am, and I won't be here and I can check into hotels under an alias."

Mitnick decides to give me a primer on checking into hotels anonymously. The Kevin Mitnick system, so to speak. It's ingenious. "You find out a person that went there. You always go to a hotel that keeps you on database. So if you check in again and say, 'Oh, I stayed here on blah-blah-blah date,' they look in the computer and they don't ask you for your driver's license. You've already been verified. And I already do this prior to going to where I'm going."

"How would you find out somebody who had already stayed?"

"Their name? Social engineering them. 'Hi! I'm looking for Jones that was in there a month ago. Could you check it in the system?' If you're already in the system, they don't require ID."

"You can actually call and say I'm looking for somebody who —"

"No, no, no. You're calling from another Marriott for a billing problem, accounts payable deal from Corporate. It has to be like Holiday Inn or Marriott, where you can call an 800 number. So you're Bill from Marriott calling someplace in Alaska. You understand? Once you're known to the system, you're not scrutinized."

"So you come up and you're just Bill Jones?"

"Yeah. 'I'm Bill Jones, stayed here blah-blah date.' They bring it up. 'Oh yes. Hi, Mr. Jones! And they explain all the benefits and they go, 'Do you want to put it on your card?'

"You go, 'No. I'm going to pay cash this time.' You never use a credit card because if you're ever discovered, they can follow your trail. Unless, of course, you want to be mean and nasty and when you feel you're discovered you give it [the credit card] to somebody else to use."

•   •   •

The conversation drifts. Mitnick chats about how De Payne is the Alan Abel of the 1990s, following in the footsteps of the great prankster who has pulled hoaxes on the media since 1966. He tells me how he uses hard luck stories to win cheaper rates for almost anything, including rental cars, offering cash only after he's significantly cut the price. Finally, I get a word in edgewise. I tell Mitnick I found his childhood mentor, Irv Rubin, the head of the radical Jewish Defense League in Los Angeles.

"Oh, from the JDL!" Mitnick says, surprised. "He doesn't know too much about me as a hacker — just as a normal person involved with them back when I was a kid. My stepfather at the time was heavy into that."

"What kinda things would you do?"

"Shooting," Mitnick says.

"I remember participating in the marches," recalls the hacker. "I knew the guy that actually bombed one of these air places and then he had to skip off to Israel."

"How old was he?"

Mitnick doesn't like my questions anymore.

"I wouldn't want the government to know I was involved with the JDL because they might come up with a whole bunch of other shit. 'Oh! So he's a terrorist!' "

"Well, this is when you were eight years old."

"*They* don't care!" Mitnick thunders. "They don't take it as chronological! They take it as a whole picture. So who knows what could be twisted? They're very good at twisting stuff. I got a feeling ole Markoff is gonna put something out. I'll have to watch the *New York Times* in the next couple days."

Mitnick doesn't pause between "twisting stuff" and "I got a feeling ole Markoff is gonna put something out." For such a high-tech master, Mitnick seems to rely on his gut feelings pretty often.

"I don't know what his new story could be," I venture. "I mean, they don't usually let them write a new story unless —"

"Unless something happens."

.   .   .

"BEEP! BEEP! BEEP! BEEP!"

"Oh, fuck! What's that?" Mitnick panics. "Something's beeping in the car! I don't know what that was!"

Could it be Mitnick's scanner telling him the feds are on his tail?

"*BEEP! BEEP! BEEP! BEEP!*"

"Did you hear that?" he asks.

"It's not your beeper? The car beeper?"

"I dunno. It's something in the car."

"It's a bugged car!" I say, laughing.

"It's a bugged car!" Mitnick screams.

"It's tracking you," I joke. "My job was to get you in that car."

It's Sunday night, February 12, 1995. Tsutomu Shimomura landed at Raleigh-Durham Airport about an hour ago.

.   .   .

Mitnick starts talking about his near capture in Seattle. "A lot of people are pissed off, right? They know where I was, right? Where I was working required a clearance, and I passed the security clearance."

"That irritated certain people?"

"I think so."

"What sort of things do you have to pass for something like that?"

"I'd rather not get into it."

"But you had a clean background obviously," I say, meaning Mitnick had created verifiable documents — birth certificate, social security number, driver's license, and educational records — to establish a whole new identity.

"Yeah. They actually took a thumbprint to check. I knew that all it is is a deterrent because you can't classify fingerprints with one print. See, if you know how the system works, you can find a loophole."

"So, you weren't even afraid?"

"No. I knew it'd work. I was right."

"Why don't they do more?"

"I think probably soon, like the year 2010, they'll probably have it where you might have to get a full set of prints," Mitnick prophesizes. "And then when you get stopped by Mo Jo Cop, he scans it and it checks NCIC [the National Crime Information Center] right away. Wouldn't that be scary? And how about when the government decides we don't want cash. We want to put it all on a plastic card. Your net worth. Then whenever the IRS wants to tax you, they just take it out.

"Hold on a sec, this guy's gonna take my stuff."

Mitnick's talking to somebody else. "Hold on! I'm gonna go on that one, I just have to get something."

.   .   .

"You were talking to somebody?"

"I'm at a library and someone took my spot somewhere so I had to ask them to move," Mitnick replies.

"So they don't mind you having a phone in the library?"

"No. I'm in a section where they have all the research computers, so I'm out here researching."

"What are you researching?"

"Stuff. I'm trying to find out the formula to Coca-Cola. I want to know what I'm putting into my body. Is that such a bad thing?"

"Well, the formula is sugar, sugar, and caffeine, isn't it?"

"I want it down to the real formula, the secret formula."

"What's that funny noise?"

"It's the up arrow key," Mitnick says. "I'm reading mail. Junk mail."

"What kind of system is it?"

"God! Always a question! I don't know what type of PC it is. It's not even marked."

"But do you have modem access at the library?"

"No. That'd be nice," Mitnick reflects. "You can search on articles and CD-ROMs, phone book directories, and all that sort of stuff."

"They have CD-ROM at this one?"

"Yeah. That should narrow it down for you. It's pretty cool."

The hacker's fingers click the keys again.

"I'm on Infotrack right now," Mitnick says. "I'm looking at Poulsen."

"Well, there might be a match between us," I say, meaning he may find a reference to an article I wrote.

"Oh yeah," Mitnick remembers. "Because of that 'Last Hacker.' Why did you call it that title?"

"You never read the story. It was the last line in the story."

"Hey!" Mitnick laughs. "Turn on your modem and I'll find it on your PC."

"It's not there anymore."

"Not there? What do you use, WordPerfect or Word?"

I pause a second. I'm not sure I want Mitnick to know what program I'm using.

"Word."

"I use WordPerfect."

"Uh-oh. We're incompatible."

"It's OK," Mitnick says. "I have a conversion program."

.   .   .

Mitnick's feeling clever and in control. He didn't just outsmart the feds by passing a security clearance in Seattle. He also led them on a wild goose chase to Israel just by pretending to be hot for some Israeli girl.

"Idiot [Neil] Clift comes to the conclusion, 'Oh! He's going there, he's on his way.' So then they phone up the authorities in the States and say, 'Oh! This guy's on the way to Israel.' They notify the Israel law enforcement people that I'm on my way."

"Do you actually know this person?"

"No! No! But they [the FBI] believe I did. Right? [I did it] Just to see what the reaction would be. And of course, they took it hook, line, and sinker."

"They [the FBI] just think you know her?"

"I *know* they do! It's great!"

"What does she look like?"

"I have no idea. I just know her e-mail address," Mitnick pauses, sounding perturbed at himself. "I shouldn't have told you. I should've kept that secret."

.   .   .

"I don't like this," Mitnick interjects. "This guy walks back here, checks me out, then walks away. That's weird."

"Some guy's checking you out?"

"Yeah, because I guess anyone on a cell phone is suspicious, you know?"

"They got a call," I joke. "Find the guy with the cell phone. He's back researching things on the terminal."

Mitnick doesn't find this funny.

"Yeah, well, he'd have a lot of libraries [with a full CD-ROM setup] to call — a *lot* of libraries!"

The truth is, in Raleigh, North Carolina, there are only two.

.   .   .

"I've got call waiting and somebody's been calling me over and over again and I haven't been picking it up," I tell Mitnick.

The hacker jokes that I'm working for the feds, trying to keep him on the line so they can trace his call. "The guy at the company says,

'We got it, so hang up! Call Jim there in the Sacramento SCC [switching control center]!'

"Jim?" I ask, puzzled.

"Jim, that's the guy that handles Mill Valley [my hometown] evenings," Mitnick responds as if it's common knowledge.

"Really?"

"Yeah, serious as a heart attack."

"Why up in Sacramento?"

"Because at night and on the weekends they cut over to Sacramento. Yeah, the good ole guy's here at the DMS 100 [telephone] switch." Mitnick chuckles. "Does what he's told. You know what I'm saying?"

"Yeah, I probably do."

Has Mitnick wiretapped my phone?

.   .   .

We've been chatting for two and a half hours straight, except for the short break when Mitnick's battery died and I forgot to hang up the phone. I'm hungry and decide to spend some time with my family. We say goodbye, but before the call ends I ask Mitnick why he seemed so suspicious the other night. "You said I didn't tell you something the other night."

"Yeah, you still didn't," Mitnick says, sounding cool and distant.

"What?"

"You didn't tell me what state Markoff thinks I'm in."

Markoff has been telling other hackers that Mitnick is in Colorado.

"Well, I can't," I answer.

"He didn't tell you you can't, did he?" Mitnick prods.

"No. But he didn't tell me anything. I had my own sources."

"I want to have fun with him," Mitnick laughs, imagining the possibilities. "Wherever he thinks I am, I think all the calls should originate from there. It'd be interesting to see what he thinks. I'm just curious. I hope it's a nice place."

IV.

February 15, 1995

"*Yes, hello?*" *mumbles a groggy Lewis De Payne. It's well past midnight, the morning of February 15, 1995.*

"This is a collect call," says the operator. "Caller, what's your name?"

"Kevin."

"Will you pay?"

"Yeah," says De Payne.

"I just was arrested by the FBI tonight. I'm in jail in Raleigh, North Carolina."

"Wow. OK."

"I just thought you ought to know," Mitnick warns his hacker buddy. "I'm in custody, the FBI and U.S. Marshals."

"Really? Wow. That was when?"

"Tonight, about four or five hours ago."

"Wow!"

"Do you have three-way calling?" Mitnick asks his friend.

·   ·   ·

Five hours later, at 8:30 A.M., Pacific time, Ivan Orton, the prosecutor in Seattle, calls to tell me the news. David Schindler, the Assistant U.S. Attorney in Los Angeles, phones around 9:30 A.M. By noon one of my hacker sources calls back with the inside scoop. Mitnick, it seems, was arrested by a Japanese security expert who had the help of a reporter.

I think back. Just two days ago, on Monday, I had returned Markoff's Saturday afternoon call. He wasn't in, but he phoned back while I was out to lunch, and left what seemed at the time a strange message. Markoff said his father was ill, thanked me profusely for returning his call, and told me to "take care." The odd thing was he sounded happy. He'd never been personal or emotional before, certainly not in a phone message.

To check if Markoff has been in Raleigh all week, I phone the San Francisco bureau of the *New York Times* and explain that Markoff has been trying to reach me. The receptionist says I'm not alone. John Markoff has been out all week on a big story, and even she doesn't know where he is.

About noon, I reach William Berryhill Jr., Chief Marshal of the Eastern District of North Carolina. In his southern drawl, Berryhill runs down the facts as he knows them: Mitnick's early-morning arrest, his appearance a few hours ago before a federal magistrate, his scheduled detention hearing Friday morning. Berryhill is friendly, but he explains there isn't a lot more he can say. "On the average John Doe, the Raleigh-Durham Task Force would issue the press release," explains Berryhill. "But because this guy is so high profile it's coming directly out of main Justice."

Several hours later, just before I drive to the airport to hop on a red-eye, David Schindler returns my afternoon calls. John Markoff was in Raleigh, North Carolina, as the capture unfolded, and by the tone of Schindler's voice, the government isn't too happy about what happened.

·   ·   ·

By midafternoon, just fifteen hours after his capture, Kevin Mitnick is making waves on the Internet. The Well has created a discussion group, or "thread," for its subscribers to post their comments publicly about what the provider calls the "Netwide Security Incident."

At precisely 2:32 P.M, Bruce Katz, heir to the Rockport shoe fortune and the Well's eccentric CEO, launches the thread with a description of his company's critical role in Mitnick's arrest.

#1

Announcement from The WELL Management
February 15, 1995
2:30 PM

On January 27 it was discovered that The WELL was experiencing unauthorized entry to its computers. This was first noticed as an accumulation of files in several seldom used accounts.

... By Monday we had contacted Computer Emergency Response Team (CERT) and leading security specialists, including Tsutomu Shimomura. ... Shortly after that we brought in specialists and equipment. ... We initiated round-the-clock staffing to monitor any unauthorized activity in detail ... we found private files and proprietary source code from other systems and sites being transferred through The WELL. ... [W]e contacted other sites involved and cooperated with the US Attorney's Office to identify the individual(s) responsible for these system violations.

With the help of computer security specialists and with the voluntary cooperation of various sites, authorities succeeded in arresting a suspect at 2am EST, Feb. 15.

We have learned a great deal about security during the last few weeks and we will be taking a series of measures to tighten the WELL's security. But having said that, it also needs to be said that public computing systems are by their very nature impossible to entirely secure. This is especially true in an open system like ours. ...

We have pledged not to mention the other sites whose systems were compromised, but suffice it to say that the files that were stolen from their systems may have represented millions of dollars worth of information. ...

Bruce R. Katz
CEO, The WELL

So the Well, known as the most pro-hacker, anti-government provider on the Internet, helped bring Shimomura and the FBI together to track Mitnick. Who would have thought it possible? Within minutes of Katz's disclosure, a Well member jumps on the bandwagon and launches a warning and a damage report:

#7

CHANGE ALL YOUR PASSWORDS NOW! . . .

Well
Netcom
CO Supernet. . .
Motorola
Intermetrics
Berkeley

But some begin to wonder why so much is being made of the break-ins. David Lewis, a former Well employee, asks why something wasn't done about the Well's compromised security months ago.

#32

Interestingly enough . . . WELL Support was aware of probable hacking problems as early as November. This one is wondering why it took so long to have WELL technical folks respond. . . ."

No sooner is that concern raised than a members says that hacking the Well is "hardly big news. . . ." But it is big news to Well management, apparently. One Well manager curtly replies to Lewis that he's asked the staff and "no one knows, or remembers, what you are talking about." Well management considers the attacks a very serious matter. So too does the FBI. Another user posts the FBI's latest update on the arrest.

#62

[From the FBI in North Carolina]

PRESS RELEASE

At 1:30 a.m., today, February 15, 1995, agents of the FBI arrested KEVIN MITNICK, a well-known computer hacker and federal fugitive. The arrest occurred after an intensive two-week electronic manhunt led law enforcement agents to MITNICK's apartment in Raleigh, North Carolina. . . .

In this latest incident, MITNICK is alleged to have electronically attacked numerous corporate and communications carriers located in California, Colorado, and North Carolina where he caused significant damage and stole proprietary information. One of the attacked sites was the San Diego Supercomputer Center (SDSC), and Tsutomu Shimomura, a system administrator at SDSC, provided significant assistance to law enforcement personnel during the investigation. . . .

At 5:05 P.M., Lewis logs on to defend himself. Well management is making him out to be a liar or a kook. He's saying that the Well's thousands of subscribers have been vulnerable to attack since at least last November, and the Well knew all about it. He's not backing down.

#69

This is the story from November:

. . . a user (name I don't recall) called for assist on downloading an ftped [a common protocol for sending large files over the Internet] document. I checked his home dir for the doc, which wasn't there. He said "it will be." Puzzled, I looked again, and the file — a HUGE file was being put in his home dir. I asked him if anyone knew his password — he said no — but "Someone has yours". He told me [the person] had the root password or root access . . . I watched a new ftp [File Transfer Protocol] session start up and another large file get dumped into his account [clear evidence that an unknown intruder had gained total, or 'root,' access at the Well].

At the same time Pei/I [Hua-Pei Chen, the Well's technical manager] were noticing a LOT of ftp activity in/out of the WELL which couldn't be accounted for . . . I reported the whole incident to WELL Support — all staff at the time knew of the situation — and . . . nothing more came of it.

There's probably email floating around in staff accounts or in the Support archive . . . late Oct to early Nov.

By 5:23 P.M., Chip Bayers of *Hotwired*, the online 'zine published by *Wired* magazine, notes that the FBI press release makes no claims that Mitnick stole software but instead alleges he caused "significant damage and stole proprietary information." Minutes later, another contributor to the thread issues a general word of caution on FBI claims. When it comes to government or corporate press releases, Bill Mandel warns, "significant damage" means little, citing the FBI's hyped Bell South case.

The Bell South debacle had made headlines a few years back. In the highly publicized case the federal government claimed a "stolen" proprietary manual was worth $70,000. It nearly succeeded. But at trial, the defense showed the manual could be ordered for $17 and the case was promptly dismissed. Ever since, sophisticated cyber-citizens have viewed federal hacking indictments with skepticism.

But the lessons of the Bell South case must have grown hazy in the minds of most Well regulars. They seem to take the FBI's press release at face value. There's no sense of "innocent till proven guilty," no sense that the government's claims might not be supported by fact. At 5:44, Bruce Koball, who helps organize the Computers, Freedom and Privacy conferences, begins to tell his inside story. There's an irony to the group's involvement in Mitnick's arrest that seems to go unnoticed.

CFP is famous for putting on conferences that encourage open dialogue between FBI agents, hackers, libertarians and journalists about hacking, freedom, and privacy in cyberspace. It's considered the Switzerland of cyberspace, a free zone for ideas. Hackers are featured attendees, and a common topic is the invasion of rights in cyberspace by overzealous feds. But all that seems to be forgotten in the excitement of the moment, as Koball proudly tells of his small role in the hacker's capture.

#85

Since this hits the press tomorrow, I might as well tell my little part of the story. . . .

On Fri 27 Jan of this year Jim Warren and I got mail from Gail [a Well conference manager] asking about an unusually large amount of storage (over 150 MB) in a comp account that had been granted to the Computers, Freedom and Privacy conference. . . .

. . . The files contained email addressed to tsutomu@sdsc.edu I didn't recognize the name until later that evening when the 28 Jan issue of the New York Times landed on my door step.

On the front page of the biz section was an article by John Markoff detailing the break in that had been suffered by Tsutomu Shimomura. . . .

Well, alarm bells went off in my head, and I immediately contacted Gail, who put me in touch with Pei [Chen]. I also contacted Markoff. . . . He immediately put me in touch with Shimomura. . . .

I then put Shimomura in direct contact with Pei and advised Pei that law enforcement should probably be called in as well. From there on, Shimomura, who was already on a crusade to catch the intruder, worked closely with Pei and the tech staff to help law enforcement catch him. . . .

. . . WELL management acted in an exemplary fashion in a difficult situation, striking a balance between the interests of the users of this system and a sense of duty to help law enforcement deal with a serious threat to the entire Net community. . . .

· · ·

At 7:32 P.M. Chris Goggans questions whether Mitnick was the first or the last hacker to crack the Well. Goggans ought to know. He's

the editor of the online hacker quarterly *Phrack*, and is renowned
online as Bloodaxe, a notorious Legion of Doom hacker:

#114

Here is my question regarding these events (which are by no means
over with the sole bust of kevin mitnick since he was not even
CLOSE to being the sole perp [perpetrator] with regards to hacking
The WELL). . . .

Now that we have all openly admitted that the well was cracked
WIDE OPEN, will all of the happy admins, please reassure all of us
that THE ENTIRE SYSTEM will be reinstalled from distribution
CD's, and that patches will be reinstalled on ALL WELL MA-
CHINES before the event grows fuzzy in peoples recollections?

. . . Telling everyone to change their passwords now is like telling
everyone that its over. It aint. . . ."

At 7:35 P.M Hua-Pei Chen, the Well's technical manager, rejects the
story that the Well was broken into last November.

#116

I SINCERELY do not remember you [Lewis] mentioned anything
about root access/pass-words on the well. . . .

Again, I don't think any SPECULATION is going to help us at all.
Spreading rumors or doubts will also help nothing. . . .

But an hour later at 8:36 P.M. Lewis stands firm. The Well had been
hacked last November. He's sure of it.

#138

Pei:

Everything I posted is very above-board. Not one word was made up.

At the time it was clear that the individual I spoke . . . [to] was
convinced that the individual in question had access to many
parts of the WELL. Other things that were known at the time: there
were unreasonably high LAVs [load averages] which at the time

were *specifically* related to multiple ftp sessions. Some of those ftp sessions we could not identify the source of. . . .

This I reported. I created a temporary directory in the support home directory and deposited the files in question there, waiting for anyone who wanted to look at them . . . and I decided after three days to remove said temporary files after no resolution had been made.

I was very vocal about my perception of the situation at the time. I mentioned it to most of the staff — and specifically all of Support. . . . In my mind, there is no doubt that the WELL has been insecure since that time. . . .

.   .   .

It's hard to imagine why a former Well employee would make this up, and I know he isn't. Lewis is talking about my Well account. I told him that I believed a hacker had root access at the Well, and he didn't dismiss my claim out of hand. He acknowledged the ease with which a hacker could crack an inherently insecure Internet site like the Well.

Now it's clear from his public post that he independently witnessed a hacker gain root access at the Well. But in August of 1994, Well employees told me a very different story. Then, they claimed it was impossible to hack universal, root access.

Somehow I think Kevin Mitnick and a lot of other hackers would disagree.

The Front Page

New York Times, February 16, 1995

A MOST-WANTED CYBERTHIEF IS CAUGHT IN HIS OWN WEB

By John Markoff
Special to the New York Times

Raleigh, N.C., Feb. 15 — After a search of more than two years, a team of FBI agents early this morning captured a 31-year-old computer expert accused of a long crime spree that includes the theft of thousands of data files and at least 20,000 credit card numbers from computer systems around the nation.

"He was clearly the most wanted computer hacker in the world," said Kent Walker, an assistant United States attorney in San Francisco who helped coordinate the investigation. "He allegedly had access to corporate trade secrets worth billions of dollars. He was a very big threat."

I'm sitting in the Atlanta airport, eating my runny eggs and chalky biscuits after a sleepless, red-eye flight, staring at the dark brooding eyes of Kevin Mitnick.

The hacker had joked with me that the government would turn his case into a billion-dollar heist and he was right on the money.

The onetime parole violator is now the world's first billion-dollar hacker, his mug glaring out from the *New York Times* front page for the second time in a little more than six months. But Mitnick's multi-billion-dollar crimes are only half the story. Tsutomu Shimomura's dramatic detective work is what makes the Mitnick saga a digital confrontation of cybergalactic proportions. Above the image of Mitnick on the front page, Markoff recounts yesterday's hearing in Raleigh, when Mitnick met Shimomura for the first time in person.

"Hello, Tsutomu," Mr. Mitnick said. "I respect your skills."

Mr. Shimomura . . . nodded silently.

I skim the 1,500-plus-word story, looking for Mitnick's billion-dollar crimes, but all I find is the small print on the 20,000 credit card numbers: The FBI has no evidence Mitnick used any of the cards. Could Mitnick, described in the *Times* as a grifter, a burglar, a hardened computer criminal, have had 20,000 credit cards and not charged even a dollar?

Markoff's cyberbust coverage is overwhelming: a good chunk of the top left corner of the front page and virtually an entire inside page — easily a hundred inches of newsprint. There's not just the 1,500-plus-word news story. There's another 2,100-word feature that profiles Shimomura's role in the hunt. There's even an illustrated 300-plus-word sidebar headlined "Tactics of a High-Tech Detective," a step-by-step depiction of Shimomura's detective work, that includes illustrations of the car Shimomura and his team drove and a cartoon of Mitnick behind bars.

Impressive work, considering Markoff had to file the nearly 4,000 words within twelve hours of Mitnick's arrest. The writing is polished, especially Markoff's detailed profile of Shimomura's deft detective work.

HOW A COMPUTER SLEUTH TRACED A DIGITAL TRAIL

By John Markoff

Raleigh, N.C., Feb. 15 — It takes a computer hacker to catch one.

Mr. Shimomura, who is 30, is a computational physicist with a reputation as a brilliant cybersleuth . . . made it his business to use his considerable hacking skills to aid the Federal Bureau of Investigation's inquiry into the crime spree. . . .

The story of the investigation, particularly Mr. Shimomura's role, is a tale of digital detective work in the ethereal world known as cyberspace.

Markoff's "Computer Sleuth" article reads like a cyberthriller. Two dozen times the reporter repeats Shimomura's name. There's no doubt who's the star. The FBI agents and Sprint technicians who worked the case are unnamed bit players.

But while Markoff skims over the roles played by the FBI and the phone company in the capture, he finds plenty of space to speculate on Mitnick's crimes. He even finds room to name the companies he believes Mitnick hacked.

Among the programs found at the Well . . . was the software that controls the operations of cellular telephones made by Motorola, NEC, Nokia, Novatel, Oki. . . .

Oki? That was the software Markoff previously had claimed was hacked by Mark Lottor, the federally indicted hacker, with the help of an unnamed accomplice. Was the Oki software part of the billions of dollars of swiped trade secrets alleged by the Assistant U.S. Attorney?

The *Times* presents its facts in an odd fashion. For instance, the main story and sidebar conflict on the "crime" that led the *Times* coverage. Markoff says the 20,000 "stolen" credit cards are from "computer systems from around the nation." But next to a graphic of dozens of credit cards, the sidebar reveals the numbers are in fact from Netcom, a single Internet provider based in San Jose.

I return to the part of "Computer Sleuth," where Markoff describes the San Francisco Assistant U.S. Attorney's role in the capture.

Subpoenas issued by Kent Walker, an assistant United States attorney in San Francisco, had begun to yield results from telephone company calling records. And now came data from Mr. Walker showing that telephone calls had been placed to Netcom's dial-in phone bank in Raleigh through a cellular telephone modem.

THE FRONT PAGE   295

Federal subpoenas served on phone companies pinpointed Mitnick dialing from Raleigh into Netcom. That's not a trivial fact. Not just anybody can look at the results of subpoenas or court-ordered telephone taps. At some point in San Francisco, it appears, Shimomura must have officially been made part of the FBI investigation.

Reading on, Markoff says that by 1 A.M. Monday, Shimomura was sitting in the passenger seat of a Raleigh Sprint technician's car, holding a cellular-frequency direction-finding antenna, and watching a "signal-strength meter display its reading on a laptop computer screen."

Why doesn't Markoff say whose equipment Shimomura is using? Is this Sprint's setup, or the Oki software Mitnick might have wanted from Shimomura's computer?

.   .   .

After a bumpy flight, I'm in a rental car headed toward Raleigh, the rain beating down mercilessly. I've got a map on the seat, but it's not much help. Duraleigh Road suddenly appears right in front of me after a billboard advertising cellular phones. I turn left, and the rain falls harder, turning the windshield into a gray sheet. The second time I pass by I see the small, brightly colored sign by the road for the Player's Club. I dash into the manager's office with my briefcase over my head. It's easy to tell I'm in the right place.

"I'm with *Newsweek*," a woman announces gruffly, a camera slung around her neck, her pockets stuffed with lenses and equipment. "I understand it isn't apartment 202?"

She doesn't even have to mention Mitnick's name.

The manager shoots her a tough look. "This is private property."

While the *Newsweek* photographer argues with the manager I take a look around. "Let the Games Begin," trumpets the bold red lettering on the wall. "Definitely not your ordinary features," reads the blurb. "Definitely not your ordinary community."

There's an air of fantasy that makes the Player's Club seem more like a health club resort than an upscale apartment complex. The bright colors, the allure of sport and youth. There's even a red surfboard hanging incongruously on the wall.

The *Newsweek* photographer finally leaves, and the manager is hesitant when I, too, introduce myself as a journalist. The FBI has ordered her to say nothing.

"I guess he wasn't here long?" I ask.

"He was here a couple of weeks," she says quietly.

I ask what she thinks attracted the world's most famous hacker to the Player's Club. She's happy to talk about the upscale apartments. "We have an outdoor pool, complete with weight room," she begins. "It's a fifteen-minute drive from the airport. There are phones in every apartment. There's central air conditioning."

As she's talking, I glance out the window. The entrance has a storybook feel, picturesque birch trees and pretty shrubbery, a cascading waterfall splashing beneath a slate walkway with red iron railings. I remember how Mitnick told me he loved the water, and how he phoned me one day from the beach.

The manager leaves for a minute and I read on about the "spacious covered patios and decks, sparkling Eurostyle kitchens, Waterpick showerheads, and convenient breakfast bar."

I arrange the Polaroids of Mitnick the deputy U.S. Marshal in Los Angeles gave me on the desk. The manager's assistant shakes her head at a photo of a tubby hacker and another of a trimmer, bespectacled hacker.

"That's him," she whispers at the third Polaroid, pointing to the image of a smiling, fit, handsome man without glasses, nothing at all like the picture on the *New York Times* front page.

"I saw him a couple of times."

.   .   .

The road floods red with rain, the clay soil bleeding across the street. I'm careening through the afternoon downpour on my way to downtown Raleigh, barely able to see the car in front of me, water spraying up like the wake from a power boat.

The U.S. Marshal's out but I decide to wait. I make some calls, and an hour and a half later the secretary invites me in. U.S. and North Carolina flags stand proudly in the corner of the cavernous office, anchored by a big oak desk at one end. Marshal Berryhill is big too, a tall broad man with a full head of hair, a ready smile, and a blue and orange tie battling his navy blue jacket. He shakes my hand, introduces his quiet chief deputy, and offers me a seat. We chat briefly about the southern hotel they recommended yesterday, and then I pop the question.

"I've heard that a reporter was part of the FBI investigation. Did you deputize John Markoff?"

Marshal Berryhill shakes his head.

"I am only speaking of since I've been Marshal," he booms in his deep voice. "I have never, ever deputized a journalist and made him a part of an investigation."

That's a long time. Berryhill just told me he's been the Marshal in Raleigh for the last thirteen years.

"Sprint couldn't have deputized him?"

Marshal Berryhill shakes his head. "Sprint has no federal law enforcement deputizing power."

He leans his big frame forward slightly. "My best suggestion is you speak with the FBI."

"Who would you suggest?"

"John Vasquez is the agent in charge. He should know the details of how it transpired."

Ten minutes later I take the elevator down and stand in the tiny waiting room by the bulletproof glass window, my notebook and pen in my jacket pocket. Behind the glass, I can see FBI agents passing back and forth. So what if FBI agents generally don't talk, I think. What can it hurt to try?

"Excuse me," I call out. "I'm looking for Agent Vasquez."

A few seconds later a handsome, muscular Hispanic man in his late thirties moves cautiously over. I introduce myself, and he eyes me carefully. But when I show him the front-page *New York Times* article, he's fascinated. He had no idea he'd busted such a big-time fugitive.

I ask Special Agent Vasquez if the FBI deputized John Markoff. "We didn't do it."

He doesn't sound surprised by my question.

"Do you sometimes bring journalists along for the bust?" I ask.

"We don't bring journalists along on investigations." He grins broadly behind the glass, flashing his teeth. "That's a no-no."

Half an hour later, I'm sitting in the waiting room of the U.S.

Attorney's office, writing up my notes from my last two interviews, waiting for Assistant U.S. Attorney John Bowler.

He apologizes for the delay and takes a seat across from me. The room is hardly private; a couple sits nearby reading magazines waiting to see another government attorney. Bowler appears to be in his late thirties, medium height, balding, dressed in a conservative suit. He's got a friendly, honest face. When I ask him what crimes he suspects Mitnick committed, he says he can't really talk about the case. But what about citizens becoming part of a federal investigation?

"There's no legal barrier for citizens helping law enforcement," Bowler replies cheerfully.

"Did you know John Markoff was present during part of the stakeout?"

His face clouds. "I didn't know he was there."

Bowler suddenly grimaces. "Let's go off the record for a second."

But just as abruptly he stops himself.

"I shouldn't be talking off the record," Bowler snaps angrily. "I don't know how he [Markoff] was there. You should ask Shimomura why he was there."

"Is it up to Shimomura how an FBI investigation is run?" I ask the assistant U.S. Attorney in Raleigh.

Bowler pauses. "That's an interesting question," he considers for a moment, as if the question were an intellectual exercise. "It's certainly unusual."

I start to ask the question again, but Bowler stands up and says he has to get back to work.

And then he's gone.

The Evening News

Tsutomu Shimomura and Kevin Mitnick aren't the only ones to get their fifteen minutes of fame. On Thursday, February 16, John Markoff's cyberspace reporting thrusts him into the public light. He's Noah Adams's featured guest on the National Public Radio show *All Things Considered*. The popular radio host asks Markoff, "Now, I'm curious here. They watched him [Mitnick] steal, for example, 20,000 credit card numbers from rich people. But did he ever use them? What was he doing with all this information, all these things he was stealing?"

Markoff acknowledges Mitnick doesn't seem to be in it for the money, and then narrates the Raleigh court scene. The reporter describes how he and "Tsutomu" arrived for Mitnick's hearing, and afterward, Markoff says he just wanted to introduce himself. "I'd never met him." It's an intriguing statement. Markoff wasn't just a spectator, he helped capture Mitnick and staged the defining scene in his story, when Mitnick utters the great line "Hello Tsutomu, I respect your skills."

Finally, Markoff tells Adams that he wonders whether Mitnick was trying to get himself captured. "I could see he was doing things that were going to get him in trouble . . ." volunteers the reporter.

How did John Markoff "see" things Mitnick was doing?

·   ·   ·

The legend of Kevin Mitnick is about to go global. Kevin Mitnick is the prime subject on the February 16, 1995, *CBS Evening News with Dan Rather and Connie Chung*. Rather leads off the broadcast with a flourish: "High-tech detective work has led authorities to the world's most wanted information highway robber. His 'modem operandi': breaking and entering codes at will and escaping through the Internet — that is, until now."

The *CBS Evening News* segment provides a snapshot of the increasingly notorious Mitnick reputation — billions of dollars of stolen trade secrets, thousands of swiped credit card numbers, the biggest, baddest hacker of all time. But the network adds its own spin. CBS neatly sidesteps Mitnick's lack of a profit motive by quoting a Justice Department spokesman who, without ever mentioning Mitnick, insists hackers are more profit-oriented and malicious than ever before. And CBS flatly states, "Mitnick was working the phones even as agents pounded on the door." Does the network really know Mitnick's last phone calls were malicious or criminal?

The facts of Mitnick's case seem less and less important. It's the message that counts, a message that seems to play right into popular sentiment. To the government and the press Mitnick has become something larger than himself, a symbol of all that is feared and wrong in cyberspace, an argument for a new crackdown on the information superhighway, a warning that walls need to be built and locks need to be installed. On the Well, many subscribers are so convinced of Mitnick's guilt that they're clamoring for his head.

"Could he be convicted and sentenced under the 'three strikes' bill?"

"Innocent till proven guilty . . . in the eyes of the law . . .In the eyes of this user he is guilty as sin."

"Kevin Mitnick, Three Strikes Poster Child. It's a concept."

But Emmanuel Goldstein, editor of *2600*, asks his fellow Net citizens to consider what they're reading more carefully.

> . . . A lot of what some of you are saying is unsubstantiated and bordering on hysteria and witch hunting. . . . Read the NY Times piece very very carefully. Oh, it's good writing; kept me on the edge of my seat. But there's a lot that's very wrong here. . . ."

A few minutes before nine Thursday night, Douglas Fine, a journalist who has written about hackers for *Spin* magazine, asks online why the Mitnick story made the front page of the *New York Times*. He wonders how the lengthy profile of Shimomura was ready the day the story broke, and he asks whether others see a new hard line toward hackers as enemies of "the people." Finally, the journalist notes the *New York Times* left out the word "alleged" when discussing Mitnick's supposed crimes.

Shortly before midnight, Goldstein weighs in with his analysis of Markoff's *Times* story.

In reading the opening paragraph of this morning's story, Mitnick is ... "accused of a long crime spree that includes ... at least 20,000 credit card numbers from computer systems around the nation. ..." Even I got the impression Kevin was doing some bigtime credit fraud from *that* description. Let's look a little closer. ...

As far as I can see, the only computer system we're talking about here is Netcom, not "computer systems around the nation". Netcom is currently saying that this ... happened recently and it never happened before. This is false. As is common knowledge in the hacker world, Netcom's credit file was compromised last summer and bits of it were displayed over IRC [Internet Relay Chat]. We reported this in the autumn issue of 2600. ... Netcom is not up front about its security problems and they have had massive security problems. ...

Fifth paragraph: "On Christmas Day, he broke into the home computer of ... Tsutomu Shimomura. ..." Correct me if I'm wrong, but shouldn't the word "allegedly" be in there someplace? ...

Now let's take a look at the technique used to find Mitnick. "Mr. Shimomura had flown ... to Raleigh, where he helped telephone company technicians and Federal investigators use cellular-frequency scanners to home in on Mr. Mitnick."

Does this mean they were monitoring cellular calls? How exactly was this done so that other cellular calls were not also monitored? What are the legalities involved? These are very important questions that go beyond the Mitnick case ... a criminal case in Holland a few years back was thrown out when it was proven that there was no way to have obtained the evidence (monitoring cellular calls) without invading the privacy of others.

The article finally admits 14 paragraphs in that there is no evidence to suggest that Mitnick was engaged in credit card fraud (an allegation strongly hinted at in the lead sentence) and that he "seemed more concerned with proving that his technical skills are better than those whose job it is to protect the computer networks he has attacked."

This leads me to ask the same question I've been asking ever since I found out he was on the run: what exactly is he being accused of doing in the first place? Violating probation is the only concrete thing I hear. . . ."

Goldstein is right to question the law. Eavesdropping on cellular calls without a warrant is illegal. Strict statutes regulate the use of scanners for monitoring and eavesdropping.

A few hours later, at 4:48 A.M. on Friday, Goldstein uploads part of FBI Special Agent LeVord Burns's affidavit.

On January 18, 1995, I was advised by Andrew Gross . . . [that] on 12/25/94 . . . [t]he intruders made a copy of Shimomura's home directory which included personal files, E-mail, security tools and other data. They also took copies of software relating to cellular phones and other security type proprietary software. One of the files copied was called "Berkeley Packet Filter" or (BPF) . . . developed under a research grant from the National Security Agency (NSA) . . . a network monitoring tool with the ability to filter packets from an Unix computer. This tool is unique in that it can be compiled and inserted into an Unix operating system without shutting down the machine with a re-boot. I was advised by Gross the cellular telephone proprietary software cost is between $500,000 and $1,000,000. . . .

Is LeVord Burns saying Shimomura had over half a million dollars' worth of cellular source code and an NSA "packet filter" program designed to eavesdrop on computers? Why would Shimomura have proprietary cellular telephone code? And did the FBI really believe the Berkeley Packet Filter was some valuable spy program? Could Shimomura's assistant, Andrew Gross, have been misunderstood by the FBI? The BPF is a freely available software package anyone can get on the Internet. It doesn't cost a cent.

But before the Well's subscribers have a chance to react to that disclosure, they've got something new to think about. Friday morning, Markoff's latest article is uploaded to the thread, and like his Mitnick story, it too delivers a frightening conclusion, sort of like a tsunami following an earthquake. According to John Markoff and the *New York Times*, Mitnick didn't just steal billions of dollars of trade secrets. He also nearly destroyed the Well.

HACKER CASE UNDERSCORES INTERNET'S VULNERABILITY

By John Markoff
San Francisco, Feb. 16 — In his final weeks of freedom, Kevin D. Mitnick . . . had been putting severe strains on the Well . . . investigators say.

And just a few hours before his arrest, they say, he delivered a last electronic blow that nearly destroyed the Well and the electronic community it served. . . .

It was as if the hacker were underscoring the larger meaning of what has been called the most notorious Internet crime spree yet: the vulnerability of any computer on the global Internet network, if a sophisticated computer criminal puts his mind to mischief. After attacks were discovered Jan. 28, Well officials, with some misgivings, had been allowing Mitnick to come and go unimpeded so that investigators could surreptitiously monitor his activities. . . .

But early Wednesday, as federal agents closed in on Mitnick 3,000 miles away, he logged in one last time to the Well . . . and erased all the accounting records for the on-line service, Well officials said.

The Show

Shimomura steps from the sixth-floor elevator like a rock star arriving for his concert. The signature Oakley sunglasses propped on his black mane, a windbreaker, a practiced look of disinterest, and a tall, slim woman at his side. John Bowler, the federal prosecutor, guides Shimomura and his companion past the throng of reporters into the courtroom and a front-row seat.

The time is Friday morning, February 17, ten minutes before Kevin Mitnick's eleven o'clock bail hearing. I grab the seat two rows behind Shimomura. His Birkenstock sandals are on the floor. He's crossing and recrossing his legs, Buddha-style, like he did in his *Newsweek* photo, waiting like nearly everyone else for the preceding hearing finally to end.

Suddenly, the magistrate barks out his decision, and the courtroom erupts, a herd of print and TV reporters rushing toward Shimomura.

"Hi, Tsutomu, I'm Jessica Gerstle from NBC News."

She doesn't have to say she's in television. She's pretty, a perfect porcelain doll face, impeccably dressed, maybe twenty-two. She slips her cellular phone into her bag as she speaks.

"I've just talked to print media," Shimomura says eagerly. "You're the first person I've talked to in TV."

Jessica isn't shy. "We'd love to do a three-part series on you for *Dateline*."

Shimomura nods, inviting her to continue.

"Tsutomu, some people outside the computer world look at hackers as the last rugged individualists," she begins what sounds like a prepared question. "There are people who like Kevin Mitnick."

"He did nothing imaginative," Shimomura snaps, clearly irritated at the question. "Nothing interesting, nothing new that I can see."

Shimomura tosses out John Markoff's name while answering a question, and John Johnson, a reporter for the *Los Angeles Times*, quickly picks up on it.

"What was John Markoff's role?" asks the reporter.

"John wrote the book on Kevin," Shimomura informs the crowd of journalists and network TV scouts.

"The third member of our team was John Markoff," volunteers Julia Menapace, the woman who accompanied Shimomura into the courtroom. She's casually dressed in jeans, taller than Shimomura, with long brown hair. She doesn't work for the feds or the San Diego Supercomputer Center. She's Shimomura's girlfriend.

"So what did John do?" the reporter asks.

"We primarily would ask him, 'If you were Kevin in this situation, what would you do?'" Menapace replies.

She pauses for emphasis. "He [Markoff] was also a victim," Menapace reminds the reporters. "His e-mail was read on the Well."

It sounds incredible, but it's true. FBI agent LeVord Burns's affidavit, which reads like the transcribed notes of Shimomura's assistant, Andrew Gross, mentioned Markoff not once but twice as a victim. The crime committed against Markoff? Mitnick read his e-mail. And then the prankster made the reporter's e-mail accessible to the rest of the world.

The crowd shifts, and I find myself standing next to the star.

"Hi Tsutomu. I'm Jon Littman."

He pauses, then shoots a look of recognition. Shimomura knows something about me, and he says it loud enough for other reporters to hear.

"Kevin got into your e-mail at the Well."

"Yeah," I reply, unsurprised. "He first got in it in April or May."

The answer fascinates Shimomura. He's interested. He ignores the rest of the crowd. I move closer.

"I'll bet it's been crazy for you?" I ask him.

"It's a zoo," Shimomura shakes his head.

The voice booms out across the courtroom. "Is there a John Markoff here?"

It's a bailiff or a marshal, a black man who just emerged from a door at the back of the courtroom. He's walking toward Shimomura, carrying a piece of paper. My mind races. Why would a bailiff or a marshal be calling out the name of a *New York Times* reporter?

But John Markoff is nowhere to be found.

"So when did you start your investigation?" I ask Shimomura.

He's right next to me now, my body shielding him from the media throng.

"I started tracking around Christmas."

"When did you know it was Kevin?"

"Around the end of January. A bunch of data was recovered on the Well —"

But Shimomura is no longer looking at me. His eyes zero in across the courtroom.

"There's Kevin!" Shimomura says deliberately.

Everyone looks up, following his voice. It's as if Shimomura is narrating the scene, pointing the media in the right direction.

Mitnick is perhaps fifteen feet away when I turn. His legs shackled, his wavy brown hair tied in a short ponytail with a yellow rubber band. He looks stocky and fit in green government-issue sweatpants and sweatshirt. He's only ten feet away now. Shimomura is right next to me.

"Hi, Kevin," I say.

Mitnick looks over, sees Shimomura and me.

"Hi," Mitnick responds in that familiar voice.

What does Mitnick see? He knows Shimomura helped catch him. Could he be wondering about me now too?

Shimomura and I sit down in the front row. He's wearing a T-shirt from a cross-country ski race, cotton khaki pants, his bare foot crossed over his knee, inches away.

Shimomura's leafing through his card collection. Associated Press, ABC's *PrimeTime Live* ... He pauses at Jessica Gerstle's NBC card.

He catches me looking. I whisper.

"Was it tough to catch Kevin?"

He leans toward me, sweeping his black strands over his ear. "Kevin wasn't very difficult to find."

"Why not?" I ask.

"He didn't do anything that was very difficult," Shimomura scoffs.

"Why wasn't it difficult?"

"Just follow the bytes." Shimomura shrugs. "It's not terribly hard."

Ten feet away, Mitnick's tall public defender, John Dusenberry, hands his client a silver pen at the table.

"What do you think of Kevin?" I continue.

"I only followed him for four days." Shimomura turns to me. "Do you know why he came to Raleigh?"

"No. How about you?"

"We were more concerned in localizing him than [in] what he did," Shimomura whispers, raising a finger to his lips, stopping me before I can ask another question. Kevin Mitnick is standing before the court.

"Mr. Mitnick, I know your lawyer," Magistrate Dixon begins. "He practices regularly before my court. . . . You have a right to a hearing. Your lawyer has informed me you intend to waive [that right]."

"Yes, I do," Mitnick declares in a clear voice.

"Do you now waive . . ."

"Yes sir," Mitnick says.

Mitnick's attorney, Dusenberry, addresses the magistrate. "We understand that in exchange for his waiver, Mr. Bowler will not oppose my modifications."

"We would not oppose that he . . . be part of the general [prison] population," Bowler responds. "The defendant agreed no other phone access there other than his mother, his father and attorney . . . the calls will be placed by law enforcement."

Dusenberry pleads. "Your Honor, we ask that he be allowed to make phone calls at least once per day. This is a very technical case, Your Honor."

"I would agree to that," consents Bowler.

The magistrate smiles. "Why don't we agree to calls to Mr. Dusenberry daily?"

"Could we have the other counsel permitted to have daily contact?" asks Dusenberry.

Magistrate Dixon rules. "I think it's also fair that he have unfettered access to the attorneys Monday through Friday."

Shimomura is reading the note I've just scribbled to myself,

big announcement. is jm here?

.   .   .

Walking slowly in his chains, Mitnick is led out of the courtroom as the media descends on Shimomura.

"Did you ever talk to him before?" asks a reporter.

"I believe I might have," Shimomura reflects. "I believe I had contact with him in the past."

Mitnick's already revealed to me that he phoned Shimomura months ago, trying to trick him out of information. Now Shimomura seems to be admitting Mitnick approached him in the past. Does that cast a new light on the Christmas hack story? If Shimomura knew Mitnick was after his machine, why didn't the "keeper of the keys" protect it?

"Do you think he had some kind of problem?" a reporter asks. "Was he obsessed?"

"I think you'll have to ask him," Shimomura responds curtly.

"Do you think he was blamed for everything that happened on the Net?" asks another.

The question irritates Shimomura.

"He was a pain, he caused a lot of people a lot of grief . . . a lot of things we've seen him do . . . getting card numbers, reading files, stealing software."

"Is there any evidence he sold the software or used the credit cards?" I ask.

Shimomura looks at me critically. "I don't know. We don't know."

"How did you feel about him reading your files?" another reporter asks.

Shimomura straightens up.

"It's not a very polite thing to do."

"Are you a hacker?" I ask.

Shimomura is caught off guard. He pauses a moment.

"What's a hacker?" Shimomura reflects.

"Old-style hacker," I reply. "Someone who creatively pursues knowledge and information."

Shimomura hesitates again, staring at me as he stared from the pages of *Newsweek*.

"You'll have to ask someone else." Shimomura shrugs, glaring at me.

"And what would they say?" I ask.

"It depends on who you ask."

Meet the Press

"**S**o, I guess all his cell phone calls made it easy?" I say to Shimomura as we walk down the hall to the Department of Justice press conference after the morning courtroom hearing.

Shimomura turns to look at me. "That's sort of what he does, isn't it?"

"Voice calls?" I ask, wondering if Shimomura heard Mitnick talking with me.

Shimomura shakes his head. "We didn't get any of those."

Shimomura and I enter the cramped, windowless room just as the press conference is getting under way. Half a dozen middle-aged Department of Justice officials crowd behind a podium and microphone, smiling for the cameras and dozens of reporters from CNN, ABC, the *Los Angeles Times,* the Associated Press, and countless other news organizations and papers.

"Can you sort of put this case in perspective?" asks a reporter. "Is this truly the biggest one that exists? It certainly seems like it today."

"I won't comment as to ranking . . . except to say that this certainly is a significant investigation with the FBI's program . . ." replies Jim Walsh, a local FBI agent.

"Is law enforcement still ill-prepared to deal with this type of problem?" asks the reporter.

"To some extent, that's probably true," admits Walsh. "We're probably trying to catch up as best we can."

"Do you think you would have been able to catch Mr. Mitnick if this individual [Shimomura] had not, basically, taken it upon himself to get people together and go after him?"

"I'm really not going to comment other than that I think Mr. Shishomura's [sic] assistance and involvement is pretty well established."

A TV reporter voice lobs a fat one for a sound bite. "It's been said for a long time that hackers basically do this to prove that they could do it, and, for the most part, cause little damage. . . . What is your advice to people who think they may want to hack?"

John Bowler, the Assistant U.S. Attorney, fields the question. "I think there's been some perception that this was an adolescent crime in the past and that it carried very little punishment. . . . This is a serious crime and it's going to be treated as a very serious crime, both by prosecutors, officers, and, I would anticipate, by the courts."

"Is the public behind you on that?" the reporter asks. "Is this crime perceived as being in the same rank as drug crime or street crime?"

"I wouldn't want to comment on how it compares to drug crime or street crime, except to say the financial damage caused by this crime is taken extremely seriously. . . ."

"Was there financial damage caused by this particular crime that you can point to?" drawls a local reporter.

But Bowler's got no comment. In fact, he and the other Justice Department officials have got very little else to say. Just as the reporters start asking why Mitnick's telephone access is being monitored and restricted, the Justice Department emcee cuts off further questions.

But the press hasn't gotten what it came for. It's hungry for the real story. A local reporter stands up.

"We have asked Mr. Shimomura, because of a great deal of press interest in his activities, if he would join us. Would it be all right with you if he answered a few questions?"

The Justice Department officials announce the end of their press conference and the media heaves forward, circling their microphones and cameras around Shimomura. Off to the side, John Johnson of the *Los Angeles Times* asks Shimomura's girlfriend more about Markoff's assistance in the criminal investigation.

"Did you [Shimomura and Menapace] have an agreement with John Markoff?" asks the reporter.

"I'm not sure what was agreed," Julia Menapace says. "Markoff and Tsutomu are old friends."

The slender woman smiles knowingly and looks toward Shimomura. "They ski together."

"What questions did you ask him [Markoff] when you wanted to know something about Kevin?" the *L.A. Times* reporter asks her.

"When we wanted to know about his habits. If there was radio silence, did it mean he'd gone out to eat?" Menapace continues out of earshot of Shimomura. "We'd ask him, 'In this situation what would you do if you were Kevin?' "

"Go out for fatburgers?" another reporter asks.

Menapace smiles. "I don't think he was eating fatburgers anymore. I think he was mostly walking to local places."

Tsutomu Shimomura's girlfriend sums up the *New York Times* reporter's role in the investigation of Kevin Mitnick:

"John essentially was our Kevin expert."

.   .   .

"Spread around. Right! Move your chairs. Relax!"

Shimomura invites everyone to gather round. No dull fed, this cyberdude. He's making quite an impression, and nobody can believe how little clothing he's wearing.

"You thought it would be warm in North Carolina?" asks an incredulous local reporter.

"Actually, I was wearing shorts yesterday."

"We noticed that." A couple of local reporters chuckle. "You left in kind of a hurry."

"Yeah. I knew I wouldn't be here long." Shimomura glibly reminds the group of his speedy tracking abilities.

"Do you want to start?" prods another reporter.

"All of you basically know the story at this point," Shimomura says into the microphone. "John Markoff, an excellent writer for the *New York Times* . . ."

"Right," a few reporters respond in unison.

"Correct," says Shimomura.

"Thank you very much," a local reporter jokes, as if Shimomura's press conference is over, as if everything that could be said about the story has already been written by Shimomura's favorite reporter.

"So was it Christmas Eve?" another reporter encourages Shimomura.

"The first phase of this was an attack on my systems starting about 1400 hours on Christmas Day, 1994. . . . Andrew Gross and I flew back to San Diego . . . to go assess damage, figure out what happened. . . .

"By New Year's . . . we had discovered there was basically a new attack being used. The intruder . . . had used IP spoofing . . . IP source address spoofing, which John Markoff wrote about. . . .

"IP address spoofing," repeats Shimomura to a confused local reporter's question. "John Markoff had a piece . . . on it on the twenty-third of January. . . . On the twenty-eighth, a bunch of my files were discovered . . . at the Well. . . . You guys heard about it. Markoff has a piece on the Well in the paper [*New York Times*] this morning. . . ."

"His [Markoff's] second piece was on January 28, which coincided with the day . . . my files were found on the Well . . . and . . . many other files . . . including source code for proprietary information belonging to many companies. . . ."

"Did you say information or code?" I ask.

"Some password files off UNIX systems . . ."

"At those corporations?" I ask.

"Correct. . . . I think John had Apple . . . the telephone source code intrigued us because we knew that Kevin . . . had been after this stuff . . . the past nine months. . . . I sent up a person, Andrew, again, to investigate further at the Well. . . ."

"And then you went skiing?" asks a reporter.

"I went to give a talk, it was a conference, then thought about going skiing again, hoping that would be the end of it. It was not the end of it. I got a phone call on Sunday, February sixth. . . . On the seventh I came down to San Francisco. And on the eighth, we started investigating the Well. . . ."

"Did you meet with the U.S. Attorney there, Kent [Walker]?" I ask Shimomura.

"We met with the [Assistant U.S.] Attorney on the eighth, I believe."

"Was that the first federal involvement that you're aware of in this particular instance?" asks a local reporter.

"In this particular round, yes. Actually, I think FBI Washington may have known something about this. . . . I think, LeVord."

"What was the purpose for your meeting with the U.S. Attorney? . . ." asks John Johnson of the *L.A. Times*.

"We were deciding . . . we would attempt to pursue and apprehend this person, now that we had a good idea as to who it was and working out what support we would give them, what support they would give us, and ground rules versus realities. . . ."

Ground rules versus realities. What an odd choice of words.

"What were the ground rules?" asks the *L.A. Times* reporter.

"Ground rules were 'Don't do anything illegal,' " says Shimomura.

"What was illegal?" I ask.

"It's a long list," Shimomura dismisses my question. "It's not for discussion here."

.   .   .

"We met with Justice, established our ground rules — what was legal, whatever — start monitoring at the Well and proceeded to try to figure out where he was coming from. . . . By Thursday . . . Netcom was one. So Thursday afternoon, we moved our operations down to Netcom in San Jose. . . .

"We discovered there was a lot of traffic from Denver and from RTP [Research Triangle Park in Raleigh]. And we attempted to get trap and trace orders . . . for their dial-ins at Denver and RTP. We never got the ones for Denver. We did get the ones for RTP. I think those were in place Friday."

How does Shimomura get trap and trace orders? The phone company can't just reveal trap and trace information to ordinary civilians.

"We got a few traps and traces. We got one that appeared to be valid. However, when we traced it down, it kinda just looped . . . suggesting to us that Kevin had monkeyed with the switch."

"But the trap and trace, that was done by the federal people?" suggests Johnson.

"It was done by the feds," Shimomura answers.

"And then they'd give you information . . ."

"Or they wouldn't give us information."

This surprises the *L.A. Times* reporter. "There were times they [the feds] didn't give you the information?"

"Right," Shimomura responds. "But this was something they had to do by going to get an order to allow them to do it like they would with any sort of tap.

"We would go to them and say. . . . We think we can get a better idea of what is going on by getting a trap and trace on this number. . . . Anyway, that didn't actually get us very far, except pointing us, getting us in touch with Sprint Cellular here."

Not very far? In Shimomura's own words the federally ordered traps and traces moved him all the way from California to Raleigh, North Carolina. Why won't he give the FBI any credit?

"After spending about five hours just looking through records, we determined that there was a particular phone number. . . . So, we obtained a court order to append these records. That was late Saturday night, early Sunday morning."

Shimomura must be talking about the FBI again.

"I left San Jose in the morning [Sunday], got here seven P.M–ish probably. Anyway, on Sunday night, some Sprint technicians and myself went out to the cell site and started our search there. . . ."

"You found that the feds and the phone companies were all very happy to work with you throughout?" drawls a local reporter.

"Uh-huh," Shimomura concurs.

"I mean, there was no hesitation, no 'Who are you? What are you doing?' "

"Not at all."

"Had you had any interface with them prior?"

"I've dealt with feds before. . . . And Sprint was amazingly helpful here. Sprint guys met me at the airport, picked me up at the airport, and we went out and did our thing.

"So, Sunday night we went out, acquired his [Mitnick's] radio [signal] using some equipment they had and some I'd brought along, and proceeded to track him and narrow him down to three apartment buildings in the complex where he was arrested."

What was this equipment Shimomura brought along. His souped up Oki?

"How long did it take from being picked up to finding the apartment?" I ask.

"Oh, I got dinner. . . . The actual time . . . hunting for him was less than thirty minutes."

"You mean hunting for him in that apartment —" asks Johnson.

"In the car," Shimomura corrects him.

"And this was his car, the Sprint —" I say.

"Yeah," Shimomura replies.

"And what was the actual technical equipment in the car?" I ask.

"We had some cellular test equipment. You should contact them for the details. He brought some equipment. I brought some equipment."

For a technical guy, Shimomura is very vague about his equipment.

"And how many people were driving around with you?" I ask.

"We had, I think two or three people."

"All from Sprint?" I ask.

Shimomura stumbles over his answer.

"Sprint and mostly — yeah."

What a strange reply. Shimomura was about to reveal someone else, but then he caught himself. Sort of. Who does Shimomura mean by "mostly"?

Who was the third man in the car tracking Kevin Mitnick?

"Were there federal agents with you?" asks a reporter.

"Not really. Well, we had a federal agent with us. . . . He disappeared that evening."

That gets chuckles, and makes nearly everyone forget about the "mostly."

"What did the FBI agents do after you got here?" I ask.

"What do you mean?" Shimomura asks, staring intently at me, perturbed by my question.

"What was their participation?" I repeat.

"You should go ask them about that," snaps the cybersleuth.

. . .

Shimomura wraps up his tale.

"So, continuing from Monday morning to Wednesday was basically getting all the legal work done, everything else done in order to go find him. That's something the feds mostly did. That's what they specialize in. He's in one of these three buildings. Go for it."

The feds "specialize" in paperwork and slapping on the handcuffs? Something tells me the FBI might describe their work differently.

"What was the actual distance you'd narrowed it down to?" I ask.

"Less than one hundred meters," says Shimomura. ". . . As we got closer, our vision got better."

"I saw a newspaper article that said he actually left some taunting voice mail messages for you with a British accent," begins a television reporter. "What was your reaction?"

"It seemed like a pretty silly thing to do. . . . If you're trying to get away with something, leaving more trails like that really doesn't help."

"How do you know it's him?" I ask.

"Well, we didn't know then."

"Are you sure it's him now?"

"Well . . . We suspected it was Kevin about . . . January thirtieth. Sometime around the end of January. . . . This past Friday, we were monitoring his activities. We managed to hear an exchange between Kevin and one of his cohorts, where he was complaining about John Markoff having put his picture on the front page of the *New York Times*. . . . That was sort of a giveaway."

A giveaway to what? That Mitnick knew his enemy? But how does this prove the voice mail was Mitnick? Or that he performed the IP spoof attack for that matter?

The reporter continues. "Was he cocky, arrogant in the way he approached you by going into your home computer?"

"My guess is I think he was after particular tools that he thought I might have. . . . I'm a security researcher. That's one of my hats, and so he thought that perhaps I had information on vulnerabilities he could use to break into more systems."

"Was one of those tools for the NSA, a monitoring tool you were developing for the NSA?" asks a reporter.

"It was not developed for the NSA," Shimomura declares. "But, we can take that one offline."

Why doesn't he want to talk about it on the record? Could it be because the program, contrary to the impression given by Shimomura's assistant and the FBI, doesn't cost a dime?

"When he came into the courtroom today, it looked to me like you guys met eyes for a second. . . . Does that make you feel good?"

"Not really."

"Why's that?

"He's caused a lot of people a lot of grief . . . and clearly this kind of behavior is not acceptable and *we* will not tolerate it . . . but I wish there was something more elegant we could do about it."

"Do you think he has some skills that could potentially, if he could be rehabilitated, that could be useful to some arm of the government?" I ask.

"I don't know," Shimomura replies curtly. "I don't know his skills. From what I've seen, he doesn't have a whole lot of technical expertise. . . . He gets tools from others and a lot of assistance from others."

"If he doesn't have technical expertise, what's his technique?" I ask.

"Persistence. A lot of persistence. We didn't really study Kevin very much. You should ask John Markoff for details since he wrote the book on Kevin. . . ."

.   .   .

A local reporter is puzzled by how little evidence the government seems to have of Mitnick's great crimes. "Looking at the search warrant that was turned in today . . . [t]here's no actual information, other than the Toshiba. . . . Basically there's a lot of technical equipment, a *News & Observer* [newspaper], a Yellow Pages, and a Toshiba computer. I'm wondering what they really have on him."

Shimomura answers like a government official. "We have a fair amount of evidence, but the details of that you should take up with Justice."

"Did he eliminate any files before he opened the door?"

"We don't know."

"Speaking of that question, it seemed like Markoff's story today, that he was zapping out files from the Well . . ." another reporter asks.

Shimomura's girlfriend, Julia Menapace, steps in to answer this one. She's been sitting dutifully at his side throughout the impromptu conference, hardly saying a word. "The Well lost their customer billing information as a result of Kevin's actions," the thin, longhaired woman declares.

"What does that mean, that they 'lost it?' " I ask.

"It was deleted," Menapace says definitively.

"All of their customer billing?" I ask, surprised.

"At least for that day. . . ."

Shimomura jumps in to rescue his girlfriend.

"You should contact them for more information on that. Also, John Markoff had this piece out this morning . . . which may talk a fair amount about this."

Eight times now. Eight times Shimomura has mentioned John Markoff in his press conference.

"Has Hollywood called you yet?" Johnson of the *Los Angeles Times* asks.

Shimomura hesitates for several seconds. It's his longest pause yet. Everyone laughs.

"Umpteen hundred voice mail messages, right," Shimomura jokes.

.   .   .

"What was it that would attract Mr. Mitnick to their [the San Diego Supercomputer Center] work and your work?" a reporter asks. "You said that you think he was just looking for new ways to penetrate security systems?"

"I think so. And to defraud cellular systems. We believe that he's shown a great interest in cellular systems recently, like in the past year or so."

Is the security expert saying Mitnick may now have learned about defrauding cellular phones from Shimomura himself?

"How damaging can these tools be that he took from you?" asks a reporter.

"Well, tools are tools. The same tools. . . that he took, that he could use perhaps to sniff networks are the same tools that we used to monitor him and to catch him."

A reporter asks Shimomura why he chased Mitnick in the first place.

"I was asked to do this out of a personal favor by someone at the Well."

"Someone at the Well? Who was that?" I ask.

"I, uh, Barlow."

How bizarre. John Perry Barlow is a legendary libertarian in cyberspace, a Wyoming native famous for his Grateful Dead lyrics and battles for freedom and privacy in cyberspace. Barlow helped found the Electronic Frontier Foundation, a civil rights group that got its start by defending unjustly accused hackers. And Barlow made a name for himself a few years back when he wrote an amusing account of a befuddled FBI agent, clumsily searching for crime on the Internet, who made the mistake of wandering onto his western ranch. Could Barlow, a self-proclaimed crusty descendant of the frontier men, a guy who wears cowboy boots, a ten-gallon hat, and a red handkerchief around his neck, really have invited Shimomura and the FBI into town?

Big Time

riday afternoon, the Well's thread heats up, the focus shifting to just how close the FBI got to the Well. Patrizia DiLucchio asks,

#365

If Mitnick has been "reading the electronic mail of <WELL> users" and the FBI is now investigating this case, does this not mean that the FBI can subpoena that mail as evidence. Further, since the WELL has been cooperating with the FBI, becoming a little brother to Big Brother as it were, has the FBI been reading the email for weeks now?

Some begin to wonder whether the Well might have trampled the rights of innocent bystanders in aiding Mitnick's capture.

Larry Persons (#427) asks why, if the government is limited in its right to search or wiretap, it appears to be all right for the Well to let the FBI potentially see, or for Well management itself to potentially see, a subscriber's private information without a warrant.

He wonders if the Well is violating the Fourth Amendment. And he's concerned about the FBI, Well management, or other parties violating his civil rights and privacy in the name of Mitnick's supposed threat. He asks why the Well isn't "proactive" about its security. He's not so worried about Mitnick. What he really wants is a place in cyberspace free from unwarranted "intrusion by private and governmental agencies."

Has the frenzied hunt for Kevin Mitnick trampled the Fourth Amendment? At least part of the answer is to be found in the Electronic Communications Privacy Act of 1986. The legislation helped adapt federal phone communications regulations for the electronic age, and while nearly everyone agrees it's incomplete, the act is clear about violations of privacy in cyberspace. Internet providers, just like phone companies, must obey the statutes or be liable for criminal and/or civil penalties.

It's a crime to access stored wire or electronic communications without legal authorization. 18 USCS 2701 of the Federal Criminal Code states that electronic communications providers "shall not knowingly divulge the contents of any communication" stored by that service. Violations committed "for purposes of commercial advantage, malicious destruction or damage, or private commercial gain" are federal crimes with jail terms and financial penalties.

In other words, neither the Well, the FBI, nor their agents can disclose information about Mitnick's communications.

But the Well is busy with another issue: John Markoff's published claim that the Well was "nearly destroyed" by a single hacker. Just after 3 P.M., The Well uploads its official response to Markoff's article. Mark Graham, who wrote the response, knew how greatly the "damage" had been exaggerated. Only the backup for a third of a day's accounting had been erased. No data was lost, and Graham, who had watched the hacker's keystrokes when it happened, believed it was an accident.

#439

Dear Friends,

Thank you for being patient while we wrote this message, in response to an article that appeared in today's issue of the New York Times. We feel that given the issues raised, and the information presented, the article warranted a full and complete examination.

First off we want to share with you how bad all of us felt when we read the story last night. We have known John Markoff for years as a respected and honest reporter and member of the WELL community. Having said this we feel that there are a number of misrepresentations and mistakes in the article that we would like to address case by case.

From the article that appeared on Page C1 of ... the New York Times. ...

"And just a few hours before his arrest, they say, he delivered a last electronic blow that nearly destroyed the Well and the electronic community it served."

The WELL was not "nearly destroyed". Erasing files would not have "destroyed" us. In the worst case we could have re-built from backups.

". . . and erased all the accounting records for the on-line service, Well officials said."

WELL officials did NOT say this. The cracker erased a SINGLE accounting file. . . .

"It was a moment of decision at the Well, whose services and unwitting subscribers had been exposed to extraordinary invasions of privacy."

We do not think it is accurate to say that our members were exposed to "extraordinary invasions of privacy." . . . We monitored nearly every keystroke of the cracker. A total of 11 accounts were compromised by the intruder, and we have contacted all of the account holders. . . . Because of our back-ups, destruction of additional files would have had little or no effect on the health of our business.

Accusing a *New York Times* reporter of "misrepresentation and mistakes" is a serious matter. The Well must be pretty upset about Markoff's story and pretty sure of the facts to take such an extreme public stand. By denouncing the reporter the company risks a defamation suit. But in an interview, Katz would say even more about the *Times* reporter: "I only knew John Markoff a little bit. I thought he was a friend of the Well. But something happened. I heard his father was ill. I don't know if that had anything to do with it. All of a sudden he starts hugely hyping the story, saying this horrific catastrophic event happened, that the Well almost ceased to exist."

Half an hour later, Well management, responding to concerns

that it invited the FBI into the close-knit electronic community, reassures its subscribers that the Well is in control of the scope of the FBI's investigation:

#445

It has been clearly understood from the beginning that we will provide only information relating to the accounts used by the intruder. . . .

This morning I found out that in this process the authorities will issue a search warrant (not a subpoena) for those records. . . .

We have told the U.S. Attorney that we will not give them a full tape back-up, but will cooperate in providing only the files they need to try the case.

The Well has promised its subscribers it would not turn over personal e-mail, but the FBI doesn't appear to care about the Well's commitment to protect subscribers' privacy. At 4:19 P.M. one of the Well's most prestigious subscribers, former board member Howard Rheingold, a celebrated author and columnist, uploads his current syndicated newspaper column to the thread, and asks whether the zealous manhunt threatens basic constitutional protections.

#452

CIVIL LIBERTIES, VIRTUAL COMMUNITIES, AND HACKERS

By Howard Rheingold
The recent arrest of alleged super-hacker Kevin Mitnick has focused the attention of the public on the dangers of putting sensitive information online: communication networks, by their nature, will always be technically insecure. . . .

This knowledge should not cause us to act out of ignorance and fear. . . .

The Well is where the Electronic Frontier Foundation was born and the Computers, Freedom, and Privacy conferences are organized, which leads some to ask why a system famous for its defense of individual liberties . . . played a small role in making the decision to cooperate with the hacker-hunters. . . .

The safety of the wider community . . . must always be balanced by a vigilance to Constitutional guarantees. The Bill of Rights exists because Americans have always feared fishing expeditions by the State. If there is a good reason to believe a serious crime is committed, law enforcement officers are required to present their evidence and obtain permission or a warrant for a specific search. . . .

We might need police, but we don't need thought police or secret police. We owe it to our freedom to hold cybercops accountable to the Constitution and we must not let legislatures extend unreasonably the power of State authorities to snoop in cyberspace.

On Saturday, February 18, Goldstein of *2600* checks in with more analysis of Markoff's initial *Times* stories.

#556

A few rather interesting things:

1) The 20,000 credit card numbers Mitnick allegedly copied have been floating around since last summer, i.e. he wasn't the first one to get this file and he could have gotten it without ever going thru netcom. . . . [L]ots of people did.

2) The voice on Shimomura's machine was not Mitnick's.

3) Quite a few people knew about the files on Shimomura's machine. It's unlikely Mitnick was the first or last. Of course, Mitnick was still a wanted man but add these facts to the front page times story and it loses a lot of its punch. Probably wouldn't have even *been* a front page story. . . .

The next day, Sunday, February 19, the *Times* publishes another Markoff article in its "Week in Review" section, for the first time revealing Markoff's personal role in the criminal investigation. To Markoff, it's yet another opportunity to praise his friend, Tsutomu Shimomura.

CAUGHT BY THE KEYBOARD: HACKER AND GRIFTER DUEL ON
THE NET

By John Markoff
My first inkling that Kevin Mitnick might be reading my electronic mail came more than a year ago. . . .

Last month . . . I was less tolerant than I had been a year ago. I was not alone. The electronic intruder had also rifled the files from the home computer of Tsutomu Shimomura. . . .

One day this month, I watched Mr. Shimomura's computer screen as the suspect wrote a message . . . complaining that I had put his picture on the front page of The New York Times. . . . I too became emmeshed in the digital manhunt for the nation's most wanted computer outlaw.

Mr. Shimomura . . . [has] an uncanny ability to solve complex technical programs in the manner of Star Trek's Vulcan Mr. Spock.

He seems to embody the very essence of the original hacker ethic — writing programs to create something elegant, not for gain. . . .

Mr. Mitnick is not a hacker in the original sense of the word. Mr. Shimomura is. And when their worlds collided, it was obvious which one of them had to win.

But outside the *New York Times*, the public spin on the capture of Kevin Mitnick is beginning to shift. The carefully orchestrated image of a duel between good and evil is beginning to crack. The press has caught on to the existence of a third man, and on this same Sunday John Johnson of the *Los Angeles Times* is the first to report a journalist was part of Shimomura's team:

A CYBERSPACE DRAGNET SNARED FUGITIVE HACKER

By John Johnson
The group tracking Mitnick had now grown to include New York Times reporter John Markoff. . . .

"John was our Kevin expert," Shimomura said. For instance, [Julia] Menapace said, if Mitnick's signal went silent, they would turn to Markoff and ask what Mitnick would probably be doing now. If he was eating, where would he go?

"John estimated he would go to the cheapest possible place and he wouldn't worry about" the quality of the food, Menapace said.

Markoff acknowledged trading information with Shimomura, but denied being a member of the team. "I wasn't involved. I am a reporter.

Tsutomu and Julia call me a member of their team, and that's fine if they want to call me that. But I was a reporter," Markoff said.

By Sunday afternoon, Markoff's new *Times* story is what's raising eyebrows on the Well. Kevin Kelly, executive editor of red-hot *Wired* magazine, a respected author, friend of John Markoff, and Well board member, begins posting some intriguing questions about Shimomura and the image created by the *New York Times*.

#621

Having had "inside" knowledge about this event for the past two weeks (as a member of the Well board and as a friend of Markoff) the thing that I still don't get is:

How did the ultimate Genuine Smart Guy, the real hacker, let himself get hacked by the challenger Mitnick?

If Tsutomu can't keep a determined hacker out of his very valuable tool box then how is the Well supposed to?

Something is not right with the picture of Tsutomu getting hacked by Kevin.

If Mr. Security can't keep the trespassers out, then it seems the only answer for public places like the Well is some kind of encryption. Maybe.

I'd like to hear more of what happened at Shimomura's gate. It was apparently a well-known hacker target. Why did he let it get breached?

A little after ten, Netta Gilboa of the counterculture publication *Gray Areas* asks:

What proof does the WELL have that the hackers/crackers of Sept. 1993 ever left? . . . I knew of at least eight of them who had root then. . . . I can also confirm Emmanuel's statement that it is not Mitnick's voice on the audio files Tsutomu released.

Late Sunday and early Monday morning, February 20, a transformation takes place. What began as a thread about the network security break-ins has become a dialogue about John Markoff. Mike Jennings (#660) comments on a post in which someone asks,

"When did John cross over from Joe Journalist to Cybercop." Jennings responds,

> If I were in a good position to assist an investigation, I would, no matter what it said on my business card.

#661 [Jeanne DeVoto]

Well, that's not really the point, is it?

If a journalist is actively aiding LE [law enforcement] in an investigation, does it mean that information given him by sources in confidence will end up in the hands of LE officials? Would the need to aid LE take priority at any time over the needs of honest and complete reporting? Could a journalist be used by LE officials to get around the legal requirements police are expected to operate under?

I have a lot of faith in Markoff's ethics, but it's not unreasonable to raise a question when a journalist is deeply involved in an investigation such as this. The idea does bring up some issues worth exploring and imply some questions that may need answering.

#662 [Emmanuel Goldstein]

I'm glad to hear such intelligent talk — these issues are exactly what's been bothering me from the very start. I only hope we get to the bottom of all this sooner rather than later. . . .

On Monday, February 20, after a formal protest by the Well, the *New York Times* prints a correction on Markoff's story about Mitnick's near destruction of the Well:

> An article in Business Day on Friday about an attack on the Well computer network before the arrest of a computer vandalism suspect overstated the damage done. The attack did not destroy all accounting records of the on-line service; it erased all data from the file containing records of that day's connections.

But according to the Well, the *Times* correction fails to correct Markoff's error. The Well says only the back-up to one third of the day's accounting was erased. Mitnick erased no real data.

Tuesday afternoon, February 21, a scant six days after Mitnick's capture, Charles Platt, a frequent *Wired* contributor, breaks the news that Mitnick's downfall is someone else's windfall. He says an editor friend phoned to say Markoff has landed a $750,000 book deal. Platt cites Markoff's close relationship with Shimomura and his role in capturing Mitnick, and then questions the *Times* reporter's "ethics" in getting rich by selling a news story he "just helped to create. . . ."

On Friday, the *Washington Post* weighs in with an article not about Mitnick or Shimomura but about the reporter who broke the story.

MEDIA NOTES: COMPUTER THIEF SCOOP NETS BOOK DEAL

By Howard Kurtz

When FBI agents arrested fugitive cyberthief Kevin Mitnick in Raleigh, N.C., last week, it came as no surprise to computer buffs that New York Times reporter John Markoff was there.

. . . Markoff's diligence may have paid off big time. His agent reached an agreement in principle with Hyperion yesterday for Markoff for a book on the case, and sources placed the deal in the $750,000 range. Markoff would write the book with Tsutomu Shimomura, the Japanese computer sleuth who cracked the case and emerged as a hero in Markoff's coverage.

"It's a very compelling story and has number one bestseller written all over it," said John Brockman, Markoff's agent. He sent 12 publishers a one-sentence fax when Markoff broke the story and "the offers started pouring in."

Markoff's role in this whodunit has been controversial in some circles because he also became part of the story.

"I don't know if I consider myself a victim," said Markoff, 45. "It's a squishy thing. I was trying as hard as I could to be a reporter."

The Silver Screen

Hollywood calls. John Brockman, Markoff's agent, flies
to Los Angeles to sort out the offers in late February. Even Steven
Spielberg is fighting for the highly prized movie rights, according to
the *Hollywood Reporter*. Other big names are lining up. Oliver
Stone, of *JFK* fame, reports the *San Jose Mercury*, phoned the cybersleuth at his San Diego office. After thanking the big time director
for the call, Shimomura reportedly asked a friend, "Who's Oliver
Stone?"

It's a lot of action for a onetime security expert and a newspaper
reporter whose movie option on *Cyberpunk* elapsed in December.
But the future is bright. Markoff's agent, writes the *Reporter*, now
wants "several million" for the rights to *Catching Kevin*.

On March 9, *USA Today* announces that Miramax won the derby
for the movie rights to the Shimomura/Markoff book tentatively
titled *Catching Kevin: The Pursuit and Capture of America's Most
Wanted Hacker*. That same day the *Daily Variety* says Miramax will
also develop a *Catching Kevin* CD-ROM video game.

·   ·   ·

Markoff and Shimomura's "million dollar" book, film, and video
deals have eclipsed the story of Mitnick's arrest. The March 10 federal indictment of Mitnick garners no more than a brief story on

page thirty of the *Times,* hardly the sort of follow-up one would expect to a front-page scoop. And even stranger, Markoff doesn't write the un-bylined report, though it includes at least one of the old myths he helped propagate.

> Raleigh, N.C., March 10 — Kevin D. Mitnick, the fugitive hacker ... was indicted Thursday on 23 counts of fraud involving computer-access devices. . . .

> Mr. Mitnick first became known for his computer skills as a teenager when he electronically broke into a computer of the North American Air Defense Command.

If the *Times* appears to be suddenly cool about Mitnick's case, the rest of the press is gladly picking up where it left off. On March 11 the Associated Press takes Markoff's articles and Mitnick's indictment and weaves a colorful piece that makes the Raleigh case sound as if Mitnick may spend the rest of his life behind bars.

> CONDOR IS INDICTED ON 23 COUNTS

> Mitnick, who was captured by federal authorities with the help of a San Diego computer security expert, faces a possible maximum of 20 years on each of the 23 charges in the federal indictment. . . .

> Thursday's indictment, which covers only Mitnick's alleged activities during his 10-day stay in Raleigh, is in addition to parole violations Mitnick faces in California and possible other charges in Denver and elsewhere.

Four hundred and sixty years for ten days of computer hacking? That's what the Associated Press seems to be saying — twenty-three counts, twenty years maximum on each count. And the government appears serious about collecting every possible bit of evidence, the U.S. Attorney in San Francisco demanding that the Well produce "all records, in whatever format (specifically including both hard :opy and electronic formats) relating to unauthorized electronic ac- :ess to The Well between Nov 1 1994 and Feb 15 1995. . . ."

A strange thing is happening. The electronic community of the Well is slowly beginning to question the story it read in the *New York Times.* On March 10, one subscriber makes the far-fetched allegation that Markoff never wrote *Cyberpunk* — his coauthor wrote it all. The same day, Aaron Barnhart takes a blast at Markoff:

> All I can say is it's been kind of interesting talking to Real Journalists off-WELL (though I love all of you Journalists here, dearly) and discovering widespread alarm that Markoff would wait till his Week In Review piece to say, "I wanted Kevin Mitnick." And, between the lines, "I assisted the law in apprehending him."

> But this is where the Bickersonian nature of WELL chat does not do a service to this subject, so I'd best bite my tongue till I can better state why it is that what Markoff did wrong troubles me more than what Mitnick (plainly) did wrong. And actually I'm more interested in Mitnick getting a fair trial and just sentencing than in ridiculing or hurting Markoff's efforts.

On Saturday, March 11, Bruce Koball, the Computers, Freedom and Privacy organizer who sparked the investigation on the Well, begins to have second thoughts about the media monster he helped create.

> Why has this story gotten such play? Because Mitnick's victims were "sexy"? . . . No doubt about it. . . .

> But these reasons have little to do with why this story is important. . . . It's important because it has the potential to bring to the public consciousness the incredible vulnerability of computer and telecom networks at a time when great changes are afoot in their technical and legal underpinnings. It's important because it provides the opportunity to argue, in the public forum, that there are technical, not legal, solutions to these problems . . . solutions (i.e., cryptography) that are being actively suppressed by the government.

> To the extent that this story gets told and understood, we all stand to gain. To the extent that Mitnick and his ilk get demonized, and the Net and cyberspace get painted as a sinister, anarchic, lawless wilderness requiring legal intervention, we all lose.

·   ·   ·

The week of Monday, March 13, the March 20 issue of the political journal *The Nation* hits newsstands and the Net. For hackers there is a certain symmetry and justice in the article. First Mitnick was front-page news in the *Times*. Now Markoff is front-page news in *The Nation*, the headline proof that the reporter who chased after the biggest scoop in cyberspace has crossed an invisible line and become part of the news.

CYBERSCOOP!

Andrew L. Shapiro

Times*man cashing in on hype? Hackers are flaming the messenger.*

The Establishment's Story. John Markoff earned the Mitnick scoop. He's one of the best of the new breed of journalists bringing cyberspace to the uninitiated. He deserved to be the only reporter there when they nabbed Mitnick, the most wanted high-tech fugitive in the world. Was he lucky to be in the right place at the right time? Sure. But he also cultivated his sources. One of them was Shimomura, who brought Markoff along for the bust. Now the two are reported to be writing a book — for a price in the high six figures — to reveal just how the cybercaper unfolded. Along with movie deals (sources say Spielberg is interested), Markoff could make millions. Is he worth it? You bet he is.

The Critic's Version. John Markoff is cashing in. He's getting rich on unethical journalistic practices and on unwarranted hysteria about the danger of computer crime — at the expense of an arrogant yet harmless young man who'll be behind bars for a long time. Markoff and the *Times* violated their readers' trust by failing to disclose from the start that Markoff had assisted in the investigation, that he himself had been a target of Mitnick's computer crimes, that he had a long-standing rivalry with Mitnick, and that he was friendly with Shimomura. Furthermore, Markoff overhyped the Shimomura-Mitnick showdown in his February 16 story to create a sensational drama ripe for exploitation in a print and screen sequel to his 1991 book, *Cyberpunk,* one-third of which was about Mitnick. That's why Markoff described Shimomura in the *Times* as a "brilliant cybersleuth" who has "an uncanny ability to solve complex technical problems in the manner of Star Trek's Vulcan Mr. Spock," not to mention "a deeply felt sense of right and wrong." That's why he described Mitnick as a "chameleon-like grifter who is a master at manipulating human beings."

The Reporter's Response. "I simply had a very good inside seat," Markoff tells me during a phone interview. "I am a reporter. It was a chance to get a good story. I don't think I hyped it. I reported it as straight as I could." Markoff shrugs off the claims about violations of journalistic ethics. "Tsutomu and I are friends," he says, adding that Shimomura has been a trusted source over years of reporting. Markoff maintains that any information about Mitnick he gave the investigators was available in *Cyberpunk*. He admits there were uncomfortable moments, such as when he first joined the investigators in Raleigh and Shimomura did not immediately identify him as a reporter. "I became very nervous," says Markoff. "I didn't run up to Agent Burns and say, 'I'm Markoff.' Tsutomu was vague; he said something like, 'He's with me.' The F.B.I. was not pleased." Markoff says that he told his editors at the *Times* everything about his role in the case, and that it was up to them to decide what to disclose in his scoop. The editors ran a straight news piece, and asked Markoff to tell the story of his own involvement in a first-person essay for the February 19 "Week in Review." There he revealed for the first time that he had been covering Mitnick since the early 1980s, that his files had been "vandalized" by Mitnick and that he had had an unusual role in the case. "I too became enmeshed in the digital manhunt for the nation's most wanted computer outlaw," he wrote. Was it wrong not to include this information in the breaking story three days earlier? "I don't know if it was the right call," Markoff concedes.

A Journalism Professor's Question. Why didn't the *Times* just add a few lines to the first article, explaining Markoff's personal entanglement in the case?

The Newspaper's Excuse. "It was an issue of space. We had ten pounds of stuff that had to go into a five-pound bag," says *Times* assistant managing editor Allan Siegal. "It would have been a useful full disclosure, but it was not a grave omission. If I had it to do over again, I'd have found a paragraph to squeeze out." As for Markoff's desire to continue covering the case despite his plan to write a book with Shimomura, Siegal says the *Times* has "explicit rules about people writing about others with whom they have a commercial or business relationship. We don't allow that." If Markoff's plan to help Shimomura tell the full tale of the great hacker hunt predated the February 16 story, these rules would have precluded Markoff from writing that scoop, right? "I wouldn't want to speculate," Siegal answers.

There were problems with the *New York Times* defense of Markoff. By the newspaper's own rules Markoff would have been precluded from writing his February 19 article (in which he compared

Shimomura to Mr. Spock of *Star Trek*), since it came a full three days after his agent began soliciting million-dollar deals with Shimomura, an individual with whom Markoff clearly "had a commercial or business relationship."

Siegal of the *Times* confessed if he'd "had it to do over again," he'd have "found a paragraph to squeeze out" to mention Markoff's personal role in the original February 16 story, but at the time "it was an issue of space." The *Times* editor complained that there simply wasn't room.

He forgot to look at the bottom-right-hand corner of the page on which Markoff's story ended. Underneath Markoff's thousands of words was a six-and-a-half- by seven-inch filler advertisement for the *New York Times*. Normally newspapers only run their own ads as a last resort to fill up a space when a story comes in short. There was plenty of room. So then what was the real reason why the *Times* didn't reveal Markoff's personal involvement?

.   ▪   ▪

John Markoff goes online with his side of the story. He promptly dismisses the usefulness of the online dialogue, and then issues a statement.

First, Markoff criticizes *Nation* writer Andrew Shapiro for portraying him as having assisted the government. While Markoff admits freely sharing information with FBI agents and Justice Department officials, he says his "information" was all five years old and taken straight from his book.

"I did not 'want to get Kevin,' " announces the reporter, strangely adding that he had never told that to anyone. But Markoff told me he was considering trying to capture him more than six months ago, just before he put Mitnick's picture on the front page of the *New York Times*.

If Markoff didn't plan to "get Kevin" he certainly had to know that if Mitnick was captured, his newspaper stories about Shimomura's pursuit would make the beginnings of a riveting book. But Markoff declares that too is false. He says he never discussed a book about Shimomura's capture of Mitnick until after his articles were published on February 16. I remember our lunch in Chinatown, and Markoff's excitement about the idea of writing a book on Mitnick.

Markoff's cryptic statements only seem to raise more questions. He admits he was skeptical "it was actually Kevin" and that it was only on the Saturday before his arrest that he became certain he was after the right man. The reporter never clarifies whether the "it" was the Christmas IP spoof or some other alleged Mitnick hack.

Finally, Markoff ends his post with a lengthy reference to his fifteen years of writing "realistically" and objectively about hackers. But he writes that the years of reporting have made him "tired of spoiled . . . kids" who lack the patience to program themselves and opt instead to take from others. He quotes from his new role model and coauthor: "As Tsutomu likes to say, that's not acceptable behavior."

.   .   .

But while Markoff defends himself against charges raised by *The Nation* and the *Washington Post,* nearly everyone skirts the larger implications. Who is Tsutomu Shimomura, and how has he managed to control the media?

After Mitnick's arrest, one of my hacker sources sends me an on-line version of a surprising 1993 *Communications Daily* article about Shimomura.

IMMUNITY NEEDED:
MARKEY PANEL SEES DARK SIDE OF ELECTRONIC FRONTIER

Last year, Congress, concerned about cellular phone users' privacy, passed legislation outlawing scanners that pick up cellular channels. . . . At a hearing on privacy, computer cracking and related topics, it took Tsutomu Shimomura about 2 min. to take a new cellular phone out of its box, turn it on and set the device to test mode — thus turning it into scanner that enabled those in House hearing room to hear snatches of live cellular conversations.

Shimomura needed congressional immunity to conduct the demonstration, which otherwise would have been illegal. An FBI special agent was standing by to make sure no other laws were broken. . . .

What an amazing story. Just a couple of years ago, Shimomura needed immunity from prosecution to show the U.S. Congress that he could transform a cellular phone into an illegal scanner and eavesdropper.

I think back to my lunch in San Francisco with Markoff, when he unmasked Mark Lottor as one of the two mystery hackers he profiled in an old *Wired* article. Markoff stopped short before he named his other source, but he had already let the cat out of the bag. I dig up the article, and am immediately struck by its timing. "Cellular Phreaks and Code Dudes: Hacking Chips on Cellular Phones Is the Latest Thing in the Underground" was researched in late '92 and published in January of '93, just months before Shimomura testified under immunity before Congress about illegal eavesdropping.

Paradoxically, the article celebrates hackers. Markoff waxes philosophical on the new cellular hackers, comparing them to the first phone hackers, who tweaked the latest technologies for the challenge. But there's plenty of technical description too. Markoff talks about a "disassembler," a program that reveals nearly a hundred secret commands for controlling the Oki phone and turning it into a scanner. He also gets a firsthand demonstration of how to eavesdrop on cellular calls at a location that sounds an awful lot like the conference room of the San Francisco *New York Times* bureau.

Markoff acknowledges that what he's watching and listening to is "highly illegal." Congress recently outlawed the manufacture of cellular scanners, writes the *Times* reporter, and the Electronic Communications Privacy Act of 1986 makes it a crime to intercept cellular calls. Perhaps that's why Markoff disguises the identity of the hackers. But he's already told me one of the masked individuals, "N.M.," is Mark Lottor. It's not too hard to guess who the other might be:

Meet V.T. and N.M., the nation's most clever cellular phone phreaks. (Names here are obscured because, as with many hackers, V.T. and N.M.'s deeds inhabit a legal gray area.) . . .

V.T. is a young scientist at a prestigious government laboratory. He has long hair and his choice in garb frequently tends toward Patagonia. He is generally regarded as a computer hacker with few equals. . . .

. . . On a recent afternoon, V.T. sits at a conference room table in a San Francisco highrise. . . . Suddenly, voices emerge from the phone's ear piece. . . .

What's going on here? V.T. and N.M. have discovered that every cellular phone possesses a secret mode that turns it into a powerful cellular scanner. . . .

But free phone calls are not what V.T. and N.M. are about. "It's so boring," says V.T. "If you're going to do something illegal, you might as well do something interesting." . . .

V.

The Well

Saul Katz, the recently retired seventy-eight-year-old
founder of the Rockport shoe empire, is surfing the Well, the Internet provider his son, Bruce, bought a few years ago. He reads in a
conference session that usage seems abnormally high. Katz phones
Bruce, the Well's Chief Executive Officer, and tells him that he too
has noticed the system seems to be slower than usual.

"Do you think somebody could have hacked in?" asks Saul.

"No, absolutely not," replies Bruce, who helped launch the family
shoe empire by selling pairs from the back of a VW bus.

But three days later, Bruce Katz gets an urgent call from the Well.
His father's hunch was right. A hacker had indeed cracked the Well
and gained root access. "I was in Aspen skiing with Bill Joy [the
founder of Sun Microsystems]," says Katz. "He had been talking
about Tsutomu's talents in security. Suddenly I said, 'I gotta find this
guy.' "

Other people had the same idea. On January 27, a Well technician had stumbled upon a bloated account belonging to the organizers of the Computers, Freedom and Privacy conference and
alerted Bruce Koball, one of the group's organizers. Koball discovered the account crammed with Shimomura's files. It meant nothing
to Koball until that evening's *New York Times* landed on his door-

step. Koball saw Markoff's Shimomura story and put two and two together. He contacted Well technical manager Hua-Pei Chen and Markoff. The reporter took over from there, putting Koball directly in touch with Shimomura.

.   .   .

This is no ordinary break-in. The Well appears to have been used as an Internet drop point for a hacker's treasures, hundreds of Shimomura's e-mail messages, code for the Oki cellular phone, and tools for hacking, or perhaps security. How could the Well not call in the government? Nobody really knew what was on Shimomura's machine and how dangerous his files might be in a hacker's hands. Shimomura's close friend Brosl Hasslacher, a physicist at Los Alamos National Laboratory in New Mexico, would later explain to *Rolling Stone* magazine: "Tsutomu has built software that can literally destroy an alien computer. They are essentially viruses that can, for example, tell the computer to sit in one register until it literally melts the circuitry in the chip or command the hard drive to hit the same track 33,000 times — until it destroys the drive."

Katz quickly calls a meeting of his board of directors to debate whether to hire Shimomura. The board knows it's taking a big risk by inviting Shimomura to investigate. Even the slightest government intrusion into cyberspace could be fiercely debated on the Well. A champion of libertarian causes, the Well helped spawn the Electronic Frontier Foundation and organize the Computers, Freedom and Privacy "civil rights" conferences. Its members consider themselves privacy advocates and staunch opponents of federal attempts to regulate cyberspace.

But Katz sees the intrusions as a wake-up call, a warning that the Well can no longer ignore its poor security. And even if the FBI ultimately becomes involved, Katz wonders whether that would be such a bad thing. His board members don't seem overly concerned. CERT, the federal government's emergency response team, isn't worried. Even the Electronic Frontier Foundation, that defender of hackers and privacy, thinks Katz is doing the right thing.

"I wanted to keep the FBI out of the Well," says Katz. "I grew up as paranoid as anyone in the 1960s. But you know it depends whose ox is gored. If something happens to you, the police become your buddy. It seemed like the FBI were going to be our ally in this. They would help protect our interests."

Andrew Gross arrives at the Well February 1, and begins assisting Hua-Pei Chen in monitoring the illegal intrusions. He's hired as a paid consultant at less than fifteen dollars an hour. He, like Shimomura and Julia Menapace, Shimomura's assistant and girlfriend, swears to maintain the confidentiality of the investigation. "We didn't want our staff to know, and the staff didn't know [about the investigation]," Katz says. "We kept it small. It was amazing, but we kept it secret."

Mark Graham, the Well's president of networks, is in charge of the monitoring. "We set up Andrew and Tsutomu in a technical staff room. They brought in two laptops. We had to make fast decisions how we were going to do this. I felt we should work with authorities but we had to be responsible to our members, I decided to do seven-by twenty-four [round the clock] monitoring. We had a high degree of ability to monitor his activities. We brought Pete Hansen [a UNIX expert] down from Oregon. We pulled shifts."

Shimomura arrives the evening of February 6. Shimomura's got three powerpacked UNIX microSparC laptops with two gigabytes of storage — over $30,000 of computing power. Two units are set up to "snoop" on the Well, and the third is left free to develop monitoring tools. "He was really into this thing," recalls Katz, impressed by Shimomura's zeal. "He was here to catch this guy."

Law enforcement seems uninterested. Claudia Stroud, a Well vice president, furiously calls the FBI in Los Angeles and Washington, D.C., but they seem to be always playing telephone tag. The FBI keeps telling her to just send them "the data." "We were begging the FBI to come in and they couldn't have given a shit," says Katz. "The problem was the FBI didn't know how to help."

When the investigative team discovers the contents of the intruder's files, Katz starts phoning up the corporations whose operating source code has ended up on the Well. He finds the experience amusing. He gets an executive secretary on the line and she tells him the CEO doesn't have time to talk. That's when Bruce Katz drops his bombshell.

"Why don't you tell him that I'm in possession of the complete source code to your new product and I don't know what to do with it."

.   .   .

Kent Walker, the boyishly handsome San Francisco U.S. Attorney, and the two middle-aged FBI agents sit around the crowded conference room table in Sausalito, California. The secret meeting is being held across the street from the Well at its holding company, the Rosewood Stone Group. The date is Tuesday, February 7. Shimomura sits at one end in his usual shorts and Birkenstocks, his cellular and Palmtop by his side. He's joined by Julia Menapace and Andrew Gross. The Well has called in its San Francisco attorney, John Mendez, to advise vice president Claudia Stroud and technical manager Hua-Pei Chen.

Mendez helped sell the Well on cooperating with the feds. It made sense to him. He was a "fed" himself not too long ago, the former U.S. Attorney in San Francisco and a onetime boss of Kent Walker. But none of this eases Claudia Stroud's concerns. She feels a "certain sympathy" with Mitnick, and knows she isn't alone. Part of her job is gauging the mood of Well subscribers, and she knows if they ultimately condemn the Well for straying from its traditional philosophy, she'll have one big mess on her hands.

Sure, Mitnick and perhaps some other hackers may be traipsing about the Well. But Stroud knows this is hardly big news. The Well has been hacked on and off for years. When Katz bought the Well in 1991, he considered it no more than a big BBS, a computer bulletin board system. There were 10,000 users and security was not a high priority. By early 1995 neither the size nor security of the Well has changed. At best, the small Internet provider has grown to 12,000 users.

Mired in vulnerable UNIX technology like all Internet providers, the Well is wide open to a number of attack techniques. And Katz is the first to admit the Well's technology lags behind most Internet providers. The Well doesn't even provide access to the World Wide Web, the Internet's navigator for widely dispersed pictures, sound, video, and text. The Well's interface is right out of the 1970s, com-

plete with cryptic UNIX shell commands. Subscribers join the Well
and rub shoulders with an eclectic mix of journalists, hackers, industry insiders, and libertarians. It's a hip café in cyberspace, a place to
chat with a select crowd and make contacts with movers and
shakers. The Well isn't a computer or its stored online conversa-
tional threads. It's an attitude, an outlook, a style.

The current break-ins are prodding the Well to do what it probably should have done long ago; junk its outmoded computers for a
$120,000 SparC computer, spiff up its interface software, and join
the rest of the Net. Stroud empathizes with Mitnick's predicament.
But she wonders. What may happen if the hacker discovers they're
helping out the FBI? What if Mitnick decides he wants revenge?
Stroud wants the new computer and system up and running as soon
as possible.

"We can only do this for so long," Stroud warns Walker. "You've
got about a week before we get our new SparC computer and move
everything over. We can't continue to monitor forever."

.   ▪   ▪

Walker listens carefully to Stroud's concerns. That's why he's here
today, to see how he can help.

"What do you need?" Walker asks Shimomura.

The two men talk for several minutes, and Walker is clearly taken
with Shimomura. He's spied his little Palmtop computer, which
seems to Walker to have "all the relevant information in the uni-
verse," this sort of "great cyberspace briefcase." But it's Shimomura's aura that strikes Walker, "his laser-like focus on the issues."
All of the technical people Walker knows consider Shimomura
a genius, and Walker himself is no novice to high-tech investigations.
He lays claim to the nation's first antipiracy prosecution and also
worked on the Kevin Poulsen case.

Mendez, for his part, is impressed by the federal cooperation
Walker is willing to provide. Telephone records. Quick telephone
traps and traces. If Shimomura wants something, Walker will make
sure he gets it. Walker knows Markoff has lots of good inside information, so he punches up the *New York Times* San Francisco bureau
number and puts the reporter on speakerphone. Months later,

Walker won't be able to recall whether it was his idea or Shimomura's to include the reporter in the investigation. The federal prosecutor asks Markoff to fill in the group about Mitnick's background, his personal quirks, his travel habits. And most importantly, when the hacker is most likely to be online.

The Assistant U.S. Attorney sees nothing unusual about asking a reporter to actively assist a federal investigation. He knows Markoff's information is good. Markoff tells how Mitnick eluded capture in Seattle by picking up law enforcement calls on a cellular scanner. Markoff describes Mitnick's habit of riding Greyhound buses. Markoff chats about the people Mitnick associates with, and gossips about De Payne, who he says is currently dating Mitnick's ex-wife. Markoff even banters with Walker about the FBI's suspicion that the hacker has been hiding out in Colorado.

Ten minutes later, Kent Walker thanks the New York Times reporter for all of his help and says goodbye. "He was called, he participated," said John Mendez, the former U.S. Attorney in San Francisco.

.   .   .

The next afternoon, Wednesday, February 8, John Markoff arrives at the Well at about two o'clock. He won't leave for two hours.

Shimomura is talking excitedly about how someone left him a taunting voice mail. "We were all huddling around listening to this [tape recording]," recalls Mark Graham. "Tsutomu was wired. I remember leaning over trying to listen to the voice mail. Markoff was just trying to get the background, writing notes, trying to get the chronology of facts."

No one seems to think it strange that the New York Times reporter knows more about the secret investigation than the Well's own staff. "You have to realize things were happening awfully fast," says Katz. "I didn't think we needed a confidentiality agreement with Markoff."

Claudia Stroud says hello, and Markoff chats with the Well's public relations man. Stroud doesn't consider asking why Markoff is there. He's a customer, one of the celebrities on the Well.

Markoff greets Hua-Pei Chen and Mark Graham, but he spends

most of his time talking with Shimomura about the investigation. The threats on his voice mail aren't the only thing Shimomura finds interesting. Back on February 1, at 7:20 P.M, Chen watched the hacker roam the bowels of the Well, enter a subscriber's home directory, and type "grep" on the subject line in the mailbox, searching for any file containing the letters "itni." Two days later, on February 3, at 6:07 P.M., she watched the hacker grep the subject line of the subscriber's e-mail again. Then, on February 5, at 1:27 A.M., the hacker did something different. He had root access and could do whatever he wanted. He entered the subscriber's home directory and sent a message the subscriber was not likely to miss. After all, how often do people send themselves e-mail?

On February 8, the monitoring group remains intrigued by the unusually addressed e-mail. It's the only e-mail message they've found that Mitnick left for someone at the Well. Shimomura finds it puzzling. So does Markoff. The reporter tries to make sense of it. Mitnick seems to have a secret communication channel with Jon Littman, a journalist Markoff happens to know.

"We all thought it was interesting," says Chen. "It was out of the ordinary. We all said, however, that we shouldn't look at it."

.   .   .

Markoff calls Robert Berger, chief technology officer of Internex Securities, a tiny Menlo Park, California, Internet provider, and tells him he has a security problem. Markoff explains that Mitnick has broken into his Internex e-mail account, and that "Tsutomu" is working "on tracking it down." Markoff would later say that Shimomura phoned Berger first, and that Markoff phoned as a reporter, and out of concern for his own e-mail. Berger, when reinterviewed, said, "I think the person I first actually talked to was Markoff, but Tsutomu might have left a voice mail originally."

The investigators are already in contact with Mark Seiden, a security consultant to Internex and a close friend of Mark Lottor and Shimomura.

What happens next is extraordinary. Mark Seiden transfers and copies 100-plus megabytes of files stashed on the Well.

"I figured rather than nickel-and-dime, I would transfer [the intruder's] whole tool kit and figure out what else was in his bag of tricks," says Seiden. "Shimomura and Gross were up to their necks trying to write tracking programs." Seiden says he transferred the file from the Well to an Internex machine "using the same methods the intruder was using."

The Well doesn't even know it's happening. Nor the FBI.

Seiden starts digging around the intruder's loot, and soon finds something interesting: a huge chunk of the customer data base of Netcom, an Internet provider in San Jose, California — over 30,000 customer records and 21,600 credit card numbers. "It was pretty old, from January or February of '94," says Seiden. "It was unclear that Mitnick had stolen it directly, as opposed to trading it or finding it lying around."

Seiden quickly phones Gross and Shimomura at the Well before dawn on Thursday morning. Netcom looks like another good place to track the intruder. Markoff knows Mitnick's accomplice, Lewis De Payne, maintains an account on Netcom. There are even stories that the government monitored De Payne's account not too long ago. Mitnick's allegedly hacked into Netcom before. Why not now?

Emmanuel

Jim Murphy, a Sprint cellular technician in Raleigh, North Carolina, sits alone in a vast Sprint cellular switch room the afternoon of Saturday, February 11. He's been given a seven-digit number that the FBI thinks is a cellular number. Murphy doesn't recognize the prefix, but just the same he searches through the subscriber database, and just as he suspected, nothing comes up. So he searches to see if it is a number a subscriber may have called, a terminating number.

Bingo! Murphy finds some calls, but they're weird. Calls coming in and out on the same GTE Durham trunk line, bouncing back and forth repeatedly before they fail. He's never seen anything quite like it. Murphy phones Burns, and offers a few possible scenarios. But it's guesswork really, since the agent hasn't given Murphy a clue as to who or what he's up against.

Murphy finishes his routine duties at about 10 P.M., and works for half an hour on the odd call before driving home. But the night's not quite finished. Agent Burns phones again, and he doesn't want to talk on Murphy's cellular line. Murphy wolfs down his second pork chop, drives to the nearby strip mall, and parks in front of the pay phone at the pharmacy. He waits in the cold booth, while a Washington agent struggles to conference him in with Burns and another man. But the FBI can't seem to make the connection.

•   •   •

Murphy sets up the conference call back at the Sprint switch. First Burns at his home near Washington, D.C., then Tsutomu Shimomura, somewhere in northern California.

The conversation starts slowly, but soon Murphy is learning about the suspect he's helping to pursue. "So Mitnick's very familiar with phone switches," Murphy thinks out loud. "If he [Mitnick] knows translations, he could have accessed GTE's switch to get this call loop going. When they get a call failure, it usually goes to a recorded announcement. When his fails, it gives him a Netcom access number. It just looks like a call failure."

Murphy talks with Shimomura for a couple of hours. He's hooked now. Shimomura faxes him hundreds of Nationwide Netcom access phone numbers, and a list of suspected Netcom log-ins by Mitnick. If Murphy can match the log-in times with actual mobile calls, they can profile the hacker's excursions on the Net.

Murphy punches in a search of local Internet access numbers, and the calls flash across his screen; "a bunch of calls" made by one cellular customer, from one mobile number — 919-602-6523.

Murphy tells Burns he's got "activity" but he needs a subpoena to go any further. No problem. Within minutes Kent Walker, the San Francisco Assistant U.S. Attorney, phones Murphy and asks for the appropriate wording. Half an hour later, Walker faxes the subpoena to the Raleigh switch and Sprint headquarters in Chicago.

Murphy's in high gear now. He's got three terminals searching the last twelve hours of calls processed through Sprint's switch — calls to Minneapolis, Seattle, Denver. The hacker seems to be dialing the Internet all over the country, but Murphy notices that nearly all the cellular modem calls originate from one local Raleigh cell site. The Sprint engineer checks activity on the cellular number. It, too, seems suspicious, with dozens of calls to Internet access numbers in just the last twelve hours. And not a single incoming call.

Murphy and Shimomura pore through the records over the phone. The pattern is clear. Mitnick's suspected access times on the

Net and the local mobile calls match perfectly except for a consistent three-minute gap they chalk up to timing differences. Murphy figures the mobile calls to Minnesota, Seattle, and Denver are "bogus long distance calls," a simple technique Mitnick is likely using to disguise his whereabouts. And though the technician knows it's technically possible, he can't believe the local calls are faked. The hacker's gotta be in Raleigh, pretending to be all over the country. It's Murphy's call, but after nearly five hours on the phone with Shimomura he's as sure as he's going to be.

"All these seem to be originating in one spot," Murphy tells Shimomura.

"You sure about that?" asks Shimomura.

"Yup," says Murphy.

"I'll be on the next plane."

.   .   .

Joe Orsak, a senior maintenance engineer with Sprint Cellular, gets a call Sunday at about 1 P.M.

"Do you have the Cellscope?" his boss asks.

"Yes."

"Get it ready."

Orsak plugs the equipment into his Blazer, turns it on and drives out to a cell site just a few miles from his house. He circles the building. If the antenna and cable are properly connected, the signal strength readings won't vary more than -15 dBms. He takes a couple passes and gets a range of -35 to -50, not bad at all. It's ready for action.

At about 7 P.M., Orsak and Murphy pull up at Raleigh-Durham Airport in a big white Ram Charger with the Sprint logo. Orsak left his Blazer back at the cell switch.

"He looked like a Japanese surfer guy from California," recalls Orsak. "Oakley sunglasses, shorts, T-shirt, black gym shorts, sandals. I was thinking, 'Is this the guy?'"

But Murphy's impressed by how quickly Shimomura gets down to business.

"He's the best," Shimomura says of Mitnick. "But I think we're better."

Orsak is just trying to keep up. "Shimomura jumps right into telling us who we're looking for, giving us the background, saying he was the world's most wanted hacker," recalls Orsak. "He didn't think Mitnick was doing it professionally, like espionage, like selling from one company to another."

The Sprint technicians shuttle Shimomura to pick up his teal blue Geo Storm rental car and lead him back to the switch. Shimomura is making quite an impression on the Sprint technicians. "Shimomura showed us his Palmtop hookup to his Oki phone just as soon as we got back to the switch," recalls Orsak. But while Orsak is intrigued by the rig, he knows it's just a toy compared to his Cellscope. Shimomura's Oki 900 scanning rig may be great for eavesdropping, but without an antenna it can't lead them to Mitnick.

FBI agents John Vasquez and Laythell Thomas are waiting for Shimomura and the Sprint technicians at the Sprint cell switch. "They had to be there before we could show Shimomura the call records," recalls Murphy. "He [Shimomura] was a consultant at that point. We couldn't show call records unless they were there."

Murphy shows the group how to read the Sprint call detail records, and they settle in, waiting for the hacker to begin his nightly routine. The agents are ambivalent. Special Agent Vasquez ducks out after roughly half an hour and leaves Thomas to accompany him and Shimomura on the surveillance operation.

About eleven o'clock, Orsak drives Shimomura over to the cell site in his red Blazer, Thomas following in his car. Shimomura continues demonstrating his Oki 900 scanner as Orsak drives, putting the custom monitoring software through its paces. "Why don't you give me one?" the Sprint technician jokes. Shimomura takes him seriously, saying he can get the software and interface cheap from some guy he knows in California. Orsak makes a pit stop at a BP gas station. He grabs a Coke and some peanuts. Shimomura buys bottled water, a Mountain Dew, and potato chips. They figure they're in for a long night.

About 11:30 P.M., they arrive at the cell site, a tiny-one room prefab building crammed with powerful radios and relay racks, temperature controlled at a constant sixty-five degrees. The fluorescent-lit room hums like a beehive. The refrigerator-sized emergency battery buzzes, and the air conditioners whir incessantly. The cell site is a hub, a local Sprint cellular link, logistically the best place to base their tracking operations. If Mitnick is indeed calling over this cell site he's probably not more than a few miles away.

The plan is simple: monitor at the cell site until Mitnick dials up, and then track him with Orsak's Cellscope. Murphy has already co-ordinated with a technician at the competing CellularOne. If Mitnick switches to CellularOne's radio band, they'll phone Murphy, who in turn will page with the new channel. But that's really just backup. Orsak's programmed the Cellscope to scan the seventy local channels — both Sprint and CellularOne. The scope scans a hundred in about a second. And if it fails, there's always Shimomura's Oki 900 rig as a backup.

Orsak's the expert on the Cellscope, an advanced scanner with full direction finding capability. Shimomura seems to have never seen one before, so Orsak gladly shows him the basic operations: how to hit the space bar to continue scanning, how to read the MIN, the number being dialed, and the signal strength. Thomas, meanwhile, remains disinterested. After about half an hour, the agent announces he's leaving for the night. Orsak and Shimomura can't believe it. How could the FBI be so nonchalant when they're on the tail of the world's most wanted hacker? How could the FBI call it quits before the night's surveillance has even begun?

Around 1 A.M. Murphy phones Orsak. He just got a call from CellularOne.

"We've got activity! Let's roll! " Murphy exclaims, reading the three-digit channel to Orsak.

They jump in the red Blazer. Orsak punches in the frequency and reaches into the back to adjust the Cellscope's volume control. Static crackles through the Blazer. Orsak tones it down and pulls a quick right out of the parking lot, heading west on 70 toward the airport. The laptop sits on the front console between them, the signal strength weak, only about -105 dBm. A mile and a half down the road, near the airport, the modem static fades. The reading slips to -115 dBm, the scope is silent. They've left the local sector's 60-degree slice of air.

"We've gotta turn around," Orsak says with a shrug.

A mile back on 70, the crackle of the modem resumes.

"There it is again," Orsak says, turning on Duraleigh.

"Ninety, ninety-five," Shimomura calls out the readings.

Suddenly a message flashes across the Cellscope.

NO SAT

"He hung up," Orsak explains.

The code means the handoff was lost or the caller just hung up.

Orsak parks in front of a little library in a small shopping center and they wait, Shimomura nervously playing with his Oki and Palm-top, cruising the channels. They pick up a couple of very brief Mitnick calls, both data, just a minute or so long.

Modem breath suddenly courses through the Blazer again, and the familiar MIN pops up on the laptop window: 602-6523. And this time the call doesn't die. The bar graph shows the signal's strong, around -90 dBms. Mitnick's online again, and he's not far away.

Orsak revs up his Blazer and continues on Duraleigh. He pulls into an apartment complex, but the signal fades again. The signal's north, back where they came from.

They've got to be close, very close. If only Mitnick would stay online just a little longer! Orsak exits the complex, drives back along Duraleigh and turns at Tournament Drive, entering the Player's Club complex. Halfway around the ring that circles the apartments, Orsak takes the antenna from Shimomura and points it toward the driver's window. He's passing right by what looks like the manager's office, the reading leaping from -60 to -40 dBms.

"Look for lights in the windows!" Shimomura cries. "Don't let him see you, don't let him see you!"

But the windows in the Blazer are tinted, and the small aluminum antenna is black. Orsak's not worried about being spotted, and it's so late the apartment units all seem dark.

Orsak keeps driving and pointing the antenna. Half an hour, that's all it took. Half an hour to track Kevin Mitnick to his neighborhood.

.   .   .

Shimomura is back at the cell site telephone, trying to rustle up some help from the FBI. "He told Walker we had found him, we were one hundred percent sure that it was Mitnick," says Orsak. "I could tell Kent Walker told him he'd get the wheels in motion. Shimomura was very concerned about getting him right away."

Meanwhile, Murphy pages FBI Agent Thomas. "Thomas was calm," says Murphy. "They wanted to come out in the morning and put it [Mitnick's apartment] under surveillance. We were pumped up. We thought they'd be right there. We were kinda upset, thinking they were taking their time. They said, 'We are the FBI. This won't be the first bust we ever made.' "

Murphy conferences in Shimomura, trying to convey the urgency: "He [Shimomura] said, 'This guy is wily. You missed him by minutes a few months ago. He may not be around in the morning.' We started to get upset. Thomas was tired. He wasn't about to be pressured by us amateurs."

Meanwhile, Shimomura gets a page. It's John Markoff, just in at the Raleigh-Durham Airport. He talks to the reporter briefly and passes the phone to Orsak, asking him to provide directions. Orsak doesn't have any idea who he's talking to. Ten minutes later, Markoff shows up in a purple Geo. He's intrigued by the equipment at the cell site.

"What does this do?" asks the curious Markoff. "How does this work?"

Orsak explains the radio gear to the *Times* reporter, walking him through the building. Then, Orsak checks his page. Murphy's sent him Mitnick's channel.

" 'That's Mitnick! That's Mitnick! That's him all right!' " Orsak recalls Shimomura saying.

"John's eyes get real big, and he's going, 'Is it him? Is it really him?' " But Shimomura's worried.

"I don't know, maybe we shouldn't go," Shimomura begins, worried they might be spotted. But he quickly reconsiders. "Maybe we should go."

"I want to go," Markoff eagerly chimes in. "I'm going too."

They pile into the Blazer. Everyone's got a job. One team member shouts out the signal reading, while another sweeps the short antenna slowly back and forth. Orsak just tries to keep his eye on the road.

356 THE FUGITIVE GAME

"Shimomura is in the passenger seat," recalls Orsak. "Markoff is in the back, holding the antenna."

Nine months after the event, and two weeks after galleys of my book were sent out to reviewers and the press, John Markoff's attorney sent my publisher a letter, claiming parts of Mr. Orsak's account were wrong. I made numerous calls to Mr. Orsak and then received the following Pac Bell voice mail message on Sunday, November 19, at 3:13 A.M., Pacific time:

"Hello, Mr. Littman, this is Joe Orsak. I got your message yesterday and I have been talking with Shimomura and Mr. Markoff, and I'm sorry if I was mistaken about any equipment being put in their rental car or the fact that Mr. Markoff had ever touched any of it. So if this caused you any trouble I'm sorry, or if I've given the wrong impression."

According to Orsak's original interviews, as they near the Player's Club Shimomura directs Markoff, "Point that way, point that way."

.   .   .

The next trip was in a Geo. "Shimomura said it would be a good idea to change cars," says Orsak. "I remember us joking about the ugly-colored cars."

Joe Orsak of Sprint said he put the Cellscope in Markoff's rental car. Markoff says the Cellscope was not put in his car.

Back at the cell site, it takes about ten minutes to transfer the equipment to the Geo. Orsak hooks the Cellscope into the cigarette adapter, plugs the Cellscope into his laptop, and attaches a fifteen-foot coaxial cable to the portable antenna. According to Orsak, Markoff starts up the rental car, the Cellscope begins scanning, and within a minute, for the first time, instead of modem breath, they're plucking voices out of the sky. It's Mitnick and he's talking to somebody they know.

"Is that Emmanuel [Goldstein]?" asks Shimomura.

"Yeah!" replies Markoff. "I think it is."

The team quiets down so they can hear. Mitnick makes it easy, addressing Emmanuel by name. The hacker seems in good humor, talking about the cool and rainy weather. "They were mentioning names of other people," recalls Orsak. " 'How is so and so doing?' "

Mitnick's voice, coming over the local cellular, is the loudest, but both parties are clearly recognizable. There may be a problem. The federal subpoena doesn't give unauthorized individuals the right to eavesdrop on voice calls.

Minutes later, just as Shimomura's team crosses Highway 70, Emmanuel Goldstein and Kevin Mitnick bid each other good night. The investigators motor on toward Mitnick's apartment.

.   •   ▪

Monday afternoon, Special Agent LeVord Burns sits by the coffee pot and vending machine at the Sprint switch and debates the legal issues with Shimomura. "Tsutomu wanted us to kick the door down," recalls Orsak, who along with Murphy, listened in. "Burns was talking about what warrants had been issued, what the FBI was going to do."

Burns impresses Orsak. A well-built, bespectacled black man in a suit and tie, Burns looks like the kind of FBI agent that doesn't miss details. As Burns recounts Mitnick's background, Orsak is surprised by what the agent says about Mitnick. "Burns said there were a lot of guys that as far as national security went were a lot more dangerous than Mitnick — that a lot of professional hackers are a lot more dangerous." To Orsak, cyberspace's Most Wanted Hacker doesn't sound all that threatening. "One of the more interesting things, I thought, was the FBI goes, 'As far as hackers go,' Mitnick was 'benign.' They didn't have evidence he was in it for the money."

A little later, John Markoff and Shimomura's girlfriend, Julia Menapace, who just flew in, arrive at the switch. Orsak and Murphy invite Shimomura's team, Burns, and two other FBI agents from Quantico, Virginia, out to Ragazzi's, a casual Italian restaurant nearby. Orsak spreads out a Raleigh street plan on the checkered tablecloth and pinpoints Mitnick's location.

"LeVord was telling us what his involvement was for the FBI," recalls Murphy. "It was light banter. LeVord assumed like we all did, that Markoff was just another guy out of California. Just another egghead. One of Tsutomu's."

Markoff gets everyone's ear when he mentions Mitnick inspired the hit movie *WarGames*. "Markoff was filling us in on Mitnick's typical behavior, the different people Mitnick had run-ins with," recalls Murphy. "A guy in England, a guy in Princeton, one at Digital." Then, Markoff runs through some of Mitnick's aliases. One of the phony names rings a bell with Murphy. After dinner, the whole crew heads back to the switch, and just as Murphy suspected, he finds a memo describing a recent attempt by someone using the alias to social engineer a new bunch of MINs.

Meanwhile, the FBI is bumping up against a technical problem. The agents had planned to install the FBI's own bulky scanning equipment in a rental van, but they can't find one. Murphy suggests using his co-worker Fred's minivan. Burns gives the idea the green light, and Orsak helps the agents set up and calibrate their equipment in Fred's van.

Around midnight, Fred chauffeurs the two agents to circle the cell site to calibrate their scanning equipment. Fred and the FBI agents get to talking.

"He [Fred] let the cat out of the bag," confides Murphy. "We didn't tell him not to say anything. We weren't trying to hide it, but we were also not trying to convey it. He told them Markoff wrote a book on this guy."

The boys from Quantico aren't happy.

"They freaked," recalls Murphy. "They thought Markoff would tip the guy [Mitnick] so he could write another book."

One of the Quantico agents phones the Sprint switch to confirm Markoff's identity. "Me, Markoff, Tsutomu, and Julia were at the switch," remembers Murphy. "One of the Quantico guys was on the phone. He wanted to talk to Tsutomu."

Murphy passes the phone to Shimomura.

"He [Shimomura] wasn't about to lie," says Murphy of the tense moment. "He [Shimomura] was trying to evade a little bit. He said that Kent Walker knew about Markoff being there, which of course Walker did."

Murphy, Markoff, and Menapace listen to Shimomura.

"Kent knows about it," insists Shimomura to the agent from Quantico. "He's cleared through Kent."

But Kent Walker later denied ever giving Shimomura such approval or knowing John Markoff was in Raleigh. Shimomura later disputed Murphy's account and said he "never told anyone from law enforcement that anyone had authorized Markoff's presence in Raleigh."

Probable Cause

John Markoff leaves the search team Monday night. The air's getting a little thick anyway, and it's not as if Markoff doesn't have plenty to do. He needs to get back to the Sheraton to write up his notes.

"They were talking about having gotten rid of him," recalls Orsak. "Burns and the Quantico guys. They were not pleased. Burns was saying, 'the FBI doesn't do business that way.' "

So the hunt continues, minus the reporter. Orsak drives Burns's car to the shopping center. They sit and joke about UFOs, while Fred takes the Quantico guys for a couple of tours around the Player's Club. Two Raleigh PD cars cruise up, and then the agents flash their badges and the cops go on their way. On the third pass, the van drops a lone FBI agent with a small handheld device to attempt to narrow Mitnick's location. He's dressed casually, with an average-looking jacket. "The bag looks like a camera bag," remembers Orsak. "No antenna. It's just a signal strength meter. This one agent goes on foot with it and actually walks up and down the hall in the apartment building. It's kind of like the Cellscope. But as you get closer, and the signal starts to saturate, you've got an attenuator to turn down the sensitivity."

.　　　　.　　　　.

The next day at the switch, Murphy and Orsak listen while Shimomura makes one more plea with Special Agent Burns to go along for the bust. He's been after the agent since he first arrived.

"I understand you'd want to go," says Burns. "We just don't do that."

But Shimomura presses. He's concerned about getting his hands on Mitnick's equipment. "He said he had to have physical evidence he was on Netcom," recalls Orsak. "He was concerned the FBI would grab all the goodies and not let him see that."

But the harder Shimomura pushes, the more Burns brings up Markoff.

"Can I trust you not to bring everybody in the press along?" the FBI agent asks.

But Shimomura won't take no for an answer. "The reason I was hired by the Internet companies was because I assured them that I would be there to limit the damage," Shimomura argues. "What if he's got command files built in to destroy things?"

Still, Burns is unconvinced. "We can't have a civilian in a search and seizure."

But Shimomura won't give up easily. "Who do you have that's going to be able to insure that there's damage control for these Internet providers?"

Murphy watches Burns closely. It's clear the FBI agent doesn't have an answer. "I have to clear it first," the agent says.

LeVord Burns has to call FBI Headquarters in Washington.

.   .   .

That same day, Tuesday, February 14, Assistant U.S. Attorney John Bowler phones the office of the United States Magistrate and warns Magistrate Judge Wallace Dixon he will probably ask him to issue a search warrant that evening.

A little after 8:30 P.M., Burns and Bowler arrive at the magistrate's home. The magistrate quickly sizes up the two men. He's taken aback by Burns's casual garb, but then he realizes it's perfect for surveillance. Powerfully built, Burns reminds him of a college linebacker. Bowler Dixon knows from his courtroom. Dressed in his usual suit and tie, the prosecutor appears to have just come from his office.

There isn't time to offer them a soda or tea. The magistrate invites the men into his living room and they hand him a warrant and an affidavit. What a load of gibberish, the magistrate thinks to himself. Ten pages of technical jargon detailing arcane computer and phone intrusions. He asks them to cut to the chase. Burns and Bowler run down Mitnick's probation violation, his alleged computer break-ins, the thousands of supposedly swiped credit cards, and the high-tech cat and mouse game that's led to the Player's Club. Now the magistrate is beginning to understand. He attends church near the Player's Club, works out at a health club down the road, even jogs by the complex's front entrance. What an irony, he thinks. The world's most wanted computer hacker holed up a mile away.

The affidavit in Dixon's hands puts Kevin Mitnick in building 4640, apartment 107, first rented February 4, "the precise date on which the target began operating out of the Raleigh, North Carolina, area." But in Magistrate Dixon's comfortable living room, Burns and Bowler confess they have no idea whether Mitnick is in building 4640, or in an apartment in one of the other sixteen buildings.

Upstairs, Dixon's wife is talking on the portable phone, hearing all sorts of beeps and buzzes, when out of the window she notices a vehicle parked in the driveway. "Here's where it gets a little unusual," the magistrate later recalls. "The whole time they were talking to me they had some educated person out in a law enforcement van electronically tracking the stuff at the apartment."

But the peculiar evening has only just begun. Dixon flips through the papers and notices Bowler forgot to bring the search warrant. "Bowler was anxious to move the surveillance team from my driveway to the Player's Club," recalls Dixon. "He asked if it would be OK to use my telephone and call his secretary [to bring the warrant]."

The magistrate has a solution. "I told him [Bowler] if he wanted to he could accept an alternative. He could have her prepare more [warrants]. I told them that in my view it would be permissible, OK for me to sign those warrants, so long as we had an understanding that they would make no efforts to search until they'd pinpointed him and then gotten approval. I told them that was permissible. I would authorize that."

Bowler and Burns agree to the magistrate's conditions and promptly leave for the Player's Club. Within half an hour Bowler's secretary and a co-worker arrive at Magistrate Dixon's home with a warrant for apartment 107, and something unusual.

"There was more than one blank," Magistrate Dixon later recalls of the warrants, which simply list Raleigh, North Carolina, as the address to be searched. "My guess is there were three."

At 9:10 P.M., U.S. Magistrate Judge Wallace Dixon signs the first blank warrants of his career.

.   .   .

Across from the Player's Club, the FBI sets up its surveillance team, but all is quiet. Bowler guesses Mitnick's gone offline to grab a late-night bite.

Shortly before midnight, Mitnick goes online again and the surveillance team begins tracking him to the Player's Club. But the FBI can't seem to pin down the hacker. They know he's in one of the buildings, they just aren't sure which one. The signals are bouncing between the buildings, confounding the agents.

Then, suddenly, around 1 A.M., the FBI gets a lucky break. But according to the government it has nothing to do with high technology. The governnment's story is that Deputy U.S. Marshal Mark Chapman sees Kevin Mitnick stick his head out of a door.

Marshal Chapman walks up to building 4550 and knocks on apartment 202. The time is around 1:28 A.M. The fugitive is inside, talking on the phone to his mom in Las Vegas.

Mitnick asks the visitor to identify himself.

"FBI," Mitnick hears the caller say.

The agent just wants to ask him some questions. Kevin Mitnick, the world's most wanted hacker, talks to the federal agent outside his door. He's still on the phone too. At 1:44 A.M., Mitnick says goodnight to his mom and phones his aunt, Chickie Leventhal, at Chickie's Bail Bonds in Los Angeles.

Then, finally, Mitnick opens the door slightly, demanding to see a search warrant. He tries to close the door, but a black agent jams the door with his foot, and several agents shove their way in.

Mitnick demands to see a search warrant, but he's ignored.

"Kevin, do you know how we caught you?" Mitnick recalls a U.S. Marshal taunting him.

At 1:47 A.M. Mitnick phones his attorney, John Yzurdiaga, in Redondo, California. Yzurdiaga asks to speak to one of the FBI agents and demands they produce a search warrant or leave his client's apartment. Burns finally leaves saying he's going to get a search warrant, only to return several minutes later with just an arrest warrant. When Mitnick repeats his demand Burns once again leaves the apartment to get a search warrant.

Meanwhile, the other agents ignore Mitnick's protests and search his apartment. They pull out a wallet from the buttoned pocket of Mitnick's leather jacket, emptying the contents. The FBI continues searching through Mitnick's things. Half an hour passes, and still no sign of Burns or a search warrant.

.   .   .

Here's what Assistant U.S. Attorney Bowler says happened the night of Mitnick's arrest:

> When the defendant came to the door he was actually on the telephone with someone. After recognizing Mitnick, the agents entered the apartment and performed a protective sweep of the apartment. . . .
>
> The agents then asked the defendant to identify himself. Mitnick then stated he was "Thomas Case" and produced a recently obtained North Carolina Driver's license, credit card, and checkbook all in the false identity of "Thomas Case." . . . After the defendant placed the wallet on a countertop, the agents examined the contents and discovered a series of other identification with several other false names. The defendant then hastily closed an open black briefcase. He was then handcuffed and placed under arrest.
>
> Special Agent Burns then left the apartment and placed a telephone call to the Magistrate [Dixon] and informed him of the arrest and the correct location. The Magistrate then authorized the agents to proceed with the search and instructed them to complete the blank search warrant with correct apartment and building numbers.

A copy of the warrant was provided to the defendant for his review. The defendant was advised of his Miranda rights by Special Agents Burns and Thomas. He refused to sign an acknowledge form and asked to call someone he identified as his attorney.

. . .

But the magistrate was sound asleep when he got the call after 2 A.M. from Agent Burns. And the magistrate knew exactly what Burns did and didn't say.

"Judge Dixon?"

"Yes."

"This is Agent Burns."

"You were here earlier this evening?"

"Yes, I was."

"I recognize your voice."

"We've got a fix on him, Judge. We've targeted him. We know the apartment now."

"You're good to search."

Magistrate Dixon insists Burns never told him the FBI had already entered Mitnick's apartment and begun a warrantless search without having obtained his permission. In his living room, the magistrate had specifically instructed Burns to phone him and gain his approval before beginning any search. And Dixon swears the FBI agent never told him he'd already placed Mitnick under arrest.

"No they should not have been in there," says the magistrate. "They shouldn't have gone in."

Who is to be believed? A federal magistrate or an FBI agent? Or is there objective evidence? The hacker's phone bill seems to prove the timing of his story and corroborates part of the magistrate's account. Mitnick phoned his attorney, John Yzurdiaga, within two minutes of the FBI's forced entry, not over a half an hour later after Special Agent Burns's return, as the government claimed. The Sprint phone bill also proves Mitnick's call to his attorney was twenty minutes long, twenty minutes during which Kevin Mitnick and his attorney repeatedly demanded to see a search warrant that the FBI did not produce.

. . .

About 3:20 A.M., Kevin Mitnick is driven to the Wake County Public Safety Center in Raleigh. He asks to call his mother.

"What's her name?" the federal agent reportedly asks. "Who should we say is calling?"

The hacker says nothing for several minutes, and then begins to talk.

"OK, you got me," Mitnick confesses. "I'm Kevin David Mitnick. I want you to know that I'm *not* a spy."

Afterword

f money was the ultimate measure of success, there was little doubt who won the fugitive game. Within a week of Markoff's front-page *New York Times* story his agent had brokered a package deal for the reporter and the security man with family entertainment giant Walt Disney. Hyperion, Disney's publishing subsidiary, paid an estimated $750,000 advance for book rights to *Catching Kevin*. The Miramax movie option was $200,000 with a total of $650,000 to be paid upon commencement of filming. Foreign book rights to the United Kingdom, Italy, Spain, France, Holland, Brazil, Japan, and Taiwan were estimated at between a quarter and a half million dollars. Video game rights were also sold. All told, the new business partners' revenue could approach $2 million.

If fame was the goal, Shimomura had become an instant celebrity. CNN produced a segment on Shimomura and NBC courted him for an exclusive interview with Tom Brokaw to coincide with his book release in early 1996. Markoff, on the other hand, was relegated to the backseat. Disney was buying Shimomura, the cybersleuth. The story was to be in Shimomura's words, as told to Markoff, as if the reporter had played no role in the drama.

Publicity had made Shimomura a marketable property. He was selling not only his story but his services as a hacker and security expert. By the spring of 1995, full-page "To Catch a Thief" advertising spreads appeared nationwide in five computer magazines, featuring Shimomura holding the same computer he'd cradled in his *New York Times* photo. Shimomura's reputation as a master security whiz soared. *Newsweek* named him one of the fifty "most influential people to watch in cyberspace." In May, Shimomura's face was splashed in the papers when he accepted a public challenge from Sun Microsystems to crack its latest computers. At a major Internet conference in Hawaii, Shimomura gave a riveting demonstration of how he tracked a hacker who had cracked into the Pacific Fleet Command during the Gulf War, intriguing his audience by purportedly quoting from Sun-tzu's *The Art of War,* a renowned work on military strategy by the fourth-century-b.c. Chinese general: "Engage the opponent, rather than sitting there waiting to be beat up on."

By invoking Sun-tzu, Shimomura appeared to be encouraging security professionals to draw hackers into battle. But Sun-tzu might offer a different maxim. The ancient general was principally known for advocating deception ("war is based upon deception") and avoiding hostilities: "It is best to win without fighting."

.   .   .

The fortunes of two hackers could not have taken more opposite turns.

As Tsutomu Shimomura launched his new careers as pitchman, author, movie subject, and video game designer, Kevin Mitnick sat in a Southern county jail. Mitnick wrote to me nearly every week on yellow legal paper in longhand, bemoaning the lack of a word processor as he recounted the hardships of jail. He told me he had been attacked and robbed by two inmates and barely avoided fights with several others. When he complained that the vegetarian diet he requested was limited to peanut butter sandwiches, and that his stress and stomach medication prescriptions weren't filled, he was moved to a tougher county jail.

His grammar wasn't perfect, but his writing was surprisingly frank and descriptive. Mitnick punctuated his letters with Internet shorthand, noting the precise minute he began each letter, as if he were still online. He was bitter, but he hadn't lost his sense of humor. When his jailers admitted they'd read the letter Mike Wallace wrote him, inviting him to appear on 60 Minutes, Mitnick admitted the irony of him, of all people, complaining about other people reading his mail. "Poetic justice, eh? . . ."

Once in a while he'd slip in a tantalizing comment about his case. One week he'd appear to trust me, the next he'd wonder whether I would betray him. It was strange corresponding with the man the media and our government had cast as a twenty-first-century Frankenstein. Mitnick himself didn't seem sure of who or what he was. He asked whether I felt he should be given a long prison sentence. Did I think he was evil? Dangerous?

When he was sent to his second jail, as a matter of policy the U.S. Marshals confiscated his books, his underwear, his toiletries. Mitnick was doing the worst prison "time" possible, because the Eastern District of North Carolina had no federal detention center. That meant he would have to defend himself without access to a law library, required by law in federal institutions. The nurse in Mitnick's second county jail cut his medication again, and on June 18, his attorney filed a motion in federal court stating that Mitnick "was taken to the hospital and diagnosed with esophageal spasms." The attorney argued that the "deliberate indifference" to Mitnick's "serious medical needs" violated constitutional standards.

Before a federal judge could order a hearing on the medical issues, Mitnick was transferred to his third North Carolina jail in as many months. "He [Mitnick] overextended his welcome," explained a deputy U.S. Marshal in Raleigh who preferred to remain anonymous. "It was time for a change of scenery. This happens with a lot of them. They get where they think they're running the place."

Mitnick's third county jail was his worst yet. He shared a cell with seven other men. There was no law library, radio or television, and each inmate was allowed only two books at a time. Mitnick's were the Federal Criminal Code and the Federal Sentencing Guidelines. The eight men in Mitnick's cell were forced to share a single pencil stub that was taken away in the afternoon. Mitnick was allotted one sheet of paper a day.

.   .   .

On April 10, 1995, John Dusenberry, Mitnick's public defender, filed a motion to suppress evidence and dismiss the indictment. He argued that the blank search warrants and the warrantless search of Mitnick's apartment violated the Fourth Amendment, which specifically prohibits unreasonable search and seizure.

In the government's response, John Bowler, the Assistant U.S. Attorney in Raleigh, defended the blank search warrants, not an easy proposition in a free country. Bowler prefaced his argument by claiming, despite evidence to the contrary, that Shimomura tracked Mitnick on his own until February 14, just hours before his capture. The government's response to the issue of the blank search warrants was to blame Magistrate Wallace Dixon. Bowler asserted that the FBI had wanted to execute the search properly, but the magistrate had "upon his own initiative" insisted on signing the blank search warrants.

But a judge never ruled on these arguments. The twenty-three-count indictment the Associated Press had hypothesized could land Mitnick 460 years in jail fell apart. The government abandoned its case in Raleigh, dismissing all but one of the counts in accepting a plea bargain from Mitnick that would likely get him time served, or at most eight months. The tiny story was buried in the back pages of the *New York Times*.

.   .   .

"Kevin is going to come and face the music in L.A., where, of course, the significant case has always been," David Schindler, the U.S. Attorney in Los Angeles, told the *L.A. Times*. The newspaper said the prosecutor believed Mitnick would receive stiffer punishment "than any hacker has yet received," a sentence greater than Poulsen's four years and three months.

Mitnick's letters revealed how Schindler planned to win the record prison term. Schindler was claiming losses in excess of $80 million, the amount that would garner the longest possible sentence for a fraud case according to the Federal Sentencing Guidelines. Nor would Schindler have to substantiate his claim. The government only had to "estimate" the loss. Mitnick's attorneys said the figure was grossly exaggerated, and added that the case rested on source code allegedly copied from cellular companies. There was no proof that Mitnick had tried to sell the code, and there was no evidence it could be sold for an amount approaching $80 million. But under the guidelines the absence of a profit motive was no obstacle to a long jail term. David Schindler was seeking an eight-to-ten-year sentence for Kevin Mitnick, about the same prison time doled out for manslaughter.

·   ·   ·

The jailed hacker wasn't the only one whose feats were being hyped. By August of 1995, the advertisement in *Publishers Weekly* for Shimomura's upcoming book featured Mitnick's *New York Times* photo stamped with the caption "HE COULD HAVE CRIPPLED THE WORLD." Declared the ad, "Only One Man Could Stop Him: SHIMOMURA."

The hyperbole made me flash on what Todd Young had done in Seattle. The bounty hunter had tracked Kevin Mitnick down in a few hours with his Cellscope. Unauthorized to arrest him, he'd kept Mitnick under surveillance for over two weeks as he sought assistance. But the Secret Service didn't think the crimes were significant. The U.S. Attorney's Office wouldn't prosecute the case. Even the local cops didn't really care.

When I met Young in San Francisco a couple of weeks after Mitnick's arrest, he was puzzled by the aura surrounding Shimomura and his "brilliant" capture of Kevin Mitnick. We both knew from independent sources that Shimomura had never before used a Cellscope. Young asked why the FBI would bring an amateur with no cellular tracking skills to Raleigh for the bust. If Shimomura's skill was measured by his ability to catch the hacker, then he was on a par with Todd Young, a thousand-dollar-a-day bounty hunter who never had the help of the FBI. The simple, unglamorous truth was that Kevin Mitnick, whatever his threat to cyberspace and society, was not that hard to find.

I tried to get the government to answer Young's question about Shimomura's presence. I asked the San Francisco U.S. Attorney's Office and they suggested I ask the FBI. But the FBI had no comment. I asked Schindler, the Assistant U.S. Attorney in L.A., and he didn't have an answer. I asked Scott Charney, the head of the Justice Department's Computer Crime group, and he said he couldn't comment. I asked the Assistant U.S. Attorney who would logically had to have approved sending Shimomura three thousand miles to Raleigh, North Carolina. But Kent Walker oddly suggested I ask Shimomura for the answer.

The response reminded me of what John Bowler, the Raleigh prosecutor, had said when I asked him how John Markoff came to be in Raleigh. He, too, had suggested I ask Shimomura. Shimomura seemed to be operating independently, outside of the Justice Department's control. Or was he running their show?

.   .   .

The media appeared captivated by Shimomura's spell. Except for the *Washington Post* and *The Nation,* most major publications and the television networks accepted John Markoff's and Tsutomu Shimomura's story at face value. Kevin Mitnick's capture made for great entertainment.

Not one reporter exposed the extraordinary relationship between Shimomura and the FBI. Most seemed to ignore the conflict of interest raised by the financial rewards Shimomura and Markoff received by cooperating with the FBI. A *Rolling Stone* magazine story condoned Markoff's actions, saying he had merely done what any journalist would do when presented with the possibility of a big scoop. The media critic for *Wired* suggested only that Markoff should have advised *New York Times* readers earlier of his personal involvement in capturing Mitnick.

The media functioned as a publicity machine for Shimomura and the federal government, quickly churning out a round of articles arguing for tougher laws and greater security on the Internet. But the fury over what Assistant U.S. Attorney Kent Walker described as Mitnick's "billion dollar" crimes simply distracted the public from the real issues. Privacy intrusions and crime in cyberspace were old news, and a series of Internet break-ins after Mitnick's arrest proved the capture of cyberspace's most wanted criminal had changed little.

The real story was that Internet providers, the new equivalent of phone companies on the information superhighway, appeared naive about how to investigate break-ins while protecting the privacy of their subscribers. After an FBI computer child-pornography investigation was made public in September of 1995, the Bureau revealed that it had read thousands of e-mail correspondences, and invaded the privacy of potentially dozens of citizens in the course of its investigation. Privacy activists complained that constitutional rights were being bulldozed, but the FBI announced the public should expect more of the same. "From our standpoint, this investigation embodies a vision of the type of investigatory activity we may be drawn to in the future," said Timothy McNally, the special agent in charge.

The government seemed to be promoting a hacker dragnet to make sure the Internet was crime free for the millions of dollars of commerce on its way. Kent Walker, the Assistant U.S. Attorney who left the Justice Department within weeks of Mitnick's arrest for a job with a Pacific Telesis spin-off, was one of the many government officials who claimed the FBI couldn't crack high-tech cases without people like Shimomura.

Perhaps prosecutions would increase if the FBI bolstered its force with nonprofessionals. But where would that leave the law and the Constitution?

.   .   .

A few days after Mitnick's arrest, Shimomura received another voice mail threat that reportedly sounded much like the previous ones. The cybersleuth chose not to post that message publicly to the Internet. Kevin Mitnick couldn't have left it. Who did?

In August of 1995, I flew to a hacker conference in Las Vegas and spent four hours talking with Mark Lottor, the cell phone hacker. He told me that the week before Shimomura helped arrest Mitnick, the cybersleuth saw "stuff on his screen that made him pretty certain" that the Christmas IP spoof attack was not executed by Mitnick, but by the "guy in Israel."

By this time, the statement didn't surprise me. Markoff himself had told me that the evidence overwhelmingly pointed away from Mitnick. Hackers who knew and talked to the Israeli were convinced he wrote the spoof program and launched the attack. Would Shimomura or Markoff ever admit this publicly?

I sent Shimomura a series of interview requests, and received a phone call and a fax from an attorney. He told me Shimomura would not agree to an interview, but later wrote that if I planned on printing any "critical" remarks I should contact him and Shimomura might respond. I sent four pages of detailed questions to Shimomura.

Five weeks later, John Markoff sent me two copies of what he called their joint response, a letter bearing no signature or letterhead but with a San Francisco postmark, and an e-mail sent from Markoff's *New York Times* account. The letter denied that "Tsutomu" had baited Mitnick, and insisted that Markoff had never assisted or participated in any aspect of the Kevin Mitnick investigation.

There were no comments on the Israeli and a number of other critical subjects, and only a handful of denials to the several dozen questions I had posed. The coauthors stated that if I included material on what they described as "Tsutomu's cellular telephone software development work," journalistic ethics would require me to include the following: "Tsutomu, unlike Mitnick, in all of his computer security research over a fifteen year period, has always, whenever he has found a vulnerability, made it known to the appropriate people, whether CERT, or a private company at risk, or the United States Congress." The letter is included at the back of the book.

And what of Lewis De Payne, Mitnick's old pal? In September of 1995 he was still managing the computers of a wholesaler. The government had given little indication that it seriously considered pursuing De Payne, but Mitnick's old prankster buddy still seemed to hold out hope. He sent me a fax that looked like a *Wheel of Fortune* board. When he later provided the missing letters over the phone his question read: "ANY INDICATION OF HIM [Mitnick] COOPERATING TO THE POINT OF INCRIMINATING OTHER INDIVIDUALS?"

*   *   *

When Kevin Mitnick was arrested there were two heroes, Tsutomu Shimomura, the honorable samurai, and the chronicler of Mitnick's deeds, John Markoff. Shimomura was technically superior to Kevin Mitnick, but this wasn't merely a question of computer expertise. It was a contest between two sets of values. In the end, the game was just as Shimomura said it would be, "a matter of honor."

Tsutomu Shimomura and Kevin Mitnick will be judged by their actions and their motives. They both hacked and they both had an apparent disdain for the law. We can guess why Kevin Mitnick hacked. He had a troubled childhood, a mean streak, and an obsession with the technology that society embraces. Money or crime never seemed to be the driving forces behind Kevin Mitnick. But Tsutomu Shimomura's underlying motives remain unexplained. We know he worked for the Air Force and the NSA. Could this have been another undercover assignment for U.S. intelligence? Or was it just a hacker's vendetta, a simple case of revenge?

By late October 1995, the ultimate punishment for Mitnick's alleged crimes had yet to be determined. Would the Justice Department succeed in convicting Kevin Mitnick of massive computer fraud, or would the failure in Raleigh be repeated? Would the government be forced to plea-bargain a slap on the wrist of the world's most dangerous cybercriminal?

In one of Mitnick's last letters from jail, he wrote me something I'll never forget. It was a typical Mitnick remark: wry, humorous, and flippant.

"Tsutomu thinks he's got his man. No cigar!"

Epilogue to the
Paperback Edition

In the aftermath of Kevin's capture, attention turned to the hacker's pursuer, Tsutomu Shimomura. *Newsweek, The New Yorker,* and other national publications criticized the cybersleuth, questioning whether he was really the white knight in this supposed tale of good and evil. But surprisingly, the most damning revelations came from Shimomura himself. In his January 1996 book, he wrote that in December a year before, Mitnick and "possibly some of his cronies" had broken into his computers and stolen software he'd written, "which if abused, could wreak havoc on the Internet community." It was surprising enough that Shimomura acknowledged that he had written the dangerous program. But why would the highly skilled security expert have left it vulnerable on the Internet for hackers to copy?

Security experts spoke of the basic methods Shimomura could have easily employed to prevent the attack. Any of a handful of readily available products and techniques would have made the attack impossible. Some postulated that Shimomura may have baited the hackers. But as criticism of the security expert escalated, it became increasingly clear that Shimomura held himself accountable to a different standard. He kept repeating mantras such as "tools are tools" and seemed to see himself as the digital equivalent of the inventor of the A-bomb. He knew his "tools" could be used for good as well as evil and couldn't understand what all the fuss was about.

In his defense, there was no evidence his software had caused major break-ins or disruptions on the Internet. Nevertheless, Shimomura defended his actions in a question-and-answer session on his publisher's World Wide Web site, with self-serving answers to carefully prepared questions such as "Tsutomu, people have said you should be criticized for not maintaining better security on your own system." Remarkably, Shimomura revealed on the Web that he had no proof that Mitnick had broken into his San Diego computers. His only evidence was that Mitnick appeared to have copies of stolen software half a day after it was taken, but many other hackers also had copies. Shimomura acknowledged that "Mitnick probably did not write the program that was used to break into my computer" and hypothesized, "Instead, he probably used a program written by another, more skilled programmer, who has not yet been apprehended."

Shimomura's retreat raised new questions. If he had no proof Mitnick had broken in and thought that he didn't even write the "brilliant" attack program, why did Shimomura think Mitnick had "probably" used someone else's program? What proof did he have that his fixation with Mitnick was not a case of mistaken identity? Even the supposed Mitnick "Kung Fu" voice mail threats to Shimomura that had infused the story with a sense of danger no longer seemed to be solidly grounded in fact. After some digging, I determined that the calls had not been made by Mitnick; another infamous phone phreak had left the messages as a racist, tasteless bad joke. When the messages had been publicized by the *New York Times,* and mistakenly interpreted as part of the attack on Shimomura, the phreak rode out the prank and left a tantalizing final message after Mitnick's capture, proving that it couldn't have been Mitnick. So there it was. If Mitnick was not the mastermind, not the designer of the brilliant attack, not even the rogue behind the death threats, it was hard not to find Shimomura's snap accusations troubling: for if Mitnick did not hack Shimomura, or leave the taunting messages, it's worth asking whether Shimomura had tracked and captured the wrong man.

What some found surprising was how Shimomura boasted about his own character faults in his book. He admitted that he had persuaded Markoff to mislead the Bureau and pretend he was on Shimomura's team. Then, when an FBI agent caught wind of their ruse, Shimomura arrogantly suggested the agent trick his superiors into thinking Shimomura had been up-front about the deception, what he called "plausible deniability." The FBI agent angrily informed Shimomura that he had "lied" and "endangered the operation."

And Shimomura had crossed other lines. Markoff later argued that because Mitnick wasn't paying for his phone calls, he couldn't complain about Shimomura intercepting his conversations in Raleigh. But what about the other person on the line, Emmanuel Goldstein? He did not appear to have broken any law. Though without a court order from a federal judge the FBI couldn't reveal his name or the fact that the conversation took place, Shimomura published Goldstein's name and parts of his intercepted conversation with Mitnick.

After Mitnick's capture, Shimomura included potential evidence in the federal investigation on his Web page. Characterized by the FBI as an independent consultant to the Well and Netcom, Shimomura could only have legally wiretapped on the Internet as an "agent of a provider of wire or electronic communication service." That may have given Shimomura the right to snoop for the Well or Netcom; it didn't give him the right to publicize transcripts of wiretaps. At least one Internet provider, aware of the criminal penalties for unlawful disclosure of intercepted communications, demanded that he remove the disclosed wiretaps from his Web page.

By the summer of 1996, Shimomura had disappeared from the radar screen, his meteoric rise to fame matched only by the swiftness of his decline. Miramax abandoned its attempt to make a feature film on the cybersleuth, and *Wired* magazine, which just a few months before had featured Shimomura's exploits on its cover, downgraded the man the *New York Times* had only recently dubbed a hero to its list of the "Tired 100."

·   ·   ·

In June of 1996, sixteen months after his capture, Kevin Mitnick considered crying uncle. David Schindler, the lead Assistant U.S. Attorney in the case, had told him he could spend forty years in prison if he went to trial and lost. Schindler's calculation was based on a kind of double jeopardy and the hypothesis that Mitnick was responsible for $80 million in losses, a fantastically exaggerated sum. He told the hacker he could face a nationwide revolving door of trials, asserting that he had no control over the other authorities that might want to try him in San Diego, San Francisco, Seattle, Dallas, and North Carolina. In addition to those threats, Mitnick had another problem. John Yzurdiaga, his attorney, had taken his case on a pro bono basis, and was losing time and money on the defense. He advised Mitnick to accept the government's proposed guilty plea — an eight-year sentence, with the potential of future prosecution for other crimes. Even if Yzurdiaga had the time to go through a protracted trial, he wasn't convinced he could beat the deal.

But at a scheduled status hearing on June 17, 1996, attorney Richard Sherman stunned Schindler with the news that he was replacing John Yzurdiaga as Mitnick's new counsel. Mitnick wanted to exercise his constitutional right to a trial, and Sherman was the toughest attorney he could find. Sherman had publicly reprimanded Schindler for the crimes committed by Justin Petersen while he was an FBI informant and also sued the government on De Payne's behalf to get back belongings confiscated in a 1992 search. There was no love lost between the two men. Schindler had not appreciated Sherman's letter to Janet Reno on De Payne's behalf describing his Petersen undercover operation as "illegal and contrary to Bureau policy." And Sherman, a former Assistant U.S. Attorney himself, had not enjoyed being investigated as an alleged murderer by FBI agent Stan Ornellas, who sometimes worked with Schindler. The allegation was subsequently dropped.

Schindler warned Sherman there might be a conflict of interest since he had previously represented De Payne. Sherman responded that if he knew of any conflict he should apprise Judge Mariana Pfaelzer immediately, since if it were determined that Sherman couldn't represent the hacker he would be left without counsel. But

Schindler left without airing his allegation in front of the judge or her clerk. The next day, June 18, Sherman wrote Schindler, complaining about the prosecutor's failure to raise his conflict of interest before the judge. "On behalf of Kevin Mitnick I demand that you indict him at the earliest time in Los Angeles, California." He asserted that Schindler was the head of the "nationwide Mitnick investigation or Task Force" and the attorney who would determine "when and where" Mitnick might be indicted. "Let's get this matter tried," he implored. Two days later he fired off another letter, this time copying his correspondence to Judge Pfaelzer. Kevin had told him that Schindler had warned that if he reneged on the plea, the prosecutor "would notify other federal jurisdictions across the country that Mitnick was now available for prosecution." Wrote Sherman, "The clear meaning of those threats was that you would encourage his indictment in other jurisdictions. . . ."

Schindler promptly wrote back on June 20, 1996, rejecting the charge that he'd threatened Mitnick and denying that he could decide "when and where" Mitnick was indicted, though the previous year he had told the *L.A. Times,* "Kevin is going to come and face the music in L.A., where, of course, the significant case has always been." Four days later, Schindler replied to Sherman's second letter, copying his correspondence to the judge and asserting that "there was a signed plea agreement in this matter which provided Mr. Mitnick with transactional immunity for a number of criminal acts occurring throughout the United States. . . . Frankly, it was a very good deal for your client."

On June 28, 1996, Sherman angrily answered Schindler's letters. He called Schindler's statement about each jurisdiction making its own decisions, with Schindler merely an observer, "totally untrue," described the plea bargain as a joke, and repeated his demand for one trial in Los Angeles. Schindler replied, dubbing Sherman's "righteous indignation" disingenuous, and said his office would "prefer to litigate this matter as professionals and we invite you to adopt a similar perspective." But when the news hit the papers that Mitnick would be represented by new counsel and was preparing for trial, De Payne got cocky and called Schindler a "moron" and a "shriveled up penis" on the Internet. He gleefully speculated what might happen "when the defense subpoenas Tsutomu Shimomura and Justin Petersen to testify!"

.   .   .

"The feds called me out of the blue," Ron Austin recalled. They wanted to talk about Mitnick.

Austin met Special Agents Ken McGuire, Kathleen Carson, and another federal agent at the FBI's office. They slapped down a piece of paper on a desk. "I wonder if you could shed some light on this?" McGuire asked pointedly. It was a formerly PGP-encrypted message between Austin and Mitnick. Austin wondered if the government had actually broken the code, but the agents said a decrypted copy had been found. As Austin began to explain the e-mail correspondence he had with Mitnick, he mentioned that he had been working in Sherman's legal office. Carson said she was going to have to talk to Schindler about this, and left the room to call the Assistant U.S. Attorney.

A few days later, on July 24, McGuire phoned Austin and "wanted to know all about Sherman. When he started working there, how he met him, the purpose of the meetings." Austin told the agent that Sherman had revealed his legal strategy for Mitnick's case, and that Austin had even typed and edited one of his legal letters. The U.S. Attorney's office had apparently instructed the FBI agent to learn whether Austin was part of the defense team. When Austin told McGuire that Sherman had informed Austin of his strategy for the Mitnick case, the FBI agent asked, "Was that in his office or in the hall?" Regardless of Austin's whereabouts, the FBI inquiries about his work for Mitnick's new lawyer appeared to raise questions of attorney-client privilege.

.   .   .

Soon after McGuire's phone call, the government filed a motion to disqualify Richard Sherman as attorney for Kevin Mitnick, and included a declaration of agent Ken McGuire. The motion and supporting documents were filed under seal. Austin, responding to what he believed were government misrepresentations, filed his own letter in rebuttal under seal on August 3, 1996.

On Monday, August 12, 1996, Judge Pfaelzer heard oral arguments on the government's motion to disqualify Sherman. Christopher Painter, another Assistant U.S. Attorney, argued that De Payne could be a future codefendant of Mitnick. But Pfaelzer was not persuaded. She chastised the government, reminding them they'd had a grand jury for four years and still she didn't "have any indictment" and promptly denied the motion to disqualify Richard Sherman.

.   .   .

On Friday, the thirteenth of September, David Schindler asked Austin to come talk to him. Usually the prosecutor wanted to meet at the U.S. Attorney's office, but Austin arrived as requested at the FBI building, took the elevator to the fourteenth floor, and followed the FBI agents and Schindler down the hall. Ten people were present, including two prosecutors, agents McGuire and Carson, two FBI techs, and other federal officers. They stopped at an office with a large pink photocopy plastered on the door showing Mitnick at his fattest and meanest. "Mitnick Task Force," announced a sign on the door. Austin peered in and saw a white board with a photo lineup including De Payne.

Austin found it all amusing and began to laugh, prompting them to move to another room, where Schindler pulled out a new PGP message between Austin and Mitnick. But Austin said he felt the prosecutor wasn't really interested in the message. He seemed to just want to put Austin in the mood to talk. Schindler wanted to know about Sherman, and what crimes the government should investigate against Lewis De Payne.

"Lewis never discussed crimes," Austin told him. "He always discussed things in the third person. I don't know how you'll ever prove anything."

"You just leave it to me," Schindler said, flipping on a couple of tapes, one with Mitnick faking a Swedish accent, and another with De Payne asking someone to ship something to an address. "Well, you know we're going to be indicting De Payne, so you might get a subpoena to testify before us," Schindler informed Austin. As the hacker left the building he wondered why Schindler had shown him this "Mitnick Task Force" room. Perhaps, he thought, they'd set the whole thing up to scare Sherman into making a deal. Maybe there was no Mitnick task force after all.

.   .   .

On the evening of September 25, 1996, I was at home preparing for a 6 A.M. flight the following morning to Los Angeles to see what I could learn about the secret Mitnick grand jury hearings being held that day. The phone rang and a Sprint automated operator asked if I wanted to accept the collect call. It reminded me of the many calls I'd received from the Metropolitan Detention Center from Kevin Poulsen. But this was another Kevin.

He chuckled. "Do you recognize my voice?"

I did, of course, but after that initial bit of humor Kevin Mitnick sounded little like the spirited prankster I'd known before his arrest. He knew about the grand jury hearings scheduled for the following day because the main witnesses were to be his mother, his father, and his seventy-year-old grandmother. He figured he and De Payne would be indicted by the end of the day, and Sherman would be forced to represent his prior client and drop him. Since Mitnick was indigent, he'd have to get a federal public defender — or be stuck with a federal panel attorney. He considered it all a ploy by Schindler to deprive him of strong counsel and to attempt to get De Payne to testify against him. "They'll do anything to win," he groaned.

After mentioning in passing that "the government is taping this call," Mitnick explained why he refused to go along with the government's deal. I'd already confirmed his story with other sources and learned what the government had filed under seal. Schindler had offered Mitnick "transactional immunity" for specific crimes in a written plea, but in June, when Mitnick pressed for a definition, the government had revealed that it left open the possibility of future prosecutions beyond those to which he'd already confessed. And the eight-year cap first dangled before the hacker was merely an eight-year recommendation. A hanging judge could sentence him to forty.

After nineteen months in jail, Kevin sounded tired and beaten down. "They put me in the hole for a week and said they'd only let me out if I agreed not to ask for bail and not to ask for a preliminary examination of the case," Mitnick recalled angrily of his arrest. "I had to give up critical rights just to get out of the hole." He continued his rant, saying the FBI had lied about the search in North Carolina, and was incredulous that Shimomura's statements to Agent Levord Burns, initially included in the agent's search warrant, had now become part of the official record that would be presented before his sentencing judge. "Do you really believe the cellular code Lottor and Shimomura reverse-engineered is worth a million dollars?" he asked. It sounded far-fetched to me. Nor could I believe that the government still failed to realize that Shimomura's software had been sold to hackers who might use it as he had, to eavesdrop.

Without an attorney, Mitnick was hoping to use the Internet as a medium to publicize his "persecution" by the government and solicit funds for his legal defense. He was sorry he couldn't reply to the hundreds of kind letters he'd received and the money he'd been sent for cigarettes and candy, but "anything I say might be used by Schindler."

When I mentioned De Payne had called Schindler a moron on the Internet, he sighed. "It's the same old pattern. It isn't helpful for my case." His only hope seemed to be in learning new facts about his nemesis. "Shimomura was working closely with this guy Walker" — the former Assistant U.S. Attorney in San Francisco — "the one who said I stole billions," Mitnick said, adding that he wanted to know more about Shimomura's relationship with the prosecutor and the FBI. "Shimomura saw my file, my confidential FBI file."

The hacker said he wanted to go to trial and call Shimomura to the stand. "This is a case where the victim of the crime is the one gathering evidence," said Mitnick. "Where's the chain of custody to show that he didn't tamper with the evidence?"

The next morning, shortly before 10 A.M., on Thursday, September 26, I sat outside the Los Angeles courtroom where the Mitnick grand jury was being held. The elevator opened and David Schindler, escorted by a team of federal agents and assistants, wheeled by a cart of documents. Ten minutes later, John Yzurdiaga appeared for a different case, pulled me aside, and angrily told me, "Sherman got Mitnick indicted. He asked for it."

The lawyer pointed out a short, balding man in a light camel jacket at the receptionist's bulletproof window and said, "That's Kevin's father."

"Can you believe this!" Alan Mitnick moaned, shaking his

head, after I introduced myself. "The way they've blown this thing out of proportion. Personally, I think that they've hyped this thing so much that they feel they can't back out." We talked awhile, and then Christopher Painter, Schindler's fellow prosecutor, came out to speak to Mitnick Sr.'s attorney, Sam Galici. Mitnick Sr. had presented the government with a motion demanding that it disclose whether he had been the subject of surveillance before he testified to the grand jury.

Ten minutes later, Schindler joined the conversation, smiled, and casually dropped his hands. He claimed there had been no surveillance on Mitnick Sr.'s line, though court records documented that Pac Bell had tapped a phone Mitnick's father had used. Schindler said Mitnick Sr. didn't have to testify before the grand jury. "All we want to do is talk to him."

"Would you agree not to call him before the grand jury?" Galici asked.

Painter answered that one. "That depends on what he says."

Mitnick Sr.'s surveillance motion had achieved its goal. If the government didn't wish to reveal any possible wiretapping, Alan Mitnick didn't have to testify against his son. Minutes later, though, Kevin's grandmother, Riba Vartanian, arrived. Slowed by arthritis and accompanied by an attorney who had cost her several thousand dollars, she wasn't prepared to fight the government. She handed me a document prepared by the government to give her immunity for testifying against her grandson. Half an hour later, she emerged after talking to Schindler outside of the grand jury.

"They don't know what they're doing," her attorney said with a shrug, disgusted. The elderly woman seemed puzzled. "They asked me when Kevin became a fugitive. How do I know?" she said, clutching her purse. They wanted to know when she had moved to Las Vegas, and if Kevin had called her there. She seemed unsure. But whatever she said, her statements appeared irrelevant. Kevin's aunt, Chickie Leventhal, of Chickie's Bail Bonds in Santa Monica, had apparently talked to Schindler the night before and identified her nephew's voice on a tape recording of an alleged attempt to social engineer a copy of a company's software.

Kevin's mother, a slender woman in her early fifties, was downstairs in the waiting room wearing a purple sweater dress and flashy costume jewelry. She too had been forced to hire an attorney and travel from Vegas. She hadn't talked to Schindler, but Mitnick's father believed the prosecutor had an agenda apart from getting the hacker's immediate family to betray their kin. "They're trying to break his support network, wear him down," he charged. "That's what it's all about."

A few hours later, Schindler faxed a press release and a federal indictment to reporters at the *Wall Street Journal,* the *Los Angeles Times,* and numerous other members of the media. Richard Sherman, Mitnick's attorney, was not faxed a copy of the indictment, and the hacker had no idea he'd been indicted.

The twenty-five-count indictment against Mitnick and De Payne was most remarkable for what it didn't say. Though De Payne was indicted on fourteen of twenty-five counts, specific crimes alleged against De Payne were included in only one count and, notably, there was no charge of conspiracy against either defendant. The government alleged De Payne had made a pretext call to con Nokia Mobile Phones into mailing its software to a Compton, California, hotel, but I recalled that Mitnick and De Payne had claimed that the call was a prank to gauge the FBI's reaction. Although no software was ever picked up, the government still considered the social engineering attempt a crime. De Payne's main offense appeared to be "aiding and abetting," allegedly providing Mitnick with cellular phones with "stolen" electrical serial numbers and allowing him to use his Netcom account to transfer some of his fraudulently obtained proprietary software.

Notably missing were any charges that Mitnick had a profit motive or had stolen or used credit card numbers. There were no charges related to any Christmas break-ins or death threats against Tsutomu Shimomura. Nor did the government mention or give the smallest credit to Shimomura. A close inspection revealed what appeared to be a surgical removal of charges that might have been tainted by Shimomura's involvement. Mitnick's alleged break-ins to the Well in Sausalito, for example, weren't included. But if the strategy was to prevent Shimomura from being called by the defense, the government may have left a door open. Netcom, in San Jose, one of the sites where Shimomura had intercepted Mitnick's communications, was listed in the indictment as one of the victims.

The indictment, including charges for unauthorized access devices, computer fraud, wire fraud, and interception of wire or electronic communications, appeared disorganized and seemed to lump together alleged serious felonies and the equivalent of hacker misdemeanors. The major alleged offenses were the misappropriation of copies of the proprietary software of Motorola, Nokia, Fujitsu Ltd., Novell, and NEC Ltd. But the indictment was laid out in such a way that it appeared at first glance that Mitnick had copied the software of Sun Microsystems, too. Boilerplate language stated that each of the six "victim companies" spends "substantial sums in developing its computer software" and, in all but one case, licenses its "proprietary software for a fee."

The actual counts of the indictment, however, made it clear that Mitnick's alleged crime against Sun was at worst the unauthorized possession of two hundred passwords on Sun's computers. Indeed, eight of the counts were for having unauthorized passwords on the computers of Sun, Novell, Fujitsu, NEC, Motorola, and the University of Southern California — the hacker equivalent of speeding tickets. Instead of charging those as misdemeanors for "trafficking in user names and passwords" under Title 18, 1030, Schindler claimed they were 1029 access device violations, each with a twenty-year maximum penalty. Nine counts were for eight social engineering phone calls by Mitnick and one by De Payne to arrange the transfer of a victim company's software. Six counts documented the alleged illegal transfers, and one count was for either preventing the use of or damaging the computers of USC and creating a loss of more than $1,000.

Nokia, Europe's largest maker of cellular phones, acknowledged Mitnick had illegally transferred the source code that operates its cellular phones and other wireless products from Salo, Finland, to USC. The company detailed the second social engineering "prank" call De Payne allegedly made four months after Mitnick already had the goods. De Payne was apparently impersonating K. P. Wileska, the company's president, and an official indicated that the company knew immediately that the caller's accent didn't match that of the Fin.

Motorola, a $30 billion corporation, clarified the indictment. Far from getting accounts to internal Motorola systems, as claimed in the indictment, Mitnick had used an ordinary packet sniffer program to pilfer common Internet accounts, mainly on university systems used by Motorola employees. "No confidential information was compromised," said an official. "It was a nuisance, not a major loss." The revelation raised the specter that the government may have wrongly characterized the other company accounts Mitnick garnered as being on internal corporate systems. Mitnick's misappropriation of Motorola's software, the centerpiece of the indictment, was also considered overblown by the company. "He did move a block of code, not considered critical at the time, and we subsequently found no pattern of abuse or fraud," said the official. Nor did the official see how cellular source code taken from Motorola or any other of the victim companies could have profited Mitnick. "The contest may have been more important than the result. Like his Digital case, this software was of no use to anybody else."

The billions of dollars of losses Kent Walker, the former U.S. Attorney, had trumpeted in the *New York Times* had apparently dropped a thousandfold to "millions" in the government's press release. The social engineering counts seemed to belie Mitnick's status as the nation's most wanted hacker. Oddly, some of the most detailed parts of the indictment described Mitnick's low-tech telephone tricks and numerous aliases. But the government press release ignored this contradiction, publicizing the "vast scope of Mitnick's alleged computer hacking while he was a fugitive from justice" and writing of how criminals using a lone computer and modem can "wreak havoc around the world." It was an ironic choice of terminology, since Shimomura had described his own program as one that could "wreak havoc on the Internet community." And there was more irony in the indictment's repeated references to Mitnick using "unauthorized" hacking programs. What were Shimomura's hacking programs? Authorized?

The last line in the press release warned ominously that "the investigation is continuing." Friday afternoon Mitnick phoned again, and I asked why he thought there was no charge for his alleged break-ins to the Well. "They intend to indict me in Northern California," he answered drearily. "They're saving charges to indict me later. They'll save a San Diego charge to indict me in San Diego too. Schindler told me if I didn't sign the plea he'd drag me around the country."

Mitnick still didn't even have a copy of the indictment, and was now left without an attorney. Sherman had informed him that he'd have to solely represent De Payne to avoid a possible conflict of interest. At Mitnick's request, the Raleigh public defender's office was on the phone to the Los Angeles public defender's office. Normally, Los Angeles would be eager to take on a high-profile defendant. But Maria Stratton, head of the office, informed Raleigh that one of her forty-three public defenders had represented Lenny DiCicco, a codefendent in Mitnick's 1989 case. Although DiCicco was not involved in the new California indictment, Stratton refused to represent Mitnick.

Mitnick, scheduled to be arraigned with De Payne on Monday, September 30, still had no attorney. The press began to kick in. Schindler provided Reuters with the juicy quote that played in papers around the country. "The statutes provide for sentences in excess of two hundred years," said the Assistant U.S. Attorney, adding that a judge would have to decide the ultimate sentence. Some papers quoted Schindler, while others just flatly announced the authorities' claim that Mitnick could face as much as "two hundred years of prison time." A spokeswoman at Nokia believed Mitnick's crimes were serious but termed the government's statement "ridiculous."

The idea that someone like Mitnick, whose problems began to spin out of control when his probation officer wouldn't let him work with computers, could be handed a life sentence for his hacking escapades seemed Kafkaesque. But then this was the Kevin Mitnick case. Government hyperbole and hardball tactics were par for the course. And there was every indication that the game was only going to get rougher. "I figure they'll keep indicting me" — in other jurisdictions — "for five years," Mitnick told me the night before his arraignment. "Justice isn't the issue. They're sending a message."

October 1996

Notes

Prologue and Part I

Based on interviews with the following individuals: Jim Murphy and Joe Orsak of Sprint Cellular; Tsutomu Shimomura; Mark Lottor; Kevin Mitnick; Justin Petersen; Intrepid; the maitre d' at the Rainbow Bar and Grill; Grant Strauss; Phillip Lamond; Erica; Kevin Poulsen; Detective Bill Spradley, LAPD; Ron Austin; anonymous friends of Justin Petersen; Henry Spiegel; Lewis De Payne; Susan Headly (Thunder); Allan Rubin, Mitnick's former attorney; Mark Kasdan of Teltec; Bonnie Vitello, Mitnick's ex-wife; Reba Vartanian, Mitnick's grandmother; Bob Arkow, Mitnick's boyhood friend; Chris Goggans; Drunkfux; Eric Heinz Sr.; Ed Lovelace, California Department of Motor Vehicles; anonymous Beverly Hills detective.

Visits to Raleigh, North Carolina, Henry Spiegel's Hollywood home, Oakwood Apartments, Teltec, Malibu Canyon Apartments, and Lewis De Payne's apartment allowed for firsthand physical description. Technical and background information was culled from: the FBI record of items seized in De Payne's apartment; a copy of the Pacific Bell SAS manual; interviews with Graystone Electronics, the makers of the Cellscope; the Mitnick federal indictment; *Newsweek;* the *New York Times;* the *Los Angeles Times;* the *Los Angeles Daily News; Spectacular Computer Crimes,* by Jay Bloombecker; Adam

Mitnick's death certificate; Los Angeles criminal and civil court files; *Cyberpunk,* by Katie Hafner and John Markoff; Joseph Wernle's Sprint and MCI phone bills; a copy of Chris Goggans's videotape of Petersen at Summer Con '92; Lewis De Payne's computer records.

Part II

Based on interviews with: Ron Austin; Justin Petersen; Kevin Poulsen; Fernando Peralta, Social Security Administration; Kevin Mitnick; Lewis De Payne; David Schindler, Assistant U.S. Attorney, Los Angeles; Bonnie Vitello; Richard Sherman, Lewis De Payne's attorney; John Markoff of the *New York Times;* Kevin Pazaski of CellularOne; a Well technical support person; Brent Schroeder; Neil Clift, English security expert; Todd Young of the Guidry Group; Mrs. Young; Mark Lottor; Ivan Orton; Detective John Lewitt, Sergeant Ken Crow, Detective John Moore, and Detective Linda Patrick, Seattle PD; David Drew, manager of Lynn Mar apartments.

Source material and research included: visit to Seattle; Todd Young Cellscope demonstration; Richard Sherman's letter to Janet Reno; Ron Austin's memo to the FBI; *Wired* magazine article, "Cellular Phreaks & Code Dudes"; transcript of Petersen bail revocation hearing; Lewis De Payne's recording of his oath with Mitnick; the *Los Angeles Daily News;* the *Los Angeles Times;* Joseph Wernle's phone records; Petersen and Austin federal indictments; Petersen's memoirs; federal statutes; *Spectacular Computer Crimes;* Susan Headly; the *London Observer,* "To Catch a Hacker"; Special Agent Kathleen Carson's September 1994 letter to Neil Clift; Lewis De. Payne's e-mail; congressional testimony on Oki scanner; promotional copy of Mark Lottor's altered Oki scanner software/interface; Young affidavit; Graystone Electronics interview; Seattle court documents.

Part III

Based on interviews with: Kevin Mitnick, Ron Austin, John Markoff, Neil Clift, Lewis De Payne, Mark Lottor, Kevin Poulsen, Tsutomu Shimomura, Peter Moore of *Playboy* magazine.

Source material included: Internet "copies" of Shimomura's voice mail tapes; Peter Moore's *Playboy* e-mail; *U.S. News & World Report; Wired* magazine; Shimomura's January 25 Internet post; CERT briefing; interviews with the Los Angeles Metropolitan Detention Center, the Federal Correctional Institute at Lompoc, and the Federal Bureau of Prisons; *Spectacular Computer Crimes; Murder in the First* (movie); the *New York Times;* De Payne's Internet post to 2600; *Newsweek;* Captain Ziese's Internet post; Rik Farrow, Unix security expert.

Part IV

Based on interviews with: Ivan Orton, King County prosecuting attorney; David Schindler; U.S. Marshal William Berryhill Jr., Raleigh, North Carolina; Bruce Katz, Well Chief Executive Officer; Hua-Pei Chen, Well technical manager; John Markoff and the *New York Times,* San Francisco bureau; the Player's Club apartment manager and staff; Special Agent John Vasquez; John Bowler, Assistant U.S. Attorney, Raleigh, North Carolina; Jessica Gerstle, NBC; John Johnson of the *Los Angeles Times;* Julia Menapace; Tsutomu Shimomura; Kevin Mitnick; Special Agent Jim Walsh.

The following publications, organizations, articles, transcripts, documents and book provided source material: Lewis De Payne tape recording of his conversation with Mitnick; *All Things Considered* radio broadcast; CBS Evening News; the *New York Times;* LeVord Burns's FBI affidavit; the FBI; radio transcript of Shimomura press conference; *The Hacker Crackdown,* by Bruce Sterling; federal statutes; *The Nation,* "Cyberscoop"; *Wired;* Communications Daily, "Immunity Needed, Markey Panel Sees Dark Side of Electronic Frontier"; "Civil Liberties, Virtual Communities, and Hackers," by Howard Rheingold; the *Washington Post;* the *Hollywood Reporter;* the *Daily Variety; USA Today;* the *San Jose Mercury;* Associated Press.

Fair use or permitted quotations were made of public posts by: Patrizia DiLucchio, Larry Person, Bruce Katz, Mark Graham, Hua-Pei Chen, Claudia Stroud, Emmanuel Goldstein, Douglas Fine, Netta Gilboa, Mike Jennings, Devoto, Charles Platt, Aaron Barnhart, Bruce Koball, David Lewis, Chip Bayers, Chris Goggans.

Part V

Based on interviews with: Bruce Katz; Bruce Koball; Claudia Stroud; Mark Graham; Kent Walker, Assistant U.S. Attorney in San Francisco; John Mendez, attorney for the Well; Hua-Pei Chen; Robert Berger, Chief Technology Officer of Internex Securities; Mark Seiden, Internex Securities consultant; Lewis De Payne; Jim Murphy; Joe Orsak; U.S. Magistrate Wallace Dixon; John Yzurdiaga, Mitnick's attorney; David Schindler; Kevin Mitnick; anonymous deputy U.S. Marshal in Raleigh; Ivan Orton; Todd Young; John Markoff; Emmanuel Goldstein; anonymous hackers; Mark Lottor.

Source material included: Well intrusion records; Rockport Company, Inc.; *The Hacker Crackdown;* FBI affidavit; government court filings; Mitnick Sprint phone records; the *Washington Post;* CNN; RDI Computer Corporation; Kevin Mitnick's 1995 letters to the author; Wilson County Jail; Mitnick's motion to suppress; the *Los Angeles Times; Rolling Stone* magazine; Hyperion Press *Publishers Weekly* advertisement; *The Nation.*

Afterword

Draws on interviews with: Todd Young; an anonymous deputy U.S. Marshal in Raleigh, North Carolina; John Yzurdiaga; the San Francisco U.S. Attorney's office; the FBI; David Schindler; Scott Charney, Department of Justice; Kent Walker; John Bowler; Mark Lottor; Emmanuel Goldstein; Lewis De Payne; Wilson County Jail authorities; anonymous hackers.

Source material included: the *Washington Post; The Nation; Rolling Stone; Wired;* the *San Francisco Chronicle;* the *San Francisco Examiner; Publishers Weekly;* RDI Computer Corp.; Sun-tzu's *The Art of War;* Mitnick's 1995 letters and sketch to the author; Government and Defense motions re: U.S. v. Kevin Mitnick; the *New York Times;* the *Washington Post;* the *Daily Variety;* the *Los Angeles Times;* Markoff/Shimomura letter of October 13, 1995; Mark Lottor; De Payne fax to the author.

Following is the unsigned October 8, 1995, letter to the author from John Markoff and Tsutomu Shimomura:

.   .   .

October 8, 1995

Jonathan Littman
38 Miller Avenue Suite 122
Mill Valley, California 94941

Dear Jonathan,

This is in response to your separate letters to us. We apologize for not being more prompt, Tsutomu was travelling on business and did not receive your September 5 letter until recently. As you know we have a contract with Hyperion for Tsutomu's account of his participation in the arrest of Kevin Mitnick, and at the request of our publisher we have decided not to participate in other books on the same subject.

First, in response to your September 7 request to John Markoff, for permission to reprint his March 14 Well posting, he is not willing to give permission.

However, we do think it is appropriate to respond to several points where you have received inaccurate information.

Our responses are not intended to be a comprehensive answer to your list of questions, but only to protect you from including libelous material in your book.

Tsutomu was not asked by any governmental, military or intelligence representative to assist in the capture of Mr. Mitnick. All of his actions were taken in response to requests for assistance from both The Well and Netcom to deal with extensive and persistent break-ins.

Tsutomu's decision to tell John Markoff that he was travelling to Raleigh on Sunday morning was done without contact with any law enforcement agency. Markoff flew to Raleigh independently six hours later after discussing the possibility of a story with his editors at the *New York Times*. Markoff did not at any time assist or participate in any aspect of the investigation into Kevin Mitnick's activities; Markoff was there only as an observer in his role as a newspaper reporter.

Moreover, in Raleigh on Sunday evening the Cellscope equipment was never placed in Markoff's car, and there was never any discussion about taking it out of the Cellular One engineer's van or about placing it in Markoff's car. Markoff parked his car near the cell site that night and then later drove back to his hotel.

Tsutomu never told anyone from law enforcement that anyone had authorized or cleared Markoff's presence in Raleigh.

Tsutomu was informed by the Justice Department that his actions on behalf of the Internet providers and the cellular telephone company during the course of the investigation were covered under their fraud detection and prevention exception granted to these organizations under the ECPA.

Tsutomu did have discussions with the National Security Agency about funding computer security research, the results of which were to be placed in the public domain, however no research grant was ever made. Tsutomu was not aware of any statements made in the search warrant until many days after the arrest.

Tsutomu did not lure Mitnick or anyone else into breaking-in to his computers. The attack was entirely unprovoked.

No copies of any files allegedly stolen by Mitnick were provided by Tsutomu to anyone other than the legitimate owners.

The first discussion of the possibility of a book on the subject of Kevin Mitnick's arrest took place on Thursday February 16, when John Markoff received a telephone call from John Brockman, a New York City literary agent, proposing a collaboration between Markoff and Shimomura.

You will remember, we hope, that after his July 4, 1994 article about the hunt for Mitnick, Markoff did not wish to pursue the subject of Mitnick's life as a fugitive and referred a free-lance article on the subject proposed by Playboy to you.

Also please note that you are inaccurate in stating that Tsutomu requested immunity before testifying before Congress on April 1993.

We realize this is a delicate issue for you because of your involvement and communication with Kevin Mitnick during the period he was a fugitive. However, since your questions suggest you believe there may have been something inappropriate in Tsutomu's cellular telephone software development work, if you do include material in your book along this line, journalistic ethics require you to include the following: Tsutomu, unlike Mitnick, in all of his computer security research over a fifteen year period, has always, whenever he has found a vulnerability, made it known to the appropriate people, whether CERT, or a private company at risk, or the United States Congress.

Sincerely,

(signed)
John Markoff
Tsutomu Shimomura